Railroad in the Clouds:

The Alaska Railroad in the Age of Steam, 1914-1945

Railroad in the Clouds:

The Alaska Railroad in the Age of Steam, 1914–1945

By

William H. Wilson

PRUETT PUBLISHING COMPANY
Boulder, Colorado

©1977 by William H. Wilson
All rights reserved, including those to reproduce this
book, or parts thereof, in any form without
permission in writing from the Publisher.

Library of Congress Cataloging in Publication Data
Wilson, William Henry, 1935-
  Railroad in the clouds.

  Bibliography: p.
  Includes index.
  1. Alaska Railroad—History. I. Title.
TF25.A4W54   385'.09798   77-24368
ISBN 0-87108-510-0

First Edition
1 2 3 4 5 6 7 8 9 0

Printed in the United States of America

Acknowledgments

At The Alaska Railroad I am especially indebted to John E. Manley, now retired as General Manager, for access to the railroad's archives, and to Mrs. Bernadine Prince, the Chief of Office Services, now also retired. Mrs. Prince's knowledge and counsel were so important to my project that this book could not have been written without them.

H. Theodore Ryberg, Director of Libraries at the University of Alaska, and Paul H. McCarthy, University Archivist and Curator of Manuscripts, were helpful and encouraging. These two librarians understand what historians are trying to do.

Alaska's late Senator Ernest Gruening and Charles J. Keim, formerly Dean of the College of Arts and Letters, University of Alaska, aided my study at critical times. Most academic historians who read these lines will be surprised to learn that the University of Alaska's history department was, prior to a basic reorganization, in the College of Business, Economics, and Government. While I was a member of that department, two former deans of the college, William M. Dickson and the late Leo M. Loll, Jr., encouraged me and arranged for some helpful financial assistance. A friend, Bill B. Janes, read an earlier version of this manuscript, making valuable suggestions. I am grateful to John E. Clark, J. J. Delaney, and Arnold Nordale for informative interviews.

Maps and photographs were obtained with the assistance of Renee Blahuta and Beverly Davis at the University of Alaska Archives, M. Diane Brenner at the Anchorage Historical and Fine Arts Museum, A. Louise Bremner at The Alaska Railroad, and Zelma Doig at the Alaska Historical Library. I am grateful to all of these resourceful archivists, and especially to Mrs. Bremner, who has charge of the prints and negatives from which the bulk of the photographs in this book were drawn.

I am indebted to the staffs of the Library of Congress, the National Archives, the Federal Archives and Records Center, Seattle, the Seattle Public Library, and the libraries at the University of Washington, North Texas State University, and Texas Woman's University.

Grants from the Johnson fund of the American Philosophical Society and from the American Association for State and Local History during the summer of 1966, together with grants from the Institute for Social, Economic, and Government Research, University of Alaska, assisted the research for this book. A Fellowship for Younger Scholars from the National Endowment for the Humanities during part of 1968 allowed me to substantially complete the research and begin writing. From 1969 through 1973, released-time grants from the North Texas State University Organized Research Funds aided the completion of the original manuscript.

Chapter Six first appeared in a somewhat different version in the *Pacific Northwest Quarterly* 58 (1967): 130-41. I am grateful to Robert E. Burke, Managing Editor of the *Pacific Northwest Quarterly*, for permission to include it here.

Throughout the research and writing of this book my wife, Katharine, was a superb critic, typist, and companion. As the dedication suggests, the late Leo M. Loll, Jr., gave greater inspiration than words of acknowledgment convey.

Introduction

Alaska intrudes on the national consciousness now and again. During one of those intrusions — the era of the Taft and early Wilson administrations — federal policy swung around to federal construction and operation of a railroad from the south-central Alaska coast to its storied, gold-rich interior.

Thirty years later the Japanese invasion of two Aleutian islands, the dramatic construction of the bare-bones "Alcan" highway, and a frantic military buildup in the territory once more pointed attention northward. In between those bursts of interest, the railroad's executives labored to build the line through a vast, inhospitable land, to develop Alaska's railbelt resources, and to strengthen the flimsy roadbed to meet even light traffic demands.

This is the story of that railroad, from its beginnings in 1914 through its workhorse role in supplying strategic Alaska during World War II. Built through an area largely innocent of any transportation line, built on the rotting remains of failed private ventures in "civilized" areas, it lost money until the late 1930s. Grudgingly, Congress voted the appropriations to keep it rolling.

Important as the railroad was for itself, it was bound to the larger issues and problems of a remote and difficult land hampered by harsh climates, forbidding terrain, and a small, scattered population. Thus, the story also involves the land The Alaska Railroad served. The relationship of land and railroad was rarely easy and was sometimes explosive. Yet, for good or ill, their fates were entwined. That reality made the railroad a nexus of the history of Alaska.

Author's Note

Purists will soon discover that I have rounded off The Alaska Railroad's mileages to the nearest mile or half mile. Such approximations avoid many decimals and are more than enough for finding precise map locations. Further, the 1964 Good Friday earthquake not only destroyed many of the railroad's Seward installations, it also forced the relocation of the Seward dock, changing the true mileage from Seward of every point on the line.

Contents

Alaska's Railroad Beginnings	1
The Lure of Coal	13
The Birth of the Alaskan Engineering Commission	23
Beginning the Alaska Railroad	37
The End of the Beginning	75
Town Building on the Last Frontier	101
The Railroad and the Steamships	123
The Commission and Its Critics	135
Rough Roadbed, Tough Transition	155
Noel Smith to the Rescue	169
Otto Ohlson and His Era	195
By Land, Sea, or Air?	207
Goodbye, Red Ink	227
War, and an Era's End	253
Notes	263
Bibliographical Essay	269
Index	275

To the Memory of Leo M. Loll, Jr.

Alaska's Railroad Beginnings

When four travel-weary federal railroad commissioners reached Seward, Alaska, on September 15, 1912, they touched a land strewn with the bones of promoters' railways: the Alaska Pacific, the Valdez & Yukon, and dozens more. Those pathetic remains rested on the firm belief that railroads would develop the northland just as they had brought population to the agrarian west and wealth to the industrial east. In Alaska the proposition had not worked. Most of the eight operating lines were nothing more than links to tidewater or navigable streams for some successful mining ventures. By "stateside" standards these short line roads were simply appalling. They charged passengers twelve cents and more per mile in return for poor service, at a time when four cents was a high fare. They maintained their rights-of-way just enough to keep wobbly trestles from collapsing and wavy track from sinking out of sight into the boggy tundra. They carried little more cargo and human freight than was directly involved in mining. No factories, and few rich farms, lay along their routes.

By 1912 the failure of unassisted private railroad enterprise to move beyond the mining frontier made the transportation question Alaska's foremost economic problem. Most men who thought about the matter had concluded that some form of federal railroad assistance was as necessary to Alaska's railroads as the land grants had been to the building of the transcontinentals.

Understanding Alaska's railroad difficulties begins with a look at the Great Land itself, and looks can be deceiving. The map shows Alaska as part of the North American continent, but to see the territory in transportation terms the observer must mentally cut it and a 250-mile-wide strip of the neighboring Canadian Yukon away from the land mass and set them adrift, an island of continental dimensions with its nearest railroad port — Skagway — 1153 miles from Seattle. Alaska's first, and for many years only, connection with the rest of the United States was by water. Scheduled airplane flights beginning in 1940 reduced travel time but did nothing to diminish Alaska's insularity. Not until late 1942, with the completion of the rough-hewn Alaska Highway, did the territory have a tenuous land connection with the outside world.

Before the Klondike gold craze of 1898 swept the country and turned attention to the remote, forbidding interior, Alaska had known mostly a maritime development. Russians and Americans in turn exploited the great seal herds that annually migrated to breed on two rocky islets in the Bering Sea. In 1878, a little more than a decade after the purchase of Alaska from Russia, American investors built two salmon canneries, the forerunners of a large, oligopolistic industry that forty years later would pack a catch valued at over $51 million. In 1892, the year that territorial gold production first crossed the million dollar mark, almost ninety percent of its value came from coastal Alaska.

There were compelling climatic and geographical reasons why land transportation remained unimportant except to a handful of hardy explorers, trappers, traders, outfitters, and prospectors in the interior. Great mountains stand behind most shores along Alaska's coastal arc from the southeastern panhandle to the Alaska Peninsula. The only two panhandle ports giving access to the interior are Skagway and Haines, at the head of Lynn Canal. However, access from these two ports is even difficult, leading over high passes and through Canadian territory. Farther west — at Cordova, Valdez, Whittier, and Seward — adequate ice-free ports exist, but all of them suffer from stiff land or sea winds at times, or from fogs or low, overhanging clouds. The North Pacific Ocean moderates their winter temperatures, which rarely fall below zero Farenheit. Summers are cool, and when the wind blows they are uncomfortably chilly.

The great interior river valleys, cut off from the seas by the coastal mountains and the awesome Alaska Range to the south and by the arctic range to the north, are semiarid. Although the thin soil will support luxurious timber stands and vegetation, much of the land drains poorly, is boggy, and is underlain by permanently frozen ground. Summers may be clear and warm, with temperatures occasionally approaching 100 degrees, but they may also be cloudy, blustery, and rainy for days at a time. The interior's extreme winter temperatures in the forties and fifties below zero (and colder) usually are accompanied by clear, calm conditions. They may persist for a month without significant warming.

Alaska's insularity, its remoteness, its tradition of littoral development, and its uncongenial climate and terrain do not entirely account for the interior's slow development. The sheer size of the Great Land was itself a limiting factor. Glibly recited statistics of bulk, such as, that Alaska has an area of 586,400 square miles, or that Alaska is one-fifth the size of the contiguous forty-eight states, or that it is more than double the size of Texas, often produce only disbelief or stupefaction. To grasp Alaska's size effectively, imagine a map of the territory, excluding the southeastern panhandle and the Aleutian island chain, spread over an identically scaled map of the first forty-eight states. If northernmost Point Barrow were placed against the Canada-Minnesota border near the Lake of the Woods, then Alaska's Seward Peninsula would come to rest in the Black Hills of South Dakota, the tip of the Alaska Peninsula would lie in the vicinity of Lubbock, Texas, and the eastern Alaska border would stretch from Lake Superior to near Paducah, Kentucky.

In the interior, the 2,300-mile Yukon River drains a watershed of 333,000 square miles of arctic and subarctic regions. But it and its main tributaries, for years the only means of bulk transportation, are frozen fast for eight to nine months of the year. Occasional periods of low water during the navigation season plague boat operations. The dependable modes of travel, before rail and air, were dogsleds, snowshoes, and human feet. During gold rush days feed was too expensive to allow much use of horses. No wonder the nineteenth century promoters, industrialists, and empire builders believed in both the vital necessity and near impossibility of throwing steel rails across this vast land.

The event that shifted the national focus to Alaska's interior occurred on August 16, 1896, in the Canadian Yukon. In the afternoon of that day George Carmack, a "squaw man," and two Indian companions, "Skookum" Jim and "Tagish" Charlie, discovered incredibly rich gold-bearing ground while prospecting along Rabbit (now Bonanza) Creek. The setting could not have been more romantic had it been contrived: here were the two natives, the disreputable white man "gone siwash," a pan holding four dollars of gold in an area where ten cents to the pan was good prospects, and a little creek draining into a third-rate tributary of the Yukon that gave its name to a great region, a glorious experience, and an era — The Klondike.

The Klondike rush of 1897-98 was romantic, too — one of the nineteenth century's last heroic adventures. More prosaically, it closed the curtain on the shameful, if understandable, political and economic neglect of Alaska's 4,298 white inhabitants, the only ones who counted in those days. While the problems of Reconstruction, urbanization, industrialization, and continental expansion absorbed the country, Alaska languished; but no longer, for the only practical routes to the Yukon Territory lay through Alaska. The northland's transportation problem suddenly became that of the nation.

The majority of stampeders gained the gold fields by one of two Alaska routes. The most popular and legendary passage lay for some twenty miles through Alaska, from Dyea or Skagway at the head of Lynn Canal to the summits of the coast range. Twenty-eight thousand of the thirty-four thousand who reached the Klondike traversed either the Chilkoot or White passes during the winter of 1897-98. They paid phenomenal freight rates. The basic rate for general merchandise at the beginning of the 1898 season was $12.50 per ton from Seattle to Skagway or $15.00 to Dyea, not burdensome in the depreciated dollars of a later time, even when the second class fare, $35.00 to Dyea, was added. The stampeders quickly discovered, however, that the basic rate was only the first of a series of staggering freight charges. Canadian authorities required each argonaut to have one ton of groceries and supplies. Usually the gold seeker's "admission fee" of staples was bulky enough to be charged on the "measurement" basis, a minimum payment of half again the basic rate. Then the wharfage charges at the Pacific Coast ports had to be paid, with an additional lighterage charge from ship's side over the tidal flats to the beach at Skagway or Dyea. Later, wharves and warehouses were built in Alaska and fees assessed for their use. Those adventurers who hired packers found that they had only begun to pay. For the final ascent of the Chilkoot, the packers demanded one dollar a pound, or a ton-rate of $2,000, a price as rarefied as the heights above Dyea. The Canadian import duty added to the freight charges. Next the prospectors paid that most common of all Far North transportation charges — the sweat tax. A lack of labor and boats for hire on the Yukon side of the pass forced most of them to manage their own outfits on the descent to Dawson.

The second route to the gold fields stretched nearly 5,000 miles from Seattle northwestward to St. Michael on the bleak coast of Norton Sound, then eastward through Alaska, up the Yukon to Dawson. The trip was a fairly comfortable six to eight weeks' steaming from Seattle (versus half that time tramping through the passes), but the two thousand passengers who went the distance to Dawson paid dearly for their rides. During the 1898 season, the second class fare to St. Michael was $125, the first class fare $25 more, and freight was $200 per ton, with transshipment privileges at St. Michael. Intense competition pared prices well below the public rates for those shippers who knew how to take advantage of the situation. The river steamers charged fifty-three cents per ton per running hour, with a minimum of $136 per ton from St. Michael to Dawson. This drove the published basic rate up to $336 per ton. Charges and duties similar to those of the pass routes were piled on top of that. Better boats for oceans and rivers and tramways over the passes and around river rapids helped the transportation problem, but only railroads could solve it.

While national attention turned northward and rushes to Nome in 1900 and Fairbanks in 1903 sustained the Klondike drama, a comparative flood of Alaska bills was issued from an aroused Congress. Acts for civil and criminal procedures, for telegraph lines and wireless stations, for local taxes, for agricultural investigations, and for mineral exploitation poured out. The first, the Alaska homestead and railroad act of 1898, was also the most important. To assess this act fairly one must keep a firm grip on the realities of late nineteenth and early twentieth century Alaska, and of the popular reaction against railroads in the United States during the same era.

News of the Far North's rich gold fired millions of imaginations, but few of the people who talked about Dawson, Nome, or Fairbanks actually went there. Alfred H. Brooks, dean of Alaska geologists, carefully calculated that only sixty thousand stampeders, 75 percent of them United States citizens, set out for Dawson during the Klondike rush. Of those, some fifty thousand reached the Klondike or Alaska, but their numbers were quickly reduced by an outflow of eight thousand from the Klondike in 1898 alone. During the nineties the white population of Alaska had enormously increased, but was only 34,056 in 1900. By 1910 little net change had occurred. In that year the white population stood at 36,400 and would not significantly increase until the military boom of the 1940s.

To the tiny and numerically stagnant white population should be added Alaska's relatively small role in total gold and mineral production. In 1906, the peak year for Alaskan gold production under the $20.67 price, the territory's share of the national value was just over 20 percent. In the decade of high Alaskan production beginning with 1900, it averaged some 15 percent. Another excellent year for total mineral production in the territory was 1906, but production was only about 2 percent of the national value. Finally, there was the popular revulsion against railroads which persisted side by side with the belief that railroads were necessary to development. Farmers, urban businessmen, even some railroad executives, had deplored rate-making practices and other rail abuses. Moralists decried the lavish land grants, construction allowances, and corruption of the transcontinental era. Federal regulatory bodies had been established, were growing in power, and soon would enjoy augmented authority. By 1898 it was difficult indeed for congressmen to vote a bounty to a railroad.

The homestead and railroad act in its final form dealt more with settlers than with railroads, perhaps because more legislators would vote for a bill purporting to open up commercial sites and homesteads. The railroad provisions scarcely were generous in comparison with grants to railroads in the states. The right-of-way was narrow, 100 feet on either side of center track. There were detailed regulations about the filing of locations. A railroader was supposed to complete his line within four years or forfeit his rights to the unbuilt segment. The license tax section of the 1899 Alaska Criminal Code added another provision: a $100 tax per mile per year on each operating mile.

The four-year completion requirement and the annual $100 per mile tax have been the subjects of much unnecessary handwringing. Historians who have explained how subsequent Congresses exempted Alaskan railroads from the four-year limit and the tax have nevertheless deplored the inhibiting effect of these provisions. Congress originally intended to prevent promoters from indefinitely tying up valuable rights-of-way and to provide the federal treasury with some revenue. In practice, extensions of time and forgiveness of taxes for periods of several years usually were granted to roads with some construction. Once, an overzealous district attorney closed a railroad on the Seward Peninsula because it could not afford the tax or wangle a forgiveness from Congress. Apart from that one incident, it is difficult to understand how the restrictions really mattered (except to the treasury, which received the tax on only the White Pass & Yukon Railway's 22.4 Alaska miles until the levy was repealed in 1914).

The White Pass & Yukon was the first railroad to scale Alaska's alpine rampart and reach the interior. Taking advantage of the new railroad law, Close Brothers of London financed the narrow gauge line from tidewater at Skagway to the head of steamboat navigation on the Yukon at Whitehorse in Canada's Yukon Territory, a distance of over 100 miles. The White Pass chose for its construction contractor Michael Heney, a brave and hard-driving man who worked prodigiously and drove his subordinates to perform wonders of labor.

Time was of the essence. The railroad act was passed in May 1898, and by the end of that month Heney had surveyed to the summit of White Pass. By February 1899 he had thrust the track twenty miles to the top of the pass, 2,800 feet above Skagway. One and one-half years later, on July 29, 1900, the last spike was driven home.

Working in a White Pass construction crew was an experience more enjoyable in recollection than in reality. The crews worked over mushy ground in spring and through clouds of mosquitoes in summer. They blasted a narrow ledge for the rails from sheer canyon walls while the snows and bitter winds of early winter whipped around them. Heney paid a maximum of $3.50 for a ten-hour day, while the Dawson mines paid $15.00 per day and board for labor as needed. Penniless and disgruntled Klondikers seeking passage money home, some newcomers, and various unfortunates worked for him when necessary. When they had made enough, or when news of fresh gold strikes or rumors of strikes reached them, they gladly left him. More of their kind took their places. During the peak of employment in 1898, Heney worked a force of one thousand. Thirty-five men, one for every three miles of track, perished on the White Pass road during construction days.

Heney's efforts returned handsome profits to the White Pass road because the Klondike placers continued to yield gold with increasingly refined mining methods. In 1901 the road showed net earnings of just under $1,290,000. It hauled almost fifty thousand tons of freight. About one third of the railroad's tonnage moved on the steamboat service organized by the company in 1901 to control traffic on the Yukon River to Dawson, 460 river miles north of the Whitehorse railhead. The White Pass carried 24,365 passengers. It accomplished its work with 268 freight cars of all types, 17 locomotives, and 11 passenger cars. In 1903 Chicago investors paid $750 for each share of its $10 par value stock and received a dividend said to be 60 percent.

By 1911 tonnage on the vest-pocket railroad had fallen to less than 22,300, and earnings were down. Neither of the federal railroad commissions seriously considered it for the first stage of the government line to the Alaska interior. The railroad was too far from the Fairbanks area and ran through foreign territory; also, the region lacked a broad resource base. None of these factors, however, should detract from the achievements of the White Pass. Its construction through the awesome country from Skagway to the summit on an extremely steep 3.9 percent grade showed that it was possible to breach the mountains with a railroad. Its earnings demonstrated that a railroad so built would pay, provided that it was tied to active mines on the interior end. Its operation proved that northland railroads could move the interior closer in time to the United States: it helped to cut Chicago-Dawson travel from two months to nine days.

The White Pass also offered some lessons less willingly learned by Alaska railroad enthusiasts. The road was expensive, costing $10,000 a mile to build at turn-of-the-century prices. Early-day profits were earned at the expense of users: the passenger fare in 1913, for example, was eighteen cents per mile, though tourists paid one-half that rate. To keep trains running with heavy loads in winter required a snow fleet and associated maintenance costs. The small traffic volume warned of the limited tonnage for a railroad depending primarily upon subarctic mines and their satellite enterprises.

The Copper River & Northwestern Railway was the most important, physically and financially, of the tidewater-to-interior lines. A standard guage road, it was owned by the powerful Alaska Syndicate. The Syndicate owned or dominated the fabulously rich Kennecott copper mines tapped by the railroad; the Alaska Steamship Company, the northland's largest water carrier; and twelve salmon canneries. J. P. Morgan and Company and the Guggenheim family controlled the Alaska Syndicate, although several minor stockholders participated. The Syndicate was a vortex in the economics and politics of Alaska.

The Copper River & Northwestern, the 195-mile "iron trail" made famous by Rex Beach's novel, ran east from Cordova on Prince William Sound, skirted the base of the Chugach Mountains, leapt from island to island over the Copper River delta, then swung north to Chitina, where it turned east once again to the mines at Kennecott. A reconnaissance line was surveyed from Chitina north to the Yukon Valley, but that portion of the road remained unbuilt. The Copper River line was a monument to the vision, bravery, and tenacity of the legendary Heney — "Murray O'Neill" in the Rex Beach novel. His partners in the venture, E. S. Graves, president of the White Pass, and Erastus C. Hawkins, the English line's chief engineer, shared Heney's qualities. With his own and White Pass money, Heney began building in 1906 from Eyak (now Cordova) toward the copper mines. The Alaska Syndicate was building, too. Expensive failures, including a spectacular storm that smashed an artificial harbor, forced the Syndicate to abandon Katalla and Valdez and take in the White Pass group. The English backers of the White Pass had no stomach for a financial duel with the Syndicate and did not object. The Morgan-Guggenheims retained Hawkins as engineer and Heney as contractor at cost plus 6.5 percent, with orders to build in a hurry. That was in 1907. In 1911 the first ore-carrying train moved the 195 miles from the Bonanza mine to the ocean.

The test of Heney and Hawkins came fifty-three miles out of Cordova, where the violent Copper River surged through a narrow canyon between the faces of two great glaciers. Here the river had to be bridged. When the summer sun shone on the serried glaciers, giant bergs would come crackling away from the masses of ice, crash into the river, and plunge downstream with tremendous force. One engineer guessed that the two glaciers were really one because they stood so close together, and that the river had merely hollowed out a trough for its own passage. He also surmised that when Heney and Hawkins sought footings for their bridge piers they would discover ancient ice beneath the roaring river. Heney and Hawkins instead found hardpan and built their ice-proof bridge, the most famous of many bold Copper River spans.

The road was a marvel of maintenance. When winter winds of up to eighty miles per hour sometimes drove snow deep over the tracks along the delta, a rotary plow with two pusher locomotives would ram into the thick, white, swirling mass while the train dogged behind. Looking back, the trainmen in the caboose watched the snow obliterate the cut. There were times when not even plows could get through and the road was blocked for days. During "spring breakup" ice jammed against the bridges and occasionally carried away steel spans. When summer came, tracks built on the moss-and-rubble covering of a glacier's toe heaved and sank as the ice beneath melted away.

Some sections of the Copper River line were constructed to the standards of a first class eastern road of the day, earning for it the reputation of the best-built railroad in Alaska. In other places the road had not followed the specified grades and curves but had been pioneered through on a steep and twisting roadbed. A pile trestle stretched over the Copper at Chitina, where the line made its bend eastward to the mines. It was far below the level of the permanent steel bridge designed for that place, so the heavy ore trains ran down a 4 percent grade, crossed the trestle, then puffed up a 4 percent grade to reach Chitina. Every year at "breakup" the swollen river tore away the trestle and interrupted rail service to the mines for two weeks. The railroad redrove the pilings and rebuilt the trestle each spring rather than pay the price of a steel structure.

The Copper River road was a common carrier, but its real function in the eyes of its owners was to carry their ore. Anyone else who wanted to use it paid dearly for the privilege. In 1914 Alaska's delegate to Congress revealed that the CR & NW charged thirty-four dollars a ton for mining machinery carried 131 miles, while the transcontinental rail charges from New York to Seattle on the same ton were thirty dollars. The passenger fare was 12½ cents per mile. Even with its stiff rates the road made no money until fiscal year 1916, when wartime demands for copper put it in the black. Huge operating expenses and interest on the construction and equipment costs of $90,000 per mile gobbled up its income and left it with net deficits of over one million dollars in some earlier years. In fiscal year 1912 it carried less than 20,300 tons of freight. Although the CR & NW was a vital link to the Alaska Syndicate's enormously profitable mining, smelting, and water transportation companies, it is not surprising that the Morgan-Guggenheims wanted the government to buy their railroad and relieve them of its burden.

The railroad that the government did purchase was the Alaska Northern, a tumbledown standard gauge line terminating in the Kenai Peninsula town of Seward on Resurrection Bay. The ghosts of this near wraith of a railroad would haunt the builders and operators of the Alaska Railroad for decades. An understanding of that bedevilment begins with a look at the construction of the Alaska Northern, called the Alaska Central in its early days. The Alaska Central was the only surviving tidewater-to-interior line built on shoestring capital. In some respects the ingenuity of its location, organization, and construction compensated for its meager financing. It was the brainchild of John E. Ballaine, a young Seattle newspaper and real estate man who early saw the value of an "All-American" or trans-Alaska route to the Yukon. In 1900 Ballaine began the investigations that led him to select Resurrection Bay as the port site. He projected a line running north to Turnagain Arm of Cook Inlet and along Turnagain's north shore to near the junction of Knik Arm. After entering the Matanuska-Susitna Valley, the Alaska Central's projected route led north through Broad Pass of the Alaska Range and struck the Tanana, the Yukon's largest tributary, near the present town of Nenana. The route was essentially the same as the one later followed by the Alaska Railroad.

Ballaine chose Resurrection Bay and the site of Seward for the tidewater port after an extensive study of other possibilities. He considered Cook Inlet and western Prince William Sound only; the competition and construction problems at Valdez and elsewhere were too formidable. After poring over an array of maps and explorers' reports, he rejected Ship Creek, the head of navigation for ocean vessels on Cook Inlet, because the harbor experienced rapid silting and thirty-five-foot tides. During the winter it was filled at times with ice pans large enough to pierce a steel hull. He also rejected Portage Bay, a blunder, though it was a reasonable move when viewed from the standpoint of Ballaine's immediate interests.

Portage Bay lies along the eastern side of the spiny neck of Kenai Peninsula. From there it is a mere fourteen miles to the head of Turnagain Arm, sixty-four miles north of Seward. Portage Bay was tantalizingly close to Turnagain; a road from there would save mileage. However, two mountainous ridges stood in the way. One, possibly two, tunnels would be necessary at a cost prohibitively expensive to Ballaine's pioneer line. The valley meadow between the mountains had in the past been a deep lake formed by Portage glacier. The glacier had retreated but could advance and dam the valley waters again. Compared with Resurrection Bay, Portage Bay had little hinterland, nor could it tap the potential mineral and scenic riches of Kenai Peninsula. Yet, forty years later a line driven through the mountains with wartime haste proved successful. During the intervening years Ballaine's route drained maintenance funds while the Kenai areas it tapped failed to fulfill his hopes.

In choosing the route that he did, Ballaine rejected the experience of other tidewater lines. Their lesson was that access to bonanza mines — the Dawson gold placers or the Kennecott copper — was required to attract large capital and enjoy immediate tonnage. Instead, Ballaine adopted the visionary belief that inland Alaska would develop diversified resources including gold and other metals, timber, coal, and agriculture to sustain the industrial population. His Alaska Central was meant to haul a wide variety of resources. Ballaine secured the best Alaska resource information of the time, but the best was primitive. He could not have known the full value or extent of the region's natural wealth. Some of it, such as the agricultural land of the Matanuska-Susitna and Tanana valleys, was described only briefly and tentatively. The richest resource, gold, lay still undiscovered in the gravel and muck of the Tanana hills around the site of Fairbanks. Ballaine's decision was a compound of necessity, careful decision, intuition, and hope.

In March 1902 Ballaine and others organized the Alaska Central and sent survey parties into the field to make the preliminary location. George W. Dickinson, former general manager of the Northern Pacific, was president. Senator George Turner of Washington and other politicians served with General Manager Ballaine and his brother Frank on the board of directors. Ballaine's Seattle real estate transactions had given him a keen appreciation of land values. Even before sending construction crews to Resurrection Bay, he dispatched Frank to establish the Seward townsite and claim or purchase as much land at the head of the bay as he could.

In August 1903 the crews began building the Seward terminal, wharf, and dock, and by the end of 1904 had completed 18.3 miles of track. The next year Ballaine sold his construction company, and with it control of the Alaska Central, to others. The new group built to mile 47 and graded several miles beyond. In the summer and fall of 1909 the Alaska Central bondholders foreclosed the bankrupt property, reorganizing it as the Alaska Northern Railway. The renamed line struggled on to Kern Creek, mile 72 at the head of Turnagain Arm, where the tracklaying of the financially exhausted railroad ceased forever.

By 1914 the Alaska Northern was sad and dishevelled. Its officers had largely ignored maintenance while concentrating instead on intramural struggles for corporate control. This was so much the worse, for the line was pioneered through with sixty-five and seventy-pound rail laid over untreated native spruce ties. There were 10° and 12° curves and a 2.5 percent grade against traffic to tidewater. Cuts, fills, and tunnels were dangerously narrow, and native timber trestles sagged over glacial streams. High trestles were built in the Placer River Canyon at miles 48 and 50 as alternatives to costly sidehill and tunnel work. One was an incredible four-story loop that crossed over itself and looked like a doughnut from the air. Both were rickety because the native timbers, mediocre framing members at best, were held by spikes, not bolts, and the spikes had shaken loose from the weight and movement of trains. Elsewhere, slides and floods had undermined or obliterated a roadbed virtually innocent of riprapping or ballast. Winter operation in the mountainous, windy country was entirely beyond the railroad's resources. During the summer a citizen's operating committee ran a little gas car once or twice a week to mile 47 and back again. Occasionally a trailer with freight or express for an isolated miner or prospector tagged along. Since 1911 the company's creditors had been lobbying for the railroad's sale to the federal government, while the 500 residents of Seward lived largely on hopes. In fiscal year 1912 the Alaska Northern hauled a miniscule 257 tons of freight and carried only 2,611 passengers.

The Alaska Central-Alaska Northern failed despite the Fairbanks gold strike of 1902, despite other rich gold finds along the projected route, despite the rapid growth of farming in the Matanuska-Susitna and Tanana valleys. There were several reasons why. President Theodore Roosevelt's conservationist-inspired coal withdrawal in 1906 dashed hopes for immediate large tonnage from the highly regarded Matanuska coal fields. The panic of 1907 further constricted the already tiny trickle of capital into new railroad ventures. At one time J. P. Morgan and Co. might have refinanced the Seward line as a narrow gauge, but Morgan's partners in the Alaska Syndicate, the Guggenheims, vetoed the suggestion of a railroad to the interior in competition with their Copper River & Northwestern. Finally, the Alaska Central-Alaska Northern management was a nest of speculation and intrigue, although exactly how much money and energy it diverted from the business of railroad building will never be known. In any case, the failure of the Seward route confirmed the lessons of the White Pass and Copper River railroads. Lacking generous government aid, a private road had better not build toward the interior without bonanza mines within its reach and big money at its back.

The second railroad purchased for the government system was the little Tanana Valley Railroad, a thirty-four mile narrow gauge mining road. It began at Chena, the head of steamboat navigation on the Tanana, and wound among the mining camps of the Fairbanks district to Chatanika, a gold rush town on the river of the same name. A spur line ran 4.7 miles northeast to Fairbanks itself.

The TVRR was strictly an interior road designed to link the booming Fairbanks placers with a navigable stream and capture the lucrative overland freighting business from teamsters charging up to ten dollars per ton mile. Its president was an attorney, Falcon Joslin, fired with visions of farmers growing diversified crops on what he claimed were the "unlimited"[1] Tanana Valley farm lands. His other dream was of a railroad — his — passing through the Tanana Valley, linking Nome on Seward Peninsula in the west with the port of Haines on Lynn Canal in southeastern Alaska. Only dreams could cross that many miles of bog and barren, so the accomplishments of Joslin and his railroad were much more modest. Financed by English and American capital, Joslin's line built from Chena to Gilmore and laid the spur to Fairbanks in 1905. Two years later, only five years after gold had been discovered in the district, it ran through to Chatanika. Construction wages were a baronial $7.50 per day but might vanish quickly in a town where no coin smaller than a quarter circulated and sandwiches could cost a dollar apiece. During the youthful days of the Fairbanks placers, the railroad served the mines well and made money. In 1909 its net earnings were $115,902.77. Its ton-mile rate was fifty-eight cents, stupefyingly expensive when compared with the transcontinental rate of about one penny, but cheaper than the nearest local charge, one dollar by winter sledge.

Fairbanks at its early-day peak held perhaps five thousand souls. Four or five towns in the creeks were bustling places with banks and telephones and trading populations of about one thousand. Farmers grew fresh produce for market. In 1909 $9.5 million of gold came out of the ground. But it would not last. The Fairbanks mines were the victims of their environment in which precipitation was eleven or twelve inches a year. Water for sluicing and for stripping away soil from ancient streambeds was abundant only during spring and early summer, when torrents from melting snow rushed down the hillsides. The quartz veins of the district were unsuited for large lode mines; thus, no corporate giants similar to those at the Juneau mines moved in to sustain the boom. Most of the trees had been cut for the mines, and some workings had closed down because of the fuel famine. High transportation, labor, and other costs of doing business in the subarctic made it difficult to work any but the richest ground. Fairbanks gold production fell two-thirds in the next five years, and the prosperity and population of the region went down with it.

The TVRR suffered from the general decline. In 1914 it hauled 27,832 passengers, only about half the number it had carried four years before. In 1914 its net earnings were $22,319.69 and dropping sharply. Freight was down almost one third from the fifteen thousand tons of 1909 and 1910. In part, the road was feeling the effects of the automobile competition that would eventually destroy it. Twenty autos a day ran over an improving wagon road to the creeks.

Jerry-built construction was taking its toll. Untreated spruce served for ties, bridges, and trestles. The TVRR's report to its bond and stockholders for fiscal year 1916 warned that extensive renewals and heavy repairs to rolling stock, heretofore neglected, were necessary and would continue to be required. Although the line enjoyed spacious terminal grounds and good facilities, the roadbed rested mostly on earth fill and was in poor condition. The run-down equipment included four engines, twenty-one cars, three coaches, a snowplow, and miscellaneous items. Not enough rolling stock was available to carry all the fuel wood offered. The heaviest, best engine saw no service: it stood idly in the yards because the flimsy roadbed would no longer accept its weight. In 1916 the road could not pay the interest on its bonds. Unable to raise new capital, it was on the brink of physical and financial collapse.

From these essays in frontier railroad building came one inescapable conclusion. If the federal government wanted a tidewater-to-interior line, it would have to underwrite its building or build the road itself. While Alaska's railroads were born, struggled, and died, other developments were convincing two successive national administrations that only the government could build the road.

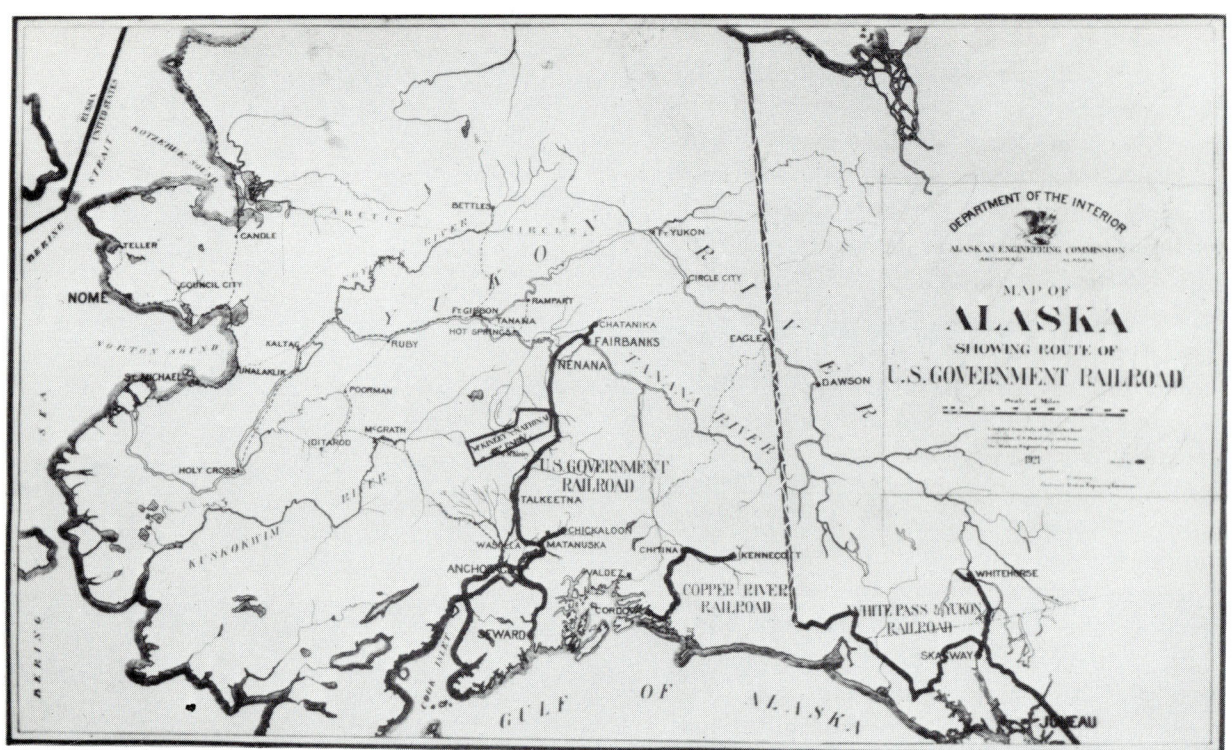

A 1921 Alaskan Engineering Commission map showing The Alaska Railroad, the Copper River & Northwestern, and the White Pass & Yukon.
The Alaska Railroad

The route of The Alaska Railroad.
Edwin M. Fitch and Praeger Publishers, Inc.

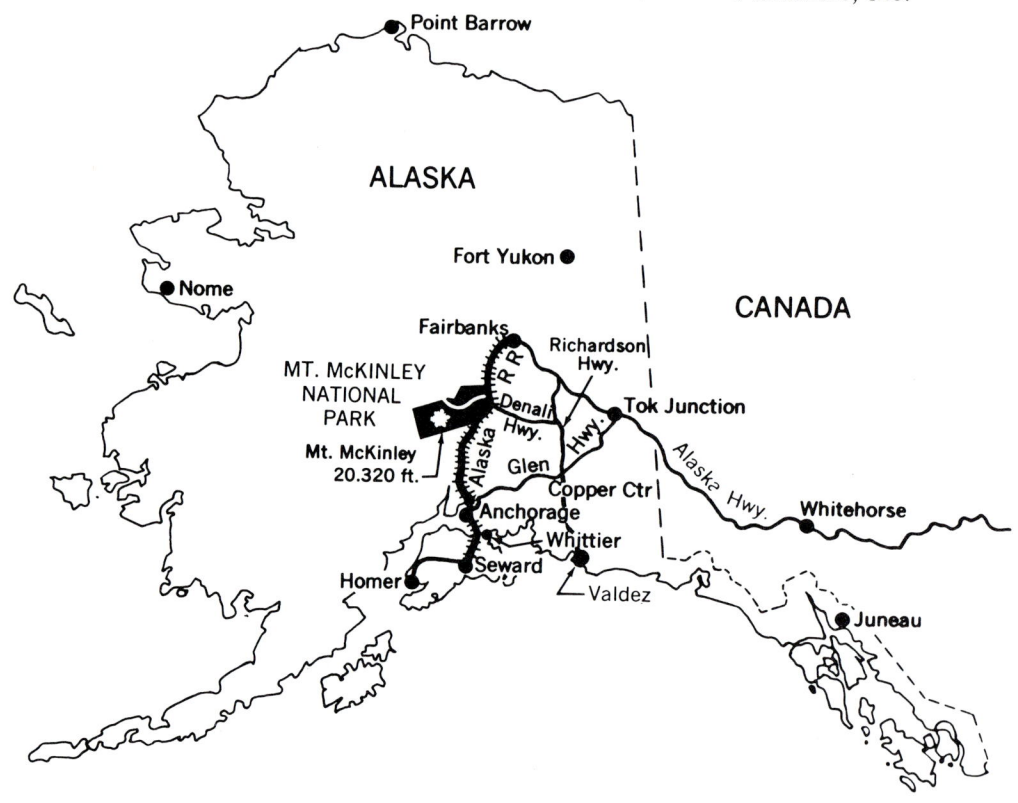

Route map of The Alaska Railroad from Seward to Fairbanks. *The Alaska Railroad*

The Lure of Coal

The coal lay folded into rock, bound where the violent primeval pressures had formed it. It lay in black scars across bleak cliffs, exposed by centuries of wind and water. Long before men discovered Alaska's great fields, they knew that some coal was there. They found it in abundance in much the same way as they found rich gold: sometimes by chance, sometimes by intuition, sometimes by careful prospecting.

Coal worked only a little less magic than gold. Although it could not drive men mad in the search or possession of it, Alaska coal bewitched them powerfully. It led a shrewd and wealthy man into a damaging blunder, helped to besmirch official reputations, and hastened the downfall of a president and his party.

Coal and gold and railroads assumed mingled roles in Alaska's transportation drama. The story was played out in committee rooms, on the floor of Congress, in legal offices, and in the private sanctums of cabinet members and presidents. It began in earnest with the last of the Far North's great gold rushes, deep in Alaska's interior. It opened in a familiar episode of gold and isolation, this time in an area reachable by an all-Alaska railroad.

In the summer of 1903 the flush point of the gold fever was on the south bank of the Chena River, a small, sluggish tributary of the Tanana. There the straggly collection of log and frame shanties called Fairbanks lay on a flood plain, ringed on three sides by the high, domelike hills of the Tanana-Yukon basin, with the broad Tanana Valley opening southward to the distant towers of the Alaska Range. The rich green hills covered with spruce and birch and the jagged white peaks were picturesque, but Fairbanks stampeders were more likely to be preoccupied with the high cost of their supplies.

Fairbanks was a paradigm of the Alaska transportation problem. Merchants fretted over goods that arrived during the three-month navigation season or not at all and over the investment and storage required to secure a years' inventory in a brief time. A trunk railroad from the Alaska coast would bring year-round service. It would also lessen the prospectors' dependence upon the White Pass line and its steamboats and save the duty on goods shipped through Canada: eighteen dollars per ton for sugar, twenty dollars for rice. An all-Alaska railroad would reduce freight charges by cutting distances and promoting competition. The total basic charge for freight from Puget Sound into the Fairbanks district was ten cents a pound or $200 per ton, compared to a landed cost of 4¾ cents per pound at Dawson, Yukon Territory.

Although the "all-American" railroad would reduce prices and improve deliveries to the Fairbanks distribution point, only a network of high-grade roads would cut the cost of freighting to the creeks. In 1903 it sometimes cost as much to move freight from Fairbanks thirty miles or so to the mines as it did to bring it to Fairbanks, four thousand water miles from Puget Sound. The transportation charge of twenty or more cents a pound at the final destination was a crushing burden considering the price levels: twenty-five cents bought a pound of butter or coffee at retail in Seattle. Roads built by private subscription helped, as did the better ones constructed by the Alaska Road Commission after 1905. The Tanana Valley line helped still more, although even the doughty TVRR required feeder roads. In any case, the roads fanning out from Fairbanks needed a railroad from the coast in order to realize their full effectiveness. The local roads and the tidewater-to-interior line were as mutually dependent as the trunk and limbs of a tree.

No one would build that trunk until he could garner a greater tonnage than promised by the merchants and miners of the interior. The floundering Alaska Central was evidence enough that any railroader had to have tonnage — heavy, daily, paying tonnage — within easy reach before essaying a railroad into the wilds. Many Alaskans pinned their hopes on coal.

In the minds of its advocates, coal was the greatest of Alaska's bounties after salmon, gold, and copper. It would fuel the Pacific fleet, preferably at a port in one of the territory's own superlative harbors; if not, then Alaska coal could be laid down at established Pacific ports for less than eastern coal could be carried to the west coast. The country's proud dreadnoughts, and its western industries, could run on Alaska coal. Of course, Alaska coal would feed territorial canneries, homes, and future industries, halting the disgraceful importation of the "outside" product. Charles H. Merillat, an attorney for the Alaska Central, was specific. Alaska coal, he said, could be delivered to the United States Navy for seven dollars a ton, or $2.20 per ton less than the cost of eastern coal.

"If any of you gentlemen have an appetite for blood-stirring fiction," a cynical Congressman Frank Mondell told his colleagues in 1919, "read the descriptions of the tremendous value of the Alaska coal fields as written in official documents some few years ago."[1] It would be easy enough, in view of the coal's failure to find a large market, to charge up the claims in its favor to typical western extravagant promotionalism. A detractor could say that Roosevelt's withdrawal of Alaska coal lands from further entry in 1906 was not very critical for the future. The Navy's gradual conversion to oil, the rise of the California oil industry, the opening of the Panama Canal and the dramatic reduction of transcontinental freight rates on coal, and the nationwide depression in the coal industry after World War I all could be marshalled to show how vain were the hopes for Alaska coal.

Granting these arguments, it did appear for a time that some Alaska coals could be extensively developed. One of the Alaska Central's survey parties rediscovered the huge Matanuska River fields while running a reconnaissance up that stream for a branch line to the Copper River. Steaming tests conducted over the years proved the Matanuska product to be the equal of the best eastern naval coal. But steaming qualities were not mining qualities. Later, coal operators learned that the beds were badly folded and faulted, that rock dams sometimes interrupted the seams, that the coal was often larded with bone, and that normal handling could reduce it to powder. Alfred H. Brooks, head of the Geological Survey in Alaska and a sympathetic friend of the territory, admitted that Alaska coal seams were bent and broken. Eastern coal operators who enjoyed "practically horizontal" and "continuous beds" were "somewhat dismayed" at Alaska's coal, he said.[2]

That was in 1921. In 1906 the qualities of the Matanuska coal were more mysterious and could inspire greater romance. To Alaskans, the withdrawal was a craven surrender to eastern coal interests who wished to throttle potential competition. Or it was mindless pampering of visionary conservationists who wished to make Alaska the plaything of their vaporous theories. In reality it was neither. The fact remained that the withdrawal, together with the suspicion cast over coal claims previously located and the lack of federal incentives to rail building, sounded the knell for all roads not linked to bonanza mines. Even before the withdrawal, federal officials began reexamining their refusal to grant substantial aid to Alaska's faltering railroads. Theodore Roosevelt vaguely requested "just and feasible" assistance in his 1904 annual message.[3] Aid proposals from the executive and other respectable sources increased with the years. None of them were adopted, partly because of a new, powerful element on the Alaska scene — the Alaska Syndicate.

The Copper River & Northwestern Railway was a minor adjunct of the Syndicate, which was formed for the purpose of owning or controlling a wide range of the productive resources of Alaska. The Syndicate's objective of rational, unified development in a remote, difficult country was laudable, but it required excluding the harassing, disorganizing effects of competition. Sometimes competitors were eliminated, or at least badly squeezed, by genteel methods long in vogue in the upper echelons of business. At other times the squeezing was left to subordinates whose techniques, as in the famous Keystone Canyon shooting, lacked sophistication. Either way, the Syndicate was certain to enhance its rapidly developing reputation as the corporate ogre of Alaska.

Most of the Syndicate's real and fancied adventures in Alaska's economics and politics do not concern us. The background of its involvement in railroads and coal is quickly told. In 1900 Stephen Birch, a mining engineer who had accompanied an army expedition along the Copper River two years before, bought a number of copper claims. He interested the famed Guggenheim mining family, who, with J. P. Morgan & Co. and others, organized the Alaska Syndicate in 1906 to provide development capital. The Syndicate's first interest was its fabulous copper holdings. To exploit them with the assurance of water transportation to the Guggenheim smelter at Tacoma, the Syndicate acquired steamship and lighterage companies which it consolidated under the Alaska Steamship Company. It also bought and sold canneries and other properties, extinguishing and creating corporations as it went along.

The Syndicate was determined that no other railroad would build to the interior in competition with its Copper River & Northwestern from Cordova. Although the CR & NW had not crossed the Alaska Range into the Tanana Valley, its backers were determined that if or when any railroad breached the mountains, it would be theirs. When the time came, the Alaska Syndicate would extend its unified, comprehensive mining and other operations into the interior along with its railroad.

To hold its prime position the Syndicate employed three means. Violence was the least necessary and most politically damaging. Syndicate employees used it twice. On one occasion Copper River construction crews drove another railroad's workers from the Cordova area. Another time the deputized leader of an armed band shot and killed a worker on a rival railroad attempting to build through the Keystone Canyon near Valdez, the site of an abandoned Syndicate right-of-way. The slaying in the narrow gorge was the more unfortunate because the challenging railroad was a petty promotional line attempting a route that the vastly more resourceful Syndicate had already surrendered though not in title. The Syndicate lost more face during the deputy's trial, at which time charges of bribery and other irregularities were freely made.

The second Syndicate method was to lobby and maneuver against bills for significant federal aid to any other railroad. Able, articulate David H. Jarvis, the Syndicate lobbyist, asked Congress to imagine the disastrous effect of government aid to one railroad upon all other lines that did not receive federal largesse. The few bills that emerged from committee usually lacked wide or determined support and were easily defeated by the Syndicate's friends in Congress. In its congressional struggles the Syndicate worked with other established roads in Alaska; even, in a measure, fought their battles, for they had an equal interest in withholding federal aid from an upstart competitor. Yet it had no compunction against using its power to squelch existing Alaska railroads when any of them stirred with life.

In applying its third technique, the Syndicate employed its intimate ties with the New York financial community to ward off any large new investment in Alaska railroads. John Ballaine of the Alaska Central had an occasion to know at firsthand. The story is complex, but this is the essence: Ballaine had been forced off the Alaska Central's board of directors and was in danger of losing his entire interest in the railroad. The Morgan-affiliated Canadian bank which held most of the Alaska Central's stocks and bonds was in receivership. In a desperate attempt to regain control of the Alaska Central, Ballaine in 1908 or early 1909 approached the ebullient George Perkins, a Morgan partner who was also the bank's representative on the Syndicate. Ballaine proposed to Perkins that the Morgan bank recoup its losses in its Canadian affiliate by refinancing the Alaska Central and underwriting its completion to the interior as a narrow gauge, the new line to be under Ballaine's direction. Perkins sent a traffic expert to Alaska to reconnoiter, then visited the territory himself in the summer of 1909. In meetings with Ballaine at Seward and later at Seattle he waxed enthusiastic over the possibilities along the Alaska Central's projected route. After Perkins' return to

New York he cooled noticeably and, in a final interview with Ballaine toward the end of the year, told him that the deal was off. As Perkins explained it, the partners in the Alaska Syndicate had agreed to finance new enterprises in competition with Syndicate ventures only by mutual consent. The Guggenheims refused to permit competition with their Copper River line. The Tanana Valley, they said, was "their territory." There would be no more railroad building in Alaska until the coal fields were reopened, Perkins declared, then he closed the conversation with a snap: "We will not allow the Alaska Northern to build into the Tanana Valley."[4]

Perkins had mentioned coal in his last interview with Ballaine, for the Syndicate still had hopes of exploiting the Bering River coal fields adjacent to the Copper River line. The Syndicate's effort to add coal to its resource development program would, soon after the Perkins-Ballaine interview, explode in the traumatic Ballinger-Pinchot affair, would sunder the Taft administration's developing Alaska's political and economic program, and would rend the Republican party itself. A look at some essentials of the Ballinger-Pinchot controversy will clarify its relationship to the Alaska railroad problem.

The conservationist, or Pinchot, faction was not composed of the preservationists and landscape mystics who inhabited the demonian dreams of the developmentalist group. The conservationists were properly horrified at the flagrant waste, the denuded forest lands, the eroded soil, that seemed inherent in the American march across the continent. They believed in private enterprise, however. They had worked with grazers, water power companies, and other users of the public domain. They merely wished to withdraw what remained of the country's virgin lands, study and classify them, work out a rational plan for their exploitation and renewal, and open them to private development under careful federal supervision. All this took time. The elaborate steps in the conservationist process exasperated Alaskans and others who wanted to develop the territory as speedily as the great continental west had been opened up. The conservationists had little sympathy for rapid, relatively uncontrolled exploitation. To them, Alaska existed for the nation, not for itself. It was the country's last natural treasure house.

The greatest of the conservationists, Gifford Pinchot, had revolutionized conservation practices within the Roosevelt administration, the upper echelons of which were sympathetic to his ideas. Growing congressional opposition during Roosevelt's second term and William Howard Taft's ascension to the presidency in 1909 marked the setting of the conservationist star. One firm indication of the new order was Taft's appointment of Richard A. Ballinger, a progressive, development-minded westerner, as secretary of the interior. When Ballinger took office a group of coal land claims in the Bering River field, the so-called Cunningham claims, were moving toward patent. That is, they were in the process of passing from the public domain into private hands. They had been located well before Roosevelt's November 12, 1906, withdrawal order and so were unaffected by it.

The 1900 and 1904 coal land laws controlling the Cunningham claims appeared to assume that coal land locators were either angels or idiots. Under their provisions, a locator could claim but 160 acres, an area much too small for a commercial coal mine. Before locating he could not agree to a combination for commercial development with any of the other 160-acre claimants all about him. Nor was he to be a dummy entryman, that is, a person who claimed the land with the intention of conveying it to someone else. Once he and his neighbor claimants moved their claims to entry (a step in the patenting process) they could, for the first time, gather round and discuss the possibility of combining their holdings. The laws cast doubt on whether any of the coal entries in Alaska could have been made in good faith.

The Cunningham claims were entered neither by saints nor by mooncalves and were therefore tainted in the eyes of the law. As later investigation revealed, the Cunningham claimants intended, illegally, to consolidate their claims before locating them. What was worse, Daniel Guggenheim and Clarence Cunningham had arranged for Guggenheim to receive a half interest in the claims as soon as the entrymen received their patents. The Guggenheim-Cunningham deal was legal but in the conservationists' view was an immoral surrender to the interests.

Late in 1909 the story broke. The Morgan-

Guggenheim Alaska Syndicate — a corporate monster — supposedly was gobbling up the riches of the last frontier with federal connivance. Hysteria and bureaucratic duplicity mounted quickly in both the conservationist and developmentalist camps. Pinchot, merely a bureau chief as head of the Forest Service, dramatized the conservationist cause when he attacked Secretary Ballinger and the course of conservation policy under Taft. Reluctantly, for he well knew he was making a martyr, Taft fired Pinchot.

In the joint congressional investigation that followed, conservationists succeeded in swinging the spotlight to largely irrelevant issues of administrative deviousness. Louis Brandeis, the brilliant counsel for the conservationists, was able to prove a damaging charge against Taft. Brandeis showed that Taft could not have read a key document which he claimed to have seen before he cleared Ballinger of certain charges. The document was completed at a later time but was predated to agree with the president's claim that he had seen it before exonerating Ballinger. Next, Brandeis demonstrated that Taft's letter of exoneration was founded on a memorandum written by a man in Ballinger's department. The president and the Republican majority on the committee fumbled with lame explanations while the conservationists savored a moral triumph.

The majority report cleared the administration, as it was expected to do. But Ballinger, the Guggenheims, Attorney General Wickersham, and the president himself, were badly tarred. Ballinger resigned in frustration in 1911. That year the General Land Office routinely cancelled the Cunningham claims.

In 1911 it would have been a sanguine man indeed who predicted the private construction of a tidewater-to-interior railroad in Alaska. Private capital was scarce. Federal coal policies meant that existing roads imported coal for their engines or, as in the case of the TVRR, burned wood. Interior gold production had reached a plateau. The Alaska Northern had begun its campaign for federal purchase, to be followed the next year by the Morgan-Guggenheim interests on behalf of the Copper River & Northwestern. The Ballinger-Pinchot controversy had discredited the Taft administration and its Alaska policy. The policy, which stood little chance of congressional enactment, included a federal guarantee of the bonds of a private trunk line to the interior. Besides the railroad bonding scheme, the old program had included an appointive commission and a coal leasing bill. The commission would have given the territory a unified administration and provided Congress with systematic legislative proposals for Alaska. Unfortunately, the commission plan had been applied to the Philippines so it smacked of paternalistic guidance for "backward" peoples. Probably more efficient and practical than a legislature superimposed upon the burgeoning bureaucracy in Alaska, the plan was too radical a departure from traditions of territorial government. The railroad proposal faced the united opposition of all existing lines. The coal lease bill was one the conservationists had long sought. Leasing of coal lands would have given them greater control over the resource than the old patent system, but they had not succeeded in shoving a lease law through Congress.

Nineteen-eleven was the watershed year for a new Alaska policy. Taft's appointment of Walter L. Fisher to succeed Ballinger as secretary of the interior in that year prefigured the policy's redirection. Taft was a genuine conservationist; so was Fisher. It was simply that the portly, relaxed Taft was uncomfortable with the spare, dedicated Pinchot and other conservationist zealots. Once he had rid himself of the Pinchot crowd, of the men with ideas "of lunar character,"[5] Taft was quite willing to proceed with a moderately progressive program wholly unsuited to the fervent immediatism of a Pinchot.

Responding to pressure from congressional Progressives, Taft soon developed a new Alaska policy unsullied by Ballinger-Pinchot. His most dramatic signal was the administration's assumption of leadership in the Alaska railroad question. In the year of his appointment the new secretary of the interior visited Alaska and returned with a recommendation that the government purchase the Alaska Northern. It was an inferior railroad, Fisher admitted, but it was projected through a potentially rich region and could be purchased much more cheaply than the Copper River & Northwestern. On February 2, 1912, Taft sent a special message to Congress asking for government construction and ownership of an Alaska railroad. In August Congress passed a "home rule" bill providing for a territorial legislature. The measure carried a significant rider, Section 18, granting a Taft request. The rider authorized the president to appoint a commission to study and recommend those Alaska railroad routes that would best "develop the country and the resources thereof for the use of the people of the United States."[6] From the welter of defeats and frustrations, public and private, Taft and Congress had at last seized the initiative. There would be no letting go.

Two railroads the United States government did not buy: one, the Copper River & Northwestern, is shown in the shape of a train passing in front of the Childs Glacier. *Pope Collection, University of Alaska Archives*

The famous "million dollar bridge" spanning the Copper River, one of the CR & NW's great construction feats. Photograph taken August 30, 1910. *Pope Album, University of Alaska Archives*

The White Pass & Yukon, except for its first 21 miles out of Skagway, passes through Canadian territory, one reason it was not purchased. Here, near Skagway, the track parallels the gold rush "Trail of 98." *Pope Collection, University of Alaska Archives*

A White Pass & Yukon train at Lake Bennett, in the Yukon Territory. *Pope Collection, University of Alaska Archives*

An Alaska Central special northbound from Seward with an unseasonable snowplow attached, 1906. *The Alaska Railroad*

The Alaska Central, later the Alaska Northern, was purchased to form the first seventy miles of the government railroad. Here the Alaska Central's engine No. 1 arrives at the port of Seward, 1904. *The Alaska Railroad*

The Alaska Northern's old No. 1 in service on the Seward Division of the Alaskan Engineering Commission during the construction days. *The Anchorage Historical and Fine Arts Museum*

Gasoline car pauses at mile 41 on the Alaska Northern about 1915, probably with an Alaskan Engineering Commission survey crew. *The Alaska Railroad*

Gasoline car on the Alaska Northern, mile 26. After the financial collapse of the Alaska Northern a summertime "citizen's car" ran along a portion of the route. This may be the car pictured here. *Peterson Photo, Alaska Historical Library*

An Alaska Central tunnel at mile 53, in the rugged Kenai country. The narrow and wavy roadbed and narrow tunnel were typical of the Alaska Central—Alaska Northern. *Peterson Photo, Alaska Historical Library*

The Birth of the Alaskan Engineering Commission

The law specified the men who would serve on the Alaska Railroad Commission: an army engineer, a navy engineer, and a civil engineer unconnected with any Alaskan railroad. To insure that respected, learned Alfred H. Brooks would be included, Congress designated him by his title. Taft appointed, in addition to Brooks, Major Jay J. Morrow of the Army Engineers, chairman; Leonard M. Cox, a civil engineer with the navy; and Colin M. Ingersoll, a private consulting engineer. Congress asked the commission to report its findings to the president by December 1, giving the four men a scant three months to organize, procure supplies and equipment, arrange transportation, travel to, through, and from Alaska, and whip their material into presentable shape. August 31, the date of the appointment, was climatically the beginning of autumn in Alaska's interior. On that day the commissioners were scattered from coast to coast with all of their formidable tasks facing them.

They left Seattle on the tenth of September. They visited Seward, the Matanuska-Susitna Valley, Katalla, Valdez, Fairbanks, Cordova, and the transportation routes in between. They left interior Alaska as the northern winter was closing in: horse sleds carried them near Isabelle Pass of the Alaska Range. They rode parts of the White Pass from Skagway and the Grand Trunk Pacific from Prince Rupert, British Columbia. On November 17, two months and a week after their departure, they were back in Seattle. Following two more stops at Vancouver and Ottawa for further study of Canadian railroad conditions, the commissioners returned to Washington early in December.

On January 20, 1913, they handed their report to the president. The report was a collation of government documents, material gathered during hearings and interviews at every stop, and the commissioners' often hasty impressions. Morrow, Cox, Ingersoll, and Brooks made two major recommendations. They urged a line from the Chitina railhead of the Copper River & Northwestern to Fairbanks. This railway would open up the mineral and agricultural resources of the Tanana Valley, while an extension of the CR & NW would tap the Bering River coal fields made famous by the Cunningham claims. Secondly, they recommended a railway from the end of steel on the Alaska Northern through the Matanuska-Susitna Valley, over the Alaska Range, and into the Innoko-Iditarod mining area of the Kuskokwim Valley. A branch line would run to the sprawling Matanuska coal fields. They asked for a quick start on both routes.

Congress' charge to the commission was generously broad, but its meagre appropriation of $25,000 precluded elaborate surveys over the variety of possible routes to the interior. The commission's limited travel funds, scarce transportation, the lateness of the season, plus a national prejudice in favor of an "all American" route confined consideration to the following ice-free ports: Seward, Valdez, Cordova, and Katalla. The virtual obligation to reach either or both the Matanuska and Bering coal fields precluded Valdez, for there were no easy grades from that port to the coal. Construction and operating costs over the high, difficult passes would have been excessive, and the commission was extremely cost-conscious. The prohibitive costs of a harbor and terminal at Katalla, where a breakwater built by the Alaska Syndicate had gone down before a storm, militated against that port. That left Cordova and Seward. Again, costs were controlling. The commission estimated that construction from the Copper River line 313 miles to Fairbanks would cost less than $14 million, versus over $17,700,000 for 391 miles from the end of the Alaska Northern. The estimated operating costs were less by some $280,000 per year on the route from Cordova. The commission's estimates were attacked by partisans of the Alaska Northern, but the assumptions on which they were based seem reasonable enough.

Squabbling aside, the commission's conclusions were open to this challenge: it had recommended a line through the agricultural Matanuska-Susitna Valley, so why not extend that road 275 more miles to the Tanana-Yukon Valley through the mineralized Broad Pass and Nenana River country? Then there would be no need to construct a railway across the barren land between the CR & NW's railhead at Chitina and Fairbanks. The Bering River field still could be tapped by a short line from the Copper River road.

The answer is that the commission's choice rested on another element than cost: immediate tonnage. The commissioners doubted whether an extension of the Alaska Northern route offered any prospect of regular, heavy traffic. They rested their case on coal, but their best judgment could be little more than a guess. They projected a possible market for Alaska bituminous of half a million tons per year. Their estimate assumed that full-scale mining could conquer the known problems, faulted beds and friability. If the market could be developed (the commissioners took an unblinking look at the obstacles), the Bering River coal adjacent to the Copper River line could be brought to tidewater for less cost than the Matanuska product. Meanwhile, the CR & NW enjoyed the heavy ore haul from the Kennecott mines.

What was more important for the future, the commissioners demonstrated that federal construction and operation were vitally necessary to a successful trunk line. Any new private railroad would run a deficit so large that stockholders would desert it in droves. Not that they intended to say so. Indeed, they wriggled out of any overt conclusions about public versus private ownership by saying that Congress had not asked them to decide the question. Their figures decided it for them. The commissioners began by assuming that if the railroad were to achieve its "immediate object" — "the development of the interior" —[1] the average freight rate could not be more than five cents per ton mile and the passenger rate not over six cents per mile. In this they were probably right, since ton-mile and passenger rates in the United States were substantially lower. The trouble was, the existing Alaska railroads were charging much more: the Copper River's passenger rate was 12½ cents a mile, and its freight rates varied from 3½ to 14½ cents per ton mile. Any assertion that building to the interior would itself create business sufficient to cut rates to the commission's maximums had to be based on faith sublime.

The commissioners had the faith. They assumed that although the Fairbanks-upper Yukon region had shipped an average of twenty-four thousand tons over the past ten years, a completed railroad would stimulate business so much that the railroad alone could expect forty-five thousand tons of inbound freight a year. Their estimate of less than a $14 million construction cost worked out to $44,600 per mile. The estimate was wildly optimistic, given the $90,000 per mile cost of the Copper River and the later $119,000 cost per mile of the completed Alaska Railroad. The commission blandly used its estimate to compute the interest on construction costs.

The commissioners had figured in their estimate a $100 per mile tax, a tax that was later repealed in 1914. Deducting the $100 per mile charge, a privately constructed Cordova-Fairbanks road paying 6 percent interest on its bonds would have lost almost $493,000 per year, even under the commission's rosy estimates. The commissioners assumed that a line constructed by the government, or by government-guaranteed bonds at 3 percent, would break even. Its income, in other words, would equal its operating expenses and interest charges. But the commissioners made no allowance for a depreciation reserve, capital expenses, or profits, matters of more than passing concern to investors. They did not suggest where the government might find the altruists who would invest in, then operate such a railroad.

The federal treasury would have to finance the deficits hidden in the commission report — that was inescapable. A federally subsidized private line or federally operated road were the alternatives. William Howard Taft followed the report's implications very nearly to their conclusion. "The necessary inference," the chief executive told Congress, was that the government would have to build the line or guarantee its construction. It followed, he wrote, that the government "should own the roads, the cost of which it really pays." Taft was too much the Sumnerian individualist to accept either subsidized operation, which he did not consider, or federal operation, which he vigorously rejected. "I am very much opposed to Government operation," he wrote, "but I believe that Government ownership with private operation under lease is the proper solution of the difficulties here presented."[2]

Taft's opinions no longer mattered. When he transmitted the commission's report, he was a lame duck president, repudiated in the rousing Democratic victory of the previous November. Taft's nemesis, Woodrow Wilson, coupled a belief in an aggressive, responsible national state with faith in the vast potential of Alaska. In December 1913 the lean-faced, bespectacled president stood before applauding congressmen and told them, "Alaska, as a storehouse, should be unlocked. One key to it is a system of railways." He stood for federal control: "These the Government should itself build and administer, and the ports and terminals it should itself control in the interest of all who wish to use them for the service and development of the country and its people." Although he did not directly refer to coal, Wilson discussed the related mineral resource problem in general terms, reflecting the continuing uncertainty about the real worth of Alaska's known resources. "How the tempting resources of the country are to be exploited . . . must be worked out . . . not upon theory, but upon lines of practical expediency. . . . We must use the resources of the country, not lock them up."[3] Four times congressmen applauded the president's nine sentences on Alaska. The applause was a good index of the popularity of the ideas those sentences expressed.

Wilson caught the infectious enthusiasm for Alaska displayed by his secretary of the interior, the Canadian-born lawyer and journalist Franklin K. Lane. A westerner, Lane was "not afflicted with the conservation disease," as the *Fairbanks Daily News-Miner* put it.[4] At the same time, he favored controlled development over unprincipled rape of the land. He was excited about the possibilities of an Alaska provided with a set of federal ground rules to insure free and fair private competition. Lane's thoughts, as expressed in his 1913 annual report, were repeated so often by advocates of Alaskan development that they are summarized here. Variations occurred, of course, but generally, Alaska boosters agreed with Lane in saying: 1) The North Country stood on the threshold of rapid development. The resource and railroad boom in Canada was one proof. The climatic analogy with productive Scandinavia, already a labored and trite analogy, was another. 2) Private railroads had failed to open up Alaska; only a government road with rates and service keyed to development rather than immediate profit could do that. 3) If Alaska were developed, the nation would benefit in material and spiritual ways not reducible to nice calculations on the income of the railroad. 4) One of Alaska's great resources, coal, should be developed through a leasing and royalty system, with a maximum holding of 2,600 acres, or the average of all coal operations in the United States.

A variety of railroad bills, including one by the territorial delegate, James Wickersham, had been introduced. By the time of Wilson's State of the Union Address they had moved through hearings and were ready for debate. The hearings were mostly a rehashing of ideas about Alaska, but some witnesses added a few new twists. Alfred H. Brooks declared that people would pour into Alaska because of population pressures in the first forty-eight states. "As a nation," he opined, "we are getting land hungry." Delegate Wickersham urged Congress to authorize the road and thereby break the power of the Morgan-Guggenheims. The opposition was too fragmented to have much impact. Alaska railroad men might disapprove of government ownership in general, but each hoped that the government would consider purchasing his line. A few pessimistic voices were heard in the general chorus of praise for Alaska's potential. Charles V. Piper, a grasslands expert in the Department of Agriculture, foretold a "calamity" if homesteaders rushed to Alaska in the belief that they could open it as their forefathers had exploited the prairies. Oliver L. Dickeson, president of the White Pass, glumly asserted that the Far North did not have enough traffic to accommodate both a government line and a private railroad that needed to make a profit. A federal road to the interior would shortly bankrupt the private line. Therefore, the government should treat all railroads alike by either purchasing or subsidizing all of them.[5]

Opponents on the floor of Congress hammered away at government ownership, trotting out the bugbear of socialism. Because of the notorious inefficiency of federal enterprises, the railroad or railroads would cost much more than the $35 million authorized under the bill. Others repeated the oft-expressed doubts about the worth of Alaska's resources. Congressional defenders of the government railroad adroitly overcame both arguments. In the first place, they said, new territories always carry the stigma of being underpopulated and nonproductive. The Mississippi basin and Oregon country had suffered terrible slanders before their resources had been appreciated and developed. Later they returned their bounties to the nation. So would Alaska. Second, the government's venture in rail-building in Alaska was no precedent for federal operation elsewhere, but was a necessary consequence of federal failure to frame a coherent policy for a distant region. Ninety-nine percent of Alaska's land was still federally owned, much of it withdrawn from private entry. That bespoke a great federal responsibility.

The argument that the government should "do something" for Alaska was especially effective. "The public wants something done toward the development . . . of the great Alaskan domain and its resources," Representative Frank E. Guernsey of Maine intoned. "In Alaska we will build a railroad over government land, and thereby enhance the value of public property along that road."[6] Alaska's delegate effectively employed a variant of the "do something" theme, the anti-Syndicate argument. During his five-hour tour de force on January 14, the redoubtable James Wickersham was learned, denunciatory, cuttingly sarcastic, and witty by turns. Frequently interrupted by applause and sympathetic questions, he was accorded a thunderous ovation at the end. Wickersham saved his sharpest shafts for the Morgan-Guggenheims. "When people inquire what is the matter with Alaska it may be answered: The Alaska Syndicate." Who would control Alaska? Wickersham asked. Would the federal government act as trustee for the little people, or would the Alaska Syndicate control? The choice, he said, was "Government or Guggenheim."[7]

Exhortations to "do something," whether for Alaska or to the Alaska Syndicate, distorted fact. In truth, the government had done a great deal for Alaska. In the nineteenth century the government had promoted exploration and mapping in the Far North. From the gold rush to the end of the progressive era, Congress had provided a judicial and legal system, land laws, agricultural experiment stations, a branch of the Geological Survey, a telegraph, a system of territorial government, and many other benefits. Whether all this assistance was desirable or effective is not the issue. The point is that it had established a solid tradition of federal aid to Alaska. In the absence of such a tradition, a proposed federal railroad in the territory would have seemed too radical and novel for serious consideration. As for the Alaska Syndicate, it had at first worked for the united development of territorial resources, albeit under a single head. Even before Wickersham spoke, it had abandoned comprehensive exploitation for concentration on copper and water transportation. Since 1912 it had been trying to sell the CR & NW to the government. The Syndicate itself had but two years more of life.

When the bill came to a final vote, the House passed it 232 to 86, the Senate 46 to 16. The lopsided vote was a thumping affirmation of continued federal concern for Alaska. It was a victory for Wilsonian progressivism as well as a demonstration of the continuity in Alaska policy from the later Taft administration through the early Wilson years. President Wilson held the signing ceremony on March 12, switching souvenir pens with a jocular "I guess I'll change engines."[8]

In its essentials, the act empowered the president to locate and construct by the means of his choice a railroad or railroads connecting at least one Pacific port with the great interior rivers and one or more coal fields. Though none of the existing private lines was mentioned, the president could buy or lease any necessary private property, including rail lines, docks, terminals, telephones, and telegraphs. There were but two significant limitations on the president's authority. One held the aggregate mileage to one thousand. The other restriction authorized a maximum expenditure of $35 million (slightly less than the Alaska Railroad Commission's total estimate) and appropriated $1 million for immediate expenses. The same provision effectively settled the bond issue question by opting for strict congressional control of future funds. The law allowed the president either to lease or operate the completed line in the absence of any congressional action, and for the use of Panama Railroad equipment no longer needed at the Isthmus. Other clauses provided for rate regulations, joint transportation agreements, land withdrawals, annual reports, and the like. An explicit provision for a commission was deleted because congressional disagreements over its powers and personnel were unresolvable.

The act was unprecedented. Unlike its approval of the Panama Canal, where heavy commercial and naval traffic was virtually certain, Congress had committed itself to a project without promise of return. It had granted the president power "to do all necessary acts and things in addition to those specially authorized . . . to enable him to accomplish the purposes and objects of this Act." It had obligated itself to spend up to $35 million on a single public work in a year when federal expenditures totalled only $735 million and the interest on the public debt was a mere $22 million. Ernest Gruening, Alaska's late senator and a vigorous critic of federal action and inaction toward Alaska, termed the act "an extraordinary example of Congressional response to executive leadership. In the relative magnitude, in that day, of the undertaking, the concern shown for its objectives, and the speed of its enactment, it was also an unprecedented event in federal legislation for Alaska."[9]

After the bill was law, two final acts remained in the preconstruction drama. One was the Alaskan Engineering Commission's survey and report. The other was President Wilson's selection of the "western" or "Susitna" route and his decision to purchase the Alaska Northern to form the first seventy-two miles of the line.

Wilson created the Alaskan Engineering Commission. He staffed it on the advice of Secretary of the Interior Lane, formerly a member of the Interstate Commerce Commission. Lane's department was one of the most active in Alaska. Later, Wilson would give Lane formal control of the A. E. C. For chairman Lane recommended William C. Edes, a man who enjoyed a large reputation as a locating engineer. To serve with Edes he chose Lieutenant Frederick Mears, chief engineer of the Panama Railroad and an engineer officer with wide experience. Thomas Riggs, well known in Alaska and the Yukon as a mining engineer and as engineer of the International Boundary Commission, was his third selection. In choosing two men who knew railroads but not Alaska, and one man who knew Alaska but not railroads, Lane hoped to avoid the appearance of favoring any particular Alaska railroad interest. He need not have bothered; both he and the commission were bitterly, repeatedly accused of doing precisely that.

During May and June 1914, the commissioners sent men north from Seattle to launch their surveys. Another full-blown engineering survey less than one and one-half years after the weighty report of the Alaska Railroad Commission was not, as might be supposed, an example of bureaucratic waste and bumbling. Because of time limitations, the first commission could not survey the intriguing Portage Bay route. The commissioners had made a fairly complete study of the "eastern," or Copper River, road and its projections, but not of the "western" route north of the lower Susitna Valley. Further, their report could be faulted on various technical grounds. For example, they had computed construction and operating expenses two or three times over on some sections of the "western," or Seward, line and its branches. This mistake grossly inflated the cost estimates for that route. For another example, they had assumed that differing rates would produce greater or less traffic, yet they calculated income from the various rates at a constant freight and passenger volume. Finally, the report had recommended a politically impossible route: the Alaska Syndicate's Copper River & Northwestern. It had left open the question of purchase, true, but had raised the spectre of an operating agreement between the government railroad from Fairbanks to Chitina and the Morgan-Guggenheim line from Chitina to the Pacific. After Ballinger-Pinchot, any deal between the government and the CR & NW, though permissible under the railroad act, would have blown up a terrible political storm.

The Alaskan Engineering Commission's work during the summer of 1914 was the most elaborate single survey in Alaska up to that time. Nine locating parties, a reconnaissance party for the Kuskokwim and Iditarod country, and a topographical party to study the Portage Bay vicinity, left Seattle during May and June. After beefing up with casual labor in Alaska, most survey parties totalled fifteen or twenty men, while those headed for the Iditarod country and Portage Bay had six and seven respectively. One hundred and twenty-eight pack horses followed the surveyors into the field.

The commission concentrated on the "western," or Seward-Fairbanks, route, dividing it into three districts, each with a commissioner in charge. Seven of the nine locating parties worked there. Surveyors and supplies were shunted around on a fifty-foot sternwheeler built to the commission's own specifications, plus on another large river boat borrowed from the boundary survey. The pretext for all this activity along the projected Alaska Central-Alaska Northern route was that it was the less familiar of the two partially built all-American lines. Yet, the commissioners could have uncovered enough information without creating their elaborate administrative structure and without running ground location surveys for well over 120 miles, in addition to extensive preliminary surveys. Granting the distances and transportation problems, a few preliminary survey teams under the general supervision of one or two commissioners would have told them what they wished to know.

Although they struck the pose of professional objectivity required by the occasion, the commissioners obviously intended to favor the "western" route. They did so on their own responsibility. Neither Wilson nor Lane ordered them to go to Alaska, spend large sums in an elaborate engineering charade, and bring in a report for the Seward-Fairbanks route. The president, although at times a conceited and arrogant man, was unlikely to make decisions without at least some review of the relevant data. The written record reveals a secretary of the interior eager for his commissioners to take the initiative and relieve him of railroad questions great and small. Besides, Lane wanted to draw the teeth of the Alaska Syndicate by buying its railroad and placing its copper corporation on an equal transportation footing with other businesses.

The commissioners may have wished to balance the record with a report as preferential to the Seward-Fairbanks route as the previous commission's had been toward the line from Cordova. A sense of fairness and balance probably is part of the explanation, but it is not the full story. Three other circumstances influenced them. The first was the Ballinger-Pinchot controversy. All of the commissioners were perceptive men and Riggs, as his later appointment as governor of Alaska showed, had connections in the Democratic party. Such men would have grasped the implications of Ballinger-Pinchot, including the Alaska Syndicate's blackened reputation. They would have realized that another endorsement of the Copper River railroad would have left the Wilson administration at a political dead end, unable either to buy the Syndicate's line or to controvert two expert reports.

Second, Edes, Mears, and Riggs firmly believed in the long-range, diversified development of Alaska. They were convinced that the some 150 homesteads in the Matanuska-Susitna Valley augered well for the future. There was mining on Kenai Peninsula and in the Willow Creek district, where operations would expand as soon as transportation reached them. The "western" route passed through the Nenana lignite coal fields, where the sub-bituminous lay ready to end Fairbanks' fuel famine and revive the declining gold placer industry. The resulting mining boom and ready rail transportation would be a boon to Fairbanks farming. A stock-raising industry around Fairbanks, the commissioners wrote, was an eventual "certainty."[10] In contrast, the land between the northern end of the Copper River line and Fairbanks was sadly unpromising.

Third, the commissioners were greatly excited by the close relationship between the Matanuska coal fields and Ship Creek on Cook Inlet. Ship Creek was a fine summer construction port for a line to the coal fields only seventy-five miles away. Coal proven in steaming tests could be brought down from the mountains along the Matanuska over an easy 0.4 percent grade.

True, Cook Inlet filled with floating ice at times during the winter, but nobody really knew how serious the problem was. Perhaps it was not even serious. The tides were high, but then the tides at Liverpool and Hull were high. Unlimited anchorage and storage room were available, and a harbor could be maintained by dredging. Ship Creek looked more promising than Portage Bay, where there might be too little room for a coaling station. It looked more promising than Seward, with the longer haul, the 2.2 percent grades against the coal, and the nearly $1 million needed to put the tottering Alaska Northern in shape for light trains. After all, a primary purpose of the government road was to reach that coal and bring it to tidewater. Independent estimates showed that Ship Creek coal would better compete with eastern coal at San Francisco than would coal shipped from Seward or from the Bering River field via Cordova.

The Alaskan Engineering Commission did not deny the difficulties. Its estimate for new construction on the Seward-Fairbanks line was $22,621,798, soberly realistic when compared to the Taft commission's less than $18 million. The second commission was much less impressed with the physical condition of the Alaska railroads than the first. Although it favored the Seward-Fairbanks route, it was in near despair over the Alaska Northern. The one virtue of that railroad was its relatively low value.

On the other hand, the commissioners optimistically adopted all the happier cliches about territorial prospects and the railroads' positive role in development. Alaska's mineral wealth had "already been proven." Its agriculture could support "a large population," a fact easily demonstrable "to those willing to listen." Its coal supply had "practically no limit." All Alaska lacked for probable "rapid development" was "reasonable transportation." The commissioners predicted "a few lean years" for their railroad, but quickly forecast eventual success. "Take the history of many of our western railroads," they wrote. Those lines had "started through a country in many instances less promising than Alaska, and now who would dare question their success?"[11]

No one dared question whether a government railroad would be built in Alaska. The questions now were "where?" and "by whom?" When Chairman Edes returned to Washington at the end of November, he was primed to press for the Seward route in conferences with Wilson and Lane. Beginning in October, interested parties importuned the president and the secretary to purchase one railroad or the other. J. P. Morgan made an offer of the CR & NW. Representatives of the Alaska Northern did the same for their line. The commissioners, the president, and the secretary discussed the problem. Falcon Joslin of the Tanana Valley line was one among several supplicants for the construction contract.

A careful observer would not have been surprised by Wilson's announcement on April 10, 1915, that the government would build over the "western" route. The president had told Congress more than one year before that the federal government "should itself build and administer" a trunk line system. He was not a man given to changing his mind. That settled the question of public versus private construction and operation. As for the choice of a line, Wilson's experts had come down on the side of the Seward-Fairbanks route. The "western" route also had the virtue of economy. An appraised price for the Alaska Northern, $1.5 million versus $17,693,595.89, J. P. Morgan's asking price for the Copper River, brought the total estimated costs of the Seward route $5,854,823.89 under the Cordova line. Further, the CR & NW appraisal placed the estimated total cost of the Cordova-Fairbanks line alone within $3.5 million of the $35 million allowed by Congress. Finally, the Democratic president could scarcely have bought a railroad involved in the attempted Bering River coal grab, a "Republican scandal." Wilson made his decision informally in February.

As early as February 17, Alaska's governor, J. F. A. Strong, was writing to a friend, "I am unofficially advised that work will be begun this spring on a line between Ship Creek on Cook Inlet to the Matanuska coal fields."[12] Ten days later the commission submitted an outline of work in the Seward and Ship Creek areas. Weeks before the formal decision, Mears was in Seattle organizing work parties and buying equipment and supplies. Eight days after Wilson's announcement, Mears left Seattle. He reached his construction base on the twenty-sixth. A stampede town was waiting for him on the mud flats of Ship Creek. Wilson had apparently delayed his executive order to give the commissioners time to organize the elaborate expedition required to build a construction base from scratch at Ship Creek and to refurbish the dilapidated terminal at Seward. The delayed announcement helped to give the initial appearance of a rapidly and smoothly working machine, though the commission's image would change for the worse soon enough. Twenty days after his first executive order, the president placed the commission under the "supervision and control of the Department of the Interior."[13]

Why Wilson ordered the purchase of the Alaska Northern is less understandable. The price of the collapsing railroad brought the total estimated cost of the Seward line, terminals and branches, to within $440,463 of the estimate for the Portage Bay route and its facilities. The extra maintenance costs of sixty-four additional miles interspersed with trestles, tunnels, and snow sheds were obvious. The operating costs of trains over two summits of several hundred feet were equally apparent. Perhaps the commissioners had doubts about adequate anchorage in Portage Bay, though they had none about the rail route itself. Possibly Wilson wished to spite the Alaska Syndicate by purchasing the rival road. The lure of diversified development on Kenai Peninsula may have decided the matter.

Wilson and the commissioners may have worried about propaganda from the Alaska Northern bondholders had they built from Portage Bay or paralleled the private line from Seward. If the later shrill attacks on the government railroad are any guide, pandemonium would have broken loose, and cries of virtual confiscation without compensation would have rent the air. Not that the Alaska Northern bondholders deserved any better. By 1915 most were Canadians who had enveloped themselves in such a complex of contracts and agreements that only an acute legal mind could have penetrated the maze. Joseph Cotton, the brilliant attorney retained by the government to supervise the Alaska Northern's sale, passed a harsh judgment. There were, he wrote, "an awful lot of crooks at some time or other in the Alaska Northern and almost every step taken in the financial history of the property was taken to defraud somebody."[14] The federal government knew that it was not rewarding virtue and smiting evil when it bought the Alaska Northern.

Nor was the government building in response to a boom, or even a modest increase in economic activity. In 1914 Alaska's mineral production had slipped to a tiny 0.85 percent of the national total. Production seemed to have stabilized territory-wide, with only the new coal leasing law offering hope for immediate expansion. No other industries appeared to reinforce the economy. Some officials with high hopes for agriculture bravely waved isothermal lines in reports purporting to show how comparatively mild Alaska's climate was, or, at least, how it was really no worse than Scandinavia's. But the Tanana Valley suffered from shorter growing seasons than places of comparable latitude in Scandinavia. Alaska lacked Scandinavia's proximity to large populations demanding its resources, lacked Scandinavia's centuries-old settlement and development, lacked its productive forests, and lacked its administrative competence and technical knowledge. Plenty of land as productive as Alaska's lay unused near transportation and markets in the first forty-eight states.

The state of Alaska's development argued for some other railroad approach than a trunk line to the interior. The railroad act should not have required the president to build to the interior, but should have allowed him the option of delaying the link through the Alaska Range until traffic warranted. In any case, Wilson should have chosen the Portage Bay route, buying up the Alaska Northern as a kind of hush money payment, then brazening out the failure to make any immediate improvements to that tumbledown line. Later it could have been rehabilitated as justified by local traffic. A system of wagon roads, connected with the Portage Bay railroad at the head of Turnagain Arm, perhaps too a narrow gauge along the northern and western shores of Kenai Peninsula, would have done at least as much for development as the expensively refurbished Alaska Northern. Had Congress given him greater discretion, the president could have ordered lines built from Ship Creek to the Matanuska coal fields and the agricultural lands and gold mines of the Matanuska-Susitna Valley. A narrow gauge extension of the Tanana Valley railway 107 miles to the Nenana coal would have brought lignite to the gold fields. Only the interior freight, twenty-four thousand tons per year, would have continued to move mainly by water.

The decisions of 1914 and 1915 had far-reaching consequences. General managers hounded by yearly deficits and querulous congressmen groaned under the operating and maintenance costs of the Seward-to-Portage line. The money lavished on that portion of the road was denied to needed improvements elsewhere. The Kenai Peninsula section raised shippers' costs by forcing freight over sixty-four miles of track when it could have reached the same spot after a cheaper water carry and a fourteen-mile rail haul. The Alaska Railroad would suffer enough criticism without having to endure the strictures against its distorted rate structure.

On December 2, 1913, James Wickersham had not yet played out his role in the great Alaska railroad debates. That afternoon, Alaska's delegate was sitting in the marbled House chamber, when at eight minutes past one, President Wilson strode in to deliver his State of the Union Address. Wickersham listened with glowing approval to the president's forceful invocation of federal responsibility toward the territory. Then the jubilant delegate wired to Governor Strong, "hurrah for Wilson and the opening of development of Alaska."[15] In 1915 the assumptions behind that joyous telegram were soon to be tested. The railroad was going through.

A TVRR train with an open air coach at the rear crosses a roughhewn trestle, probably over a slough near Fairbanks. *Wilson F. Erskine Collection, University of Alaska Archives*

A Tanana Mines train ready to move out from Fairbanks with a steam boiler for the gold creeks. The coach, a White Pass & Yukon original, still carries the legend "White Pass & Yukon Route" above the windows. *Wilson F. Erskine Collection, University of Alaska Archives*

The United States also purchased the tottering Tanana Valley Railroad, operating between Fairbanks and the gold creeks. In 1905, when this picture was taken, the little narrow-gauge line was still under construction. Letters above the coach windows read "T. M. Ry." for Tanana Mines Railway, the railroad's original name. *The Anchorage Historical and Fine Arts Museum*

Two locomotives pose at a junction on the TVRR. The train on the left may be running into Fairbanks from the river port of Chena, the one on the right returning from the creeks. *Terry Cole Collection, University of Alaska Archives*

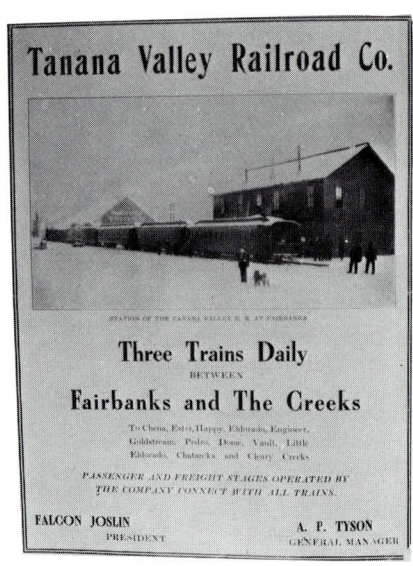

Advertisement for the TVRR. *Eugene McCracken Collection, University of Alaska Archives*

At Fox a TVRR railcar leaves the main line. *Pope Collection, University of Alaska Archives*

Two TVRR boxcars in high water, probably during the 1911 flood. *Charles Bunnell Collection, University of Alaska Archives*

In 1911 water from the Chena River poured over Fairbanks, perched on a low flood plain. A TVRR coach rests high and dry by the station, probably during the 1911 flood. *Charles Bunnell Collection, University of Alaska Archives*

Near the town of Fox the TVRR trains twisted around a tortuous switchback to gain altitude for crossing a divide 1,000 feet above Fairbanks. This trestle was part of that climb. *Terry Cole Collection, University of Alaska Archives*

TVRR railcar in what is probably a publicity photograph before shipment to the Far North. *Alaska Historical Library*

Another train on the Fox Gulch switchback. *Eugene McCracken Collection, University of Alaska Archives*

Beginning the Alaska Railroad

Rails from Ship Creek to the Matanuska coal fields — this was the commissioners' first goal. To achieve it, they squeezed most of their first construction into the thirty miles between the mouth of Ship Creek and the Matanuska River. They carved out three divisions, assigning the busiest and largest, about 230 miles of main line, to Frederick Mears. His division ran from the head of Turnagain Arm to the summit of Broad Pass, including the tracks to the coal.

Mears, the youngest, most aggressive commissioner, knew both engineering and the army from the ground up. Beginning as a chainman on the Great Northern in 1897, he later enlisted as a private, saw service in the Philippines, and was commissioned second lieutenant in 1906. The next year he married Jennie Wainwright, a general's daughter. He was chief engineer of the Panama Railroad when President Wilson named him to the A. E. C. Thirty-seven in 1915, Mears was tall, well-built, with regular features. A commanding figure in uniform or civilian outdoor togs, he was a bold man given to the articulate expression of strongly held opinions. He was the commissioner best suited to oversee the transformation of wilderness to town at the mouth of Ship Creek and direct the thousands of laborers, many of them immigrants, who wrested a railroad from the stubborn North Country.

At first the commissioners planted their headquarters where the Alaska Northern's had been — at Seward. From there they operated the Alaska Northern as a government-owned corporation under a lease from the bondholders and set about the expensive task of rehabilitating that decrepit railroad to mile 71. Although he spent little time there, Chairman William C. Edes made his headquarters at Seward.

Edes was fifty-eight when he was named chairman and chief engineer of the A. E. C. Boston-born, a graduate of the Massachusetts Institute of Technology, he had seen service with several railroads, chiefly as a highly respected locating engineer for the Southern Pacific. Edes was a kindly man who acquitted himself well with a pen but who lacked Mears' vigor and initiative. His greying, drooping moustache and tired, seamed face forecasted the illness that would force his retirement in 1919 and kill him a few years later. During his little more than five years as chairman, Edes spent about five months each year in Alaska, an equal time in Washington, and two months traveling between the two. He mastered endless details of the work in widely separated camps along his remote line and kept a loose, but guiding, rein on his subordinates. Even toward Mears, who could be demanding and preemptive, Edes remained calm and patient, while reserving all the major decisions for himself.

The third division ran west and south from Fairbanks until it joined Mears' Anchorage Division at the summit of Broad Pass. In the beginning it was merely a survey division with two locating parties directed by Thomas Riggs. The parties struggled with difficult location questions, especially with the choice of a proper line along the turbulent Nenana rushing north to the broad Tanana. Construction was not considered at first. Construction supplies could be shipped only by steamboat, from Whitehorse at the northern terminus of the White Pass railroad, or from St. Michael near the Yukon's mouth on Norton Sound. Either route required elaborate planning and the increased expense and risk of shipping in the brief river navigation season. The only justification for launching a full dress division from Fairbanks was that the completed rails would bring untapped wood fuel, and later the Nenana coal, within range of the mines. During the construction phase, the building would serve as a work relief project for the rapidly sinking Fairbanks region. From the engineer's economical viewpoint, it was better to drive the rails north to the Yukon basin, leaving the Fairbanks section until last. Sympathy for Fairbanks' plight and concern over the imminent collapse of the Tanana Valley narrow gauge to the mines decided the issue. On May 24, 1916, Edes formally designated Riggs to take charge of construction work north of Broad Pass.

Riggs was an old Alaska hand, having joined the great gold rush in 1897, three years after earning a degree in civil engineering from Cornell. For the next one and one-half decades he served off and on in Alaska as a mining and civil engineer and as engineer in charge of the fieldwork for the Alaska Boundary Commission. A Marylander of good family, educated in part in Germany, "Tommie" Riggs throve on camping out, hiking through the wilds, and swapping jokes with sourdough companions. His abundant humor and sympathy for Alaska won popularity for himself and the railroad project, but led him to overlook some of the improprieties of a few of his sourdough subordinates. Later, when Riggs was governor of Alaska, some scandals in the government town of Nenana were laid to his trusted officers and caused him intense mortification. In 1915, however, he was a lean, tough, and jovial forty-two, supervising his surveys and plumping hard for converting the Broad Pass-Fairbanks district into a full-fledged construction division.

The commission opened a purchasing office in Seattle, a move confirming the faith of that city's chamber of commerce. During the agitation for a government railroad, the chamber had formed its Alaska Bureau and lobbied for the line. It had set up a display of Alaska products and scenes in the Senate Office Building, a display so effective that James Wickersham, during his famous speech on the railroad bill, had urged his colleagues to look at it. Far from being in cahoots with the Seattle Chamber of Commerce, however, the commissioners resented Seattle's domination over their purchases. In 1916 Edes told Lane that complaints about sales to the A. E. C. from a wholesale grocer in Everett, Washington, stemmed from the underbidding of Seattle grocers who expected the business as a matter of right. The same year, the commission responded to rising freight rates from the Seattle-based Alaska Steamship Company and other lines by chartering the government troop ship *Crook*, among other ships. In 1917 the commissioners opened branch purchasing offices at Portland and San Francisco, claiming increased competition and reduced prices for their efforts. A Washington, D.C. office in the Department of the Interior rounded out the commission's organizational structure.

After late April 1915, Ship Creek was the center of A. E. C. activity. Barges and lighters plied across the broad harbor from steamers to a temporary wharf, unloading supplies from Seattle and Panama. There were almost enough leftovers from the government-owned Panama line to begin a miniature railroad. During the first year, commission stevedores unloaded four 200-class "Mogul" locomotives modified from Panama's five-foot gauge to standard rails, 2 steam shovels, 15 flat cars, 405 tons of tie plates, and a grand array of other machinery and equipment.

Mears' Anchorage Division, named for the government town established on the plateau south of Ship Creek, had four construction tasks. The first was to build a terminal on the mud flats of Ship Creek to handle the tons of material pouring in during the navigation season. The second was to build the main line to the Matanuska River, then construct a branch thirty-eight miles up the Matanuska to reach the coal — one of the line's major lures. Of less priority were building the 160 miles from Matanuska junction to Broad Pass and linking up with the Seward Division at mile 79. The line to the Matanuska Valley ran northeastward along Knik Arm on generally easy grades. Barges working the arm kept construction camps supplied. The steel reached Eagle River, thirteen miles from Anchorage, where construction of a high trestle and bridge across the river canyon halted tracklaying for 1915.

Station men, or private contractors, did most of the clearing, grubbing, and grading along a "station" of one hundred feet of right-of-way. Usually they took several stations under one contract. Many of them, especially in Mears' division, were Russians, Greeks, Slovaks, or other Eastern Europeans, with Italians, Germans, and Swedes only slightly less prevalent. They worked at a fixed price per cubic yard or per acre, eight or ten men to an association, largely with hand tools. The commission rented or sold blasting powder, handcars for hauling cut and fill materials, horses, and horse-drawn graders, but the men did most of the chopping, grubbing, shoveling. They worked in the early dawns, through the soft, cool twilights, endured the mosquitoes, and struggled to finish in the shortest time with the least debt at the A. E. C. commissary. Fading gray photographs capture the dull sameness of their daily lives. The laborers stand against a boreal background, usually stiff and unsmiling under broad-brimmed hats. Wide galluses over rough shirts, denims tucked into heavy boots, were the working clothes of the men whose toil built the railroad.

Early in 1916 crews laid the track over the completed Eagle River bridge and on to Peters Creek, twenty-two miles from Anchorage. Mears ran trains loaded with construction equipment to Peters Creek, where he had established a supply base. From there, horse-drawn sleds hauled the equipment up Knik Arm, then over the frozen Matanuska to winter camps strung out for eighteen miles along the right-of-way. By mid-February the clearing gangs were working. A delayed appropriation and shortage of funds enforced concentration on the coal branch. In the spring, station men swarmed over the line, and in July the track reached Moose Creek, fourteen miles from Matanuska Junction, fifty miles from Anchorage. Other gangs filled in the fifteen miles from Peters Creek to the junction. On August 17 the first coal train ran from the Matanuska field to Anchorage. It carried coal from the small "Doherty" mine on Moose Creek. The coal was full of dirt and bone, but it was Alaska coal.

The gangs continued building through the beautiful but rough Matanuska country, even working night shifts during the spring of 1917. On October 20 the branch reached Chickaloon, mile 38, and the line to the Matanuska coal fields was complete. By the end of the year, the Matanuska District's main line track extended fifty-two miles beyond Matanuska Junction. Earlier, the commission had capitalized on the main line's seventy-five-mile parallel with the Susitna River by establishing the Talkeetna District to push the work ahead of the end of steel in the Matanuska District. Boats supplied the working gangs from the Susitna, a wide, swift, turbulent, glacial stream. To reach the district, the flagship of the A. E. C. river fleet, the stern wheel steamer "Omineca," paddled up with 150 tons of freight from Anchorage to Croto, an old Indian village about fifty miles above the river's mouth. At Croto the Susitna broke into a maze of twisting shallow channels choked with gravel bars. To cope with this stretch of river the A. E. C. engineers designed gasoline-powered "tunnel boats," so named for their tunnel-shaped propeller housings, or for their tunnellike frame-and-canvas freight enclosures on deck. When loaded with thirty tons, the "tunnel boats" drew a scant twenty inches. Working together, the "Omineca" and the raft-like "tunnel boats" hauled 1,731 tons during 1916 alone. On the ground, there was substantial clearing and grading by the end of 1917. Hampered by the flooding Susitna and a trickle of funds, the Talkeetna District steel gang had driven but eight miles at season's end.

The wild, rugged Turnagain District held the greatest construction challenges in the entire division. Along Turnagain Arm the foothills of the Chugach Range run down to the north shore in steep alpine cliffs. On clear summer days a light breeze blows among the wild flowers, creeks splash down the slopes, and the Kenai Mountains rise beyond the three-mile blue expanse of Turnagain Arm. At this time of year the north shore is a lulling scene of tranquility and grandeur. The scene is grossly deceptive. Often, arm and mountains are overhung with clouds, and the turbulent Turnagain is opaque. At some places the tides bore in on a six-foot wall of water, and snowslides carrying trees and boulders thunder down to the sea. In the early days of the railroad, the wind sometimes blew so powerfully it stalled the four-cylinder gasoline rail cars trying to move against it. Steel had to pierce this district before the all-weather port of Seward would be linked to Matanuska coal.

The first few miles from Anchorage south to the Arm presented few problems except for bridging frequent streams. Supplying the camps was easy: steamer tugs hauled large barges from

Anchorage before the Arm filled with floating ice. The commission built a dock and warehouse at Rainbow (mile 94) and a warehouse at Potter (mile 100) and reconstructed several old Alaska Northern construction camps built for that line's advance grading gangs. The easy work ended at the Arm's rocky shore. Benches for the track had to be hacked from the rock walls; sometimes rock fills had to be built across the Arm to carry the line from headland to headland. Brawny stationmen surveying the plunging cliffs frequently refused to contract for the rock work. The commission had no choice but to work its own crews in the heaviest cuts. Pile drivers and three steam shovels worked along the shore. Powder blasts sent tens of thousands of cubic yards of earth and rock crashing down to water's edge. Yet the dirty, dulling hand labor was as inescapable here as anywhere else along the line. It went on year around because the rock was no harder in winter than in summer and could be taken out during the cold months when other work had to stop. In one five-month period, in the thirty miles between Potter and Kern, toiling crews hand excavated more than four million cubic yards of rock at an average $1.35 per cubic yard. Recalling the achievement many years after, Anton Anderson, the railroad's chief engineer, claimed that contemporary equipment would not do the job so quickly, even at a price far higher. Actual tracklaying was confined to twenty-four miles south of Anchorage. Relocation of the main line to pass through Anchorage and the virtual completion of terminal facilities there filled out the work in the Anchorage Division up to the end of 1917.

Edes and his engineers on the Seward Division faced two essential tasks. One was to operate the Alaska Northern, the other, to reconstruct it. Operation of the ANR sorely vexed Edes, who fussed over details of law and accounting. He might well be forgiven his fussing, for the vicious rivalries within the Alaska Northern had created a legal snarl that delayed improvements to the line. First, the minor, American bondholders sued to prevent purchase payments to the major, Canadian bondholders. After that suit failed, the government paid on August 25, 1915 the first purchase installment on the road it had been operating under lease since June. After August and until June 1916 the officers of the A. E. C. operated the Alaska Northern as a government corporation. In the latter month, after the final purchase payment, they turned the company over to the United States. A damage suit by John Ballaine against the Alaska Northern delayed its corporate dissolution until October 1919. Excepting technical distinctions, the Alaska Northern had operated as part of the A. E. C. since June 1915.

Some drastic reconstruction of the faltering road had to be accomplished if it were to operate much longer. Before the first payment, the A. E. C. had made only enough repairs to hold the ANR together. By that time the season was too far advanced for very much work. The commission gained a not unwelcome opportunity to rebuild the dilapidated wharf when, on a cold, windy night in January 1916, a fire swept through the wharf warehouse and quickly consumed the dock. The commission put two shifts to work, and four weeks later the wharf was rebuilt to handle the winter's traffic. By September a new, larger dock of treated piling, able to accommodate two ships at once, was substantially complete.

Elsewhere, crews laid seventy-pound rail, filled or replaced trestles, widened cuts and clearings, built a tunnel, and reduced curvature. Work progressed slowly because so much had to be done. Edes confessed to Lane in June 1917 that the Alaska Northern was nearer collapse than the commissioners had first supposed, for bridge timbers that appeared sound on the outside were rotted on the inside. Edes estimated that $4.5 million would have to be spent on grade reduction and trestle repairs to fit the ANR for heavy coal trains — assuming that they could operate through the Kenai Peninsula's terrible winter weather while the port of Anchorage was closed. By the end of the year, rebuilding the ANR had consumed $1,549,118.49, or more than $443,500 over the commission's original estimate. The work was far from finished, as the line was rebuilt only to the summit at mile 45 and could carry heavy traffic merely to mile 40. Clearing and grading went forward from Kern Creek to the end of the division at mile 79. Trains operated intermittently to Kern Creek during the year.

Most of the work was preparatory on the Fairbanks Division. Parts of this division were true wilderness. Very little of its boggy soil was suited for construction. Fairbanks, the only sizeable town, was inconveniently located at the far end of an unbuilt line. The commissioners, therefore, established a town at the confluence of the Nenana and Tanana rivers, almost equidistant from Fairbanks and the Nenana lignite coal fields. In late May 1916 a pioneer party reached the Nenana townsite and began building a dock, warehouse, and wagon roads for supply distribution. The A. E. C. established the town of Nenana with lot auctions August 24 and 25, and Riggs moved his headquarters there in December. At the close of the 1917 season, slightly over fifteen miles of main line track had been laid south from Nenana toward the coal fields. Another five miles of narrow gauge, built to take the trains of the newly purchased Tanana Valley Railroad, were pushed out to a fresh wood supply at Happy station, ten miles west of Fairbanks.

Construction conditions found nowhere else in the United States were standard fare for station men and pile driver crews on the Fairbanks Division. The ground beneath the spongy moss was permanently frozen and thawed only a few inches per year even after the station men had stripped away the thick insulating blanket of moss. Ground for trestle pilings had to be steam thawed. When the soil froze the next winter, usually to a depth of several feet, expanding ice crystals adhered to the pilings and thrust them up. When the spring thaw came, the softening earth collapsed around the piles and prevented them from falling back into place. Crews then sawed off the tops of the piles, capped them, and laid the track. On some stretches of line, roadbed and ballast gradually settled out of sight into the heaving, almost undrainable, jellylike muck. To give the track some flotation, ties were laid on large logs running parallel to the rails. Elsewhere, trains hauled fill material to soggy spots and filled as rapidly as the roadbed settled. The incessant struggle to construct a suitable roadbed explains why so little track was laid during the first two seasons.

Freakish weather too frequently delayed or destroyed construction on all divisions. One such incident occurred on the Seward Division in September 1917. Unusually heavy rains began falling on the eighth. A torrent of 7.2 inches in twelve hours was recorded at Seward on the tenth. The downpour continued, tapering but still heavy, through the next day. All that rain transformed swift, small Lowell Creek on the edge of Seward into a raging giant. Lowell Creek rose five feet above normal on a bed of uprooted trees, dislodged boulders, and spewed gravel to a depth of four feet over the railroad's trestle bridge. It swept away small buildings in the rail yards and moved about five thousand cubic yards of earth. It washed away several buildings in the town and heavily damaged the electric plant. Out on the line, water undermined more than one mile of track and took out 800 feet of roadbed. One bridge abutment collapsed into a stream, while loosened earth slid over the track in several places. The summer melt from Spencer glacier near mile 53 had been bad enough in normal times to force the commission to construct a diversion dam. When the heavy rains and rain-melted ice struck the dam, they ripped out 100 feet and smashed an additional 300 feet of pile cribbing. Alaska's vastness added to the commissioner's woes. The A. E. C. was building through country almost entirely uninhabited and unproductive, more than eighteen hundred miles from its supply base. Private construction companies could, and sometimes did, work their gangs under hard conditions when the necessities of the country required it. The commission would have created a scandal had it done similarly. Unlike private contractors, the commissioners could not escape responsibility for the towns that grew up at strategic points along their line. So they provided essential services at Anchorage, Nenana, and other points where little or no permanent settlement had existed before the coming of the railroad.

Three construction headquarters for a mere 470 miles of main line would seem to be bureaucratic extravagance except for the isolation of each from the others. For several years the most dependable way to reach Anchorage from Seward during the navigation season was by water, which took one day. Until the trains ran regularly, the trip overland required more time. In February 1917 Mears arrived in Anchorage 35½ hours after leaving Seward. His one-and-one-half-day run by rail, doublender sled, and dog team, the commission newspaper reported, was "probably a record for the 114 miles traveled."[1] When Mears or Edes wished to travel to the Fairbanks Division, they did not try to penetrate the wilderness north of the end of steel. Instead they waited at Seward for a ship. In summer, three or four ships a week might call there, although the published schedule often failed to forecast the day. If they made the trip during the ninety or so days each year that Thompson Pass above Valdez was not blocked by snow, they sailed to that town and rode in automobiles or wagons over the trail to Fairbanks. If they were traveling during early spring, late fall, or winter, they sailed instead to Cordova, rode the Copper River line to Chitina, then went to Fairbanks on whatever was running — wagon, car, sled, or a combination. Nenana was another sixty miles downstream from Fairbanks and until 1919 was reachable only by boat or sled. Five days was "good time" for a one-way trip.

Telephone and telegraph connections helped to close the distances. Anchorage and Seward were linked in September 1915, but Anchorage and Fairbanks were not connected until April 1920. Telephone and telegraph work was especially arduous in Alaska. Light wooden tripods carried the wires because freezing ground ice thrust the standard crossarm poles out of the soil in a few seasons. In the winter, shivering linemen battled snowslides, ice accumulations, forest fires, and floods to keep the wires working. They built and replaced with any available copper or iron strand. When the line once gave way at a point on Turnagain Arm, an ingenious repairman patched it with a dog harness. In 1917 it cost one dollar to talk for three minutes over the 126 miles between Anchorage and Seward.

At the end of 1917 the commissioners could boast 24.78 miles of completed main line track, 26.5 miles of siding, spur and yard track, 76.8 miles graded and ready for track, and 70.8 miles cleared but ungraded. Partly because of rising costs and unexpected expenses, they were uncomfortably close to their authorized $35 million ceiling, having spent or obligated more than $26,845,600 in three years, plus another $387,835.64 in operation and maintenance of the ANR. From January 1, 1916, the A. E. C. had hauled passengers on its construction trains at the low rate, for Alaska, of six cents per mile. As tracklaying proceeded in the Anchorage Division, the Terminal District expanded to encompass the operating right-of-way.

The many-sided labor question caused the commissioners added vexation and occasional excitement. They brought some of it on themselves, for they were as antiunion as the most hard-bitten private employer. In their opinion, the common laborer should trust in his employer for humane treatment and a maintenance wage and ignore the "agitators" who promised to better his condition. The skilled worker could demand higher pay, but owed unswerving loyalty in return. In short, the commissioners held tenaciously to nineteenth-century employer views of the labor question, although their position as government officials and other circumstances prevented them from enforcing those views as sternly as they wished.

From the first, the commissioners tried to beat down wages to a point well under the prevailing Alaska scale. The Valdez Chamber of Commerce accused them of paying their survey crewmen $2.50 per day in 1914 when the minimum for survey work in Alaska had been $3.00 plus board for eight hours. In 1915, a few days before the official route announcement, Mears recommended a wage of 37½ cents per hour for unskilled labor. With one dollar deducted for board, that made a net of two dollars per day, a dollar less than the Alaska Road Commission paid for similar work. Mears regretted that Colonel Wilds P. Richardson, road commission chairman, seemed "disinclined to lower his wage schedule." Even so, the commissioners should establish the 37½-cent wage "and stand 'pat' on it regardless of strikes."[2]

The partial 1915 season passed without serious labor problems, but early in 1916 the workmen put Mears' philosophy to the test. Trouble erupted on February 7 when the steel gang at Peters Creek struck for a basic wage of 50 cents per hour, 12½ cents more than common labor then earned. Mears was alarmed about possible violence but he behaved coolly. When thirty of the fifty men in the gang refused to leave their outfit cars and walk the twenty-two miles back to Anchorage, Mears dispatched an engine under the guard of three deputy marshals to pull the cars into the Anchorage yards, where the men were paid off. Mears tried to organize a new steel gang, but no one would work for him. Undaunted, he continued to send supplies to the head of steel at Peters Creek, where they were sledded to Matanuska to await the springtime start of construction on the branch to the coal fields. The workers in the meantime had organized a militant Alaska Federal Labor Union. On February 12 the union called out the teamsters who had been sledding supplies from Peters

Creek, effectively closing down construction preparations on the Anchorage Division. Although he could find a few men to defy the union and help him make a pretense of carrying on the work, Mears knew that the labor organization could call out any one group of employees, or all of them, at its will.

Mears urged Edes to give the strikers short shrift. Although he proposed a compromise wage schedule to throw the onus of rejection upon the workers, he predicted their certain refusal, followed by probable violence and destruction of commission property. He asked for troops and recommended shipping in strikebreakers from Seattle. From the perspective of Washington, Lane and Edes were inclined to temporize. Lane appealed to Secretary of Labor William B. Wilson, who appointed an experienced committee of conciliation to go to Alaska, take testimony, and establish a new wage scale. On March 4 the workers agreed to return pending the board's decision. Construction resumed two days later.

While the board was still gathering and weighing evidence, the union called a general strike for April 22. The walkout was so well coordinated that 90 percent of the terminal employees were off the job during the first afternoon. Four days later only the stationmen, who were independent contractors, were working. Again Mears wired for troops to provide safe conduct for men willing to work. This time Lane called a hurried meeting of the cabinet officers concerned, and they committed themselves to swift, decisive action. Lane then told Mears that forty troops were rushing to Anchorage aboard a revenue cutter from Valdez and that the district judge with them would be authorized to swear as many men as needed. Mears also appealed to the district attorney for an injunction against the strikers' entering the terminal grounds or persuading others to stay off the job. Neither the injunction nor the troops were needed because the strike was a short one. When it began, the strike leaders probably hoped to inspire the plodding conciliation commission to finish its business and to influence the members in labor's favor. At any rate, that was what happened. On the twenty-seventh the committee recommended many classes of wages higher than Mears' suggestions. The commission accepted; the union balked for two days, then capitulated. The longest strike in the railroad's history was over.

The strike sharpened the commissioners' sentiments against organized labor. Edes responded more calmly than Mears, which was usual, but his attitude toward labor was, if anything, less friendly. When Mears wired that he would "sooner or later" have to raise the wage for common labor to 42½ or 45 cents per hour, Edes, with one eye on the budget, urged a basic rate of no more than 40 cents an hour, 2 cents less than the offer Mears had made in his draft compromise scale. A week before the April strike Edes wrote his chief engineer at Seward that "there seems to be a determined effort by a lot of bums to handle the labor question. It is evident that we must squelch some of this I. W. W. activity on [sic] the start and give them to understand that we will handle our own business."[3] Edes even toyed with the idea of shipping in laborers from Seattle, though his workers were not striking at the time. The only purpose of the usually cautious chairman would have been to break the union, an action fraught with unforeseeable consequences. He also approved the use of labor spies who attended and reported on union meetings. There would have been much less trouble, Edes and Mears maintained, but for the radical agitators, Republicans, and sourdough Alaskans who created disaffection among the contented foreign laborers making up the bulk of workers in the Anchorage district. The only real labor grievance, they insisted, was that under the law men could work only eight hours per day on government jobs. Had the laborers been able to work ten hours they would have been happier because they were earning more.

There was some truth in Edes' and Mears' contentions. Organizers who belonged to or sympathized with the Industrial Workers of the World had arrived at Seward late in 1915, determined to form a union. A few local Republicans hoped for political dividends from trouble on a government project under a Democratic administration. Edes masterfully typed certain disgruntled Alaskans when he wrote about those old-timers who "are fond of telling you how they have helped to build up the country. Just what they have done is not quite clear." Those sourdoughs had convinced themselves that they deserved high wages only "because they have been here for a number of years. These men are largely backed up by the pioneer merchants, who see in high wages. . .an excuse for charging high prices."[4] The eight-hour law possibly did reduce pay because the commissioners, had they been able, might have set a standard ten-hour day at the same hourly rate.

Edes and Mears held part of the truth, but only a part. The commissioners' 37½-cent wage was low for Alaska when they announced it in 1915, and it became ever less attractive as wages rose and the labor market expanded in other parts of the country. Even before the first stoppage in February, Mears had forecast a labor shortage for the 1916 season. It was then that he had appealed for a basic wage of up to 45 cents. Besides, the strikers' cause was extremely popular. At various times during the winter and spring Mears had wired Washington about support for the workers' demands from a local newspaper and the Anchorage Chamber of Commerce, in addition to the Republicans, sourdoughs, and socialist agitators who fomented the trouble. With such a wide spectrum of support for labor there was little community sympathy left for the commission.

As for the agitators whom the commissioners so roundly condemned, their success requires more explanation than mere glibness of tongue or the gullibility of the laborers on the Anchorage Division. The overt grievance — low wages — and the resentment against the commission's paternalism had to be compelling for 957 men to pledge themselves to the new Alaska Federal Labor Union, established in February during the first, brief strike. Only 420 commission employees of all types worked in the Anchorage Division in February, and most of them outside of the office force probably joined the union, along with local casual laborers and unemployed persons. The Alaska Labor Union (the "Federal" soon was dropped) not only throve, but it moved rapidly to the left. At first affiliated with the conservative American Federation of Labor, the ALU had, by April, moved nearer to the I. W. W. Its leaders were not commission employees, but they kept a strong hold on the membership. Sometimes they used tough tactics. Mears and the district attorney reported incidents of union members forcing railroad employees off their jobs. Yet coercion, like agitation, was hardly a primary cause of the April general strike. More likely, the wage scale and a sense of alienation from a seemingly indifferent commission were critical. Mears was so insensible to the emotions of the employees, despite reports from his labor spies, that he wired Edes on the day before the April walkout: "Doubtful if strike will be successful as men working are apparently satisfied."[5] The next afternoon those men, grim-faced and carrying angry placards, picketed the depot grounds at the foot of C Street.

Nor did labor-management relations improve over the long term. A. E. C. workers did secure steadily increasing wages and benefits, but only because of the wartime manpower shortage, not because the commissioners had abandoned their hostility to organized labor. On the other hand, leaders among the crews were many times totally lacking in company loyalty, no matter what benefits they received. Of the two commissioners, Mears alone became more than routinely concerned for the workers' welfare. In May 1917 he established a successful "Sunday court," going to his office on Sabbath mornings to hear employee grievances. Labor relations relapsed with his second and final departure in 1923. They remained bitter and brambly until after General Manager Otto F. Ohlson's arrival five years later.

The federal eight-hour law of August 1, 1892, prohibiting federal workers or workers under federal contracts from working more than eight hours, grieved the commission almost as much as its own employees did. The season of long days began early in April; from then until late September the construction crews could work ten hours and enjoy abundant sunlight during leisure time. They could accomplish more by working ten-hour days during the short construction season, an important consideration to the commission. Mears was even more upset by the eight-hour limitation on harbor and train crews. The tide controlled unloading at Anchorage, so the longshoremen clambered aboard barges and lighters as the tide rose, sailed out to the one or two freighters in the roadstead, and unloaded the cargo swung out from the decks of the big ships. Their work regularly ran more than eight hours. Train crews were on the job over eight hours, a common practice among railroads. When the crews worked overtime, Mears certified that an extraordinary emergency had existed. His alternative was to arrange for a relief crew to take over before the first crew's time reached eight hours. The first procedure was deceitful, the second would have been expensive. Both were absurd. After weeks of falsely certifying to extraordinary emergencies, Mears blew up. He predicted to Edes that the Alaska line "would be the laughing stock of the entire railroad world" and asserted that rather than operate under the eight-hour law "it would be better to abandon the idea of Government construction and operation of railroads in the beginning and admit failure."[6] Edes solved the problem by suggesting the changing of stevedores and trainmen from the "labor and mechanic" category to the exempt "operating" status. Completion of an adequate dock in September 1919 all but ended the troublesome lightering system.

The commission's most successful evasion of the eight-hour law involved the contracts for station work. The station system itself was a proven method of letting small contracts for clearing and grading in preference to direct hiring of large numbers of laborers on "force account." Some details of the A. E. C. station contracts were novel, however. Instead of dealing with one contractor who would in turn hire laborers, the commission wrote contracts with a gang of men who joined a partnership to complete the work on a given station. Because each man was technically a member of the contracting firm, none was considered a laborer under the terms of the eight-hour law, and he could work as long as he liked. Only those laborers hired to supplement the partnership's work were subject to the law. West coast labor unions loudly complained about the commission's deft dodge on the grounds that it violated the law's intent.

For all the maledictions they exchanged with organized labor, the commissioners' paternalism had its soft, generous side. The tents or log huts in the construction camps were primitive, but they were snug and dry. The most elaborate structure was the bunkhouse, its roof covered with earth or tar paper, its chinks filled with moss. Inside, a central stove warmed a room filled at either end with rows of cells four feet square, eight feet deep. These were the "muzzle-loading" bunks, room enough for a man and his duffle. Two coal oil lamps glowed over the windowless room, over men hunched about the stove, over men clambering up to their "muzzle loaders." In the towns, bunkhouses and mess houses were frame buildings of finished lumber. In the smaller camps the commission hired its own cooks, while it contracted for food service at remote layover points with heavy traffic. Either way, the food came from commission stocks. It was good food, "extraordinarily good,"[7] wrote New Yorker Joseph P. Cotton, the commission's counsel, following an inspection trip in 1917.

From July 1915 the A. E. C. provided medical care and injury compensation, programs steadily expanded by law and executive order. The commission built two hospitals, the "base hospital" at Anchorage, a severely plain, white frame building with a simple pitched roof, perched between A and B streets on the steep slope overlooking Ship Creek. Two stories and a basement, 100 feet long by 42 feet wide, the ugly little boxlike structure served the hospital needs of the railroad, of Anchorage, and of the surrounding country for a generation. The Nenana building was quainter and cruder, with its two-story screened porches and its first story built of logs. When they were completed in 1917, the hospitals ranked with the best in the territory.

Trainmen and foremen, together with officers, department heads, and other office workers, could rent the dozens of comfortable frame cottages built at the commissioners' order. The neat houses ranged down several streets in the Anchorage townsite and circled the head of "Government Hill," the promontory north across the railyards from the town. All employees could take advantage of the commissaries. These were large warehouses in the towns where necessities sold for the landed cost plus 10 percent, more cheaply than they could be bought at the stores. The retail merchants campaigned against the commissaries, held them to selling essentials, and were able to curtail their operations beginning in 1917. Though the commissioners maintained that the commissaries simply enabled employees to buy those things needed to make them fit workers, the commissaries helped to control private retail prices and increased the wage-earner's buying power. During the early years, employees and their families could count on the commissaries for good food and clothing at reasonable prices.

A lack of money at critical times was second only to labor as a source of official headaches. The commissioners complained less about the amount of money they received than about the timing of appropriations from Congress. Their attitude derived from the commission's funding system, for the A. E. C. did not have the authority to sell stocks and bonds as did a private

45

railroad. Instead, Congress annually appropriated a portion of the authorized $35 million, which usually became available after the beginning of the new fiscal year. But the commissioners needed their money — or the assurance of it — during the preceding winter. In the wintertime they were planning the work of the short summer season and buying supplies to be sledded into advance camps before breakup turned Alaska's frozen earth into quivering bogs.

Because they had to plan during November for next July's needs, the commissioners made a bold decision. They would guess the amount that Congress would give them and use their guess as the basis for orders, bid advertisements, and labor recruiting. Such anticipation of income was risky enough for a government agency, but the commissioners quickly overspent even their own estimates. Even they had not anticipated the massive expense of constructing a railroad in the wilderness. With the help of a deficiency appropriation in 1916, their scheme worked well enough for a time, but they soon came close to a scandal. By early 1917 the commission had spent $800,000 it did not have and its creditors were demanding payment. To ease the strain Edes requested $7.5 million for fiscal year 1918 and asked for $3 million to be made available immediately. In the Senate his request collided with the famed filibuster against President Wilson's proposal to arm United States merchant ships on the high seas for defense against belligerent naval vessels. Edes pleaded. The money was needed for salaries, he said. The House then passed a joint resolution giving Edes his $3 million, and the Senate suspended its armed ship bill debate long enough to concur.

Mears was angry. In his mind it was Congress' fault that the commission had been caught short, and he began gathering a bulky report to Lane on the construction snags caused by the congressional appropriations system. Edes stopped him short. In a painfully frank letter the calm, fatherly chairman gently rebuked Mears for his independent action, telling him how well Lane understood the commission's problem but how little he could help it. Then he phrased an admission most difficult for the head of a government agency. "Instead of planning work and figuring that the money will be forthcoming anyway, we should see what money we have, and if necessary, modify our plans. Fortunately, we have not been called upon for an exact statement of liabilities from the Appropriations Committee. It might be an embarrassing one to make. I do not think they would have accepted as an excuse for incurring liabilities exceeding our existing funds, that their method of making appropriations was all wrong. You certainly appreciate that we have not kept strictly within the law on this matter."[8]

On other occasions the commissioners suffered frustrations that were not of their own making. In 1916 they asked Congress to pass a law giving them jurisdiction over sanitary and public health matters within five miles of any location survey. The laws of Alaska were inadequate, they said, because the territorial code provided for punishment only after detection of a violation. The commissioners wanted broad and effective regulatory powers to prevent violation (such as stream pollution, a threat to public health) either in the townsites or in any uncontrolled settlements springing up along the right-of-way. Their bill as drawn was mild, but in its passage through the Interior Department a bureaucrat as zealous as he was anonymous made two changes that caused the commissioners painful embarrassment. First, he added a clause granting the commission general police powers within five miles of the railroad work and in the townsites. Second, he struck out the five-year limit and replaced it with a phrase making the bill perpetually effective. Territorial Delegate James Wickersham attacked these broad powers of indefinite duration and succeeded in having them stricken from the draft bill. Then Wickersham, with much less justification, denounced the commissioners as power-hungry graspers planning to seize permanent control of Anchorage and the construction line. Edes and Mears were surprised by the changes in their original draft, thrown off balance by Wickersham's attack, and never effectively corrected a widespread impression of their covetousness. The bill passed the Senate but failed to clear the House Committee on Territories. Thereafter, the commission relied on its own regulations and Alaska's public health legislation.

In reality, Edes was less eager for power than the commission's critics supposed. He refused to create a townsite police or allow the swearing of commission employees as deputy marshals in townsites, even though the commission was responsible for the administration of the towns. He demurred when Mears advanced a scheme for a new judicial division in the Anchorage area. While he accepted the argument that a court at Anchorage would be convenient to the railroad and the new population in the construction zone, Edes reminded Mears that court location involved Alaska's bitter town rivalries. "I think we should keep absolutely clear of these semi-political matters as we will only be cursed for our trouble," he wrote.[9]

In other activities the commissioners suffered less frustration and enjoyed more accomplishment. One of these was purchasing the narrow gauge Tanana Valley Railroad out of Fairbanks. By buying the destitute little line, the commission reduced its own rail charges from Chena and gained the first leg of a narrow gauge link with Nenana, where coal from the lignite fields could be rushed to Fairbanks' fuel-starved mines. In view of the later charges that the sale resulted from bribery or blundering, it would be well to remember that the commissioners entered into it with eyes wide open. Riggs knew the railroad's rotten condition, "deplorable"[10] he called it. He knew, even while recommending the sale, how badly the TVRR needed basic repairs to its roadbed and rolling stock. Although he voiced the usual hopes for a resurgent mining industry, Riggs obviously wanted to buy the road as a service to Fairbanks. The TVRR was the only year-round, large-volume transportation link between Fairbanks and the mines, an almost indispensable hauler of mining machinery and, hopefully, of coal. It could be saved only by an infusion of funds far beyond the company's resources. Had the commissioners chosen to be ruthless with the Tanana Valley line, they could have paralleled it for the Chena-Fairbanks distance or purchased only the yards and a few miles of track west of Fairbanks. As the TVRR's anxious president well knew, the commission could dictate its terms, or worse yet, stand by while the road collapsed, then pick it up for junk value. The negotiated sale price of $300,000 was more than $90,000 under the A. E. C.'s conservative estimate of the railroad's value and vastly less than the TVRR's own valuation of its property and equipment — $2,118,790.29. The real gainer from the 1917 transaction was the Fairbanks region, which was assured of wintertime transportation. The commission at once began to refurbish the nearly exhausted railroad.

Nineteen seventeen was also the year that the commission began work on an ocean dock at Anchorage. The work seemed to be the beginning of the fulfillment of the commissioners' hopes for a full-fledged port at the construction camp, hopes born of despair over the steep grades and physical condition of the railroad to Seward. The commissioners keenly felt the lack of a permanent dock for their own operations. Besides, they believed that Anchorage could become a short-haul coal port in its own right. Their problem was securing expert endorsement of their faith in Anchorage to justify the expense of dredging. The first expert to be approached, the engineer in charge of the dredging division of the Panama Canal, was disappointingly pessimistic. He despaired of Anchorage's thirty-six-foot tides and its huge, tide-borne ice pans during the winter. He questioned the commission's scanty information about the nature of the material to be dredged (this was in March 1915). Although he admitted that a sea-going dredge could be moved from Panama to Anchorage, he pointed out the unavailability of supporting tugs or barges. Clearly another expert was required. He was finally discovered in William Gerig, a respected dredge expert. Gerig, a small, scholarly man with a greying Van Dyke beard, turned on the problem with all the force of his considerable intelligence. He argued the feasibility of constructing a long dock about one thousand yards north of Ship Creek, then dredging out a deep basin where steamers could ride at any stage of the tide. Problems of floating ice and silting could be minimized by the proper construction and equipment. The commissioners gladly accepted Gerig's recommendations and subsequently retained him to supervise the reconstruction of a dredge Gerig had designed five years earlier for a "stateside" railroad. The reconstruction was to be carried out on the commission barge *Sperm*.

The years through 1917 saw the commissioners alter and expand their organization to accommodate their increasingly diverse activities. Early in 1916 they established general storekeeper's and telephone and telegraph departments. They added a land and industrial department, charged with supervising townsites, leases, and economic development, in April. On February 2, 1917, Lane approved the creation of an accounting department to have charge of all bookkeeping and commission funds. A month later a

47

department of health and sanitation was added.

During 1916 the commissioners changed two headquarters locations to bring them closer to the important construction work. The major move shifted the general headquarters from Seward to Anchorage, effective January 1, 1917. At Seward the headquarters was isolated at one end of the line, situated on the relatively small sixty-acre tract purchased from the Alaska Northern, and surrounded by land held at speculative prices. Anchorage offered larger terminal grounds on government land and was closer to the critical construction work toward the coal fields. On the Northern Division, Riggs moved his headquarters from Fairbanks to the new Nenana townsite to be nearer to his principal construction effort along the Nenana River.

By early 1917 construction, organization, the labor force, and the money flow seemed to be reasonably well controlled. Things were far from rosy, a pessimist could say, but he would have to admit the A. E. C.'s progress and adaptability. Ironically, some of the pessimist's worst fears were about to be realized.

The Alaskan Engineering Commission's Seward Division embraced the Kenai Peninsula from Seward to the head of Cook Inlet's Turnagain Arm, including the Loop District, shown in a bird's-eye view. *The Alaska Railroad*

The construction years, 1915-1923: Survey party moves its camp across Portage Glacier, probably during the 1914 surveys preceding the start of construction. *The Alaska Railroad*

The Loop District combined the works of God and man in an awesome way. Sublime mountains, glaciers, and valleys seemed to allow trestles, tunnels, and track to exist on sufferance. Photos at left, *National Archives;* above, *The Alaska Railroad*

Because the Alaska Central—Alaska Northern had pierced most of the Seward Division, there was little construction to undertake. But reconstruction, required by the false economies of the ACR—ANR and by deterioration, proved to be an enormous task. Here a work crew reinforces a trestle in the Loop District, September 4, 1920. *The Alaska Railroad*

Benching and trestling along the north shore of Turnagain Arm was difficult and expensive. Even experienced station contractors refused to tackle some sections of the line on Turnagain. When no escape from snowslides was possible, the Turnagain shore sprouted ungainly snowsheds. *The Alaska Railroad*

Trestle built over the Turnagain flats to escape snowslides, 1919. *The Alaska Railroad*

A pile driver at work on Turnagain Arm. *The Alaska Railroad*

Looking south across Turnagain Arm to the Kenai Peninsula, November 28, 1919. *The Alaska Railroad*

A construction camp on Turnagain Arm. *National Archives*

A station contractor's cut 14 miles south of Anchorage. *National Archives*

Grade near the water on a stretch of rough Turnagain country, with the trail at extreme right. *The Alaska Railroad*

Two views of Rainbow Camp, mile 89.5. Above, *The Alaska Railroad;* below, *National Archives*

Hand labor for a station crew on Turnagain Arm. *The Alaska Railroad*

A saddle tank engine and a string of dump cars filling the grade between Potter and Rabbit creeks, near Anchorage. *The Alaska Railroad*

An ever-present threat along Turnagain: a washout leaves sagging track near Peters Creek, October 7, 1916. *The Alaska Railroad*

Laying the last rail between Seward and Anchorage, September 17, 1918. *The Alaska Railroad*

A rare moment of triumph for Thomas Riggs, right, Governor of Alaska and former railroad commissioner, as he rides the first through train from Seward to Anchorage. *Sexton & Thwaites Photo, Alaska Historical Library*

Triumph to disaster: Passengers from Anchorage walking over a snowslide at the head of Turnagain Arm. A train for Seward awaits them on the other side of the slide, November 29, 1918. For several years, through track did not mean dependable through operation. *The Alaska Railroad*

A caboose caught in a snowslide at the head of Turnagain Arm, January 5, 1920. *The Alaska Railroad*

On the morning of April 6, 1921, a snowslide thundered down on the Seward-Anchorage train, ripped out a bridge near mile 49, and dropped two engines, a rotary plow, and two cabooses into a ravine. The plow and engines are almost entirely obscured by snow. *The Anchorage Historical and Fine Arts Museum*

Pile driver at work on a Ship Creek bridge at Anchorage, probably 1916. *The Alaska Railroad*

Gathering piling along the right-of-way, probably north of Anchorage, March 1917. *The Alaska Railroad*

Sternwheel steamer *Omineca* at Anchorage, with ocean steamer *Northwestern* in the background, about 1920. The *Omineca* was a jack-of-all-trades workhorse, often used for carrying construction materials to Croto on the Susitna River. *The Alaska Railroad*

Dinner time at Wasilla, mile 160, about 55 rail miles north of Anchorage. The steel gang coming in for a meal on May 4, 1917. *The Alaska Railroad*

Part of the Anchorage Terminal Reserve, the site of the stampede town. A pile driver is in the foreground, and the "Government Hill" housing area in the background. *National Archives*

The Anchorage yards showing trains loaded with construction materials, ready for "the front." Anchorage is in the left background. *National Archives*

Driving piles and digging ditches on the Nenana River, spring 1918, were wasted effort. The Nenana cut a new main channel, forcing the relocation of 21 miles of track south of Nenana town. *The Alaska Railroad*

Dragline excavator loading ballast near Nenana, August 24, 1917. *The Alaska Railroad*

Steam shovel No. 2 working 17 miles south of Nenana, July 14, 1919. *The Alaska Railroad*

On the Fairbanks Division, working a gravel pit near Fairbanks, October 13, 1917. *The Alaska Railroad*

A narrow-gauge dinky and dump cars working between Fairbanks and Nenana July 26, 1919. *The Alaska Railroad*

A relic from the old TVRR, restenciled "U.S." for work on the narrow gauge between Nenana and Fairbanks, about 1919. *The Alaska Railroad*

Mile 449, about 21 miles from Fairbanks, July 26, 1919. *The Alaska Railroad*

The emblem used—probably unofficially—on some of the Alaskan Engineering Commission's Susitna River construction supply boats. Drawn by an unknown artist. *National Archives*

Four methods of moving supplies and equipment to "the front": a river boat with eagle emblem on the pilot house at Talkeetna, mile 227, about 1918. *The Alaska Railroad*

During the long Alaska winter, supplies moved best by horse sled. Here eight tons of hay, grain, and car wheels pass camp 166, March 30, 1917. *The Alaska Railroad*

Caterpillar tractor and trailers move supplies near Broad Pass, in the Alaska Range, about June 1921. Construction crews called this ensemble "the cat and her kittens." *The Alaska Railroad*

The Talkeetna River bridge, March 10, 1919, in the final construction stages. Typical of The Alaska Railroad's timber bridges. *The Alaska Railroad*

Where there was no track and an engine was needed, construction forces had to improvise. Here horses haul a dinky overland from Healy south toward McKinley Park. About 1921. *The Alaska Railroad*

The Riley Creek bridge under construction, winter 1921-22, with construction camp in foreground. *The Alaska Railroad*

The Chulitna River through the south end of the Hurricane Gulch bridge, 1921. *The Alaska Railroad*

Hurricane Gulch bridge under construction, with crane lifting a girder, August 1921. *E. F. Bryant Collection, University of Alaska Archives*

The bridge nears completion, August 8, 1921. *The Alaska Railroad*

First regular train over the Hurricane Gulch bridge, mile 284, August 18, 1921. *The Alaska Railroad*

The view from the bridge, the Chulitna River and the Alaska Range. *The Alaska Railroad*

Trestle approach to the Tanana River bridge, the last uncompleted link, July 30, 1922. *Charles Bunnell Collection, University of Alaska Archives*

American Bridge Company crews at work on the girders of the Tanana River bridge, 1922. *The Alaska Railroad*

The bridge with falsework piling frozen in the river ice, February 1923. *The Alaska Railroad*

The bridge a few days before completion, February 1923. *The Alaska Railroad*

The End of the Beginning

The Great War hit the railroad hard. Wartime demands decimated its labor force and damaged its resource development work. Wartime and postwar exigencies swung the commissioners away from concern for railbelt resources and ever more intensely to other interests. These included construction, labor troubles, a cumbersome administrative structure, operations, organization and operation of the River Boat Service, and the railroad's multi-faceted relationships within the territory.

Even before the United States joined the war, the 1916 preparedness boom drew men from the railroad. During 1917, the A. E. C.'s peak employment year, a shortage of unskilled labor and track men hampered construction. Nineteen eighteen was an employment disaster. That summer the working force averaged 2,800 compared with 5,675 in 1917. About half of the commission's clerical and engineering forces enlisted in the armed services. Many left with Mears when he resigned in January, 1918, to accept a colonelcy and command of the 31st Engineer Regiment, which served on the French railroad system. Women filled some jobs; others went begging. Worse, high wages elsewhere and faltering appropriations perpetuated the labor shortage through the 1920 season, although white-collar employees began returning shortly after the end of the war. During 1919 the commission took the desperate step — for that time — of hiring native laborers to flesh out the working force. In August, 1919, the labor force reached the year's high — 3,084. In July, 1920, it climbed to 3,748, almost 2,500 below the best month in 1917. Workers' quality declined along with their quantity. "We have to take what we can get," Edes complained in August 1918, "and allow a man to call himself a carpenter, for instance, who cannot frame a bridge but can nail on a board." The official report for 1920 declared that "labor has been inefficient."[1]

The railroad's problem was the territory's, for the war accelerated central Alaska's population decline. Anchorage's population skidded from 3,928 in 1917 to 1,856 three years later. In 1910 over 3,500 people lived in Fairbanks, but the town numbered only 1,155 in 1920. By 1919 population had declined so rapidly that the steamship companies would have either raised their increasing rates still more or sharply reduced their service to Seward and Anchorage had not the A. E. C. contracted with them to carry commission freight.

The commission, caught in the vise of labor scarcity and wartime inflation, repeatedly raised wages. It offered fringe benefits such as mess meals at or below cost and free transportation to Seattle. During every year of the labor shortage save 1919 the commissioners rearranged the budget and grudgingly granted general increases. Their raises neither proportionately equalled the soaring wages outside Alaska nor matched the spiraling cost of living.

From 1915 to 1919 wages for common labor rose from 37½ to 55 cents per hour, or 68 percent. But by 1918, war industries and the city government in Seattle were advertising for laborers at fifty cents per hour and more. The near-parity seriously devalued A. E. C. wages

75

because of Anchorage's himalayan living costs, about 25 percent above Seattle's. Edes' grumbling over having to take what he could get in skilled labor indicates that Alaska wages were not competitive at any level. The commission's coal mines suffered a dearth of competent labor though mine wages were 10 percent or more above the Washington scale. In the spring of 1920 railroad wages rose again, but the labor supply remained "short."[2] Laborers transported from Seattle sometimes jumped ship and forgot their contracts with the commission when they learned of jobs at Cordova or Valdez. In desperation the A. E. C. began shipping workmen directly to Seward to shield them from the seductive wages at other coast towns.

During the war the commissioners inculcated patriotism and feelings of fierce loyalty among their men. Employees who did not enlist oversubscribed to war bonds and contributed heavily to a service hospital in France. They served as conscription registrars and on the price interpreting committee of the Federal Food Administration. The A. E. C. filled columns of the *Alaska Railroad Record* with food conservation regulations and exhortations. It gave space in its buildings and in the *Record* to the activities of the Anchorage branch of the Alaska Loyal League, a patriotic and quasi-military organization comprised mostly of commission employees.

Most workers were patriotic enough, but the disaffected, the disloyal, and a band of labor radicals played upon the relatively low wages. They also battered away at the A. E. C.'s self-image of unity and mutual loyalty. Before the United States entered the war, members of the militant Industrial Workers of the World had controlled the Alaska Labor Union at Anchorage. When spring arrived they moved up and down the line, speaking with evangelistic fervor and agitating for a strike. Their articles in the Seattle labor newspapers warned workers away from A. E. C. track gangs. Their most articulate leader, the voluble Lena Morrow Lewis, declaimed to a May Day, 1917, audience at the Anchorage labor temple upon the merits of the red flag, which "carries with it vigor, and courage and is the symbol of labor itself." She declared, "We are looking forward to the day when the working classes will be the dominant triumphant class."[3] For a brief time the radicals had a large following.

"I am fearful of the effect of this constant incendiary preaching on these men," read one of Edes' worried letters to the Department of the Interior. "Is there any way that a lot of irresponsible trouble-makers can legally be prevented from interfering with the operations of the United States Government?"[4] he asked in another. Not unless they violate the law, the department replied. Edes' informers dogged the radicals on the line and in their meetings but discovered nothing indictable. The Seattle employment office tried not to hire any "Wobblies." Early in June, conservatives captured the union, and the I. W. W. lost its base of operations in the Anchorage Division.

A strike flared up briefly in July at the Nenana construction base deep in the interior. Here, workmen felt the pinch of Alaska's sharp seasonal employment most keenly. Here, north of the mountain parapets, spring lagged weeks behind the coastal warming, while winter closed in ahead of "freeze-up" to the south. The busy season was four months at best, the slack season long and cheerless. "The thought of an idle winter hangs like a black pall over the mind of the laborer,"[5] wrote Thomas Riggs, though he moved against the strike and its leaders with swift ruthlessness.

Early in 1917 a persuasive "Wobbly" and recent migrant from Dawson, one Charles Lestor, organized a union in the Fairbanks district. On the fifth of July his union acted: some men of the steel gang at Nenana struck for higher pay. Workers from other crews joined them until, by the seventh, eighty-three men had quit. Riggs, the United States attorney, and the marshal mounted a four-pronged offensive against the strike. The marshal clapped Lestor and three German confederates in jail, while the attorney told a mass meeting at the Nenana movie house on the night of the tenth that he would repress any strike against the railroad during wartime. Next, government officials played on the Germans' involvement in the strike to stir up patriotic sentiment against any labor disruption. Riggs displayed his genuine sympathy for the strikers' cause by discussing the workers' demands with them. Finally, and most effectively, he played on local fears of a complete work stoppage. He wired Edes at Anchorage to send him a telegram reading, "If strikers interfering with railroad construction you will be prepared to stop all work within your district." When he read Edes' telegram to the Nenana mass meeting the effect was electric. Within two days the Germans were packed off to Fairbanks and internment, the hapless Lestor was convicted of treasonable utterances, and the striking workers dissolved both union and strike. Riggs and the lawmen "were prepared to form a vigilance committee and hang a few if necessary," but their "firm" policy, combined with getting the town of Fairbanks "worked up" against the strikers, rendered more extreme measures unnecessary.[6]

The still nervous commissioners appealed for increased troop strength at Anchorage, and the War Department, after some hesitation, beefed up the infantry detachment from 40 to 100 men. The soldiers spent most of their duty pulling guard in the terminal grounds and out on the line. No further labor flare-ups occurred, although discontent remained. Early in the morning of January 15, 1918, an arsonist fired the Nenana engine house. Kerosene-fed flames swept over the plank floor, consumed a flatcar, and melted the fittings on three locomotives. The culprit may have been someone with a grudge against the commission, but more probably he was a "Wobbly," or that especial A. E. C. fear, the German agent. Whoever he was, he never was caught.

Pressures for patriotic loyalty and conformity placed every alien's job in some jeopardy. Simmering citizen resentment against alien employees heated rapidly after the April declaration of war. Not only were Germans enemy aliens, but the prevalent Swedes, Danes, and Norwegians were transmuted into neutral allegiants. On the Anchorage and Seward divisions the railroad's special inspector investigated all complaints of sympathy for the enemy. In suspicious cases the A. E. C. replaced doubtful workers "with men of known loyalty,"[7] whether or not the inspector had uncovered enough evidence for a court prosecution. Because job jealousies doubtless inspired some complaints, and because the special inspector equated indifference toward the war with disloyalty, some of the apparent handful of firings may have been unjustified.

On the Northern, or Fairbanks Division, more sourdough camaraderie prevailed, and few firings were based on nationality until after Riggs resigned April 25, 1918, to accept the governorship of the territory. His successor in office, though not in title, was Frederick D. Browne, the engineer in charge. Browne was an able engineer, but a martinet who expected absolute obedience to regulations and loyalty to the organization. Browne's extensive firings for "pro-German leanings" were related to an administrative scandal at Nenana and animosity between Riggs and the district attorney. He also was sensitive about charges "that an American citizen had no chance on the railroad" because of the "very strong German element fastened to the pay rolls," rolls that "in some places savored of the roster of a German military company." His blows fell most heavily on clerical and "around camp" employees. Of twelve firings the engineer-in-charge enumerated to Edes, he listed suspected disloyalty as a partial cause in seven. In addition, he dismissed all registered alien enemies and some men charged with sedition, even though they had not been convicted. Browne claimed that he had done "great good," but in some instances it is probable that his arbitrary actions robbed the railroad of reliable and experienced men.[8]

Palpable labor unrest continued through 1919 and 1920, but very little of it related to radicalism. Despite the Seattle general strike of 1919, a high-water mark of I. W. W. power, the "Wobblies" were ineffectual in central Alaska. Their few emissaries to the Far North failed to stir the old enthusiasms. A short-lived employees' cooperative published newsletters sprinkled with references to the plight of the masses and the need for social change. It caused the commission management some anxiety but had little influence. Most workers expressed their opinions of commission wages and working conditions by taking jobs elsewhere, though the miners at Eska struck for two months. Besides raising wages, the commission worked to improve sanitary and mess conditions at the camps.

As if war, wage disputes, and "Wobblies" were not enough, deadly influenza visited the line in 1918 and again in 1920. In the earlier outbreak the A. E. C. restricted train movements and assisted railbelt communities in maintaining quarantine and health measures. The later epidemic, although confined to the district north of the Alaska Range, was much more serious. In late April, 1920, the "flu" swept the right-of-way from Fairbanks to Broad Pass. By mid-month forty-three people were dead at Nenana, a toll more than one-tenth the population. Browne called in a line doctor to help at the stricken town.

Engineers became nurses while commission and station gangs, many sick to a man, dissolved in fever and prostration. Victims in recovery found themselves in the grip of exhaustion and a strange lassitude. The disease claimed at least seventy-seven lives. Nine employees and seven contractors died, and 90 percent of the railroad's Northern Division forces were incapacitated. From mid-May to mid-June scarcely anybody worked. Despite its own incapacity, the commission spent $5,869.84 aiding indigent natives caught in the epidemic.

Through it all, men advanced the track. On September 10, 1918, the commission passed a construction milestone when crews joined the steel at mile 78.75 on Turnagain Arm. Edes pounded the last spike home. Anchorage and Seward were connected, but tenuously. The grandly rugged, mountainous Kenai Peninsula was home to some of the most hideous weather on the continent. Winds howled and snowslides roared through "Hell's Acre," north of the 1,063-foot summit at Grandview, mile 45. The ten miles of the Placer River Canyon running north to Turnagain Arm were a cataclysm of winds, snow, sleet, and slides in winter, and floods in spring. The fragile line soon buckled under the storms. A large slide north of the summit blocked the line from November until July. Later slides halted trains from Anchorage at mile 80 on Turnagain Arm. From here, dogsleds carried passengers, mail, and freight to mile 40, where the trains to Seward were waiting.

Trips from Anchorage to Seward could be grueling. In December, 1918, before the heavy snows and slides of the new year, eighty-two passengers left Anchorage bound for Seward the morning of the tenth, a Saturday. When the train entered the treacherous Placer River Canyon it encountered ice on the track. There had been a warm spell, and rain, and then a cold snap that had congealed the water on the rails. While sectionmen picked away at the ice, the train crept on to mile 58 near the summit, where the tired crew gave up at 8:00 P.M. The crewmen then decided to run back to the roadhouse at Kern Creek, mile 71, but found the track re-iced behind them. There was nothing to do but pick out the ice once more in an exhausting struggle that ended at three o'clock Sunday morning. Before noon on Sunday the passengers were up and away from Kern, and late that night they arrived at the 1,200-foot-long snowslide at mile 54. After tramping around the slide, they boarded another train and arrived at 7:00 A.M. Monday morning in Seward only to find their steamer delayed by storms. In almost two full days of travel they had come 114 miles.

The commission engineers pressed the work on the "Seward line," raising tracks, relocating trestles, widening tunnels, and building snowsheds, suffering all the while from a lack of funds and labor. Snow blockades shut Matanuska coal out of Seward early in 1919, forcing the commission to use imported coal in its buildings there. It was a humiliating necessity for a railroad begun almost four years earlier with the purpose of developing Alaska's coal markets. But at least the 1920 season was better: plenty of men and money. The secretary of the interior, John Barton Payne, added a firm order to finish the Seward-Anchorage line for regular winter operation. Widened tunnels and new snowsheds helped, but freakish Kenai Peninsula weather still could frustrate Payne's mandate. Weather especially interfered with train No. 2, which chugged out of Seward on the morning of April 5, 1921, preceded by Extra 275 comprising a rotary plow, two engines, and two cabooses.

The two trains slogged through the stormy Kenai, the passenger train twice coupling to the rotary to ease over steep grades. At dusk they were fighting a small slide and blizzard in the Tunnel vicinity. Then they fell back to a new iron and timber bridge at mile 49.3, where Trainmaster J. T. Cunningham, riding as a passenger, arranged the engines and cars for next morning's attack on the snow. He placed the passenger train south of the bridge, protected from the violent winds. To prevent the rotary's being drifted in, he parked it on the bridge. Cunningham could have done no better had he read the records, which showed that no dangerous snowslides had occurred there since the Alaska Northern built a bridge at that spot in the spring of 1907. The next morning at 8:05 some crewmen were inside the cabooses, others had walked to the rear of the passenger train for breakfast in the buffet car "Seward." Suddenly a juggernaut of snow thundered down a nearby hill and smashed the bridge as if it were a matchwood toy. The plow and engines dropped twenty-five feet to the valley floor. The cabooses wrenched loose and careened down a bank, tossing and bruising the trainmen inside. The slide interrupted through service between Anchorage and Seward for twenty-six days. It was the first of many such rude interruptions.

During 1918 in the railroad's northern reaches, Frederick Browne fought the Fairbanks fuel famine with steel. Gravel was scarce along the right-of-way, so Browne ordered a roadbed built from quavering muck, then laid down narrow gauge rail to a fresh wood supply. The cost of the wobbly road offended his engineer's sense of economy, but when the Fairbanks Gold Mining Company imported oil by ocean and river because California crude was cheaper than local wood, it was time to forget expenses and act. In the same spirit, Browne ordered the tracks built south from Nenana to the Burns coal mine at mile 363. Crews worked through the golden autumn, through the short, crisp November days, and into the dark, cold winter. The earth turned to iron, and Browne almost doubled the stationmen's prices to keep them hacking and blasting away at it. Grading and track gangs plunged on through lengthening days and softening snow to reach the mine on April 4, 1919. Then the operating crews worked frantically to ship coal north before the awakening Nenana smashed the crossing trestle at mile 370 during the spring ice run.

During the summer Browne's crews drove the track to the foot of Nenana Canyon, a dramatic gorge north of the McKinley Park station. Here they faced some of the most grueling work on the entire line. To the north, gangs worked to complete the narrow gauge. On November 3 they joined the rails between Fairbanks and North Nenana, a station across the broad Tanana from the Nenana townsite.

After the 1920 season the line gapped a mere eighty-three miles between the ends of steel. None of the great steel bridges were built, but breaks in the line were small enough for the post office to shift its winter mail contract from the Valdez trail to the railroad. From October 1, 1920, the A. E. C. trainmen took the mail sacks at dockside, then carried them to the horse sled drivers south of Broad Pass, who ran them through to the north edge of Nenana Canyon and steel once more. The mail moved from Seward to Fairbanks on a seven-and-one-half-day schedule. After May 1 the summer's mail followed its traditional sea routes to St. Michael or Skagway, then to the interior. Once the snow melted, only men on foot or horseback could cross the soft, mossy, mosquito-infested floor of the continental divide.

The next year — 1921 — two great steel bridges closed gaps in the line at the Susitna River crossing and Hurricane Gulch. The Susitna span at Mile 264 was delayed when snow fell on the site as late as the previous June 19, and again that October, when a pier containing improperly mixed cement collapsed. Even before the repoured pier had cured the American Bridge Company crews were erecting steel for the 504-foot main span. On February 2 the bridge stood clear of its falsework and four days later carried the first train across the Susitna. Twenty miles north at Hurricane Gulch the commission's forces and the American Bridge men forged the most dramatic of all Alaska Railroad bridges. At its completion on August 15, the great spandrel arch lifted the rails 296 feet over the wild chasm. Passengers on the first wooden coaches to crawl over the trestle saw one of the most breathtaking sights in Alaska beneath them — the Chulitna River — a shining ribbon 400 feet below and one-fourth mile away against the backdrop of the Alaska Range. In the eleven-mile Nenana Canyon from Riley Creek (mile 347) to Healy, contractors and commission crews hacked and blasted at the nearly sheer walls. They cut three tunnels through rock promontories rising straight from the thrashing stream. At year's end the finished track hugged the canyon's slippery sides two hundred feet above Nenana River.

Regular through service advanced with the track. Two mixed trains each week were scheduled between Seward and Chulitna (mile 274) beginning in 1921. In June the service reached Hurricane Gulch and by late September had been moved in stages to Broad Pass. On December 4 the railroad established through service over the 470 miles of main line, four days from Seward to Fairbanks with night layovers at Anchorage and Deadhorse (now Curry, mile 248.5) and McKinley Park (mile 348). Freight was transferred at Riley Creek, the head of Nenana Canyon, and again at Nenana. At the Tanana River town, passengers and goods were loaded into narrow gauge cars for a journey behind the "North Nenana Limited," a dinky confined to hauling trains on rails laid over the frozen river. At North Nenana a narrow gauge road locomotive hitched on for the run to Fairbanks. The A. E. C. used the three-foot gauge between Fairbanks and the Tanana crossing so that the Tanana Valley equipment could double on the main line during the construction phase.

As the system knit together, the original tripartite organization designed to serve scattered construction forces in the wilderness became less and less necessary. After the steel gangs linked Seward and Anchorage late in 1918, there was little need for a separate Seward Division. By December 1919, the railroad boasted 340 operating miles, even though some 85 percent of them could accept nothing heavier than a sixty-ton locomotive. An operating railroad man would have blanched at some of the line's anomalies. Diminishing construction activities maintained the right-of-way over freight and passenger trains. Uncoordinated departments sprouted beside those that were better planned. The A. E. C. reached the ultimate *ad hoc* response in 1918, creating a receiving and forwarding department to cope with heavy shipments over the Anchorage dock. By themselves, the peculiarities little concerned the commissioners and engineers in charge. Tidy administration and effective operations were not the business of construction engineers. Their case before congressional committees, the secretary of the interior, and the public rested on their ability to advance the track quickly and economically.

Yet the commissioners could not ignore the pressures for reorganization coming from their third-echelon officials. These officers wanted to clear away the accumulated administrative thickets and create a structure that would encompass both construction and operation while accommodating the transition to full operation. Thus, the master mechanic, not the railroad executives, first proposed keeping the systematic reports required for efficient operations. Mounting outside pressures for economy also forced structural changes. Although the world war prompted congressional and departmental mutterings about expenses, they would have come soon enough, with more than $24 million of the $35 million authorization already spent at the end of 1917. Snarled accounting procedures and the need to keep two sets of accounts, one for voluntary filing with the Interstate Commerce Commission, the other for the Treasury, did not help. At the budget hearing early in 1919, an embarrassed Edes admitted that he knew neither the railroad's unexpended balance nor the amount needed to meet unpaid obligations. Two commissioners resigned before the reorganization, relieving the possibility of any conflicts over authority among the managers. Riggs left in April 1918. Although he held the title of consulting engineer six months longer, Edes resigned as chairman and chief engineer on August 29, 1919, the same day that Mears assumed the dual title.

Mears issued the reorganization circular less than four months after he returned from France to the railroad. In it he abolished the three construction divisions, replacing them with Southern and Northern divisions bisected at Broad Pass (mile 315). The scope given to the Anchorage-based Southern Division presaged the centralization of all railroad administration at the Cook Inlet town. Briefly, Mears placed all the important maintenance and construction officials, plus the heads of the transportation, mechanical, telephone and telegraph, mining, and other departments, under William Gerig, the assistant chief engineer and divisional engineer in charge. Browne's Northern Division comprised autonomous hospital, townsite, and disbursing offices together with a local construction chief and the headquarters of the Tanana Valley Railroad. The TVRR operating department controlled the narrow gauge operations from Fairbanks to Chena, Chatanika, and North Nenana. The Northern Division was clearly a subordinate, not a coordinate division.

Mears' order brought some badly needed organization to the line's chaotic fiscal and storekeeping arrangements. At the same time, it reduced the authority that the heads of the three construction divisions had formerly exercised over such matters. A Supply Division at Seward assumed responsibility for all construction equipment orders, for ocean freight shipments, and for most intraterritorial employment. Its Employment Bureau met and assigned workers shipped in from Seattle. An Accounting Division was charged with the supervision of accounting, auditing, and bookkeeping in all divisions and departments. The Purchasing Division was not reorganized or relocated, but remained at Seattle to superintend nationwide purchasing, initiate ocean freight shipments, and hire laborers for work in Alaska.

Although Mears approved several administrative adjustments between the 1919 reorganization and the 1921 consolidation, the decline of the Land and Industrial Department was the most significant. Its diminishing role reflected the A. E. C. management's loss of hope for diversified economic development in Alaska and the Wilson administration's economy drive. After disastrous agricultural overproduction in 1917, the department stopped trying to attract homesteaders. At about the same time, the Mining Department and the management informally supplanted the Land and Industrial Department by dealing with private coal operators in the Matanuska field. When private developers opened their lignite mines near Healy, they worked not with the Land and Industrial Department, but with Frederick Browne, the engineer in charge. Edes added the Nenana townsite to Browne's responsibilities on September 1, 1918, and Mears confirmed the change in the 1919 reorganization. These actions not only ran counter to centralizing administrative matters at Anchorage, they also contravened the order establishing the Land and Industrial Department.

The result of these restrictions was that successive department managers administered leases and the Anchorage townsite and answered inquiries. They edited the *Alaska Railroad Record,* a useful institutional publication containing official circulars, employment statistics, and much else. Their superiors whittled away at even those few duties. In May, 1920, Secretary of the Interior John Barton Payne ordered the eight-page *Record* discontinued as an economy measure, and the little paper ceased publication with the June 29 issue. Mears objected and tried to gain permission to revive the sheet, but was unsuccessful. The commission had hesitated to abolish the Land and Industrial Department while possibilities existed that it would play a role under the various Alaska Development Board bills pending in Congress. With hopes for congressional action and the newspaper gone, there was no reason to continue. Mears dropped the development activity, rationalizing his action by the lack of a specific appropriation. Anchorage's incorporation ended the remaining townsite functions. The Land and Industrial Department, founded on high hopes four years before, faded away.

The 1919 reorganization by no means solved all structural problems, nor could other embarrassing or cumbersome departments simply disappear from view as the Land and Industrial had done. The Accounting Division continued to have difficulty tailoring accurate, clear, and comprehensive systems to the rapidly changing relation between construction and operation. In September, 1921, Trainmaster Cunningham and Master Mechanic Fred C. Ferrell toured the Northern Division. They discovered deficient equipment, unsatisfactory operating practices, and inflated payrolls. Cars on the narrow gauge lines out of Fairbanks had automatic couplers, but Ferrell found trainmen using the awkward, dangerous link-and-pin coupling method because the automatics varied in height. At the Fairbanks roundhouse, engine crews washed their engines and made many of their own repairs, while train crews cleaned coaches, built fires, fueled engines, and performed other tasks normally done by mechanics and station employees. Three men — pilot, engineer, and deckhand — manned the launch "Midnight Sun" as it plied the Tanana between Nenana and North Nenana. The pilot, an old river hand, told Ferrell that he could operate the craft by himself. Up and down the line Cunningham discovered instances of inefficiency and poor operation. Most of the lapses could be explained, even excused, by the concentration on construction, by the lingering on of old habits from the privately owned TVRR, and by the desire to transfer capable or well-known men into operations where they were released from the rapidly dwindling construction forces.

The situation was unsatisfactory from the operating viewpoint, whatever the reasons. Mears gave Ferrell almost a free hand in reorganizing the mechanical department a few weeks in advance of the general consolidation. Then on November 1, Mears abolished the Northern and Southern divisions and redesignated the organizational divisions as departments. A month later, as already noted, the railroad began its through route operations.

Truly, through operation required bridging the last two gaps in the line, at last binding Seward to Fairbanks by steel. In 1921 the A. E. C.'s construction forces attacked the first gap, the Riley Creek bed athwart the line at mile 347 just south of McKinley Park station. During December the concrete foundations were finished. That month the erection crews began from the south end, placing the pyramids of lacy steel that carried the cantilever bridge 570 feet across the creek. They built a wooden trestle another 330 feet to the high ground on the north. The bridge opened in February, 1922. Only the Tanana River remained unconquered.

The Tanana bridge site at Nenana is unmistakable on any map of Alaska large enough to show the river. After bending from northwest to southwest at Fairbanks, the Tanana runs southwest some fifty miles until it abruptly swings north. The bridge cuts across the northward arc. The first plans called for a long, low, multi-span bridge, its south end anchored to the Nenana townsite's west side, its north end striking the low elevations at the edge of the Tortella Hills opposite the town. The proposed bridge carried the main line over the river and around the west edge of the Tortellas without heavy grades or curvature. In Mears' mind, that was its only advantage. Edes had approved the plan, but the younger man never warmed to it. Mears disliked the maintenance costs associated with a 200-foot lift span designed to admit river steamers. His greatest doubts concerned the concrete piers intended to carry the structure 1,600 feet from bank to bank. Because bedrock lay far below the stream, the piers would have to rest on timber pilings driven deep into sand and gravel. The pile underpinning was not objectionable in itself, but Mears doubted whether the piers resting upon it could withstand the pressures of river ice during the spring breakup. Observations extending over several springtimes revealed that the ice crust, three to four feet thick, moved out in a solid mass at the planned bridge crossing. Each year, the thawing Tanana nibbled at the great conglomerate, freeing it from the banks, wearing it away until it extended some 400 yards across and anywhere from 300 to 600 yards upstream or downstream. Then during mid-May the rising waters lifted it, groaning and crackling, and floated it away. No piers he could build, Mears believed, would survive year after year in the midst of those gripping, pulling pans of ice.

Mears' preference for a single span without river piers led him to the site of the former Indian mission almost a mile upstream. Here the Tanana narrowed. Here a high span could cross above the channel. Modjeski & Angier, consulting engineers, translated Mears' vision into a 700-foot simple truss span rising 47 feet above mean summer high water. The Tanana structure has been compared to the Chicago, Burlington & Quincy bridge over the Ohio River at Metropolis, Illinois, designed by the Modjeski firm a few years before. At 720 feet the channel span of the Ohio bridge is the world's longest simple truss, but the sweeping bank-to-bank span of the Alaska bridge is more dramatic, for the slightly longer midwestern model is lost among the several long spans required to cross the Ohio.

Through the spring of 1922, railroad and contractors' crews worked to build the approaches. On the south side Mears ran the track past the Nenana station and docks, then around a loop to the south end of the bridge. This solution involved grades and curvature, but Mears preferred it to laying steel directly to the bridge and bypassing Nenana, an important transfer point. On the north bank he benched in the line along the south and west faces of the Tortella Hills, then joined it with the established route to Fairbanks. On May 5 the railroad's workmen began excavating the pier foundations. The work advanced rapidly, and on August 29 the American Bridge Company crews arrived to begin erecting the great steel superstructure. The concrete piers were poured by mid-September, and on November 23 the bridge carried its first train. The workmen finished their task on February 27, 1923. With its approaches, the bridge stretched 4,183 feet, contained 2,900 tons of steel, and cost about $1,300,000.

Standard gauge trains could not run through from Seward to Fairbanks until track crews had widened the three-foot rails from North Nenana to the interior terminal. They began shoving the rails apart early in April and completed the job on June 15, a month before President Harding drove the golden spike. Other major construction projects of the A. E. C.'s last years included a combination depot-hotel at Curry and a passenger depot at Nenana completed in 1922, a depot and terminal layout at Fairbanks finished at the end of 1923, and a foundry building at Anchorage, also readied in 1923. Lesser projects, remodeling, repairs, and minor line changes combined with the great and small undertakings of previous years to create a railroad temporarily adequate to the 234,067 freight tons that it carried. It was by no means a finished, first class road.

Since March 24, 1922, the railroad had been operating under an official designation, "The Alaska Railroad," with the capitalized article a part of the name. The title had been favorably discussed within the commission and the Interior Department as early as 1916, but no decision had been reached. The drab green cars at first carried only a stenciled "U. S." and a number on their sides. The words "United States" ran in block capitals above the windows of passenger coaches, with Alaskan names below. Unofficially the railroad was called "the Alaska Railroad" or "the Government Railroad in Alaska," while the construction and operation agency, or its managers, were known as the Alaskan Engineering Commission. Obviously the latter title was anomalous and could even be ludicrous when applied to the physical railroad (imagine "all aboard the Alaskan Engineering Commission!"). Secretary Albert B. Fall's titling of the railroad solved that problem but encouraged thinking about the railroad and its management as separate entities. Further, the Alaskan Engineering Commission was confused with the Alaska Road Commission after the two organizations merged in March 1923. In an August order, Hubert Work, Fall's successor, replaced the "Alaskan Engineering Commission" with "The Alaska Railroad."

The Alaska Railroad added a new dimension to its operations when it inaugurated its River Boat Service from Nenana 723 miles downstream to Holy Cross on the lower Yukon. The railroad's appearance in the river boat business climaxed a generation of rapidly shifting relationships among the steamer operators on Alaska's interior waterways. Vicious competition early gave way to combinations and alliances. They, in turn, bowed before the American Yukon Navigation Company's virtual monopoly of the waterborne trade. The railroad's appearance added a layer of jealous intrigue before the A. Y. N. and The Alaska Railroad resolved their differences.

It began with the great Klondike gold rush. Stampeders rushing from St. Michael to Dawson overwhelmed the stern-wheelers of the Alaska Commercial and North American Trading and Transportation companies. A myriad of boats appeared to carry men and supplies to Dawson and to the later rushes along Alaska's interior valleys. For a few years the independents and big companies battled one another for the prospectors' trade, but for a few years only. Corporate reorganizations and the failure of small operators in the face of declines in placer mining rapidly reduced the number of companies and their boats. In 1912 the Northern Commercial Company and its Northern Navigation Company ran eleven of the thirty-eight vessels on the Yukon and Tanana rivers. The next year the White Pass and Yukon challenged Northern Navigation with a ruling from the attorney general that the railroad, although British-controlled, could operate boats in the Yukon basin. Soon the White Pass' American Yukon Navigation Company sent its sternwheelers chuffing down the Yukon from the railhead at Whitehorse. The Northern Navigation and the American Yukon companies locked in a rate war during 1913. The Yankee firm struggled briefly with the higher costs of its much longer haul, then succumbed. After 1918, when American Yukon Navigation bought out the last independents, the "White Pass boats" ruled the Yukon and the Tanana. They met the ocean steamers at bleak little St. Michael on Norton Sound, sixty miles northeast from the Yukon's shoaly delta. They met the narrow gauge trains two thousand miles east at Whitehorse. They were not large — most were well under 750 gross tons — but they looked proud and capable while shoving a barge along the broad rivers. Mears, who had no reason to love the American Yukon Navigation Company, admitted that it "operated very good river steamers on sufficiently frequent and regular schedule to serve the country adjacent to the Yukon and Tanana Rivers."[9]

The managers of the White Pass road had never reconciled themselves to the government railroad, regarding it as a threat to their interior business. The A. E. C. moved some shipments by White Pass rail and steamer, but the traffic produced, instead of reconciliation, squabbling over schedules and deliveries. Mears did not help matters when he predicted that the completed government line would divert from the White Pass about 4,000 passengers and 20,000 tons annually, a prediction published in the 1921 report of the secretary of the interior. The A. E. C.'s inauguration of through service at the end of 1921 was the final straw for the White Pass managers. They launched a campaign to thwart the effectiveness of Alaska's new railroad. Early in 1922 they announced the suspension of steamboat service on the Tanana. At the same time, they reduced their Yukon service to a shell — two White Pass boats operated intermittently along the great river in 1922. A swarm of little local boats, frail, ungainly and dangerous, floated out to fill the need for transportation. Yet no private boat operator was willing to haul passengers, freight, and mail along the Tanana on schedule. The short 200-mile haul and the lack of financing made the venture too risky. Service was so erratic that the War Department steamer *Jacobs* had to collect stranded sourdoughs from the riverbanks during the 1922 season.

From these trials The Alaska Railroad's River Boat Service was born. By happy coincidence the War Department had reduced its interior posts and by 1922 maintained only signal stations in the Yukon basin. The two stern-wheel steamers owned by the Quartermaster Corps were scarcely necessary for supplying the stations alone. They could be used to carry all the government's business, commercial freight, and tourists if they operated under the railroad's aegis. With H. Foster Bain, director of the Bureau of Mines, acting as intermediary at Washington, the War Department transferred the boats to the Department of the Interior on September 16, 1922. The agreement provided for their recall in case of emergency or on six months' notice. The War Department handed over its other marine equipment at Ft. Gibbon, including five barges, the ships' ways, and parts. The steamers, the *Gen. Jeff C. Davis* and the *Gen. J. W. Jacobs,* were unadorned, no-nonsense vessels. The *Davis* was also an unreliable old tub, as the Army knew and the railroad was to discover for itself during the season of 1923.

An unlooked-for "gentlemen's agreement" with the much-disliked White Pass shaped the course of the River Boat Service. In its essentials, the plan called for government boats to operate on the Tanana and the lower Yukon from the Tanana's mouth down to Holy Cross. The White Pass boats would serve the upper river from Whitehorse to Tanana village, then run up the Tanana to the interchange with the railroad at Nenana. There was to be no competition, for the American Yukon Navigation stern-wheelers were to sail the Tanana itself without pause.

It had not always been intended that way. At first Mears planned a head-on fight, placing cut-rate boats on the river from Norton Sound to Dawson, or to Eagle just inside the border if the Canadians denied his request to cross into Yukon Territory. A bitter steamboat war was averted when Mears and the Canadian railroaders joined forces to haul silver ore from the Mayo mines in Yukon Territory. The ore scheme was the second element of the "gentlemen's agreement."

The arrangement was advantageous to The Alaska Railroad. Its River Boat Service controlled the comparatively lucrative lower river trade. The railroad enjoyed the immediate prospect of 8,000 tons of ore and the more distant hope for greater tonnage, a hope unfortunately not realized. Moreover, Mears' successors would have been sorely embarrassed had they attempted to operate a steamer service from one end of the Yukon to the other with two boats, one of them the inefficient *Davis*. Had they attempted to barge Mayo ore down the Stewart and the Yukon, they would have had to add boats or face a breakdown in the service. In another respect, the "gentlemen's agreement" was less beneficial, for the rate quarrel only intensified the ungentlemanly attitudes of each railroad toward the other. During the negotiations, Gerig had written to Mears that "the White Pass people are pretty tricky and therefore it behooves us to carefully scrutinize every move they make," a sentiment which the "White Pass people" thoroughly reciprocated.[10] In their bitterness toward the government railroad they did nothing to encourage tourist travel on the Yukon below Dawson during the 1923 season. Alaskans along the railbelt were convinced of deliberate efforts to block tourists from descending the river and taking The Alaska Railroad back to deep water. They complained to Secretaries Hubert Work and Herbert Hoover during the presidential visit of 1923. Lack of evidence and improving relations between the two lines forestalled an investigation by the Interstate Commerce Commission.

In the midst of the activities of the final construction year, Mears was relieved of his job. On March 26, 1923, James G. Steese, president of the Alaska Road Commission, became the chairman and chief engineer of the Alaskan Engineering Commission. The two organizations combined administratively, and Steese assumed several additional unrelated duties in what the Harding administration hoped would be the nucleus of a new, unified Alaska administrative board. The change marked a new era in The Alaska Railroad's history to be discussed in Chapter 9. What now concerns us is why Mears played no role in the reorganized management.

One reason — that there was room for but one top manager in the combined commission — gave the edge to Steese, who had some railroad experience, while Mears had no comparable experience with roads. There were personal reasons as well. Mears had been detailed to build the railroad, not to operate it. According to Charles F. Curry, chairman of the House Committee on the Territories, Mears had been offered a high salaried job at the end of World War I but remained in the army and returned to the railroad at Lane's request. In the surviving record there is no indication that Mears believed his chairmanship to be anything more than a position of high responsibility and temporary tenure. Further, Mears was an outspoken subordinate who vigorously protested decisions made contrary to his own opinions. On several occasions Mears and Fall had suffered disagreements, most recently over details of the "gentlemen's agreement." Finally, Congressman Curry probably was correct when he called Mears' reassignment "a matter of politics."[11] The A. E. C. chairman was not a pliant witness before congressional committees. James W. Good, chairman of the Appropriations Committee, may have long retained the memory of his clash with Mears over contracts and purchases made without specific congressional authorization. Other congressmen were unhappy with Mears when, in 1921, his estimates for the time and expense of completion proved wrong. Mears had no apparent political sentiments except for his dislike of left-wing radicalism, yet he was identified with the Democratic Wilson administration because it had appointed him. Mears was routinely removed from the agency to which he had given almost seven years of able service.

The railbelt journey of Warren Gamaliel Harding to drive the symbolic golden spike overshadowed all other events of 1923. During June and July the president traveled across the continent by rail, losing himself in the plaudits of admiring crowds. A number of dignitaries — Secretaries Work and Hoover among them — were included or added by prearrangement as the trip progressed. The presidential party boarded the transport *Henderson* at Tacoma for the Alaska leg of the journey. The *Henderson* first touched in Alaska on July 9, and on the thirteenth the president reached Seward. There followed an incredible round of speeches and tours along the railbelt, including an exhausting ramble up a flight of 175 wooden steps at Chickaloon. At North Nenana on July 15, a warm and sunny Sunday afternoon, the president paused to drive the golden spike. In a few gracious words he paid tribute to the railroad's builders and expressed a conviction that the line would open Alaska to development. After tapping the golden spike, Harding clumsily pounded in its iron replacement.

The party moved on to Fairbanks for more grueling speeches, exhibitions, and tours. Plans for an automobile trip over the Richardson Highway to connect with the Copper River & Northwestern were cancelled in deference to an exhausted Mrs. Harding. The president made little effort to escape adulatory crowds, either during the trip back down the railroad, or later. On July 27 he delivered a major address on Alaska to a crowd of 60,000 at the University of Washington football stadium in Seattle. He told the enthusiastic audience of Alaska's great potential and of the federal government's determination to use The Alaska Railroad and other agencies aggressively but rationally in the territory's future development.

Throughout the Alaskan journey Harding was genial, beaming, and very much in his element, a politician on the hustings. But candid camera shots, even a few posed photographs, showed lines and signs of fatigue on his handsome, fleshy face. Midway through his Seattle speech he hesitated, dropped his manuscript, and clutched the podium. Secretary Hoover retrieved the sheets, handed the top few to the president, and reorganized the rest while Harding spoke on. Though he was seriously ill, Harding filled the rest of his Seattle engagements. A heart attack followed his overexertions. During the evening of August 2, at San Francisco, he suffered a second, fatal attack. The grief was nowhere more genuine than in Alaska.

Behind the pomp and celebration, the railroad carried on an astounding miscellany of activities. For many years the most important of these involved relationships with other agencies. In general, the relationships were indifferent or poor at the outset but improved to mutual toleration and even cordiality by the end of the construction period. The Board of Road Commissioners for Alaska (later the Alaska Road Commission), at work on territorial transportation problems since its founding in 1905, was understandably jealous of the flourishing upstart. By 1915 the road commission's major highway, the Valdez-to-Fairbanks road, was a fairly good one-lane gravel "wagon road" with wooden bridges, two ferry crossings, and a steady summertime auto traffic. For all its back-breaking efforts to run roads and trails through the far-flung land, the road commission was allowed only $284,755.12 in 1915. In the same year, the railroad received a $2 million appropriation. Wilds P. Richardson, the road commission's president for many years, harped on the need for road feeders to the railroad without doing enough, in the railroad's view, toward building them. In retaliation, occasional trial balloons were raised from the railbelt, suggesting that the A. E. C. take charge of road construction in the area. Relations improved after Steese's appointment to the road commission in 1920.

The A. E. C. suffered a rocky relationship with the Post Office Department for a time. The chief postal official, a Cordova property owner, resented the railroad's location away from the Copper River port. His attitude and influence may have been the source of the post office's reluctance to pay the railroad more than "stateside" rates for mail service. Later the two agencies compromised on a payment that was not so large as the railroad wished but larger than the standard rate. Irritation continued over slow post office payment for supplies and services furnished by the A. E. C. in Anchorage. However, the post office treated the railroad no worse than the railroad occasionally treated some of its own creditors. Dealings with the Department of Justice were so frustrating that Mears decided in 1921 "to restrict our dealings with them as much as may be consistent with the interests of the Government."[12]

Associations with other agencies were more pleasant. The A. E. C. and the General Land Office worked closely together over the years. Contacts with the Forest Service, which usually involved cutting in the Chugach National Forest for railroad purposes, were consistently cordial. When, in 1921, the ranger at Mount McKinley National Park built an office and residence at Riley Creek, Mears released surplus office equipment and other supplies to him either free or at a low valuation. The next year Mears helped to wangle additional funds from the National Park Service to pay for still more equipment, some of it planned to fit out ten tourist cabins in the park. At about the same time, he gave some office equipment to the newly established Agricultural College and School of Mines, located on the main line three miles west of Fairbanks. The commission also established a temporary service to the College station. An outbound train carried passengers to College in the morning; a gas car returned them in the evening.

On the operating side, the two stern-wheelers of the River Boat Service paddled along the Yukon and Tanana rivers during the 1923 season. The crew of the doughty *Jacobs* bore the heaviest burden, for the poor old *Davis* proved unequal to the task. During the overhauling of both vessels, the *Davis* had been converted to burn the nearby Healy River coal, even though that fuel had failed to give good service in the commission's steam engines. This effort to aid a local industry collapsed when the *Davis* barely limped downstream to Tanana on its maiden voyage in early June. After switching its barge and freight to the previously departed *Jacobs*, the unhappy little boat returned to Nenana for reconversion to wood-burning. A few trips notable for the lack of fuel economy followed, then the *Davis's* wheezing boiler threatened to give way during its final, September voyage. After once again transferring freight to the *Jacobs*, it struggled back to Nenana and season's end. While the *Davis* foundered, the *Jacobs* ran barges and passengers up and down the Yukon. In July it paddled up the Tanana to ferry the presidential party across the river. It was a fruitless trip, for President Harding returned by rail, not over the Richardson Highway as originally planned. The hard-working boat then returned to duty, straining on through September to distribute the winter's freight before the ice runs began on the Tanana and Yukon. The task was a hard one, but the River Boat Service successfully completed its first year's operation.

Through the years the railroad's rail operations steadily expanded. From May (the first month of record keeping) through December 1916, the Anchorage Division carried a mere 1,975 revenue tons. Revenue passengers totaled 6,410 and paid $11,197.63 for their rides. In 1919, the first year of consolidated records, 17,329 passengers rode, paying a "large proportion of short distance fares."[13] Because the line was still building, tourism slight, and the railroad as yet a novelty, there was none of the later summit of summer travel followed by a winter trough. Passengers numbered 1,054 in January, increased until spring, dipped slightly in summer, peaked at 1,946 in October, and tallied 1,542 in December. Passenger revenue was $40,895.16. Freight tonnage totaled 13,308, with revenue at $68,629.47. Ton miles registered a low of 26,679 in August, a high of 57,235 in December.

Traffic increased dramatically with the inauguration of through service during the last days of 1921. In 1921 revenue freight totaled 28,713 tons and 1,709,737 ton miles. Freight revenue was $133,494.84. The figures for 1922 sharply increased to 40,700 tons, 4,636,077 ton miles, and $334,811.21 revenue. Nineteen twenty-one saw 33,138 passengers travel 1,967,244 passenger miles and pay $103,612.58 for the privilege. In the next year passengers increased to 37,377, passenger miles to 2,723,362, and revenue to $160,763.72.

Still another general increase marked 1923. Revenue freight went to 56,173 tons and 9,069,623 ton miles, freight revenue jumped more than $100,000 to $439,940.72. Passenger figures were less impressive, and revenues even declined slightly to $159,960.30. The number of passengers rose to 44,490 and passenger miles to 2,822,576. Operating revenues reached $905,942.46, but operating expenses of $2,706,788.54 left the line with an incredible 298.78 percent operating ratio. Heavy shipments of nonrevenue freight of 177,894 tons, three times the revenue tonnage, accounted for some of the deficit. In addition, the railroad extended free freight and passenger service to other government agencies, even though Mears had objected to the practice. This free service cost The Alaska Railroad $80,901.06 in 1923 alone.

The railroad's equipment was a miscellany reflecting its debt to another government project — the Panama Canal — and its recent emphasis on construction. Mogul-type engines surplus from the Panama Railroad were the backbone of the 30-locomotive fleet. The slightly smaller version came with 19- by 24-inch cylinders, 54-inch drivers, a total weight of 138,400 pounds, and a weight on drivers of 120,500. These workhorses served from the beginning; the larger 155,700-pounders arrived at Anchorage in 1919. Both 2-6-0 models were built by the American Locomotive Company to the Panama Railroad's five-foot gauge and had to be refitted to the four-foot, eight-and-one-half-inch standard. The Mechanical Department at Anchorage accomplished the conversion in the simplest way by pressing wide tires on the five-foot axles. The flanges then fit against the inside of the rail, but each tire overlapped the outer edges of the rails an extra 1¾ inches. This simple solution for the shop crew caused headaches for the engine and track crews when a Panama Mogul encountered high ridges of hard-packed snow next to the track while climbing a grade. Those wide, over-lapping tires rode up on the unyielding snow ridges and spun helplessly while the train slipped back down the slope. Successful assaults on some grades came only after plows had cleared the track ahead or another engine had been added to the train. The narrow cuts around Divide, twelve miles from Seward, were especially treacherous.

The rolling stock included 427 versatile flatcars from Panama, 90 ballast cars, 95 dump cars, and, as an earnest of the railroad's hopes, 143 coal cars. There were but thirty-seven boxcars, six stock cars, and eight "reefers." Passenger equipment included nine wooden coaches, five baggage cars, five "sleepers," of which two were business cars, and two combination observation-dining cars. Narrow gauge equipment included thirteen boxcars, twenty-nine flatcars, forty dump cars, four passenger coaches, and a gas-electric passenger car. Of the nine locomotives, only two or three, Mears said, were "worth anything."[14]

Thus the railroad moved toward its uncertain future. It left behind three of the most exasperating and entangling nonconstruction activities a railroad could encounter: town building, dealing with the Alaska ocean lines, and living with continuous, sometimes vicious, criticism.

From 1915 to 1923, operations mingled with construction. Here an Armstrong speeder pauses in the Kenai country. *The Alaska Railroad*

A special train in the Loop District for the filming of "The Cheechakos," an Alaska-produced motion picture about the Yukon gold rush. *The Alaska Railroad*

Operation was not all work. Here a dinky and dump cars provide parlor car service for Anchorage baseball fans to Potter Creek on Turnagain Arm, July 1, 1917. *The Alaska Railroad*

Ladies day at Potter Creek, dinky engine No. 20. *The Alaska Railroad*

Speeder on the turntable of the Anchorage roundhouse, April 29, 1919. *The Alaska Railroad*

Engine 606 with mechanical department employees crowded around, January 12, 1921. *The Alaska Railroad*

The *Admiral Watson* unloading at the newly completed Anchorage dock, October 18, 1919. *The Alaska Railroad*

Locomotive cranes No. 1 and No. 2 landing a Jordan spreader from barge *Lawrence*, Anchorage, June 13, 1917. *The Alaska Railroad*

Train leaving Anchorage for Matanuska and Chickaloon. *Lulu Fairbanks Collection, University of Alaska Archives*

Engine No. 285 working in a gravel pit near Anchorage. *The Alaska Railroad*

A trainload of Eska Creek coal. The coal fields in the upper Matanuska River valley were a prime target for construction crews. Here, about 1917, engine 225 does its hauling job. The railroad's 200 series locomotives, built in 1906 by the American Locomotive Company, were first used on the Panama Railroad, then shipped to Alaska in 1915 and 1916. These "Panama Moguls" were slightly smaller than the 600 series engines, also from Panama. Some of these engines, and much other aged Panama equipment, served The Alaska Railroad until after World War II. *The Alaska Railroad*

No. 265 on the branch to the coal fields, March 19, 1917. *The Alaska Railroad*

Running along the Matanuska River to the coal fields. *The Alaska Railroad*

The "Sourdough" coal train leaving the main line at Matanuska for the coal fields, 1917. *The Alaska Railroad*

The train to Chickaloon on the branch line, May 10, 1919. *National Archives*

Wasilla, in the Matanuska-Susitna Valley, October 11, 1917. *The Alaska Railroad*

Train from Healy arriving at Nenana, 1920. *The Alaska Railroad*

The Healy River coal mine at Suntrana, supplier of lignite to Fairbanks and the interior, October 1920. *National Archives*

Before the Tanana River bridge was completed and the track from North Nenana to Fairbanks widened to standard gauge, narrow gauge engines made winter crossings on the river ice. Here a narrow gauge train takes freight and passenger transfers at Nenana for the run to Fairbanks, 1920. *The Alaska Railroad*

No. 152 on the Tanana River. This was the type of road locomotive used for the run to Fairbanks and on the old TVRR, rechristened the "Chatanika Branch." *The Alaska Railroad*

No. 830 in shuttle service on the Tanana River ice. *The Alaska Railroad*

Railcar in service between Fairbanks and Nenana in the narrow gauge days, 1920. It ran on weekdays whenever no regular train served the two towns. *The Alaska Railroad*

An early retiree from The Alaska Railroad's narrow gauge locomotive fleet, this much-photographed little engine stood near the Fairbanks passenger station. It now rests at the site of the Alaska Centennial Exposition. An early photograph of the engine in retirement, taken in 1922. *Charles Bunnell Collection, University of Alaska Archives*

Even after the transition from construction to operation, some perennial problems remained. The Nenana River Canyon is the scene of washouts and more gradual destruction caused by the "moving mountain" underneath the roadbed. *The Alaska Railroad*

Moose prefer The Alaska Railroad's well-packed right-of-way in wintertime. Here a moose, with only its pride injured, lies caught between the ties on a bridge. *The Alaska Railroad*

Even reasonably well-ballasted track is subject to frost heaves, and sinking rails must be shimmed up until the track is reballasted. *The Alaska Railroad*

Not every railroad could arrange for a President of the United States to drive its golden spike, as Warren G. Harding did on July 15, 1923, at North Nenana. *The Alaska Railroad*

President Harding leaves Nenana after driving the golden spike. *The Anchorage Historical and Fine Arts Museum*

President Harding's train at Wasilla, mile 160.
The Anchorage Historical and Fine Arts Museum

Congressmen C. C. Crampton and Burton French on the line between Nenana and Fairbanks. Behind their Model T railmobile is the observation car "Denali." The excursion was part of the activities of the Congressional Special of June 1923, preceding President Harding's visit. *The Alaska Railroad*

A United States Army railbus hauling supplies during President Harding's visit to Alaska. *The Anchorage Historical and Fine Arts Museum*

Town Building on the Last Frontier

Frederick Mears strode ashore at the mouth of Ship Creek late in April 1915. Before him lay the Ship Creek flats, a long reach of marshy ground one-half mile wide at the creek's mouth. Two bluffs, each two hundred feet high, flanked the bottom land. They closed to form a funnel of low ground running due east away from Knik Arm. The funnel was three to four hundred yards across and one mile long, a generous space for the main yard and shop area of the future. Most of the fine stand of spruce and birch on the south rise soon would give way to the new commission-controlled town of Anchorage. The north ridge, on the side facing salt water, ended in a nearly sheer drop less than three hundred yards from water's edge. The narrow coastal strip thus formed followed Knik Arm northeastward for more than a mile, allowing ample space for docks. The high rise itself would later become the "Government Hill" railroad housing area.

The flatlands already were transformed. A few weeks before, a Forest Service ranger's cabin, a homesteader's shack, and a few nondescript A. E. C. buildings used during the survey were scattered around. Now a stampede town had sprung up, a ragged, dirty collection of tents and temporary wooden buildings. Boom prices prevailed. Potable water sold for five cents a bucket, a wagon and team rented for two dollars an hour. Sanitation was primitive where it existed at all: the deputy marshal supervised the collecting and dumping of garbage at water's edge for the outgoing tide to carry away. By June, about two thousand adventurers were on the ground, and every week saw at least one hundred more debark from steamers or hike in from the end of steel on the Alaska Northern.

The Ship Creek boom was unlike the mining stampedes that it superficially resembled. This time the federal government intended to control the area in and around the rail yards to insure that no private interest would impede the project and that the town itself would develop in an orderly way, free from the usual "hell on wheels" construction camp atmosphere. Thus began a unique experiment in federal operation of a frontier municipality thirty-five hundred miles from the seat of national government, an experiment lasting more than five years and embracing every aspect of local affairs. The experiment was a commentary on the realism of the government's hopes for the townsite, the behavior of pioneers confronted with close federal control of their activities, and the attitudes and actions of untrained federal officials who were given wide responsibility for municipal government. These often harassed officials had to balance local demands against political and economic necessities as Washington saw them.

Mears urged the General Land Office to act quickly in surveying the high, thickly timbered tableland south of the camp so that lot sales in the permanent settlement could begin. He wrote long, fretful letters to Edes filled with complaints about delays and slowed construction work. Efficiency was not his only concern. In late May, the commission surgeon warned of probable contamination of the water supply if the settlement on the flats continued much longer. Settlers in the temporary location freely criticized the government's inaction. Therefore, Mears wrote, the Interior Department must cut red tape and allow local authorities to proceed in a matter so "important from a sanitary and construction standpoint as well as from a political standpoint."[1] He also asked for regulations prohibiting liquor in the new townsite.

Andrew Christensen, the able Land Office chief of field division in charge of the surveys, seconded Mears' recommendations. Christensen had pleaded with the land office to develop a policy back in November 1914, after the government had withdrawn land at several potential townsites, but his superiors avoided action until the stampeders demanded to know why the Ship Creek site was not ready. Instructions from Washington finally reached the Juneau land office on May sixth. Christensen arrived at Anchorage with a survey party eighteen days later, good time considering the necessary preparations and transportation problems. Anchorage had no direct cable connection with Washington, so men in both places agreed to sacrifice time-consuming formalities. Mears and Christensen worked closely together, made on-the-spot decisions, and kept their superiors informed. The Alaska officials rapidly surveyed the 350-acre site and soon they received approval for a lot auction July 10.

To control the sale and lay the basis for future government, President Wilson on June 19 issued the "Alaska Railroad Townsite Regulations." These detailed rules provided for conditional sales of lots at public auction by a superintendent of sale who was to appraise all lots and have full charge of the proceedings. No lot could be sold for less than twenty-five dollars. Depending on the sale price, the purchaser was to pay either in full or one third down and the balance in five equal installments. One clause reflected hopes for high standards of sobriety and behavior on the part of rough construction crews. It required that the lots, and payments made on them, be forfeited if they were "used for the purpose of manufacturing, selling, or otherwise disposing of intoxicating liquors as a beverage, or for gambling, prostitution, or any unlawful purpose."[2] Provided a purchaser paid his bid price and improvement assessments and prohibited improper conduct on his lot, he was to receive patent to the land at the end of five years.

Christensen, the superintendent of sale, spoke before the auction began from a platform erected in the Ship Creek campsite, promising permanent improvements and heavy expenditures at Anchorage. Christensen's expansive speech and the high spirit of the occasion spurred the stampeders into active competition for business and residential lots. Bidding became so brisk that some prospective owners who had conspired to hold down prices "all lost their heads," as Christensen reported, and when he closed the sale on July 18, he had sold 655 lots at just under $150,000. Despite earlier fears that the auction system would invite speculators and squeeze out legitimate interests, Christensen could claim that the sale had "injected confidence into the people of the town." The land office, and later the commission, continued to open new additions, sell lots and tracts, and lease business sites in the terminal area. After two successful sales during November, when days were cold and a foot of snow covered the frozen ground, Christensen exulted, "I could sell lots every day if I were in Anchorage; it seems that the demand for them never ceases."[3]

Assisted by an uncompromising removal order issued to residents of the Ship Creek flats, the confident little town spread over the rigid rectangular pattern of the land office survey. The survey did not escape criticism. A student of city planning called the uniform block townsite "this T-square community of Anchorage." After comparing a five-acre recreational reserve and seventeen-acre cemetery tract, he concluded that "Anchorage has been figured to be a place to die in, but not much of a place to live in."[4] It was true that commission officials demonstrated little contact with planning ideas; they graded one winding drive overlooking Cook Inlet but only because topographical conditions dictated it. They designated east-west streets numerically, north-south streets alphabetically, and all of them unimaginatively. Clay Tallman, land office commissioner, offered the only excuse: the town had been urgently needed and was quickly laid out by men whose primary purpose was to build a railroad.

In a sense, government began before the auction, when Mears opened the Ship Creek post office. Acting with Edes, he appointed a physician to be sanitary officer and a land office special agent to be temporary townsite manager. The appointees quickly issued sanitary and fire regulations. Although some essentials of town life were provided for, important policy decisions were as yet unmade regarding other elements of an orderly, healthy community: its lighting, telephone, sewer, and water systems. Neither Edes nor Mears wished to become deeply involved in running the town because civic government was outside their experience and because the energy invested in administering Anchorage would be lost to railroad construction. Having assumed responsibility for sanitation and fire protection, however, they found it difficult to avoid the operation of a complete utilities system.

The question was not one the commission could decide at its leisure, for the new town was taking shape and people were clamoring for the right to install telephones and electric lights. The chamber of commerce, on the other hand, had resolved that lighting and telephone systems be "conducted by the government and not by private corporations." While Edes declared he was neither "advocating Government ownership" nor "hunting for additional responsibility," he wrote Lane that providing water was an inescapable part of assuming control of fire protection and sanitation, and that lighting and telephone systems should also be constructed and operated by the commission. If private parties owned and managed the lights and telephones, they would insist on rates high enough to return substantial profits. Because the commission would license and supervise the light and telephone works, the public would blame the commission for any failure. Anchorage, Edes argued, "is our child and we are responsible for its well being until it can care for itself."[5] On September 1 Lane authorized the installation of a water system, and the commission began pumping from a sand filter bed in Ship Creek to the townsite above. Electric light and power were extended in 1916, though gingerly. By 1917, from fear of overloading the plant, new users were added only after the utilities superintendent had called upon some commercial customers and persuaded them to reduce their wattage.

The telephone problem was more difficult to solve. A stampeder had shipped in telephone equipment bought on credit, certain that he could install it because he possessed the qualifications most important to an Alaska camp — he was first on the ground with the necessary supplies. Much to his dismay and the displeasure of his suppliers and creditors, the commission refused him permission to string his wire and insisted on referring the matter to Washington. On October 4 Lane told the commission to install telephones, and Mears relieved an embarrassing situation when he purchased all the equipment belonging to the would-be entrepreneur. In 1917 a sewer system to serve the business district replaced inadequate cesspools. Following the initial street work, improvements proceeded only at the request of residents, and after the townsite office had determined that affected lot owners could afford the assessments.

These actions met immediate needs, but the commission's commitment to five years' government demanded comprehensive townsite control. Every alternative to systematic federal administration confronted the fact that the town could not incorporate, govern itself, or tax itself unless the government surrendered both land titles and its conception of a model construction camp. Further, the townspeople preferred federal direction. Anchorage citizens assumed that commission utilities management would cause cheaper rates because a profit did not have to be realized. Besides, they believed that federal townsite administration would be free from "petty city politics."[6]

From the commission' viewpoint, the first arrangements were inefficient and cumbersome. The Land Office was charged with investigating and reporting all violations of townsite regulations, including the failure to pay improvement assessments. The commission was supposed to make improvements, issue assessments, and have general authority over the townsite. Because of overlapping functions and divided responsibility, policy and townsite administrative matters had to be decided in conferences between Christensen, Mears, J. A. Moore, the temporary townsite manager, and J. G. Watts, the townsite engineer.

To bring the commission's authority and organization in line with its responsibility, Christensen and the commissioners developed plans for a commission Land and Industrial Department to supervise most matters outside the sphere of engineering and construction. Lane did not sign the order creating the department until April 12, 1916, but it is evident from Christensen's role as unofficial townsite advisor that he was expecting to leave the land office to become the department's manager. Christensen was a forthright, diligent, decisive public servant whose previous experience had been in land and railroad legal matters. Mustachioed, balding, and thirty-six in 1915, he was raised on a Nebraska homestead. He had held a variety of jobs until 1901, when he was appointed to the Railway Mail Service. After winning a promotion to assistant chief clerk, he worked closely with the traffic officers of the railroads running through Salt Lake City and Ogden, Utah. Transfer to Washington, D.C., a law degree, and private practice followed. In 1908 he joined the General Land Office, was placed in charge of the Alaska coal land cases in 1910, and was named chief of the Alaska field division the following year. He had no technical knowledge of local government, but he was well known in Alaska and understood the territory's laws. As it developed, he needed calm nerves and a sense of humor more than formal training, for he had to cope with a breakdown of law enforcement involving liquor, gambling, and prostitution.

Bootleggers catering to thirsty construction crews throve in the new townsite on the strength of heavy shipments from the licensed saloon at Knik, thirty miles up Knik Arm from Anchorage. In a town of scarcely 3,000, gambling games ran wide open, and dealers worked in shifts in the jampacked back rooms of some dozen false-fronted pool halls and cigar stores along the rim of the tableland overlooking Ship Creek. Characters nicknamed "Dago Jim," "Creampuff Bill," and "The Pale Faced Kid" strolled Anchorage's dirt streets and disappeared behind swinging doors where, day and night, the click of billiards mingled with the clink of chips. In tents and cabins southeast of the built-up section, "Little Annie," "Montana Bessie," and thirty or forty other members of the oldest profession followed their calling in Alaska's newest townsite. Theirs was a sordid exile. Forced into a "restricted district," forbidden by stern local custom from mingling on the main streets with the townspeople, and dependent on a "messenger" who carried their provisions, the girls on "the line" were at the mercy of the pimps who had organized them.

Prostitution was the nexus between the frontier underworld and the world of government and law. The commission itself shared responsibility with the deputy marshal's office for planning a restricted district rather than permitting prostitutes to settle anywhere in town or attempting to keep the place free of them. The commission's responsibility began in July 1916, when it decided to sell lots and acre tracts in the district and ordered prostitutes off the sale site by the first of October. On October 2 the chamber of commerce went straight to the commission with a stiffly worded resolution. Prostitutes were overrunning the town and endangering morals, it complained. The Land and Industrial Department must establish another district. Christensen, J. G. Watts, now townsite manager, and the deputy marshal collaborated on picking a new location.

The men of the commission shared the responsibility for the restricted district, but a sheaf of information gathered by commission agents showed how a few pimps and their allies in the marshal's office reaped the rewards. The leading procurer had formed such an effective league with one of the deputies that prostitutes who refused to buy liquor from him were jailed, and if they did not acknowledge their error, were handed a one-way ticket out of town. The same pimp reportedly exacted protection money from the gambling dens. The deputy in question owned the lot upon which one of the most notorious gambling establishments stood and was openly living with a lady bootlegger who was not his wife. Christensen and his co-workers were in an unenviable situation. They believed that they had to permit prostitution, partly to protect the town's respectable women, while at the same time they had to prevent the corruption of law enforcement, graft, and liquor traffic that were its consequences.

Gambling, and the marshal's office's lax attitude toward it, agitated the commission even more because the blatant gaming preyed upon eager construction stiffs newly arrived from the wilderness isolation of "the front." Once an agent discovered a big card game in progress at one of the pool halls. The exceptional pot of between $1,200 and $1,500 had drawn such a large, excited crowd that he could not enter the back room. He stood among the pool tables, following the play by word passed from the onlookers. When he informed the chief deputy of the facts, the lawman regarded him calmly and remarked, "I guess I'll have to touch 'em up a little."[7] To the agent's disgust, the chief deputy did nothing. Doing nothing was his usual action in such cases. Exasperated though they were with the chief deputy, commission men could never discover clear links between him and the underworld. They could not decide whether he was stupidly indifferent, intimidated, or involved in illicit profits, although their evidence suggested all three.

Bootlegging flourished alongside gambling and prostitution. Commission informants and agents alleged that liquor and beer were dispensed from drugstores, general merchandise stores, and residences, as well as from "the line." The deputy marshal's office only sporadically enforced the law against the three offenses. When the deputies did move, they acted merely to assist a pimp in controlling his prostitutes, to appease the aggressive assistant district attorney periodically dispatched to Anchorage, to quiet the commission whenever its agents brought in overwhelming evidence, or to increase official revenues through fines levied with the mutual understanding that they were a business tax upon the violators.

On the face of it, the commission's remedy was simple. Because the townsite regulations provided for forfeiture of lots used for prohibited purposes, the commission could have at any time begun forfeiture proceedings by bringing charges against lot owners to the field division of the land office. Actually, the procedure was potentially so slow and cumbersome that federal officials hesitated to become involved in a series of forfeiture hearings. Besides, they wanted Anchorage to develop from a construction camp into a stable center for railroad yards, light industry, and the agricultural and mineral hinterland. But the town could not mature with the threat of forfeiture hanging over every lot, because the territorial banking board had warned against real estate loans on land so liable to loss. Even in cases of clear violation, forfeiture might be an injustice, for the regulations did not forbid leasing or assigning by quitclaim deed, and a lessee or assignee could invite forfeiture of another's lot by his illegal pursuits. Finally, if the townsite administrators moved against owners of lots given over to gambling, for consistency's sake they should also prosecute violations of sanitary or fire regulations. Yet forfeiture for such petty violations was a punishment scarcely fitting the crime. It was easier to do nothing than to determine the degree or kind of violation that warranted forfeiture.

Enforcing federal laws on gambling and liquor was more attractive than lot forfeitures but equally beset by practical difficulties. The commission found it impossible to enlist the aid of the prostitutes in its anti-liquor campaign. This was not only because the shady ladies made money by reselling whisky and beer, but also because they lived in fear of exportation. They dared not inform on their liquor-selling pimps. "The girls never squeal," one of them told Christensen.[8] The commission's sleuths failed to stop the flow of liquor through its more respectable channels because the government had to prove at least one sale, a difficult business requiring purchases by undercover agents. Successful prosecution of gambling was doubtful because the word of a participant in the game, provided that he could be persuaded to give self-incriminating testimony, was not sufficient evidence to convict a gambler. The testimony of a spectator was necessary in addition to that of a player or dealer, assuming that a jury would in any case return an adverse verdict. Gamblers, after all, provided one of the town's principal forms of amusement. Gambling convictions were understandably infrequent.

Despite these handicaps Christensen decided to conduct his own raid on a gambling den with the help of the assistant district attorney and an out-of-town deputy marshal. He did not ask for aid from the local chief deputy, of whose raids the gamblers always seemed well informed in advance. After making preparations in secret, on November 17, 1916, Christensen and his band swooped down upon a pool hall named, with whimsey and accuracy, "The Bank." They arrested fourteen dealers and players. Christensen soon discovered that arrest was easier than conviction. At the first trial before the local commissioner, the marshals, who were charged with selecting the jury, waited until the prosecution had exhausted its challenges. Then they sent in a gambler to sit in judgment on his peers. The first jury failed to agree, a second trial was held, and again the marshals managed to pack the jury. "No stronger case of gambling could be made," an exasperated Christensen wrote in despair to Edes. "People who played in the game, who paid the dealer the money and saw the dealer take his rake-off on every pot, testified. In fact, the scene in the pool hall was clearly enacted before the jury. There was no doubt whatever as to the facts, and yet the jury let him off."⁹ Christensen was further disconcerted when government witnesses were intimidated and spirited away, two undercover men were expelled from the Alaska Labor Union, and courtroom spectators demonstrated against the prosecution during the trials.

Finally, commission officials decided that the only solution to the law enforcement problem was to change the law enforcers. They appealed to the Department of Justice to overhaul the marshal's office. At the end of November the chief deputy was transferred to the insignificant Matanuska townsite, and the deputy who had enjoyed such a close relationship with underworld elements was removed from office. The change stuck despite a petition to the district marshal at Valdez, signed by some of the town's leading businessmen, praising the chief deputy's "honesty, integrity and moral uprightness" and requesting his return. Although Christensen criticized the temporary deputy marshal's lack of "initiative" and "energy," the new man was, he believed, "one with whom you can work."¹⁰ Arrests mounted, but so did public feeling against the commission. Several union members had been arrested on gambling charges, and labor trouble might erupt again at any moment. Securing convictions was as difficult as ever. On the other hand, gamblers and bootleggers realized that, convicted or not, they faced constant harassment after the loss of their comfortable working arrangement with the marshal's office. In mid-December the commission, government attorneys, and the temporary deputy marshal reached a compromise with the gamblers. The government discontinued its pending gambling cases, while the gamblers agreed to tear out the partitions of their notorious back rooms. Bootlegging also declined. After the permanent deputy arrived in January 1917, illegal activity dwindled to manageable proportions.

The perplexities of adequate schooling for Anchorage children paralleled and proved as difficult as those of law enforcement. With schools as with law enforcement, the commission faced a situation compounded from administrative oversight and divided authority, one it did not create, though it was required to assume responsibility. The school problem was impossible to solve easily because there was no way under the townsite regulations to compel residents to pay for their children's schooling. Through an oversight, schools had been omitted from the list of specific items for which the commission could assess Anchorage lots.

Some sources of financial aid existed. Under the so-called Nelson law of 1905, Anchorage residents could organize a school district outside incorporated towns. Such a district would be eligible for aid from the "Alaska fund," 25 percent of the receipts from federal licenses on businesses located in unincorporated areas, to be used annually for school maintenance. In addition, it could expect $1,000 in territorial aid for school construction and possibly more for certain operating expenses.

Territorial funds were inadequate for Anchorage's needs, as the commission and the newly formed school board quickly learned. The legislature could not help them because it was forbidden by the Alaska organic act of 1912 to write "local or special" school laws. The governor, in his capacity as ex-officio superintendent of public instruction, was reluctant to requisition the "Alaska fund" because the Nelson and other laws had been designed for hamlets or scattered settlements. They were not intended to cover the needs of a community containing, during the summer of 1916, 3,332, and a school age population of about 200. Anchorage was a metropolis by Alaska standards of the time, and legislation assumed it would incorporate and care for its own schools.¹¹

Anchorage could not incorporate. Anchorage citizens concluded that the government's failure to provide for school assessments did not relieve the commission of the financial responsibility for education. That belief collided with the convictions of Alaskans outside Anchorage and the other townsites. Most residents of the territory were uninterested in supporting schools in "government towns." An unstated but surely significant reason for the governor's reluctance to spend "Alaska fund" revenues for Anchorage was that the town contained no legal saloons. Saloons paid large license fees to the fund; thus, an appropriation for Anchorage would bestow upon the federal boomtown benefits out of all proportion to its contributions.

Although these problems later became pressing, they were unimportant in the early days. Under the comptroller general's liberal interpretation of the broad grant of power in the Alaska railroad act, the commission constructed a schoolhouse in the fall of 1915. A public subscription supplemented "Alaska fund" money which the governor had granted to tide the town over until, as everyone confidently believed, Congress would provide for carrying on the schools. The first school year passed without incident, but a crisis developed during the second half of 1916. In July the director of the Anchorage school board reported to the commission on the shortcomings of the first, hastily constructed school. The building lacked a safe foundation, paint, inside toilets, running water, satisfactory heating system, and other desirable features. Its unheated outside toilets did not conform to sanitary regulations. The school, Townsite Manager Watts concluded from his own investigation, was "entirely inadequate," "insanitary," and was generally "of an order of the early Eighteenth Century."[12] He agreed with a commission engineer's recommendation to abandon the structure and construct an adequate building. The commission decided to build a new, larger school, while the board undertook to rent the additional space needed until the completion. Other questions, however, still were unresolved.

As the 1916 fall term approached, both board and commission appealed to the governor for money. They found him unwilling to advance any significant sum for maintenance and operation. In a letter, Governor John F. Strong reminded Edes that the territory had allotted about $6,000 to the Anchorage school in 1915-16, complained that the pupil population had fallen below expectations, and charged that the board had been remiss in failing to send him regular reports as required by law. Later the board informed Strong that more than $14,000 would be necessary, and the commission reinforced the board's plea with assertions that the school would soon be forced to close. The governor refused to budge. "I cannot coax money from a fund that is exhausted," he once exclaimed.[13] Though he exaggerated the lack of funds, Strong's allocation of what was available revealed his intention to care for other districts in unincorporated areas before attending to Anchorage.

While the commission was pressing Strong to act, it was urging Lane to authorize aid for the school. Lane's refusals were as uncompromising as Strong's, and the matter became a contest between the federal and territorial governments to see which of them could force the other to assume the burden. When Mears reported on November 10 that teachers were living without pay and on credit from merchants, Lane relented and authorized federal funds until about the time of the Christmas recess. The next month the harassed school board informed Christensen that if the commission did not immediately assume fiscal responsibility, the school would remain closed at the end of the vacation. Lane capitulated, agreeing to advance funds until other financial sources were found.

Federal officials scarcely could escape the obligation to support education. They were less happy with the realization that administrative control followed fiscal responsibility. This was especially the case with Christensen, whom Edes appointed to assume operation of the school during the time commission money was spent for its maintenance. Edes told Christensen that he hoped for a permanent solution, but "in the meantime you can be school director in addition to your other duties."[14]

Christensen did not have long to wonder why the school board "appeared much relieved" when he announced that he was taking over. He had inherited a personnel problem — the principal had demoted one of the teachers from the high school to the third and fourth grades — and the board had sustained the principal when the teacher complained. Christensen decided to restore the demoted teacher to the high school, but he determined to give both principal and teacher "a good talking to." He told the teacher "to stop gossiping, complaining, and criticizing, and to bring her work up to the standard," while the principal was informed "that he must quit going to the pool halls and must get down to business." Overcrowded classrooms plagued the new director. One teacher, he wrote Edes, had charge of seventy primary students and was instructing them in half-day shifts. "It is a troublesome question," Edes agreed, "and I wish we were rid of it."[15]

A permanent source of funds to finance schooling was an equally troublesome question. Since the spring of 1916 the commission had campaigned for congressional action to return half of the lot sale receipts to the townsite for public improvements. The school crisis and congressional criticism of the commission's educational expenditures quickened interest in a way to avoid spending railroad funds for schooling. Congress solved part of the problem when it passed, on April 17, 1917, an act allowing 50 percent of the lot sale money for schools and other permanent improvements. The "fifty percent fund," as it applied to the schools, was limited to construction expenses only and did nothing to ease the shortage of maintenance and operating funds.

The previous month Congress had responded to another Interior Department appeal by repealing the school restrictions imposed upon the Alaska legislatures by the 1912 organic act. When Christensen went to the legislature in April to explain the need for special legislation, he found the lawmakers willing to extend territorial aid to Anchorage equitably with other larger Alaska towns. For the rest, the legislators believed, the town or the commission should be responsible. Working with Christensen, they quickly drew up and enacted a bill giving unincorporated towns with 100 or more settlers and a school-age population of at least 30 the right to elect a school board. The board was vested with the authority to evaluate real and personal property in its district and levy a tax of up to 1 percent of the valuation. That summer Anchorage voted in a new board under the provisions of the act. In December the commission completed the new school and, because construction costs had been reimbursed from the "fifty percent fund," donated the $45,000 building to the district free of charge.

Special problems aside, effective administration of Anchorage was a continuing responsibility requiring the consent of at least some of the governed. Commission managers were employers, high salaried, and socially important in the town. It was natural, then, for them to write of "the Anchorage Chamber of Commerce and Commercial Club, representing the people,"[16] and to form close ties with the town's merchants through the chamber and other commercial organizations. The merchants found the commission a willing partner in plans for the promotion and development of Anchorage and of the town's tributary agricultural and mining region. Relations were not always harmonious, but disagreements usually were limited to the operation of the railroad's retail commissary, which the chamber wanted closed, or to commercial opportunities in construction areas, which the commission wished to restrict. On matters of government, commission leaders and merchants generally agreed. The chamber repaid the recognition the commission accorded it by endorsing commission appropriation requests and appeals to the territorial legislature, and by printing and giving wide circulation to a pamphlet praising the commission's work.

The relationship was mutually satisfactory, but it failed to hide the fact that the chamber was not popularly elected. Both the commission and local citizens wished for a group similar to a city council which could advise on townsite management. The articles of the resulting Advisory Council called for at-large election of seven members by the adult lot-holders, a clause that cut off the large transient labor and boarding group from representation on the new body. The council was elected in September 1917. It was recommendatory only, dealt mostly with routine matters, and failed to supplant the commercial organization in the commission's confidence. The initiative in affairs of importance continued to rest with the chamber.

No other area of administration affected the residents so palpably as the financial demands of the townsite office. That office levied three types of assessments. First, it charged for townsite operation and maintenance under the terms of sale requiring lot purchasers to comply with regulations regarding streets, sanitation, and fire protection. Assessments comparable to property taxes were raised to meet ordinary municipal costs such as maintenance, garbage collection, office expenses, and engineering. Townsite Manager Watts argued that they were not like property taxes, but rather were charges levied for the services each lot received, without reference to property value. His argument failed to convince people who saw Anchorage's business lots assessed at only three times the rate for unimproved parcels on the fringes of the townsite. Opposition to the one-to-three ratio of the first assessment was so strong that townsite officials later worked out monthly service charges for eight classes of lots, each carefully defined by location. Though they maintained the service charge fiction, they in fact levied operation and maintenance assessments in proportion to lot values.

Second, the sale regulations justified assessments for improvements including sewers, water main extensions, sidewalks, and grubbing, grading, and surfacing streets. Improvement assessments, issued against benefited property on a front foot basis, were the same as special tax bills in incorporated communities. Finally, the commission compelled Anchorage residents to pay a portion of the costs of the first permanent water main. In 1915 the commission had approached the chamber of commerce on the subject, and the commercial body had authorized the installation. Owners of affected lots were to repay in four equal installments.

Watts took great pains to prove to townsite residents that commission government was a bargain. For example, in 1918 he compared the average yearly Anchorage operation and maintenance costs of about $32,000 per year with figures of $60,000 for Juneau and $35,000 for Fairbanks, towns of comparable size. Accepting the Anchorage school board's valuation of $2 million, Watts figured the total assessments of 1.93 percent of valuation, slightly below the maximum legal rate of 2 percent for incorporated towns. In any case, the commission received few complaints about assessment rates. Further, the number of delinquencies does not seem abnormally high, doubtless because the commission unhesitatingly reported delinquent lots to the land office for forfeiture. Anchorage received other benefits. By the end of 1917 the "fifty percent fund" had paid for the first two schools, the firehouse, park improvements, and some street and utilities construction. The commission repeatedly raised water rates in an attempt to erase its operating deficit, but its charges still compared well with those in other coastal towns, even though the latter were served by less expensive gravity systems.

The townsite manager and his one, or sometimes two assistants, struggled with the minutiae of administration as well as with the large issues of townsite government. A stream of regulations, including a solemn warning to dogteam drivers to stay off the sidewalks, issued from the townsite office. The office encouraged lot assignees to register there, sent assessment notices to them rather than to owners of record, and published lot installment information received from the land office at Juneau in the official *Alaska Railroad Record*. Believing themselves obligated to control roaming dogs, townsite officials also operated a pound, though it was without much legal color and was heavily criticized by "self-styled admirers of dogs," as Watts called them.[17]

During the commission's administration, Anchorage evolved from a rough construction camp into an established railroad town, though it retained its frontier flavor. Near the end of 1917 it reached a population peak it would not exceed for several years: a reasonably accurate count showed 3,928 persons living in the townsite and terminal yards. The commission contributed to Anchorage's amenities in many ways. It lobbied at Juneau for improved health and sanitation laws, ran excursion trains, founded a YMCA, encouraged gardening, athletics, and beautification, established parks and recreational reserves, and assisted with controlling the spread of influenza during the 1918 epidemic. The World War drained men away from Anchorage, and by 1920 population had recovered to only 1,856.

"Personally," Christensen had written in December, 1915, "I should think it would be a good idea to always have in mind the withdrawal from the management of these towns, so that it can be done gracefully and with dignity."[18] Almost five years later the time came for Anchorage. Did the citizens of the town desire independence from commission government? Many did not. Members of the territorial legislature, the governor, and territorial delegates to Congress sharply criticized the unrepresentative nature of commission control, but they did not live in Anchorage. Local residents knew they had a "good thing" in federal paternalism. Despite many personnel changes, townsite administration was relatively efficient, economical, scandal-free, and, for the residents, carefree. The citizens of Anchorage were loath to assume responsibility, grew increasingly apprehensive as the end of federal tutelage loomed, and threatened to balk at organizing their own municipal affairs.

Beginning in the spring of 1920, the commission and a committee of the chamber of commerce worked closely together to establish plans for local control. Using a "carrot-and-stick" technique on the balky chamber and citizenry, the commission promised the town the schoolhouse and grounds. It also threw in the "municipal block" reservation, the firehouse, the water mains, and the streets, sidewalks, and alleys. It agreed to discuss assumption of a proportionate share of town expenses, based on unsold lots and government property within the corporate limits. The concessions were not sufficiently tempting. So a commission spokesman used the stick. He bluntly informed a mass meeting that if Anchorage failed to incorporate, the A. E. C. would withdraw fire protection and its street maintenance crews. The commission, he warned, would have "no more to do with the management of the town . . . than it would have to do with the management of the City of Seattle."[19] Anchorage held its incorporation election November 2, 1920. After some indecision over blank ballots, the district judge declared that incorporation had carried by more than the required two-thirds majority.

Their Anchorage experiences prepared the commissioners for events in other townsites. Nenana was the largest, gaudiest, and most significant of the later towns. The townsite sat astride the main line on the south bank of the broad Tanana River where the glacier-fed Nenana rushed to meet it. Plenty of room was available on the flat, marshy land to plant a town among the spindly spruces. The low site flooded frequently, but little level building space was available on the higher north side, where a sixteen-hundred-foot bluff dropped down to the river's edge. The commission was trapped into the mediocre location by its own decision to establish a northern construction division. Because bulky supplies reached the interior by water only, the A. E. C. had to plat a town at the intersection of the navigable Tanana and the main line.

When government surveyors arrived on a rainy May 26, 1916, only a homesteader and his family and two or three commission employees occupied the ground. An Indian village huddled nearby. Within a few weeks a tent town squatted behind the commission's corrugated iron-and-log buildings lined up along the wharf. The location was so unpromising for a sizeable permanent settlement that Riggs tried to dampen stampeder enthusiasm and reassure jittery Fairbanks about the mushrooming town a mere sixty miles downstream. "Everybody at Nenana realizes that it is simply a construction town and that it has not the resources of Fairbanks to keep going when the railroad is completed," he said. "Fairbanks will be the same busy town always and the people of Nenana who, for the greater part are Fairbanksans, realize this."[20]

Despite Riggs' warning, a speculative craze swept the crowd at the opening lot sale on August 24. The first lot fell under Christensen's hammer for $1,600 to Harry E. St. George, a Fairbanks real estate and insurance agent. The first forty lots sold for an average $1,368. One William Casey bought a lot of $1,000 and an hour later refused an offer of $1,500. The bright, warm day, the festive audience, and Christensen's optimistic address before the sale all fired the bidding. Christensen promised little but made remarks that could have been interpreted as a government commitment to permanence. "I came here to Nenana," he intoned, "not to sell lots, but to put Nenana on the map as a town in the United States." Whatever the reasons, bidders showed even "greater signs of Americana Dementia" at the next day's sale. "Many of them," the *Fairbanks Daily News-Miner* reported, "are buying lots in the jungle and covered with a foot of water for three and four hundred dollars."[21]

The bidding was frantic compared to the sale at Anchorage the previous year. There the highest priced lot sold for $1,150, and the average for the first block of lots was a mere $225. The Nenana prices worried Riggs. "In many instances I do not think the inflation was warranted," he said.[22]

Nenana's long-range development justified Riggs' concern, but for two years the town boomed. By the end of 1916 possibly 800 people, mostly A. E. C. employees, were living there. The new town boasted the Northern Division headquarters, six restaurants, a hotel, two drugstores, a theater, a newspaper, and three pool halls. A townsite manager and a clerk responsible to the Land and Industrial Department governed Nenana much as the Anchorage townsite office directed that community. Nenana's prospects never looked brighter than at the beginning of 1918. It boasted a population approaching 1,200 and the largest payroll in the interior. Four new pool halls and a score of other fledgling businesses were in operation. The commission had installed water mains, sewers, a lighting system, and telephones. A commission fire department helped to confine two serious fires, but a much better guarantee against a holocaust was the commission's decision to sell only every third business lot, leaving a fifty-foot firebreak between each wooden building. A school and health board operated on the Anchorage model.

The bright prospects dimmed in 1918. Almost entirely dependent on construction, Nenana was hard hit by the Great War's manpower drain. By summer 1919 some residents of the sagging town complained of flooding, expensive utilities, and a stagnating retail trade. The devastating influenza epidemic of 1920 demoralized them still more. The census that year recorded only 806 persons, including 172 in the native village. The commission withdrew from town government on August 31, 1921. Construction of the great bridge over the Tanana created a brief flurry, but it died early in 1923 when workmen finished the huge span. The A. E. C.'s decision to make Nenana its river boat terminal assured the town's permanence but did nothing to lift it out of stagnation. With no mining hinterland to sustain it, Nenana had lost on its bid to displace Fairbanks as the interior metropolis.

The commission established other townsites or held lot sales at Matanuska, Wasilla, Moose, Talkeetna, and Girdwood and sold lots in the Federal and Cliff additions at Seward. But those sites were small in population and significance. Anchorage was the true test of commission townsite government. There the men of the commission assumed a major responsibility, and although they failed to create a model construction camp, they fashioned a modern community from the wilderness. They contained the caterers to human frailty who threatened to overwhelm the town, they provided education for the children, and they kept a reasonable degree of order. To accomplish all that they had to work with occasionally uncooperative officials and with ambiguous, inadequate laws and regulations. They had to live with local criticisms made in most cases without an understanding of the sometimes conflicting restrictions and responsibilities placed upon them. They had to deal with human nature as they found it. Considering these conditions, their achievements were remarkable.

The railroad towns: Seward, the southern terminus, was founded in 1903 by the Alaska Central Railway. In this photograph, about 1908, it appears much as it did when the commissioners of the Alaskan Engineering Commission inspected it in 1914. The Alaska Central dock in the foreground thrusts out into Resurrection Bay. *Alaska Historical Library*

Seward's Broadway as it appeared about 1920, looking north from near the dock area. *Signal Corps Photo, Alaska Historical Library*

The Alaska Railroad established Whittier in 1941 as the port for the Whittier Cut-off, originally a war-emergency alternative to Seward. Here the tiny townsite rests on an alluvial fan at the head of Passage Canal. Passage Canal is also named Port Wells or Portage Bay on many maps. *Alaska Historical Library*

Seward in the 1920s. *Alaska Steamship Company Photo, Alaska Historical Library*

The Alaskan Engineering Commission founded Anchorage in 1915 and administered it until 1920. On the main street of the stampede town on the Ship Creek flats, July 1915, before removal to the promontory overlooking Cook Inlet. *Nellie Brown*

Another perspective on the stampede town, with "Government Hill" on the right. The new railroad had track sitters as well as track walkers. *Nellie Brown*

The militant Alaska Labor Union parades along Fourth Avenue in the permanent Anchorage townsite, April 24, 1916, in the midst of its successful seven-day strike for higher wages. The strike was the longest in the railroad's history. *National Archives*

Fourth Avenue, about 1920. *National Archives*

A concrete mixer at work along Fourth Avenue, probably 1917. *The Alaska Railroad*

A panorama of the stampede town on the railroad's Terminal Reserve during its brief timber-and-canvas existence, summer 1915. Looking from the crown of "Government Hill" south to the tree-covered table land in the middle distance, the photographer identified 1) Housing for employees and their families. 2) Privately-owned cold storage plant. 3) Privately-owned wholesale grocery. 4) Forest Ranger's house. 5) A. E. C. kitchen and mess hall. 6) Offices of the disbursing officer, accountant, and superintendent of construction. 7) Headquarters office. 8) A. E. C. stables and corral. 9) Bachelor quarters and recreation room for employees. 10) Hospital. 14) Clearing for the new townsite. 15) Location of the new townsite. 11) Warehouse and dock. 12) Staging for soundings to determine the nature of future dredging. 13) One thousand ton scow, used as a floating dock. The Chugach Mountains are in the left far background. *National Archives*

Fourth Avenue in the spring of 1945, the year Otto F. Ohlson resigned as general manager. The Chugach Mountains are in the background. *Lulu Fairbanks Collection, University of Alaska Archives*

Part of the Alaskan Engineering Commission facilities at Nenana, founded in 1917 by the commission as its Tanana River-rail junction. The commission cottages, hospital, mess house, and cold storage plant as they appeared on April 1, 1918. *The Alaska Railroad*

The Nenana townsite, the second largest of the railroad's towns, at the intersection of the Tanana River and the main line, mile 412. This panorama probably was taken in October 1919 before work began on the bridge over the Tanana at the Indian mission, extreme left. The A. E. C. dock, power plant, hospital, cottages, and other buildings are at the extreme right. Owners of the commercial buildings to the left of the A. E. C. grounds were required to leave every third lot vacant for firebreaks. *National Archives*

Fairbanks, the northern terminus, began life as a trading post in 1901 and grew rapidly after a major gold strike in 1902. In 1904 it was still in its booming log town phase. *Laura M. Hills Collection, University of Alaska Archives*

An auto parade driving north on Cushman Street in Fairbanks, the Fourth of July, possibly 1912. *Archie Lewis Collection, University of Alaska Archives*

The Chena River waterfront at Fairbanks, July 10, 1913. *Charles Bunnell Collection, University of Alaska Archives*

Fairbanks about 1940, with the passenger station at the center left, left of the bridge and across the street from the church. *O. B. Chamberlin Collection, University of Alaska Archives*

A bird's-eye view of Fairbanks about 1929, looking north. The Alaska Railroad passenger station is across the Chena River, at the north end of the cleared area to the left of the bridge. *The Alaska Railroad*

The Railroad and the Steamships

Steamships were the railroad's lifeline. In modestly sized holds they carried railroad freight, equipment, supplies, and construction materials. Railroad officers and employees traveled in their often cramped cabins. The railroad, as a comparatively large shipper, could negotiate for special rates and privileges with the steamship companies or it could haul some cargoes in chartered vessels, tramp ships, and government transports. It could not escape the overwhelming consequence of Alaska's insularity — absolute reliance upon water transportation.

Small shippers and residents of the territory poured their wrath, in great volume and vituperation, upon the steamship lines. Alaskans resented their dependence on the water carriers. They were convinced that the steamship companies charged them exhorbitant rates, throttled territorial development with high tariffs, and provided service ranging in quality from indifferent to poor. The fact that the Alaska Syndicate figured prominently in territorial water transportation served to intensify Alaskan ire.

The Guggenheim-controlled Alaska Steamship Company dominated the Alaska maritime trade. The first company to bear the name was formed in 1895 in the halcyon days before the Klondike gold rush. The Alaska Syndicate incorporated it in 1908 to link its fabulous copper mines with the Guggenheim smelter in Tacoma. "Alaska Steam" also served as a common carrier, and in more than a technical sense. It steadily improved its service. In 1908 it installed wireless telegraphs. The next year it sent its first deep-draft vessels into the Alexander Archipelago between the spruce-covered, silvery green slopes of the Inside Passage. In 1912 it placed Victrolas on board its passenger ships. By 1913 Alaska Steam maintained 130 scheduled sailings a year from Seattle.

The Alaska Steamship Company was one of the two concerns in the trade that regularly sent its vessels to Westward, the ports west across the choppy Gulf of Alaska from the protected Inside Passage. The other was the Pacific Steamship Company. H. F. Alexander, the king of Pacific Coast steamer magnates, formed his "Admiral Line" in 1916 by consolidating four firms. While his company dominated the coastwise commerce south of Puget Sound, in the northbound trade it deferred to Alaska Steam. Except for minor discrepancies, it conformed to the rate schedule of the Guggenheim company. Alaska Steam took the lead in negotiations with the commission, and presumably with other large shippers as well.

In 1919 Alaska Steam operated twelve ships with 18,316 net tons. The Admiral Line had one more vessel, but its net tonnage was less — 14,128. Alaska Steam listed 164 sailings from Seattle, the Pacific Steamship Company, 137. By then the two lines had little competition in southeastern Alaska and no regular competitors for the Westward business. Alaska Steam virtually controlled the traffic to Nome and other points on the territory's western coast.

The commission was plunged into this developing situation, both as shipper and as recipient of a share of the abuse that Alaskans heaped upon their transportation lines. Alaskans denounced the railroad on the ground that it abetted the steamers' allegedly extortionate rates by making the freight transfer arrangements necessary to business with the water lines. They argued that the railroad should use its leverage to force water tariff reductions. They argued that the railroad, built to develop Alaska, was instead stifling the territory's economic progress.

The proper place to explore the charges against the steamships and the railroad is within the context of their dealings with one another. Those dealings and a review of the charges will be deferred a moment to present some conclusions about the railroad's role. An examination of hundreds of pages of correspondence, memoranda, and testimony about rail-ship relations exonerates the commission from the charges. Railroad officials believed that steamship rates were too high, even with the higher operating costs of the Alaska trade considered. They well knew that the water carriers were tough bargainers. Far from being the dupes or henchmen of the shipping interests, they took a practical, cynical view of their relationships with the Admiral Line and Alaska Steam. Their first interest was to secure the lowest possible rates for commission shipments in order to lower the costs of construction. Their second interest was to obtain rates low enough to permit the development of the interior. Both concerns reflected the intent of Congress — to build a railroad and to open inland Alaska for economic exploitation.

At the same time, commission officials were acutely aware of two factors inhibiting them in their railroad-steamship negotiations, factors as good as trumps in the hands of the water lines. The first was the commission's knowledge that it was not, in law or policy, the proper agency to force a general reduction in steamship rates. Congress, the United States Shipping Board, and the Interstate Commerce Commission retained the rate-making power. The second consideration, simply put, was that the railroad needed the steamship companies more than the steamship companies needed the railroad. Alaska Steam was assured of the ore traffic from the copper mines before the Alaskan Engineering Commission appeared on the scene. Both companies depended upon cannery and other commercial traffic, not upon the commission, for their livelihood. Therefore, the commission negotiated with the companies just as any other large shipper would have done. Had it threatened to use any presumed governmental powers to force general or specific rate reductions, it would have been repudiated. Had it refused to negotiate, either it would have paid full tariff rates or it would have chartered a ship to haul its own freight. The former option was unnecessarily expensive, the latter was potentially expensive and harbored many possible difficulties.

During 1915, the first year of large waterborne freight shipments, the commission used a variety of ocean transportation. The next season the regular steamship companies denied space to the railroad until late summer, when they made enough room for the road to move some shipments of supplies and construction materials. The Kennecott Copper Company may have ordered the action in a fit of pique over the government's refusal to buy its Copper River & Northwestern railroad. Increased ore shipments spurred by the rising wartime demand for copper, confusion resulting from the organization of the Pacific Steamship Company, or other causes may have been controlling the situation. Whatever the reason, Edes in desperation secured the 3,500-ton government transport *Crook* from the War Department. The *Crook* carried commission freight and passengers during part of the 1916 season and during 1917. Because the *Crook* sailed nonstop to Anchorage, it arrived in five or six days from Seattle. Commercial steamers following the Inside Passage and making regular stops required an average ten days' time for a one-way trip. The *Crook* saved money, too, about 20 percent on commercial steamship rates. Early in 1918 she was recalled to military transport duty.

Nineteen seventeen was a season of heavy A. E. C. tonnage, but the steamships handled only 11,000 of 70,000 tons. After the *Crook's* recall, they carried the bulk of commission freight under contracts negotiated by the shipping board. From their subsequent actions the steamship companies evidently wanted the business, but they did not desperately want it. Had the railroad's haul been vital to them they could have found space for the cargo in 1916. Edes would not then have been required to borrow the *Crook*.

The commission's prelude to its own negotiations with the steamship companies was partly serious business and partly charade. In 1919 its problem was to secure water transportation for 1920 at reductions from the published tariffs.

Rates were sharply higher and congressmen were crying for economy. So commission officers went about the business of investigating alternate government transportation, to be ready with shipping if negotiations failed. An element of playacting characterized their work, for they wished to impress the steamship companies with their readiness to use government transportation if no favorable contract were forthcoming. "Our experience heretofore has been that we were unable to talk business with them with any favorable result until we had some definite information as to what we could do to help ourselves," wrote H. P. Warren, the commission official in charge of negotiations.[1] In the fall of 1919 Warren worked in Seattle, studying various transport possibilities. He rejected the shipping board's surplus steamers because they were unsuited to commission requirements for a combined passenger and freight vessel with cold storage and room for bulky construction material and equipment. Besides, the railroad would have had to dispose of such a ship at the end of the tonnage-producing construction period.

Warren's continuing studies reduced the commission's choices for economical water transportation until only the commercial steamers were left. He initially favored the further use of the transport *Crook*, but he based his preference for the *Crook* on an estimated 50,000 tons of A. E. C. freight to Anchorage and Seward during 1920. After adopting a more realistic estimate of 25,000 tons, he abandoned the *Crook*. The reduced estimate meant that the *Crook* would operate economically only during the summer, when the commission could assemble enough material to fill its holds on each voyage. Yet the *Crook* had to maintain regular sailings even without adequate cargo, for the commission intended it to serve as a year-round passenger vessel, carrying seasonal laborers and employees at nominal rates. For the eight months of the year when passenger travel was heaviest, the *Crook* would haul only about 834 tons per voyage, plus a few tons of commercial freight from shippers who had bothered to inform themselves of its sailings. The commission could not, under the law, solicit private shippers in competition with the steamship companies. The commission's inability to satisfy its own freight and passenger requirements with one vessel eliminated the *Crook* from consideration. (Had Warren known that the A. E. C. would ship less than 19,000 tons including shipments direct from Panama, he would not have considered the *Crook* at all.)

Warren then fell back upon a tug-and-barge operation. The basic plan had several variations including a commission-owned tug and barge. Some schemes were more feasible than others, but all of them went to smash upon one fundamental objection: tugs and barges could not carry passengers. The deficiency was much more critical than might appear. For one thing, the railroad regularly imported seasonal laborers from Seattle. It was equally important to provide economical transportation for long-term commission employees. Low-cost transportation was an employment inducement and morale builder. "I receive more complaints from my employees regarding transportation costs [from] Seattle to Alaska than for any other one thing," Mears wired to the president of the Pacific Steamship Company. "We feel an obligation to these employees and their dependents to provide them reasonable means of transportation back and forth. It was for this reason that operation of transport 'Crook' direct from Seattle to Anchorage and return was highly successful in creating contentment and good will among our employees."[2]

With the tug-and-barge scheme deflated, Warren turned to a combination of chartered barges and commercial steamers. For the barges Warren probably had in mind a warm-weather operation, when they would carry heavy pieces and such other freight as could be gathered during the summer months. The steamship lines would carry commission employees and the remaining 10,000 tons of lightweight freight as it dribbled in during the off season. Warren argued that under the arrangement the commission would have received its freight at the least cost. He was correct. For example, a steamship and barge company bid $11.50 per ton on rails and fittings (because it did not offer passenger service, its bid on rails and other freight was rejected). The negotiated freight rate (including rails) between the commission and the steamship companies was $13 per ton. This rate increased the estimated freight charges on rails and fittings alone by $10,500, not including wharfage. From the railroad viewpoint, the barge-and-steamship arrangement was the best, but the water lines would have none of it.

125

Alaska Steam and the Admiral Line insisted on shipping all commission freight originating in Puget Sound in return for reduced passenger fares. From the steamship companies' viewpoint it was a reasonable compromise. The commission had something the steamers wanted — an estimated 25,000 tons of shipping. The steamers had the power to grant something Mears had confessed was essential to employee morale — reduced passenger rates. Why shouldn't they come together? Why not, indeed, except that it would cost the commission more money. Time after time Warren dressed up his idea in different details, until at last the steamship companies "refused absolutely to consider such a plan." There was no alternative. Warren recommended acceptance of the steamship companies' offer. Mears, who two months before had written, "it is absolutely necessary to handle our own transportation next season," wired his assent on December 20, 1919.[3]

The background of the 1920 transportation agreement well illustrates the A. E. C.'s realistic attitude toward the steamship companies. It shows how limited was the commission's power to coerce the water lines and reveals its dependence upon them. Mears capitulated partly because he was so acutely aware of the situation. All year long he lived with Alaska Steam's threat to halt its sailings to Anchorage and Seward if the commission continued to charter independent steamers for special voyages at lower rates. In delivering the threat, the vice-president of the water line even suggested ending all Alaska service except to Cordova to bring rich copper ore from the Kennecott mines. The steamship official said that if Alaska Steam reduced its operations to Cordova, the Pacific Steamship Company probably would follow suit and cease serving Alaska altogether. Had the threat been carried out, the A. E. C. would have been forced to take charge of both railroad and commercial shipping to Anchorage and Seward. If Mears had wished to build a federal transportation empire, he would have regarded the prospect with delight. He did not. Moreover, he knew that Congress would not countenance a full-fledged federal steamship line. Thus, he dared not take lightly any threat to end steamship service.

For their part, the steamship companies made important concessions, bringing the estimated costs to within $16,000 of the estimated charges for the transport *Crook* operating under optimum, but most unlikely, conditions. A 25 percent reduction in passenger fares for employees and their families was the most significant concession. The reduction saved the employees $16,703.77 and the A. E. C., which paid laborers' transportation, $16,196.87 during 1920. The water lines also granted a $13 per ton freight rate on railroad materials from Seattle to Anchorage or Seward, a rate that saved the commission an additional $84,334.78, or about 19 percent of the cost at published rates. Further, the water carriers agreed to waive penalty charges for heavy or bulky equipment. In return, the railroad gave the companies the exclusive right to ship all freight from Puget Sound. There was to be no penalty for the companies' failure to ship, except that the commission could engage other transportation for the cargoes involved.

All in all, the agreement was a bargain for the railroad. The commission gained significant reductions from the public rates and it had its water transportation for little, if any, more than alternative methods would have cost. The arrangement was a distinct advantage for the residents of Anchorage and Seward. Without the commission contract the steamship companies probably would not have maintained regular service to the two ports. At Anchorage only 6,100 tons of commercial freight and express moved in and out by steamer during 1920. The commission considered itself well served. After renewed bidding and negotiations, the agreement was continued for the 1921 season. Following that mutually satisfactory season, the railroad and steamship companies extended the contract through 1922.

A through-rate agreement with the steamship lines was the major transportation innovation of 1922. Acting on the advice of a rate committee composed of commission officials, Mears, in November 1921, proposed through rates to the water carriers. Mears wished for the announcement of joint water-rail tariffs to coincide as nearly as possible with the commission's inauguration of its own through service in December. He believed that the joint through rates would result in three significant changes in the Alaska transportation picture. First, given through rates sufficiently low, shippers in the interior would receive their freight for less money than they had been paying. Second, provided the through rates were equalized between Anchorage and Seward, interior shippers would enjoy low rates year a-round. Year-round shipping would break one curse of Interior Alaska business — the need to ship most freight during the short Yukon River navigation season via the Skagway or St. Michael gateways. Third, assuming significantly lower year-round charges, the railroad would haul the freight formerly carried on the Yukon to the Fairbanks-Nenana region. Mears estimated the diversion at 25,000 tons per year.

It was not enough to reduce rates. Lower rates alone would not easily move freight over the rails unless the commission could induce the steamship companies to surrender their weight/measurement tariff system. The weight/measurement system was a traditional, integral part of steamship operation. In applying it to a piece of freight, the water lines figured both weight and bulk. They then assessed the charges by weight in the case of heavy, compact items, or by measurement, as with light, but bulky, material. They chose whichever billing gave them the greater revenue. The standard for choice was the "measurement ton" of forty cubic feet. For example, if a package measured forty cubic feet but weighed less than a short ton of 2,000 pounds, it was nevertheless assessed at the rate for one ton, though it might weigh but 500 pounds. The system really established two differing types of tons — the familiar 2,000-pound variety, and another having nothing whatever to do with weight. In the eyes of the steamship companies, even forty cubic feet of crated air was a ton, and if anyone had proposed to ship air from Seattle to Alaska, he would have paid the ton rate for every forty cubic feet of it.

To anyone unfamiliar with transportation, the weight/measurement system seems worse than preposterous. Actually it was a simple arrangement which avoided the elaborate classification tariffs that were, nonetheless, rapidly replacing it. Under weight/measurement, the steamship company set one rate to each Alaska port. All freight, with certain exceptions, moved at that rate. Of course, bulky items consumed space without earning much steamship revenue on a weight basis. They paid their way, however, when the water lines applied the tonnage rates on a measurement basis. Either way, there was only one rate. The 2,000-pound weight ton and the forty-cubic-foot measurement ton were standard. With a little experience and a weight/measurement conversion table, any shipper along coastal Alaska could figure the freight on any item. All he needed to know was the base rate plus wharfage charges.

Despite its simplicity, the weight/measurement system would not do for joint water-rail rates to the interior. For one thing, it smacked of trickery and deceit. To cite a prosaic example, bottled salad oil weighed fifty pounds per package, with forty packages per weight ton. A hypothetical shipper who ordered a weight ton of salad oil from Seattle to Anchorage in 1922 would not pay $18.05, the ton rate plus wharfage. He would pay about $25.65 for almost fifty-seven cubic feet of salad oil, seventeen cubic feet more than a measurement ton. Had he ordered a ton of breakfast cereal he would have paid about $40.05. No shippers ordered such large quantities, but the rates for what they did order were higher by the same proportions. Some heavy commodities such as sacked ore traveled at the published rate. On the average, however, freight paid about 57 percent more than published tariffs. Then too, wharfage was assessed at so much per ton, weight, or measurement. The purchaser of that ton of cereal would have paid not $2.55 wharfage, but about $6.40 based on the measurement ton. Finally, by 1922 the weight/measurement system was obsolete and in effect on few, if any, United States lines outside the Alaska trade. There was something sinister about its survival, the attorney general of Alaska implied.

The steamship companies could have obviated these objections by producing a weight classification tariff, but such a tariff would have raised a new crop of criticisms. Shippers would have had difficulty mastering the classifications, would have accepted any reductions as their due, and would have complained bitterly of any increases. So the water lines left the weight/measurement system alone. Coastal shippers abided with a familiar, if not entirely satisfactory, rate schedule.

The defect of the weight/measurement system, next after its presumed deception, was that many people who were inexperienced in transportation failed to understand it. Failure to understand its application caused endless perplexity, anger, and dismay and possibly generated more ill-will for the steamship companies than any other single issue. The imbroglio involving a fire truck shipped to Anchorage in 1922 will serve as an example. After a serious fire early in the year, the commission and the town of Anchorage upgraded their equipment by purchasing two American La France pumper trucks. The city's machine moved with the railroad's on a government bill of lading to reduce the freight charges. In its crate it weighed five tons. At the commission's special rate of $13 per ton, the charge from Seattle would have been $65 on a weight basis. Wharfage and switching charges, a heavy lift penalty, and crane service would have brought the total assessment to $87. Instead, the commission presented the Anchorage City Council with a freight bill for $521.58. The council raised "quite a hubub [sic]" as Mears phrased it, but the council paid.[4] The tonnage and other charges based on 32 1/8 measurement tons were correct.

The commission and the steamship companies would have met an even greater barrage of criticism had they permanently maintained the weight/measurement system in the interior. For years shippers in the interior had been accustomed to a flat ton rate based on weight only. The exceptions carried at higher rates were valuable, fragile, heavy, or bulky items. Special rates below the $70 base were granted to quantity shipments of heavy staples. For example, ten tons or more of dredge timbers moved at $60 per ton, flour at $63, and sacked ore, outbound, at $22. Interior shippers would have felt the weight/measurement confusions and suspicions most keenly, for paperwork and costs would have increased: two freight manifests, one for the rail (weight) shipment, the other for the water (weight/measurement), would have been required.

The joint-rate solution was the only way to meet the objections to weight/measurement and reduce rates at the same time. Through late 1921 and early 1922 representatives of the railroad and steamship companies figured a new schedule of through rates. They signed the rate agreement on March 10, 1922. In general, the arrangement provided for rates on a strictly weight basis, with all wharfage charges included. Commodities were grouped according to the Western Classification, in widespread use on railroads in the west including, since 1916, the commission's line. The fifth class rate, or the carload rate for general merchandise, was critical because it most nearly compared with the all-water "base rate" to the interior of $70 per ton. The transportation lines set their fifth-class tariff at $42 to Nenana or Fairbanks, or 37 percent below the old rate to the Fairbanks region. The steamship proportions of the through rates were designed to yield the water lines about 80 percent of the revenue they would have received had the same shipments moved on a combination of steamship and railroad local rates. The commission did not significantly reduce its rates south of Healy, 244 miles north of Anchorage. That is, its proportion of the through rate was the same as its local class distance rate from Anchorage or Seward. North of Healy the commission reduced its proportion in order to lower freight charges to interior shippers.

During the open season, through freight moved to Anchorage, and the steamships received a higher proportion because of the longer water haul. During the four months or more that the port of Anchorage was closed, the railroad received a higher proportion in recognition of its mountain haul from Seward through the Kenai Peninsula. Finally, the railroad undertook to fashion "distributive rates" for Seward and Anchorage to develop them into the distribution centers for their respective hinterlands. It established new, lower local class distance rates from the two towns, reducing the rates about 10 percent. This shrinkage also placed the new local rates 10 percent below the commission's proportion of the through rates.

Under this arrangement a small shipper at Matanuska would find an advantage in ordering from a merchant in Anchorage who had shipped his stock into the Cook Inlet port on the steamship companies' local rates. In order to beat the distribution and steamship local rates, the small shipper would have to amass a carload (generally about 24,000 pounds of one commodity or a few similar commodities) to be shipped at the through rate. Assuming that he could assemble a carload, he could avoid the Anchorage merchant's markup by shipping his merchandise himself, but the added paperwork and the need for an agent at Anchorage to reship the goods would have reduced or cancelled the advantage. Through rates did not apply to local water shipments, so the weight/measurement system remained in effect on cargoes to Anchorage or Seward. Both the commission's freight contract and the joint through-rate agreement were continued through 1923, after renewed bidding and negotiations.

Rate reductions from 1922 levels were the principal changes in both arrangements.

This review of water-rail relationships provides the perspective for one of the most vigorous, comprehensive crusades against the steamship lines and the railroad. John Rustgard, territorial attorney general, launched his attack in 1921. Rustgard's presentation was usually strident, sometimes telling, sometimes outrageously erroneous. He developed his case at length in his biennial report for 1922-23. Anyone who is interested in his entire presentation may read it there. In brief, he accused the steamers of overcharging and denounced the railroad for its supposed collusion with the water lines. Rustgard argued that the steamship companies made extraordinary sums from the Alaska trade, up to 86 percent per year on their investment. Possibly the companies did enjoy an unreasonably high return. A careful outside examination, the federal government's 1944 "North Pacific Study," estimated Alaska Steam's average dividends at 28 percent per annum. Whether rates that brought a reasonable return would also have brought diversified economic development to coastal Alaska is another matter. Rustgard was convinced that lower rates would have developed the territory and that the behavior of the water carriers in refusing to reduce their rates was little short of criminal. Although his conclusions were dubious and some of his figures untrustworthy, Rustgard did demonstrate that rates were high on the Alaska run.

When he made his charges, Rustgard had before him a document mitigating the high rates: the report of the Alaska Territorial Shipping Board. The Alaska legislature had authorized this board in 1919 in response to skyrocketing freight rates. Governor Thomas Riggs, one of the original railroad commissioners, was its chairman. In a 1920 statement the board revealed the steamship companies' serious handicaps. The water lines accepted the burden of serving unprofitable, out-of-the-way ports and maintained expensive wintertime operations in return for about 25 percent of the territory's shipping business. "Private ships" belonging mostly to canneries, together with tramp vessels, took the rest of it. Rustgard himself pointed out the problem: "large canneries could force the steamship companies to grant low commodity rates on cannery supplies by threatening to operate their own vessels, thus further reducing common carrier tonnage."[5] According to the board, even the extraordinarily low copper ore rate that Alaska Steam granted to its holding company, Kennecott Copper, was a blessing in disguise. Without the ore business Alaska Steam would have still less incentive to maintain year-round schedules. Even so, the board believed that the copper ore rate was too low and succeeded in having it raised from three to four dollars per ton. The board confessed, however, that the higher rate would have made it possible for the copper company to run its own direct ore ships at the same or less cost had it elected to do so.

Other obstacles to economical steamer operation included dangerous navigation hazards in the Inside Passage, winter storms in the Gulf of Alaska, and high insurance charges. Rustgard and other critics trotted out another argument in reply. They tirelessly compared ton-mile rates on the Alaska run with those of international carriers or transcontinental railroads, to the disadvantage of the Alaska lines. But they forgot or minimized the low traffic densities of the Alaska trade, competition between international carriers, or between transcontinental railroads and water line carriers via the Panama Canal. International steamship companies received subsidies that the Alaska trade, defined as coastal, did not.

An examination of the problems of steamship operation serves as the backdrop for Rustgard's charges against the A. E. C.: collusion with the water lines to maintain high rates. The attorney general argued that the railroad had abetted steamship rate practices in the through-rate agreement of 1921. Rustgard based his charge on a common misunderstanding of the weight/measurement system. While examining the tariffs, he was struck by the fact that the steamship companies' proportion of the through rate was in most cases greater than its local rate for the same item. He used the example of a crate of bathtubs shipped to Nenana, which, by through rate, had returned thirty dollars to the ocean carrier, assuming that the crate had been assessed at one ton. The through rates did not reduce freight costs for the interior after all, he concluded, but were a joint water-rail scheme to milk consumers of even greater sums.

Rustgard failed to grasp the essential fact that the bathtubs, being relatively light and bulky, would move by the measurement ton on the steamship's local rate. Mears carefully explained that the crated bathtubs, which weighed 250 pounds, not a ton, had moved on the through rate at the charge for one-eighth of a ton, or $10.50. Under local rates the total cost to the shipper would have been $16.22. Other through-rate savings generally were significant. According to Alaska Steam's figures, it received 21 percent less revenue in 1921 under the through rate than it would have had the same volume of freight moved at its local rates.

In deploring the railroad's failure to battle the steamship companies, Rustgard revealed how seriously he had overestimated the muscle the commission could use on the ocean carriers. Leaving aside its lack of legal power to amend the water rates, the commission might have extralegally used a large shippers' prerogative to reduce transportation charges to the railbelt. But it was not that large a shipper. During the period under review it secured its favorable contracts on declining tonnages — 25,000 tons contracted for 1919, only 7,500 tons for 1922. During 1922 the commission handled 19,868 tons of its own freight over its docks, including the still-arriving Panana equipment. In the same year Alaska Steam alone moved 310,000 tons of cargo. Alaska Steam's traffic manager noted that the A. E. C. gave the company a bit more than 5 percent of its total tonnage. The canneries provided more than 25 percent. Therefore, the commission was not in the dictatorial position of the canneries. Nor could it presume to speak or act for other shippers.

Consider once again the experience of the Territorial Shipping Board. In its search for alternatives to the ocean carriers the board had turned to a territorial steamship line, a scheme requiring Congress' approval. It quickly discovered a congressional opposition so overwhelming that it was "doubtful whether a member could be found to even introduce" the necessary legislation.[5] Rustgard accepted the board's conclusion but thought he had found a different solution. He suggested that the commission call for bids and award its supposedly lucrative business to a steamship company not then sailing to Alaska.

The commission's business (Rustgard grossly overestimated it) would give the new firm a toehold in the Alaska trade. Presumably it would rapidly expand its business at the expense of the profiteering lines. In truth, the A. E. C. had advertised widely for bids on freight and passenger movements, beginning with the 1919 season. For the first two years it received bids on freight only from companies unable to handle the passengers. In addition, Alaska Steam and the Admiral Line made a joint bid for both passengers and freight. The commission had no choice but to reject the bids for freight only and to negotiate with the existing companies. After the first two years the A. E. C. received but one bid, a joint offer from the two steamship lines. Finally, the commission lacked the power, which Rustgard suggested it had, to specify the rates to Alaska ports other than its own.

What is surprising in water-rail relationships is that the commission stood up to the ocean carriers as determinedly and successfully as it did. To go no further back than 1920, Mears heard a rumor that the water lines would make up the recently granted reductions to commission employees by increasing regular passenger fares. He lodged a vigorous protest and secured the promise of Alaska Steam's traffic manager that no higher rates were contemplated. The commission firmly resisted every effort by the ocean carriers to raise their contract rates. Late that same year the steamship companies began to build a justification for rate increases based on an advance in the price of fuel oil. The commission responded with figures showing that the increase was slight and should not significantly affect rates. Mears regarded the joint through rates as a partial victory in the commission's struggle to persuade the steamship companies to lower their tariffs and to abandon the weight/measurement system. In 1922 he made a concerted effort to bring down both the contract and through rates. Rustgard's charges and the wide publicity given them were partially responsible for Mears' efforts. On the other hand, the commission had begun gathering supporting data for its argument early in the year, before Rustgard's complaints were widely aired.

The unique association between railroad and steamship companies had its inescapable irritations and conflicts, but both sides accepted Mears' principle that "harmonious relations" were preferable to incessant bickering.[6] The steamship companies gave the commission good service under the contract. The commission behaved with an acute sense of its responsibility and its limitations as a public agency. Rustgard remained convinced that "the Government Railroad has become an adjunct to a privately owned steamship line."[7] Mears had the better part of the argument.

From 1922 the railroad operated a River Boat Service downriver from Nenana to Holy Cross on the lower Yukon River. The service was later extended to Marshall. The first two boats, the *Gen. Jeff. C. Davis* and the *Gen. J. N. Jacobs* were castoffs from the Army, which was reducing its Alaska garrisons in the 1920s and no longer needed the vessels. The *Davis* is at the left. *The Alaska Railroad*

The *Davis* and the *Jacobs*, rear view, in winter quarters. Both photographs were taken in October 1920 while the boats were in Army service. *The Alaska Railroad*

131

At the dock near season's end, October 1920. *The Alaska Railroad*

The Tanana River waterfront at Nenana, with the *Jacobs* at dockside, 1918. *The Alaska Railroad*

The Nenana waterfront, with the Tanana River bridge in the background. At left center a sternwheeler, its plume white against the Tortella Hills, heads upstream. Because river boat traffic above Nenana virtually ceased several years before the bridge was built, the boat may be the *Jacobs*, on assignment to ferry President Harding and his party across the Tanana at the Richardson Highway in July 1923. Harding, however, cancelled the highway trip, and the *Jacobs* returned to duty with the River Boat Service. *The Alaska Railroad*

Steamer *Alice*, added to the River Boat Service fleet in 1926 by purchase from the Alaska-Yukon Navigation Company. *The Alaska Railroad*

Stern view of the *Alice*. *The Alaska Railroad*

The *Alice* shoves a barge along the Tanana River. *The Alaska Railroad*

The river boat *Nenana* unloading at Tanana, at the confluence of the Tanana and Yukon rivers. The *Nenana*, launched in 1933, was the largest of the railroad's wooden hulled, wood-burning sternwheelers. She was also the last. *The Alaska Railroad*

Tanana's wooden fronts and board sidewalks are in view as the unloading continues. *The Alaska Railroad*

The *Nenana* at Ruby, a gold rush town on the Yukon River. These *Nenana* photographs were taken in 1951 but show scenes little changed from the 1930s when the *Nenana* was new. *The Alaska Railroad*

The Commission and Its Critics

The railroad commissioners labored under a barrage of criticism from within and without Alaska. Even though they paused occasionally to return the fire, they could not answer all their detractors. To do so now would require a chapter as long as this book. An assessment of the major criticisms against the railroad will show that most of them were unjustified or overstrained. A few were reasonable. The railroad, like any other human institution, had its faults.

Criticism came from three major sources: Congress, John E. Ballaine, and James Wickersham. Congressmen were concerned mostly with the commission's soaring costs. Ballaine will be remembered as the founder of Seward and as one of the principals in the Alaska Central-Alaska Northern Railroad. He was embittered when the Alaska Syndicate refused to help him regain control of the line and complete it to the interior. Stung by the loss of the line and by the failure of his hopes for his property at Seward, he directed his drumfire attacks against the Syndicate and the government railroad from 1910 until his death in 1940.

Ballaine's long-time friend, James Wickersham, fought his own rhetorical battles with the Morgan-Guggenheims. At first favorably inclined toward the Alaska Syndicate, he went into opposition after he offered his services as counsel to its chief corporation, Kennecott Copper, and was refused. Wickersham's first Alaska venture began in 1900 following his appointment to the judgeship of the newly created Third Judicial Division. Detailed to clean up the scandalous claim-jumping situation at Nome, Wickersham did so with fairness and efficiency. In 1908 he ran for the territorial delegate position and was elected. He was reelected five times in succession. A handsome man, physically and intellectually powerful, Wickersham garnered many friends, although his political allegiance strayed from progressive Republican to independent and back again. He was a sparkling humorist, a skillful speaker, a successful lawyer, and a scholar. His *Old Yukon* is a charming melange of autobiography and Alaskana; his landmark *A Bibliography of Alaskan Literature* is a monument to his industry.

Unfortunately, Wickersham's relations with the railroad added no luster to his reputation. He attacked the commission viciously, skillfully weaving falsehood with distortion to produce the warped image of an incredibly inept officialdom. Wickersham's anti-Guggenheimism and his sincere belief that the A. E. C. had fallen under Guggenheim influence do not by themselves account for his bitter denunciations. Wickersham was known with some justification as the father of the Alaska railroad bill. Despite his formal Republicanism, he was a partisan of President Wilson. Yet, as he confessed on the floor of the House, the Wilson administration had not consulted him on railroad matters. Worse, Wilson had appointed Wickersham's political enemy, Thomas Riggs, a commissioner. To Wickersham, Riggs was part of the "Gugg crowd"[1] suborned by the wily Alaska Syndicate. Further, Wickersham seems to have had a compulsion to attack federal activities in Alaska. The largest specialized federal agency in the territory before the advent of the railroad was the Alaska Road Commission. Its president,

Colonel Wilds P. Richardson, bore the brunt of Wickersham's verbal assaults until, stung beyond endurance, Richardson angrily denounced him as "a falsifier."[2] When the railroad hove into view with its larger staff and appropriation, Wickersham shifted his sights.

Both Wickersham and Ballaine condemned the railroad's relationships with the steamship companies, condemnations answered implicitly in the last chapter. Ballaine made charges of government truckling to the Morgan-Guggenheims regarding the surveys, route selections, and line acquisitions, charges refuted in earlier chapters. Ballaine's lurid pamphlet, *Strangling of the Alaska Railroad,* was his most widely publicized, although by no means his only, onslaught against the commission. The pamphlet is the product of a mind unsettled on the subject of the Alaska Syndicate. It contains several serious distortions, as the following examples show.

In his discussion of the weight/measurement system, Ballaine attempted to prove that it worked against the commission whether goods moved by weight or by measurement in steamer holds. Taking the instance of steel rails at thirteen dollars per ton, he figured a ton of nested rails at twelve cubic feet, or more than three weight tons per measurement ton of forty cubic feet. Therefore, he wrote, the A. E. C. paid $43.33 per measurement ton. The statement was objectively true, but irrelevant. It was not possible for the shipper to opt for the measurement ton on the Alaska water lines (or on any others in the world) if his cargo were heavy and compact enough to move by weight. There was nothing sinister or unfair about it. Indeed, most shippers would have been delighted to move cargoes by weight and avoid measurement altogether. Ballaine claimed expertise in Alaskan affairs and should have known all this. He was incredibly ignorant if he did not know it, and if he knew it, he was guilty of deliberate distortion.

Ballaine tried to develop circumstantial proof that Mears was a tool of the Morgan-Guggenheim Alaska Syndicate. He was equally anxious to demonstrate Mears' commitment to Anchorage as the major railroad port despite icing and silting conditions in the harbor. Unfortunately for Ballaine, his demonstrations collided. He claimed that Mears forced the steamship companies to call at Anchorage in another effort to make Anchorage, not Seward, the main harbor. Ballaine's claim was internally inconsistent. Mears, had he been the puppet of the Morgan-Guggenheims as Ballaine insisted, could not have ordered a Morgan-Guggenheim concern, the Alaska Steamship Company, to use an inferior harbor against its better judgment.

If Ballaine's pamphlet is filled with nonsense such as this (and it is), perhaps his charges should be ignored. They cannot be ignored because Ballaine wrote or inspired many letters and magazine and newspaper articles of similar tenor. An intense man, impressive in his personal appearance, Ballaine could persuade, however briefly, with his tales of mismanagement and intrigue. He usually coupled his criticisms with assertions that he had done, and could do again, a much better job than the A. E. C. Lane was sympathetic toward him until he granted him an interview. Then Lane learned "that what he wanted was a job, one with authority that would practically make him the railroad commission."[3] For all his unreliability and self-seeking, Ballaine had an influential audience.

The most persistent charge brought against the commission was that the railroad cost too much by reason of bureaucratic waste and inefficiency. There was no denying that costs had soared beyond all expectations. Congress appropriated the last of the original $35 million authorization in 1919. Bringing the road to formal completion in 1923 required $57,896,247.74. Ballaine had projected a cost "over $50,000,000, possibly as high as $60,000,000," back in 1917.[4] At the time, Edes had indignantly rejected the idea. Ballaine's estimate of the necessary additional expenses to place the line in proper running order was excessive, but close enough to official calculations to be uncomfortable. His figure of $15 million compared with General Manager Noel Smith's sober judgment in 1925 that almost $11,879,000 would be needed.

Mismanagement was, however, a small factor in the increased costs. In one instance only did the convergence of two managerial decisions result in significantly higher expenses. The most serious decision from a cost viewpoint was building in the interior before the road had been completed through Broad Pass. When Wickersham complained of how railroad construction was "not done in a businesslike way"[5] he should have cited the expensive interior work which was of so much direct and indirect benefit to his constituents in the Fairbanks region. Had the private contractor whom Wickersham so fervently wished for been building the line, he almost certainly would have avoided the long water hauls, the payroll, the office overhead, and the townsite expenses of disconnected interior construction. He would not have bought and rebuilt the crumbling Tanana Valley road. The A. E. C. did those things because it was a government service as well as a government enterprise. Edes, Mears, and Riggs were engineers, Lane a man of wide experience. Their deliberate decision to establish a Far North construction base was a decision on behalf of industrial development, not economy.

Because they began construction in 1916, the engineering forces followed Edes' philosophy of location before Alaska experience modified the chairman's ideas. Early locations emphasized easy grades along waterways, especially the Susitna, Matanuska, and Nenana rivers. The selection of water grades in rough Alaskan country was understandable, but it left the line open to attacks by glacial streams. The routes of Edes' railroad, the Southern Pacific, experienced flooding but not rampages like the rioting of an Alaska glacial stream during spring breakup. The soggy banks of many Alaska streams were especially susceptible to sloughing and to the scouring action of ice floes. Heavy rains, warm weather, or both could bring down torrents of melted glacial ice loaded with debris. Water grades required shielding by expensive riprapping and other bank protection. The commission's pioneer construction usually did not provide adequate defenses against the ravages of glacial rivers.

The decisions favoring interior construction and water grades combined for disaster during the spring of 1918, when the Nenana River ripped out twenty-one miles of roadbed, including eleven miles of track. About twenty-seven miles south of the Nenana townsite an arm of the Nenana River veers northeast while the main channel arcs west. After running up to five miles apart, the arm and main channel rejoin about three miles south of Nenana townsite and the confluence with the Tanana. For most of its distance the arm is known as Lost Slough. Survey crews projected a right-of-way along Lost Slough, in those days an insignificant overflow channel, because it ran on slightly higher ground directly to the townsite. Shortly thereafter the Nenana began edging into Lost Slough. During the autumn of 1917 it spilled a "considerable" volume into the channel beside the roadbed. To guard against a damaging attack in the spring, crews drove a piling-gravel-and-brush dam 1,300 feet across the mouth of Lost Slough. In May 1918 the country around the Nenana townsite flooded badly. Railroad clerks and townspeople got around the A. E. C. grounds and part of the town by boat. The dam held until the twenty-seventh, when rapidly rising water stove it in. Then, as Browne described it, "a vast moving sea" spread over and around the line, crushing bridges, twisting rails, and shoving the track as much as ten feet from the grade.[6] No alternative remained but to relocate farther east. By dumping logs and gravel into a quaking swamp, Browne's crews built a new roadbed, tying it to the untroubled ends of the line before winter. The net cost of the relocation was more than $788,600.

The washout probably would never have received the attention it did had not Wickersham used it to further his end of a political feud with Riggs. Ironically, Wickersham would have been even more enraged had the commission done the sensible thing from the standpoint of economy and confined itself to a few surveys in the Fairbanks-Nenana area. Neither Riggs nor, as Wickersham had it, "the drunken inefficiency of a locating engineer" in his party should bear the blame for what happened. Nor should Edes. Railroad location engineering was partly empirical and intuitive, based on experience wrung from the engineer's own success and failure over a particular terrain. To ask him to abandon his hard-won knowledge before new experiences refuted it was asking a great deal. Many years afterward Anton Anderson, The Alaska Railroad's chief engineer, explained the locating engineer's cast of mind: "Engineers seemingly, without exception, when moved to new and far off locations are prone to locate railroad routes that could be constructed and maintained economically only if the climate and other factors they have previously contended with were duplicated in the new areas."[7]

No other serious losses could be charged to managerial decisions. The occurrence of petty grafts, thefts, and other illegalities were inevitable on any large project. Most of them cost the railroad little or nothing. Employee kickbacks to job foremen who hired them were common enough south of Broad Pass for the commission to issue multilingual oilcloth posters warning against them. North of the Alaska Range the workers were mostly sourdoughs who took care of one another without a monetary consideration. Gambling in the construction camps during the long, bright evenings was unlawful but was one of the few ways for men working in a wilderness to pass the time. In 1915 a group of Seward business houses and commission dock employees formed a ring that milked the A. E. C. of some wharfage collections before their combine was broken in December of that year. The loss at Seward probably did not exceed $30,000.

Commission officials were keenly aware of internal inefficiencies and strove to eliminate them. Malingering and materials losses would have been figured into cost estimates by men long familiar with their effects. In short, colossal corruption and mismanagement, concealed with consummate skill, must have existed if malfeasance and misfeasance are offered as explanations for the gap between estimates and expenditures. There simply is no evidence of any kind for anything of the sort. Most of the few cases of managerial failure, including two not yet discussed, are interesting for reasons other than the expense they entailed. On the whole, the commission management was remarkably efficient, hardworking, and dedicated to the success of the road. Secretaries of the Interior Lane and Payne conducted several investigations and inspections of the line. Some were open, others were secret. None of them validated the charges against the A. E. C.

Two of the commissioners come off well against their critics. Edes was not a forceful personality, but he kept a firm grip on the details of construction and on the actions of his subordinates. Although the minutae of finance eluded him, he repeatedly urged economy upon his colleagues. Edes had the misfortune to be afflicted with influenza just before the congressional hearings and debates of early 1919 over an increase in the A. E. C.'s authorization. He steadily worsened. By March he was "too weak to walk across the room"[8] and was no longer able to give his personal attention to the railroad. Edes' condition lent credence to congressional suspicions that he never really controlled the work, suspicions the modest engineer had not assuaged.

A coincident typographical error in the appropriations estimates gave Edes almost as much difficulty as his illness. What happened was this: Treasury Department rules required the commission to list certain classes of employees under the heading "salaries," certain others under "wages." The lists estimated 441 under "salaries," 1,982 under "wages." So far, so good. Unfortunately, the estimated figures on the compensation paid to each group were transposed, appearing as "salaries," $967,295, "wages," $305,455. That an active construction project requiring large numbers of laborers would pay out more than three times in salaries than it paid in wages was absurd on its face. Any congressman who thought he had discovered a lurking bureaucratic monster could have disabused himself by checking previous estimates or the annual reports. Wickersham did not check, he attacked. "Seventy-five per cent for overseeing," he charged, "and twenty-five per cent for construction work!" The delegate discovered large numbers of "non-railroad builders" and "pencil holders" on the lists. Only "pick and shovel men," he contended, really built the railroad.[9] Wickersham's charge was easy to refute. One hundred and nine of the 441 salaried employees were not in any sense supervisory or office personnel. Stationmen were not included in the "wages" list. Had stationmen been added to the "wages" column together with the 109 salaried workers, the ratio of "overhead" people would have been 1 to 10 — and that in the wintertime when relatively few station contractors and other wage hands were working. Wickersham was too intelligent to blunder into making a charge so easily refuted. He traded on the axiom that refutations never overtake accusations.

Edes was under a cloud when he relinquished his title of chairman and chief engineer on August 9, 1919. He was not a happy man. During the final year of his chairmanship he commented on Wickersham's reference to him on the floor of the House as an "amiable gentleman." Amiability, Edes wrote, "is a characteristic which possibly the Judge [Wickersham] does not place at its full value. Any one not possessing an amiable disposition and a considerable sense of humor would have had many severe shocks to his nerves in the course of five years of experience in building a Government railroad in Alaska, and being subjected to the criticisms of irresponsible, malicious parties."[10] Edes kept his consulting job with the road only a few months before resigning. He died in San Francisco in 1922.

Mears was a vigorous and forceful leader. First a member of the commission, then an engineer officer in wartime France, he assumed Edes' office when the older man resigned. J. J. Delaney, who joined the railroad in 1916 and later became its assistant general manager, remembered him as a man who got things done. Mears took care of his workers. On one occasion a group of men were walking toward their new construction jobs in the country north of Broad Pass. They arrived at a camp in the evening just behind Mears, who was traveling the line by horseback. As the men trudged up, tired and hungry, to where Mears and the camp boss stood talking, the boss waved them on. "Just keep right on walking, boys, we have no room for you here. The next camp is only a few miles farther." Then the boss told Mears that he would have the one unoccupied bed in camp. "Like hell I will," Mears retorted. "When you have found a bed for every one of these men, it will be time enough to think about me. These boys are in here on foot to help us, and they are going to have decent treatment."[11] Mears did not make a play for popularity during his stays in Alaska, claiming only a few close friends. Joseph Cotton, perhaps Lane's most trusted advisor on early A. E. C. affairs, concluded that it was just as well. "Mears is not particularly popular in Anchorage," the perceptive lawyer wrote after his 1916 inspection trip, "but he is respected and somewhat feared. I am inclined to think that is as it should be."[12]

Unfortunately, Mears did engage in a series of minor indiscretions. These were unimportant from a monetary standpoint, but as they involved reduced transportation costs and avoidance of commissary charges on personal consumption items, they were abuses of his official position. From 1915 through 1917 Mears on at least four occasions requested the Seattle purchasing office to buy tobacco items at wholesale for personal use and ship them to Anchorage at commission rates. The Seattle office also forwarded a shipment of apples to Mears on the same terms. About ten officials participated in the tobacco buying arrangement, which Gerig repeated at least once after Mears left for war service. There is no evidence that Mears continued the practice after he returned as chairman. Mears was straightforward about the purpose of the discount buying, which was "to get hold of the exact brand of tobacco and cigars that several of us like and also eliminate the profit and surcharges that it is necessary to put on in the routine of the Commissary Department."[13] The tobacco arrangement was especially ill-advised because Mears was called upon to defend the commissary before a group of Anchorage businessmen who claimed unfair competition and wanted the railroad outlet closed. Mears supported the commissary with vigor and reason. He and most other managerial people bought little or nothing at the commissary, he assured local businessmen, but made their purchases at retail in the Anchorage stores. The statement was less than candid, and Mears knew it. Mears himself saw nothing seriously amiss in his tobacco purchases, for he never attempted to conceal them from others in the A. E. C. He would have been acutely embarrassed had the purchases become public knowledge. The fact that they did not says much about the reliability of critics who claimed to have inside information about the commission's activities.

Riggs fared less well in his commissioner's job. Congressional critics lambasted Riggs for his lack of railroad experience. "He did not know whether a railroad frog jumped forwards or sideways," Wickersham quipped during a House debate. "The nearest approach that he has to any knowledge of railroad construction," Congressman Martin B. Madden chimed in, "is that. . .as a citizen of the United States he has occasionally been compelled to travel over a railroad." In reality, Riggs' railroad inexperience had little to do with the difficulties on the Fairbanks Division. Riggs was a political appointee, and not only in a partisan sense. Lane hoped that Riggs would win acceptance for the project from within the territory. He was chosen, Lane wrote in his 1919 statement, "because he had spent many years in Alaska and. . .was familiar with the Alaskan people and conditions under which work could be done in Alaska."[14] In that respect the appointment succeeded. Cotton reported that Riggs was popular in Fairbanks. Other statements by Cotton were portents of future revelations. Efficiency existed in inverse proportion to the number of Alaskans employed, he implied, and many Alaskans worked on the Fairbanks Division. Cotton found confusion at the Nenana docks, confusion he blamed on the newness of the town and the helter-skelter arrival of supplies by river steamer. The chaotic supply situation became chronic and ended in scandal.

Riggs often authorized the storekeeper to lend or borrow materials and supplies. "We have got to get along and scheme along and lend and borrow the best we can under the conditions,"[15] he told the chief steward. Getting along and scheming along with hundreds of thousands of dollars in government property might have been successful had Riggs exercised strict supervision. Instead, the auditors hastily called in during May 1918 found several instances of lax administration. A warehouse containing property worth some $250,000 had no hand fire extinguishers. Rusting coils of heavy cable lay half buried in silt. Hardwood lumber shipped thousands of miles had been shoved under the rear platform of the store building where warping and checking had ruined it. Engines in the electric plant vibrated so badly that they shook a pipe filled with live steam almost to the breaking point. These and other shortcomings were conclusive evidence of chronic administrative laxity. Riggs was remiss, but the resulting disorganization at Nenana would not have had serious consequences if his subordinate officers had been capable, honest men. Two of them were not. The best that can be said for the general storekeeper is that he was incompetent. The best that can be said for the chief engineer is that he was a scamp.

Rumors of wrongdoing were rife even before Riggs resigned in April 1918 to accept the governorship. Browne heard several of the stories from the district attorney at Fairbanks, others came from citizens. The sources and seriousness of the charges were such that he could not ignore them. Besides, he was a stickler for exactitude, correctness, and form. On May 26 Browne closed the retail store for an inventory by accountants chosen by the district attorney. Attention may have focused first on the storekeeper because the district attorney, a political enemy of Riggs, considered him an easy mark. However, he brought the storekeeper to trial on charges of embezzlement much too quickly — on June 17, before the auditors had completed their investigation. About all the prosecution could show was a large amount of informal lending of commission provisions to private concerns, transactions recorded in a separately kept "Loan Book." The defense replied that Riggs had authorized the loans. The United States commissioner dismissed the case because Riggs' authorizations removed any presumption of fraud.

The commissioner might have rendered a different verdict had the trial been postponed. Continuing investigations revealed serious lapses and errors in the storekeeper's judgment. He had loaned 14,497 pounds of beef and mutton to a meat market, entering the transaction in the "Loan Book" as of March 1918, although the loans extended over the previous four months. Sixty miles away at Fairbanks the commission was buying at retail from the same market to supply its crews on the Tanana Valley line. The favored meat market was renting a portion of the Nenana cold storage plant for $300 per year. An increase of $1,500 would have covered merely the firm's fair share of plant expenses. In May 1917 a grocery purchased potatoes at 9½ cents per pound from commissary stores, while the commission was buying potatoes on the local market for 15 cents a pound. In October, just after the Alaska potato harvest, the same grocery sold local potatoes to the commission at the 9½-cent price. At that time local potatoes could be purchased for 4½ and 5 cents per pound. Government property that could not be sold to private parties was sometimes arbitrarily condemned, then sold. Serious shortages and surpluses, elaborate and confusing bookkeeping, and an office force demoralized by low wages and some newcomers' rapid promotions, contributed to disaster at the Nenana commissary.

If the storekeeper were grossly inadequate to his task, the engineer in charge was worse. Edes wrote Riggs that the man did little work, preferring to spend his time around the poker table or "in the company of frisky ladies." One frisky lady was the wife of a contractor. Edes thought it more than a coincidence "that grain and supplies destined for other places found their way to his camp." The Nenana payroll for the winter 1917-18 was abnormally large, and many of the men attached to it were without visible means of labor. They passed the cold days in the warmth of the poolrooms. The engineer approved some curious contracts. He graded one motley group of ties mostly at first quality, grossly overpaying the contractor. When the ties arrived at the Nenana material yard, the foreman declared most of them culls and ordered them sawed up for firewood. In another instance the engineer allowed larger payments for cords of firewood containing half cottonwood than for nearby cuttings of better quality. The engineer had the foresight to quit his post before Browne arrived. Probably he had received kickbacks from the questionable contracts. "But these things cannot be proved," Edes wrote, "and it seems the best plan to forget them and start fresh."[16]

The line washout and the scandals at Nenana caused Riggs acute embarrassment. Certainly the scandals reflected on his judgment and administrative skill. Other Riggs appointees, however, performed their tasks well. Stores aside, the auditors discovered most departments in capable hands. They found some disorganization "out on the line," but no more than other investigators discovered in that difficult and rapidly changing situation. Half a century after he worked on survey and construction crews, Arnold Nordale remembered the no-nonsense attitude prevailing on the line portions of the project. After Browne arrived he tightened up the office forces, firing several incompetents, along with men dismissed with less justification for alleged pro-German attitudes. In justice to Browne, he soon rehired some of the "pro-German" workers. Browne was a capable administrator, but line construction was his forte. He designed a gravel spreader to speed the laborious handwork involved in raising a roadbed out of the muskeg. He established a system of residencies in which each resident engineer enjoyed a large measure of control over camps and other local matters. As soon as TNT became available after war's end, he advocated it in preference to dynamite.

No new scandals marred the work on the northern end. Lane ordered another audit, but not only to uncover further wrongdoing. It was also a review of all cost and accounting procedures, anticipating comprehensive systems of accounting and control. The second audit was influential in shaping the administrative reorganization of 1919.

Lane did not think highly of his commissioners despite their generally good records. Because their relations were officially cordial and no hints of fundamental disagreements survive, it is difficult to say how much Edes, Mears, and Riggs suffered with the knowledge of Lane's displeasure. His dissatisfaction had no reference to cost or corruption or to anything tangible that the commissioners did or failed to do. The secretary's unhappiness had its source in his thwarted ambitions for Alaska. He had made an emotional commitment to Alaskan development, and when the railroad failed to produce immediate results, he blamed men rather than circumstances. Lane apparently said nothing directly to the commissioners but was less restrained in his comments to others. He complained of Edes' indecisiveness and his advanced age, though only eight years separated the two men. Edes was hesitant to assume responsibility at first; however, the reluctance passed as he settled into his job. Mears and Riggs were, like Edes, personally unknown to Lane when he appointed them. They never were able to gain his confidence.

Lane tried to flesh out the commission with men he regarded as more competent, but never succeeded in luring them to Alaska. J. L. McPherson, an engineer with wide experience in the territory and sometime head of the Alaska Bureau of the Seattle Chamber of Commerce, twice refused Lane's offers. When Mears resigned to go to war, Lane asked McPherson to take his place. After Mears assumed the chairmanship, Lane again requested McPherson to take a job with the railroad as its "traffic developer."[17] McPherson did accept a Washington assignment as Lane's special advisor on Alaskan affairs and played a role in preparing the 1919 and 1920 appropriation requests. He also wrote a report on the railroad and its adjacent resources. During the war Lane asked Allan Pollok to take a "creative job" with the commission. "You see we have a fine bunch of men there, practical fellows of experience," Lane wrote, "but not one of them looms large as a business man or as a creator."[18] Lane wanted someone who would, among other tasks, integrate Alaska into his agricultural soldier settlement scheme, but Pollok refused the assignment. Lane thought no better of the commissioners' subordinates than he did of the commissioners themselves. He was uncertain of Andrew Christensen's capabilities, although Christensen was outstanding among the second-rung administrators of the A. E. C. He toyed with dismissing the examiner of accounts, Burton H. Barndollar, after the Nenana scandals, even though Barndollar had little control over Northern Division accounting.

Lane's frustrations were those of a man who wanted "to spend a few years of my life just dreaming dreams about what could be done in that huge territory, and if I only got by with one out of five hundred, I would leave a real dent in the history of that territory."[19] Lane wanted dreamers — he needed engineers. He blamed the commissioners for not being both. He was not an administrative meddler, however. Only in unusual circumstances did he interfere, leaving routine work to the Washington office force of a clerk and two assistants. An assistant secretary with limited policy and personnel authority exercised general oversight.

This recitation of the purplish side of Alaska railroad building has carried the discussion some distance from the problem of cost. To reiterate, losses by carelessness and chicanery scarcely explain the difference between the $35 million first authorized and the almost $58 million spent on a pioneer line by the end of 1923, to say nothing of the additional $11,879,000 needed to bring the road to first class condition. What did explain it, then? Apologists for costs and the time required to complete the railroad assign primary responsibility to World War I, with its inflation and manpower shortage.

Actually, most of the higher cost originated in a ternary relationship between the Alaska wilderness, the war, and the nature of the commission as a government enterprise. To take the last factor first, the cost considerations of federal construction have nothing to do with the old saw about the inefficiency of government *versus* private enterprise. They involve the railroad in its role as a federal service to Alaska. How much a private contractor would have saved depends on so many variables that fixing a dollar amount would be a futile exercise. Besides refusing to accept responsibility for Interior Alaska's economy, for the townsites, and so on, a private contractor probably would have charged higher rates and avoided part or all of the $3,400,000 operating deficit which the commission had accumulated by the end of 1922. He probably would not have displayed the patience and forbearance that the commission showed toward its small contractors. Probably he would have organized a land and industrial department, but it is doubtful whether he would have absorbed its costs as the commission did. The A. E. C. with its concepts of service and responsibility spent a good deal of money, possibly several millions — money which a private contractor would not have spent. Certainly Alaska was the better economically for the expenditure. The railroad's critics suffered from a peculiar schizophrenia regarding the commission budget. For instance, the extraordinary costs connected with aid to the interior coal mines and Browne's blatantly uneconomic building to link Fairbanks to the coal were accepted as the territory's due. When the total expenses rose beyond the authorized limits, the critics filled the air with charges of flagrant extravagance. They conveniently forgot how much the commission's special development costs had contributed to the increased expenses which they so righteously denounced.

The difficulties of remote wilderness construction drove up expenses and delayed completion. Edes confessed in 1919 that he had underestimated the problems. Materials sometimes failed to arrive because of kinked transportation lines. Except for rough lumber and some foodstuffs, everything had to be hauled at least the 1,230 miles between Seattle and Seward. Rugged country conspired with the worse-than-suspected condition of the old Alaska Northern to mock the commission's estimates. Some work along the wild, sheer cliffs of Turnagain Arm cost $200,000 per mile, with construction roads and trails consuming up to $25,000 extra for each mile. The commissioners thought it would average $110,157 per mile. To put the Alaska Northern in shape for light trains they had allowed $955,601. By the end of 1923 the cost of rebuilding the rattletrap railroad was over $4 million and climbing. If the commissioners deserve any stricture, it is for their consistent underestimation of the costs of wilderness construction. Even so, they faced real limitations on their attempts at true estimates. Inflation aside, it was difficult for anyone not personally familiar with railroad construction in Alaska to properly estimate all costs. Interviews with Alaskan railroad engineers and travels over the terrain helped, but they were no substitute for personal experience. The commissioners estimated remarkably well when allowances are made for inflation and other situations beyond their control.

The slowed construction of World War I left the line open to serious inflationary erosion. Although prices had risen fairly steadily during the two previous decades, the Great War touched off a wild acceleration. By 1920 the cost of living had soared 105 percent above the prewar level. All types of railroad costs increased dramatically.

The price of a mile of track, $9,860 in 1915, climbed to $14,264 in 1919, by which year most of the required materials were in place or purchased. Food prices skyrocketed. A case of fresh eggs could be purchased for $10.50 in 1915 but cost $20.05 by 1919. During the same years a case of condensed milk rose from $2.95 to $5.75, a pound of butter from 27 to 66 cents. Ocean freight rates were $7 per ton in 1915, $13 in 1920. McPherson estimated that inflation devoured $7,447,051 from 1915 to the spring of 1919. Wartime labor shortages slowed construction from 1918 through 1920, amounting to about a season's work loss.

Erratic congressional appropriation methods further increased costs. Instead of appropriating the $35 million in a lump sum, Congress dribbled it out over six years, usually during the spring or summer. The commissioners needed the funds by the previous fall so that they might plan the following year's work. Instead, the money arrived in the midst of construction activity already determined by the labor situation, construction priorities, and the commissioners' guesses about the funds ultimately available. The piecemeal appropriations sometimes scattered experienced crews. In the Talkeetna District in 1916 the district engineer had assembled capable construction gangs and stationmen who could have worked on bank protection, blasting, and timber cutting more economically during winter than summer. A shortage of funds forced him to disband the forces, clearly a false economy. At other times the commission staved off creditors, not a "businesslike" action. On other occasions, notably in 1919, it suspended the payroll, slowed or halted construction, and doled out partial wages and salaries on the basis of individual needs until a new appropriation became available. Then it made up the back pay. Despite Mears' objections to the annual appropriation, Congress not only refused to abandon it, but progressively tightened its fiscal control over the railroad after 1919.

Finally, we should recall the origin of that $35 million authorization. The figure was the estimated cost of the first, "Taft commission" recommendations, rounded down to the nearest million. The A. E. C. had not made it. The $35 million was in the bill creating the A. E. C. and was there regardless of any fresh recommendations that the A. E. C. might make. True, the first commission had recommended 733 miles of new construction, not the A. E. C.'s existing 550 miles of main line and branches. But its cost figure was naive even for 1912. Neither the $35 million nor the A. E. C.'s almost $23 million estimate allowed for the purchase of existing lines, for rolling stock, for new functions including townsite and coal mine operations, for uneconomical interior construction, for rampant inflation. Nevertheless, that $35 million became the symbol of economy, the arbiter of fiscal responsibility.

After airing charges of incompetence and excessive costs, the railroad's detractors focused on the lack of railbelt development. In 1917 Ballaine assured Lane that a competent railroad man "would set to work immediately to enlist capital for the building of a smelter on Resurrection bay" and in other ways quickly bring central Alaska into economic bloom. The next year he charged in a letter to President Wilson that the commissioners "are making no attempts whatever to develop traffic for the railroad," and that coal shipments were being "deliberately held back or blocked altogether." Several years later he wrote that Alaska could be developed "by the simple application of a will to do it."[20]

On the contrary, the A. E. C. was sympathetically interested in reviving and expanding the gold and other metal mining industries. It was concerned about an adequate supply of quality ties and began the railroad's long search for an alternative to the untreated Alaska spruce tie, an inferior product with low wearing, bearing, and spike-holding qualities. In 1922 the commission added sleeping cars — it already had a dining car service — and began actively seeking tourists. It continued activities unrelated to primary development but valuable in themselves. Its loan of two boarding cars to house unemployed ex-servicemen at Anchorage during the winter of 1921-22 was a useful palliative. Mears recommended a permanent army post at Anchorage — an infantry detachment had been on temporary duty there since 1916 — an arrangement desirable from the standpoint of internal security and retail trade. These and other activities, plus the commission's basic development work, counted for nothing in the eyes of the critics.

The commission's critics did not lack for other targets. They brought the railroad under heavy attack because of its allegedly high local rates. In isolated instances complaints of unreasonable rates were justified, and when possible the railroad responded with reduced charges. Most of the attacks on the rate structure had slight justification. Either they were uninformed, or worse, were outright untruths. "Oh, there has been a large percentage of increase in the government rates in Alaska," Wickersham told the House in February 1919. "The rates are excessive."[21] Probably his auditors believed him. His statement had no basis in fact. Even honest critics looked at the problem from but one parameter of the rate question. It is easy for someone who is not a traffic expert to say what a rate should be. If the nonexpert is a shipper he is ready to justify a very low rate. The rate specialist, on the other hand, is guided by certain principles in building up a rate structure. Light, bulky items — hats, for instance — take high rates because they devour space in freight cars without contributing much tonnage. Goods dangerous or difficult to handle, such as dynamite, are charged high rates, as are luxuries. Ore and coal, tonnage-producers requiring almost no care, are assessed low rates. Goods conducive to "developing" or "opening up" a country — mining machinery or farm equipment — also take low rates. Applying the principles is more than a mechanical task, for the rate specialist must consider the economic character of the territory he serves, his railroad's aspirations for that territory, the competition, and many other factors. All the factors are constantly changing in value, and the expert must be alert to their fresh effects on his rate structure. Above all, the rate specialist needs time — time to test his rates against experience, time to develop equitable relationships among rates, time to gain the confidence of long familiarity with the economic and social situation in the country that his railroad serves.

The commission suffered handicaps in the application of rate theory to central Alaska. For one thing, the A. E. C. ran a through railroad for only one and one-half years of its life, from December 1921 to the summer of 1923. From 1915 through 1921 its management was primarily concerned with construction, not operation. Territorial conditions from 1915 to 1923 were remarkably unstable, involving boom towns, wartime stagnation, debilitating influenza, and a measure of recovery at the close of the period. Rates outside Alaska rose rapidly until the early 1920s. What, if anything, a rate expert should have derived from all this is uncertain. In any event, there was no full-time rate expert and no traffic department in which formal responsibility for rates could be centered. Edes, then Mears, had the local responsibility for rates but no authority over rate policy, which remained with the secretary of the interior. The secretaries were as uncertain as anyone what rates should be, so rates continued stable with adjustments upward and downward in individual tariffs. Gerig assumed, among other duties, the day-to-day supervision of rates because he had proven himself a calm, highly capable administrator and engineer. Although at first he was not well grounded in rate matters and never completely understood them, he performed adequately in his work. Trainmaster J. T. Cunningham had been involved with traffic and rate problems from the beginning, but Mears failed to appreciate Cunningham's knowledge and abilities as fully as he might have. Not until after Noel W. Smith assumed the general managership in 1924 did Cunningham become the railroad's one-man unofficial traffic department.

The law gave the secretary of the interior the rate-making power possibly because Lane had been a member of the Interstate Commerce Commission. As with many other matters, in rate-making Lane followed the commissioners' advice. In 1915 he approved a rate schedule for the Alaska Northern which Edes had established effective June 1. Edes set passenger rates at eight cents per mile, twelve cents lower than the charges under private management. The freight rates were graduated by mileage up to mile 35 and up to a rate of $1.25 per hundred pounds. In March 1916 Edes slashed the rates, again with Lane's approval. The passenger toll fell to 6 cents a mile, far cheaper than the White Pass' 18 cents or the CR & NW's 12½ cents, but about three times higher than average rates in the "states." The new freight charges distinguished between carload and less than carload rates, but not among commodities. For the longest haul of fifteen to thirty miles they were less than fourteen cents per hundred for a carload of 20,000 or more pounds, thirty-five cents for less-than-carload — cheap rates in Alaska.

In September 1917 Lane established the rate schedule that remained in effect without any fundamental alteration until 1931. Neither his previous service on the Interstate Commerce Commission nor the railroad's slight experience with commercial freight provided much direct guidance. "It is difficult to know what rates should be charged on such a railroad as this," he wrote in 1919. The government road, he continued, was one "which is as yet in the process of building, which originates so little traffic as to be negligible, and will not in all likelihood for some years pay operating and maintenance charges."[22] Apparently Lane tried to strike a balance between the high rates on Alaska roads and rates outside Alaska. The former had not encouraged diversified development, the latter were inadequate to the government road's higher costs.

Therefore, Lane directed Edes to adopt the Western Classification, the class-distance tariff used by railroads in western United States, but with percentage increases. The increases were computed as follows: the first class rate (for items such as bookcases and baseballs), was increased 100 percent over the Western Classification. The rates for the other nine classifications were expressed as percentages of the newly-established first class rate. To take a hypothetical example, if the Great Northern's first class distance rate for a seventy-five-mile haul were fifty cents per hundred pounds, then the commission set its rate at one dollar. It set the second class rate (on items such as enameled bathtubs and shade rollers), for the same distance at 85 percent of the first class rate, or eighty-five cents. Rates for the remaining classes ranged from 70 to 20 percent of the first class rate. The railroad thus maintained a relationship among commodities while recognizing the shippers' desire for low rates and its own need for revenues to compensate for higher expenses.

The resulting rates were bargains in comparison with other Alaska roads, two to four times cheaper than Copper River and White Pass charges. Tariffs were especially favorable on items that the "little fellow" would be inclined to ship, whether he be businessman, prospector, or employee. To carry one hundred pounds of secondhand household goods one hundred miles on the government road cost 32 cents, on the CR & NW, $1.60. Canned goods were 49 cents and $1.09, flour the same, and eggs 69 cents and $2.16. The A. E. C., so much abused for its coal policy, kept coal rates from Matanuska to Anchorage extraordinarily low. They rose from 75 cents per ton in 1916 to $1.20 in 1919, where they remained until reduced to $1.00 in late 1922. The rate expressed as a percentage of the value of a ton of coal at the mine averaged 19 percent during the construction years. This was remarkably low when compared with the 87.7 average of rates in the United States. After the 1922 reduction, A. E. C. coal rates were lower than the Northern Pacific tariffs in Washington state. The commission's minimum carload was 40,000 pounds *versus* the Northern Pacific's 60,000.

It would be futile to follow the arguments between the railroad and its detractors over whether rates in general were too high. The critics usually stated the argument in terms of A. E. C. rates *versus* those on large railroads in the United States. The comparison was not apt, for traffic density had much to do with determining costs. As Lane pointed out, "the Southern Railway running immediately out of this city [Washington] . . .carries in any one hour more traffic than the Alaskan road carries in a year."[23] Anyway, each side could make a favorable case for itself by presenting judiciously selected rates for comparison. Wickersham's attacks were especially difficult to answer because of his cavalier disregard for accuracy and his habit of comparing less than carload rates on the Alaska railroad with carload rates on the transcontinentals.

The gap between A. E. C. and outside rates narrowed with time. Rate inflation outside Alaska accounted for some of it. The A. E. C. granted commodity rates, selective rate reductions, and through rates, all of which reduced the differential. At the end of the commission's life its rates in general were about 70 percent higher than those in the Pacific Northwest. The A. E. C. rates were about average when compared with those on United States lines of similar length. There were some inequities of course. Rates north of Broad Pass were higher as a rule until the commission inaugurated through service at the end of 1921. Coal rates from the Matanuska fields were proportionately lower to Anchorage than to Seward, if one accepts the distance rates of the Northern Pacific in Washington as a fair comparison. The disproportion reflected the A. E. C.'s bias in favor of Anchorage as a coal port and might have been significant had rail rates rather than mining costs restricted coal exports. The commission abolished the distinction in favor of

Anchorage in 1922. Until 1919, when Wickersham brought it to their attention, the commissioners had allowed the express company an unconscionably high rate for a train haul. The overcharges were based on dog sled operations over part of the old Alaska Northern and had not been adjusted. These exceptions aside, the commission's rates were extraordinarily low for Alaska.

None of this meant much to local shippers. They were unimpressed by the rate comparisons and were scarcely appeased by conscientious investigations of their rate complaints. Though they occasionally would argue in terms of comparative tariffs, that approach was unsatisfactory to them because it quickly bogged in a morass of subjectivism about lower traffic density, higher costs, the effects of inflation since the heyday of the river steamer, and so on. Shippers wished that the railroad would abandon all such guidelines, including its own operating expenses. The road, they said, should test its rates against one standard: was it developing Alaska?

The argument for "development rates" was simple and eminently appealing to shippers. Either a potential industry along the railbelt — lumber, agriculture, coal, gold — was developing, or it was not. If it were not, then the railroad's duty was clear. The railroad should lower its rates on the product and all items consumed in the course of its manufacture. It should continue the lowering until development began. If the product were denied a local market because low rates were encouraging competition from outside Alaska, then rates should be raised to wall out the import. George Preston, the agent of the Northern Commercial Company at Fairbanks, wrote to Mears that the rate to the interior city in 1915 had been about sixty dollars per ton. The rate was so high that it stifled development, but inflation had driven the tariff up another ten dollars. Therefore, the railroad should drastically reduce rates. Preston suggested a scant forty dollars through rate. "It was not intended or expected," he wrote, "that the railroad would accumulate profits or even pay operating expenses at the start, but that it should be operated more in the nature of a public service, somewhat analogous to the postal service, for the purpose of developing a rich new territory which, owing to unusual conditions, could not be developed in the ordinary way by private enterprise alone."[24]

Others joined Preston in the retreat from the earlier "development follows the rails" position. "As a statement of basic principle, we believe that...at this time more consideration should be given to the development of the natural resources of the country contiguous to the line than to the question of immediate profits," the Anchorage Chamber of Commerce declared. "In order that the road may be placed eventually upon a paying basis, it is absolutely essential that tonnage be created. This can only be done by the adoption of such a liberal policy as to rates as will serve to encourage development."[25]

The railroad agreed. At the end of the most comprehensive of several rates studies made by or for the A. E. C., a commission management committee reported that because operating expenses were so high, rates could not be raised to meet them. Development, the committee reported, should be the first consideration in planning rate structure.

From consultations with shippers and its own deliberations, the committee forged its amendment to the Lane rate policy. It did little with the rates themselves beyond recommending a 10 percent reduction in the first class rate. Rates, it decided, were low enough to assist development, high enough to provide some protection to local products. Selective adjustments since 1916 had eliminated most inequities. The committee did recommend certain reductions in minimum carload weights and a wider range of articles for carload shipment under headings such as "Mining Machinery," "Groceries," and "Hardware." On February 17, 1922, Secretary Albert B. Fall accepted the recommendations.

From a review of the commission's rate-making practices, it would appear that the complaints of its critics had little foundation. The rates were low for Alaska and compared favorably with short line rates outside the territory. A. E. C. officials approached the rate problem empirically and kept rates under continuous review. They conscientiously considered complaints about rates and charges, whatever their source or apparent validity. Occasionally they made rate reductions. Shippers could not reasonably have asked for more.

The commission's critics charged it with all sorts of unethical, illegal political activity. There was bitterness in Wickersham's assertion that Lane and the A. E. C. were "directly responsible for many criminal violations of the Congressional Election Laws" in Alaska.²⁶ Although his only specific complaint was against his enemy, Riggs, Wickersham suggested much more. The railroad was really Lane's partisan machine in the territory, he implied. "It has been built without touch of politics," Lane declared in reply.²⁷ While Wickersham's general charge was not true, Lane's rejoinder was no more correct unless one equates politics with rabid partisanship. Even within the equation, Lane was not entirely candid, for Riggs was a partisan appointee. It would be naive to suppose that he suspended his party activity entirely during his commissionership. Riggs excepted, the commission and its officers avoided partisan battles as much as possible. It is necessary to write "as much as possible" because many attacks on the A. E. C. were partisan, and refuting them involved the railroad willy-nilly in partisanship. A reading of the refutations makes it clear, however, that any commission defense of the administration or the party in power was tangential to a defense of itself. Surviving confidential correspondence indicates that neither Edes, nor Mears, nor any other official expressed any partisan sentiment. Had they been Democratic partisans, they would have lost their jobs at the outset of the Republican Harding administration. No political dismissals were made when Harding took office. Nor did Lane hand out political jobs on the railroad. "I have not asked them to appoint one man," he asserted, and Edes backed him up. The chairman wrote that Lane and President Wilson had done more than give him a free hand, they had insisted in writing that all jobs should be filled "solely upon the basis of merit."²⁸

While the commission may be absolved from involvement in purely partisan affairs, it certainly did not avoid politics. If to "play politics" is to develop and enlist influence to advance one's interests, then the commissioners played politics. It is difficult to imagine them doing anything else. There was nothing automatic in congressional sympathies and appropriations. The railroad's critics were many, so were its competitors for attention and funds. During trips to Washington and in correspondence, the A. E. C. management cultivated friendly senators and representatives, warned them against the railroad's enemies, and gave them information and arguments to strengthen the railroad's case with Congress. A. E. C. officials pored over the *Congressional Record* and committee hearings to sense both individual and collective congressional tempers. They granted favors, doubtless without prodding from Lane. In 1915 Senator Benjamin R. Tillman of South Carolina, a member of the Appropriations Committee, secured a place for Benjamin, Jr. on the railroad. The son of "Pitchfork Ben" kept the job for only a short time. His was hardly a "merit" appointment, as his previous experience had been in plantation management. In 1922 Mears named the station at mile 248.5 after Congressman Charles F. Curry of California, chairman of the Committee on Territories. Curry, a champion of the railroad and Alaska, responded with a warm note of thanks.

The commission tried to keep its public relations fences mended in Alaska, meeting innumerable complaints with patience and prompt investigation. Most territorial criticisms had no foundation in rationality or reality, especially the journalistic and verbal lashings directed at commission officials from Seward. The commissioners winced under blows from the disappointed town eclipsed in importance by Anchorage, but dock improvements and other assistance to Seward mollified it little. The only legitimate criticism against the A. E. C., in Seward or anywhere else, was that it assumed a paternalistic attitude. Anchorage felt the results of the commission's paternalism most keenly. For instance, Mears acted without authority when in 1922 he appointed a board of A. E. C. employees to investigate an Anchorage school official. The board heard witnesses and recorded testimony concerning the official's allegedly homosexual advances to several students. A justifiable concern for the proper education of employees' children having prompted his action, Mears wrote in defense of his intervention. The Anchorage school board, however, had long been an independent agency supposedly immune from such interference.

In general, the railroad enjoyed a good relationship with railbelt residents. It was especially concerned to have the good opinion of the "right thinking people";²⁹ entrepreneurs with some capital, large shippers, commercial organizations in the towns. The commission gained and held that opinion by consulting with businessmen concerning schedules and rates, by maintaining its liberal development policy, and by giving good service under existing conditions. Mears' efforts were rewarded in March 1921, when a rumor swept the railbelt that John Ballaine was to be appointed in his place. Whether Albert B. Fall, the incoming secretary of the interior, intended any changes, or whether the rumor merely billowed up from Ballaine's braggadocio, the territorial reaction was decisive. The Fairbanks Commercial Club, together with Austin E. Lathrop, Thomas C. Price, a territorial legislator, and other prominent Alaskans protested against the idea. Fall did not appoint Ballaine. It might be argued that the reaction was more anti-Ballaine than pro-Mears, or that somebody will always be found to oppose a change. But the protests were positive, stressing the need for continuity and experience in the closing months of the great construction project. The rumor provided the opportunity for a drive against Mears and the commission had there been any will to make one.

The commission's workers persistently criticized their employer. Workmen and stationmen chronically complained of low wages, poor working conditions, mistreatment by superiors, and employment of aliens in preference to citizens — along with a host of other grievances. The commission carefully investigated the complaints, no matter how petty, no matter how base their apparent motivation. In truth, wages and stationmen's compensation on the government road were proportionately lower than on other lines, except for a brief period from late 1921 until April 1922. During that time wages were falling inside and outside Alaska. Mears cut railroad and mine wages about 10 percent effective April 1, 1922. Trainmen often complained of defective, poorly maintained equipment and of safety hazards. The commission's own reports revealed that some of the grumbling was justified. The Panama equipment, although reconditioned, was not new. The narrow gauge from Fairbanks to North Nenana and Chatanika operated with a grab bag of equipment. Loose steps, peeling paint, and automatic couplers of such varying height that cars had to be hand coupled were among the deficiencies on the old TVRR.

Many gripes were grounded in vindictiveness or jealousy or could be readily explained. Wage and equipment complaints, however, could not be. Part of the explanation for proportionately lower wages rests with the commission's long-standing aversion to high pay. Even during the postwar labor shortage it refused back pay to striking miners, although the attorney general had ruled that they could receive it. The management's disinclination to pamper its labor force scarcely explains defective equipment, for no right-minded railroader would court the expensive and demoralizing accidents such rolling stock might induce. The best explanation, apart from disorganization in the shops during the construction phase, is the pressure for economy and swift completion.

By 1919 congressmen were wondering aloud why so little roadbed had been built to a first class standard. Congressman Madden of Illinois, powerful and economy-minded, was unsure of the line's location, but he was sure it was costing money, "more money and more money to continue the construction of a railroad in the clouds."[30] Secretary Payne insisted that the Anchorage-Seward line be brought to a year-round operating condition in the 1920 season. To comply, Mears diverted scarce labor from other tasks. The next year Chairman Curry of the House Committee on Territories urged him to complete the line for through operation at the expense of other work. Always the Department of the Interior and Congress urged economy. Under such conditions, it is not surprising that the railroad's entire physical plant deteriorated.

The commissary and related benefits were a source of employee complaint from the time, in June 1917, that the A. E. C. management restricted purchases at its Anchorage store. During the two years before the restriction, workers and their families at Anchorage could buy clothing and groceries at the commissary for less than retail. Sometimes they paid much less than in the stores on the bluff above the railroad yards. A can of tomatoes cost twelve cents at the commissary, twenty-five cents from a merchant. A fifty-three-cent pound of butter from the commissary saved the purchaser twenty-two cents of the retail price. A shirt costing six dollars "uptown" sold for four at the commissary. Prices were closer on other items, identical on a few, but the overall differences would have appealed to thrifty shoppers. Even before the commissary restricted its operations, the commission's employees began an increasingly determined campaign for what amounted to a commission department store. Under the restricted policy the commissary sold only beef. Firewood and coal were also available through the A. E. C.

Employees argued that Anchorage retail prices were too high. In relation to wages, they were. Whether they were too high in relation to merchants' profits is another matter. The employees tried to show that retail profits were exorbitant by citing the commissary's experience. The Stores Department added 10 percent to its "landed cost" when charging meat to the commissary butcher shop. During 1922 the butcher shop grossed an additional 27½ percent on sales of about $1,000 per month. It made this gross even though it sold beef for about 30 percent below the prices in the one privately operated meat market. The A. E. C. management replied that bookkeeping failed to reflect all costs and that the true gross profit or loss was insignificant. The employees argued that full commissary operation would decrease overhead. But they admitted that merchants still would make more sales to employees because of better service. They hoped for fewer mercantile establishments, each doing business at a lower profit. The verdict on the employees' case has to be "not proven." It is not self-evident. Nor did the railroad test it by reopening the commissary at Anchorage.

The employees voiced other complaints that had more substance. They maintained that the commissary ought to be restored because wage increases given in lieu of commissary privileges were followed by retail price hikes. Charges for dental work were so exorbitant, they said, that employee families took ship for Seattle to have their teeth repaired. The commission should expand its medical staff to include a dentist because employees found it difficult to leave for the two weeks required for treatment and a round-trip ocean voyage. These complaints almost certainly were well founded. For one thing, they were fairly easily affirmed or refuted on the spot. For another, they were made by representatives of the Alaska Railroad Employees' Protective Association, a responsible group formed to lobby for reopening the commissary. Finally, the complaints were made in person to cabinet secretaries Hubert Work and Herbert Hoover during President Harding's trip to Alaska in 1923. Nothing was done about them, for the management preferred the *status quo* to the uncertainties of reducing or increasing employee privileges.

The employees argued that the railroad ought to subsidize them in such a remote, undeveloped location. To this the commission replied that the commissary operated "at considerable expense" only until enough privately owned stores were established to handle the business.[31] Workers should become members of their communities and buy from local merchants. They should not plead for special privileges. The A. E. C. did briefly reopen the Anchorage commissary when grocery shortages developed in the spring of 1919. When, in 1920, prices at Nenana appeared to be climbing beyond all reason, the commissary there was reopened on a one-day-per-week basis. Commissaries remained open at camps on the line throughout the construction phase. The blandishments of the Anchorage Chamber of Commerce and other commercial bodies had little effect on any of these policies.

The employees' crown of martyrdom to high prices might have worn a bit better had none of them abused the commissary privilege. Unfortunately, some employees resold commissary supplies or diverted them to other than personal or family use. One section foreman ordered sugar, currants, and raisins so frequently that he was strongly suspected of making "mule." Even after the store closed in 1917, Anchorage employees with the right connections went on purchasing heavy clothing and groceries from the commissary.

In summary, the commission stands free of most of the charges leveled against it. The A. E. C. was not extravagant. It was not a corrupt organization; indeed, given the wilderness location, the necessary decentralization, and local initiative, it was remarkably free from scandal. The few bizarre exceptions should be viewed against the background of economy, efficiency, dedication, and hard work. The commission often went beyond its appropriations and specific authority in efforts to develop the territorial economy. The source of its failures lay outside its control — the failures had nothing to do with lack of ability, effort, or will. The A. E. C.'s rates were not exorbitant; indeed, they were low by Alaska standards. The rates on coal were so low as to be reasonable in comparison with schedules outside Alaska. The commission was not a partisan operation, although its managers well knew how to play politics in their railroad's behalf. For this realistic, calculated tactic they should be praised, not blamed. And, the commission was firm but not oppressive toward its employees. The commission had the monumental task of building a railroad in a remote, inhospitable wilderness. It drove the rails through. The accomplishment overwhelms the criticisms.

An Alaska Central rotary plow bucks a slide at mile 44 in the Kenai country. Slides, heavy snowfalls, and blizzards were common over much of the Kenai Peninsula. The Alaskan Engineering Commission and The Alaska Railroad inherited the weather conditions along the ACR—ANR right-of-way. *The Alaska Railroad*

An Alaskan Engineering Commission rotary throws a plume of snow as it steams to the rescue of a snowbound passenger train at mile 48. Photograph taken from the train on March 30, 1920. *The Anchorage Historical and Fine Arts Museum*

The snow fleet near the Loop District in the Kenai Peninsula. *Eugene McCracken Collection, University of Alaska Archives*

A rotary steams into Healy, mile 358, 1920. *The Alaska Railroad*

A Russell plow in front of the Curry Hotel, mile 248.5, about 1924. *The Anchorage Historical and Fine Arts Museum*

The snow fleet taking on water at Tunnel, mile 51, in 1946. *The Alaska Railroad*

A snow cut, probably on the Kenai Peninsula during the construction days. *National Archives*

Engine coming through a cut that towers above its smokestack. *The Alaska Railroad*

Rough Roadbed, Tough Transition

Upheavals in management shook The Alaska Railroad in 1923 and 1924. After 1924 the line operated effectively enough, but in an atmosphere of doubts and impermanence marked by labor-management bickerings. The time of troubles did not end until strong-willed, industrious Otto F. Ohlson became general manager in 1928. These were times of irony, as well as agony, for the men involved. The first two reorganizations were intended to be permanent, but the Steese and Landis administrations each lasted less than a year. Noel W. Smith was dispatched to Alaska on temporary duty but stayed on to render four years of highly creditable service. It all began with the Road Commission-Alaska Railroad merger, the president of the road organization being the head of both agencies. The merger was one of several efforts to rationalize the federal bureaucracy in Alaska.

These efforts responded to a mounting dissatisfaction with Alaska's uneven, laggard development. The pressure began with Franklin K. Lane's 1913 call for a local development board. Subsequently, the Department of the Interior and its friends in Congress urged a reorganization of the territorial bureaucracy. The various draft bills established a board comprising major bureau heads and other federal officials who could radically rearrange bureau activity and make other basic decisions subject to the approval of the secretary of the interior. Insofar as these proposals recognized the need for a special, coordinated approach to northern lands, they were enlightened and progressive. Had their sponsors confessed that Alaska required a unique federal policy because of its particularly difficult climate, terrain, and geographical relationships, their candor might have carried the day. Instead, they advanced the specious argument that Alaska was retarded because bureaucratic red tape had frustrated and defeated so many of its pioneers. Their insulting remarks about bureaucratic staff and methods increased the natural fears of bureaus threatened with a loss of their autonomy. From 1914 through the early 1920s, the bureaus worked with their own congressional friends to ward off several development board bills.

The bureaucrats were fearful and jealous of challenges to their tight little empires. Their reactions were human, if less than noble. Nevertheless, they had a shrewder understanding of the potential threats to their integrity than many of their critics. Alfred H. Brooks, the eminent chief of the Alaska branch of the geological survey, approved the consolidation of land and soil activities under a development board but opposed placing some technical services, including his own, with any such administration. A development board might well cut off a technical service from sympathetic professional colleagues in Washington, might combine it with other technical services, or might abolish it altogether in favor of organizing its own group of specialists. Other bureau chiefs held similar opinions about their own operations. There was no guarantee that a local board would be more understanding, responsive, or dynamic than the fragmented bureaus. Even the enthusiastic Lane admitted as much.

While Congress struggled with the development board proposals, the Interior Department tried temporary administrative solutions. John Barton Payne, Lane's successor, established an Alaska Advisory Committee including representatives of his own department, the Post Office Department, the Department of Agriculture, and the Shipping Board. Brooks was its chairman. The committee studied reports, held informal hearings in Seattle, and submitted a report of recommendations for territorial development. Among them was a call for a permanent interdepartmental Alaska committee, to be located in Washington. The committee would include representatives (besides those on the advisory committee) of the departments of war, navy, agriculture, and commerce, with the territorial governor, *ex officio*. It was to be chaired by the Interior Department representative. The departments agreed, and Payne established the committee with President Wilson's approval in December 1920. The committee met occasionally and made recommendations, but lacked authority. The Harding administration continued the organization, renaming it the Alaska Interdepartmental Committee. A local Alaska Council was appointed in 1922. It was as ineffectual as the Washington-based committee. At Work's request, President Harding abolished the interdepartmental committee in April 1923.

Consolidation in the field held more promise than an advisory committee. The railroad, a bureau necessarily concerned with economic development, had figured prominently in several development board schemes. So had the Alaska Road Commission. Early in 1922 Mears believed that consolidation of the two would come under the aegis of the War Department. However, most draft legislation and recommendations urged association under the Department of the Interior. The Harding administration followed that advice, and through a series of orders accomplished the consolidation before the summer of 1923. By May the railroad and the road commission were using each other's men, equipment, and supplies interchangeably. Because only Congress could transfer the road commission to Interior, the two organizations were treated separately for accounting purposes.

James G. Steese directed the merged transportation activities. Compactly built, neatly dressed, and sporting a trim mustache, Steese was, at forty-one, a successful career officer. He had graduated from West Point in 1907 and had served a four-year hitch in Panama during the construction days. After several years of teaching at West Point and forts Riley and Leavenworth, he became the assistant chief of engineers. In 1918 he won a colonelcy and an appointment to the general staff. He was appointed president of the road commission effective July 1920, in the waning months of the Wilson administration. As a Republican under the Harding regime, and as a bachelor without a family to yearn for warmer, softer climes, Steese was admirably fitted for duty in the Far North. He arrived at Anchorage on March 24, 1923, was at his desk two days later, and ceremonially accepted the chairmanship from Mears on the first of May.

From the time of his arrival in Alaska, Steese garnered titles and duties. The administrative merger of the roads and the railroad brought the total to eight tasks cutting across three departments. Among other responsibilities, he was a consulting engineer for the Sixteenth Lighthouse District and the territorial director of public works. Steese claimed quick results from the merger. There was, he wrote, "an immediate speeding up of development work upon a unified plan," with "matters. . .handled promptly upon the ground, or. . .by a single telegram."[1] Six months after he took office, the man who wrote those lines was replaced, and the consolidated operations of railroad and road commission ceased.

Their brief tenure and the railroad's problems bound Steese and his vice-chairman, Major John C. Gotwals, to limited accomplishments. The road's rickety condition was by far the most serious situation. Edes and Mears had poured their appropriations into construction, reconstruction of the doddering Alaska Northern, economic development, and operations. They had made some replacements, but only because fires, floods, snowslides, wrecks, and frost heaves had destroyed some structures or damaged them so severely that they had to be replaced. If a bridge or building withstood these ravages of climate and chance, it was consigned to quiet deterioration. High costs enforced jerry-building, especially north of Broad Pass where climate and soil conditions could undo even careful construction. Riggs had confessed to "makeshift"[2] construction back in 1918, citing ocean and river freight rates higher on concrete than the cost of concrete itself.

The line abounded with examples of makeshift work. Local contractors had cut the railroad's ties, but not always to specifications. Even a well-trimmed spruce tie lasted but five years under the best conditions, and some conditions, like some ties, were far from ideal. On the line's lower reaches the tie hackers could harvest some hemlock, a superior wood with twice the tie life of spruce. As the road advanced northward, the hemlock thinned out. North of Healy (mile 358), where it was uneconomical to ship in bridge framing, the builders were restricted to the native spruce. Some stands of spruce were good, rising sixty feet or more. In poorly drained, swampy areas there were no proud, straight-trunked, pyramidal trees but only dwarfed, stubbly specimens canted by wind and frost heaves. Weary crews hauled what lumber they had to and made do with the rest. Many pilings were undersize and all were untreated. The 800 bridges and trestles were a staggering maintenance problem, for they totaled more than 17 of the railroad's 540 miles. By 1923 most of the timbers showed some decay, especially those in dry soil. Spruce caps, stringers, bridge ties, railings, and braces were sound but badly checked. Only the hemlock timbers were relatively unscathed. The early policy of following rivers and streams at low grade left its legacy — an eroding right-of-way. The engineers had ordered dikes thrown up, but most of these, hastily conceived and built, had been overwhelmed. Glacial waters knifed into unprotected banks, and shards of earth slipped from beneath the rails into roiling streams. At Anchorage, buildings and tracks laid for a construction base poorly served the operating railroad. In Broad Pass the lightly built telegraph line collapsed each year from the weight of snow. The aging 600 class Moguls could carry but 230 tons per train over the grades from Seward to Anchorage. They doubled to haul heavier loads.

The climate dealt staggering blows. For six months every year, men and machines struggled to keep the tracks through the Kenai Peninsula free of ice, snow, and slides. Sometimes a train rumbled through snowplow cuts so deep that they rose above the engine's smokestack. Huge slides carrying boulders or trees that could smash a whirling rotary blade had to be picked and shoveled away by crews of 100 or more men. The most dramatic maintenance headache came not from the snow, but from the soil. Frost heaves, especially in the swampy region from Healy to Fairbanks, could overnight bend rails into wavy shapes like the edge of a cookie cutter. This was caused by frost penetration in the muskeg. As the sun receded behind the peaks of the Alaska Range and cold gripped the ground iron-hard, the water-logged, freezing soil exerted tremendous, but uneven, upward pressures. Along the right-of-way, cleared of insulating snow and natural vegetation, the earth froze as far as ten feet down. Track crews worked through brief days and weird twilights in temperatures eighty or ninety degrees below freezing to "shim up" the rails. They placed wooden blocks between the ties and rails and anchored the rails to gauge with cross rods. Sometimes the rails had to be shimmed day after day until blocks six or eight inches thick rested between tie and rail. When springtime came, the uninsulated roadbed thawed the swamp below and settled into it. Then it was time to pour in gravel, and more gravel, to keep the track above the quivering mass. The violent thrusts worked against bridges, too. Every winter the heaving raised pilings as much as six inches, twisting bridge structures and shoving them off grade. Track crews shimmed the rails by raising or cutting ties, although the better method would have been to shim between stringers and caps. Not enough bridge men were available for the task, nor for backfilling the piers with gravel to prevent heaving. Gotwals topped off the problems with a batch of gloomy statistics. Over the next three years, he wrote late in 1923, the railroad would need a million new ties at a cost of $1,250,000. For renewing bridges and filling in old trestles he estimated $2,000,000. Five light Mikado engines, three river boats, and other equipment would cost $750,000. And so on for a total of $5,300,000.

Active discontent at Anchorage also impeded the new administration. Local unhappiness centered in the work force and in the business community. The two shared some anxieties and, indeed, some personalities, for occupations overlapped in the small, relatively isolated town to a degree incredible in a later, highly specialized age. For instance, the railroad's chief surgeon and its yardmaster were the president and vice-president, respectively, of an Anchorage bank. Disappointment over the railroad's failure to stimulate an economic boom pervaded the town. Force reductions hurt uptown as well as in the yards. Businessmen were unhappy when the overnight passenger stop at Anchorage was canceled and service from Seward reduced to one overnight at the newly opened Curry Hotel. Cancellation of his buffet car concession in favor of a railroad dining car ended the food service operation of an Anchorage resident. Labor chafed under the 10 percent wage reduction of 1922. Tempers among trainmen in passenger service were not soothed when, in July 1923, Steese ordered them into uniforms to be purchased at their own expense. Railroad employees, Governor Scott C. Bone later wrote, displayed "a manifest lack of loyalty and cooperation during the Steese administration."[3]

Some discontents were simmering during the last days of Mears' tenure, while the others probably would have developed had Mears remained. Yet, Mears held the loyalty and trust of many employees, and the reaction against him probably would not have been as severe as it was against the newcomers. Anchorage businessmen respected Mears and knew, through long association, that he would usually deal forthrightly with them. Although he held no brief for Anchorage and did not advance its interests unless he was at the same time aiding the railroad's, the former chairman remembered the town on the mud flats, the early construction boom, and the incorporation. It was a bond of memory and association that insured a sympathetic hearing whenever an "old resident" had a problem or grievance. No such bond existed between the employees, the townspeople, and Steese. He was instead the representative of a Juneau-based agency which had not, until his own appointment, devoted enough money to railroad feeder projects. Soon after Steese arrived, certain employees and Anchorage businessmen hit upon a strategy to deal with him: they would force his replacement with someone more receptive to their wishes. In July, rumors were rife that some Anchorage residents were trying to have Steese removed. Their efforts did not end when Work relieved Steese and ended the consolidated operations. For several years some Anchorageites sought a proscriptive power over the general managership.

Relations between the railroad and its principal town had deteriorated further when, in August, Gotwals stepped before the Anchorage Chamber of Commerce to deliver a plea for community support. The vice-chairman had no gift for the apt phrase. His speech, heavy and blunt, betrayed his bewilderment and hurt over criticisms from Anchorage. He defended the location of the Curry Hotel, although later, in a memorandum, he confessed that it was too small. He regretted the high waters on the Nenana that had carried away two trestles on the Healy coal spur during 1923, but defended pile trestle replacement until funds could be had for a permanent bridge. He explained the railroad's failure to carry through the planned extension of the Anchorage dock by a reference to devastating June floods along the line. The floods had forced him to divert men, equipment, and supplies from the dock program. Furthermore, the dock extension required dredging which could not be economically performed with the present dredge. Gotwals reminded his listeners that even without the extension, the dock received inbound freight for railroad and town and handled the Mayo ore outbound. Then he warned against "misrepresentation" and "false conclusions," saying glumly that the "products of diseased, dishonest, and disgruntled minds will no doubt be continually found here."[4]

Steese recorded some accomplishments despite the deteriorating line, disgruntled employees, and the disaffection of Anchorage. Although Mears made the plans, it was Steese who inaugurated and oversaw the River Boat Service during its first season. He escorted the Harding tour as well as the sixty-six-member congressional party preceding it in June. He also arranged for the railroad's first tourist special, the *Brooklyn Daily Eagle* party, which witnessed the formal dedication of Mt. McKinley National Park in July. In September, Steese arranged a special train and itinerary for Senator Wesley M. Jones of Washington, a partisan of Alaska. Senator Jones, Territorial Delegate Dan Sutherland, and others traveled the railbelt during an investigative tour. By the beginning of the tourist season, Steese had completed negotiations for "The New Golden Belt Line Tour" with Alaska Steam, the Admiral Line, the Copper River railroad, and Galen and Sheldon, auto stage operators on the Richardson Highway. Under the plan, tourists traveled The Alaska Railroad from Seward to Fairbanks, rode in automobiles to Chitina, then boarded the CR & NW for Cordova. If he wished, a traveler could enter Alaska at Cordova and reboard a steamer at Seward. The White Pass line frustrated Steese's efforts to establish an excursion fare under which passengers would board the narrow gauge at Skagway, ride a steamer from Whitehorse to Nenana, and travel The Alaska Railroad to Seward. A few determined tourists made the trip for a $263.70 fare, no small sum in 1923.

Steese dealt successfully with other matters. One involved removing squatters and their buildings from Garden Island, a settlement not then incorporated with Fairbanks although it lay across the Chena River, north of the business district. The squatters were on land needed for a new station and approaches. They delayed and appealed to public opinion, but Steese, tactful and firm, cleared the land before the end of 1923. Steese began the first significant tie renewal program, with 150,000 renewed during the year. He and his staff worked to improve the railroad's freight handling. In all, Steese made a good record during his brief tenure.

By August Steese and his administration were under review at the Departments of Interior and War. When the Seward Chamber of Commerce wrote Work urging him to retain Steese, it received an ambiguous reply. Toward September's close it was evident that some major change was in the offing. Employee problems and the unhappiness at Anchorage did not, by themselves, force Steese's removal. Later general managers weathered storms of local and labor criticism. The railroad and road commission broke apart because little hope existed for a permanent merger. Congress had not, and apparently would not, approve a development board. Other Alaska bureaucrats had probably increased their lobbying against it after the administrative marriage of railroad and road commission. Nor had Congress approved the formal transfer of the road commission to the Interior Department. Congressional reluctance enforced a cumbersome accounting system. Exchanges of supplies and equipment were scrupulously kept and funds periodically transferred. The procedure, almost impossible to manage on a long-term basis, complied with legal injunctions against a bureau's increasing one appropriation at the expense of another. The differing natures of rail and road made for further internal problems. Train operations were geographically confined, and railroad maintenance was a year-round necessity. The road commission's responsibilities were far-flung, but much of its work was intensely seasonal. Thus, their operations were set on different cycles.

Alaska would have gained from the coordinated transportation plans emerging, through time, from the consolidated organizations. Whether one man — Steese or anyone else — could have harmonized their disparate operations is less certain. On September 29, Work ended the suspense and speculation along the railbelt. He announced that he was appointing Lee H. Landis, a veteran railroader and a civilian, to the newly created position of general manager. Steese reassumed the presidency of the Board of Road Commissioners for Alaska, ending an unhappy experiment.

Lee Landis found The Alaska Railroad in a sharp decline and left it on the brink of collapse. The problems that had developed before his arrival contributed to some degree, for the railroad's first civilian general manager faced evident difficulties. Labor continued to be demoralized. Businessmen at Anchorage who had either upheld or opposed the Steese administration spiced their quarrel with fresh acrimony, compounding railbelt suspicions and jealousies. Physically the line was frail. Worn-out equipment cried for replacement. Freight traffic rising on diversions from the White Pass and Yukon River trade and an economic revival jammed the inadequate warehouses and docks at Anchorage and Seward. Secretary Work had circumscribed the general manager's authority with a resident "Committee on Policy of The Alaska Railroad," although the committee's role was but vaguely defined. At the same time, he was urging economy on Landis. The railroad's 1923 revenue was building to $905,942.46 while Landis traveled north. The figure was below Mears' 1921 estimate of $1,170,000 total revenue after completion, but not disastrously short. The real source of red ink was the bloated operating expense — $2,706,788.54.

Despite these problems and pressures, the Landis debacle was a clear-cut case of personal failure. Even after Landis' own actions had intensified the difficulties, his successor righted the railroad and led it through some of its most trying years. Landis failed because he never intended to make The Alaska Railroad a success, but instead planned to make a record for himself at the railroad's expense. His raiding scheme might have succeeded in a mature, stable organization of the type with which he was familiar. The new general manager had been a railroader for more than thirty years. Beginning as a station agent and dispatcher for the Philadelphia and Reading at the age of eighteen, he had held a variety of minor jobs with major systems. He then switched to small lines and was general manager of the Fresno Interurban Railway when the United States entered World War I. After duty with army transportation services in Europe, he became the industrial commissioner of the Western Pacific Railroad System, from which post Work called him to The Alaska Railroad.

Ruggedly handsome, insouciant, a "regular fellow,"[5] and a lavish party-giver, Landis made an excellent first impression. An average three years' service in his previous jobs suggested a streak of instability and opportunism in his personal makeup. A longer acquaintance confirmed it. His cheery, but noncommittal, replies to requests for special rates contrasted with the straight-forward correspondence of Mears and Steese. While his general managership spiraled into crisis, he clumsily attempted to keep the loyalty of Governor Scott C. Bone and other members of the policy committee. While fear and resentment spread among the railroad's employees, he became supercilious and abrupt toward them, sprinkling his inter-office memoranda with phrases such as: "We will not prolong the discussion further" and "Make it snappy!"[6] There was a lot of Babbitry in Lee Landis.

The anomalies in the railroad's operations would have struck most men having years of operating experience. Landis was appalled at some — the hospitals and on-the-line commissaries — without appreciating the Far North context within which they operated. He did pinpoint and correct other, less justified irregularities. These contributions, though few, deserve mention. A change in accounting procedure recognizing the need for an emergency reserve was the most significant. Previously, the railroad's managers had to spend the amount appropriated for each fiscal year within that year or lose the money. During the construction years, the limitation meant little because surpluses could be spent on advance orders or new building, while shortages could be met by cutbacks and pay suspensions. Edes, Mears, and Steese freely transferred funds despite the ostensibly restricted item appropriations. The operating railroad enjoyed no such flexiblity because of closer congressional scrutiny and fewer spending options. Nor could it budget a fund for emergencies or other unplanned expenses. Soon after he arrived in Alaska, Landis secured the policy committee's unanimous recommendation for an annual lump sum appropriation "to remain available until expended,"[7] and followed with his own request to Work for a special maintenance fund. The Budget Bureau established a revolving fund beginning with the 1926 appropriation.

Landis undertook a wide-ranging campaign for tourists. His action was self-serving to the extent that he planned to add the campaign to his short-term laurels. Yet, it was the sort of work that had to be begun and sustained if the railroad expected a steady tourist traffic in the future. Early in 1924 Landis completed the negotiations for an improved "belt line" tour of coastal and interior Alaska. Each complete tour involved 140 passengers, half debarking at Cordova, the rest at Seward, the first group traveling via the CR & NW and Richardson Highway to Fairbanks, while the second rode The Alaska Railroad. The parties then traveled southbound by each other's transportation. The next steamer collected the first group at Seward and the second at Cordova, making ten days' total time in westward and northward Alaska travel. Landis issued a summer schedule with three round trips per week instead of one, a twenty-four-hour through train to Fairbanks, and a special Sunday boat train between Anchorage and Seward. The arrangement allowed for longer stopovers at Anchorage and Fairbanks, but it strained the passenger equipment to capacity. Landis appointed a young woman resident of Juneau to be a tourist agent and sent her on an eastern promotional tour. He named a Dallas, Texas, tour director as a special tourist agent. When the *Pathfinder of Alaska* published a tourism issue, he sent 2,000 copies to "the states."

Landis' economy drive absorbed much of his remaining energies. His cost-cutting campaign was scarcely to his credit, because he really cared little for the efficient and economical operation of The Alaska Railroad. What he did care about was a dramatic short-run cost reduction, the basic ingredient of his superficially good record. Had he wished for economy he would not have recommended a tourist hotel at Mt. McKinley National Park. Nor would he have charged his private telephone to the railroad, a questionable practice later disallowed by the comptroller general. Landis did eliminate many inefficiencies in the course of his economy moves, but these were merely the side effects, not the objects, of his activity. The general manager's actions were those of a man who, when asked to prune a tree, would chop it down instead.

From the first days of his tenure, Landis fired people, especially those he described as holding supervisory jobs. Some of his dismissals were seasonal, but he cut more deeply than that, lopping $27,700 in payroll and 198 employees from the December 1922 figures. A few reductions were justified. During an inspection trip to Nenana, the chief clerk found an unkept dormitory and fired the janitor on the spot. Landis dismissed a few line supervisors who were allegedly involved in employment grafting. Soon he was firing dissenters who questioned his policy decisions, replacing them with men whose chief qualification was personal loyalty to him.

Landis' personnel policy was the most apparent part of an economy program that reached into all phases of the railroad's operation. His most important savings scheme was, unfortunately, the most dubious. By slashing his maintenance expenditures for 1924 and 1925, he intended to reduce drastically the deficit for those years. Then, by carrying over his unexpended 1925 maintenance allowance, he planned for a deficit-free year in 1926. He would not ask for a 1926 appropriation and would show a dramatic improvement over the $1,800,000 deficit of three years before. As Landis' successor phrased it, there would be a "post mortem" when the ravaged railroad collapsed, but by then Landis would have realized his probable purpose — "another and better position."[8] The general manager's scheme was as unlawful as it was physically dangerous. Prior to 1926, the only way he could have held over unexpended funds was to show, falsely, that the money had been spent while it was really being kept in reserve. Noel W. Smith, his successor, believed that Landis would have hired accountants to arrange the books in the desired manner.

Landis began no development program commensurate with his cost-cutting moves. His few promotional rates — on flour from the Tanana Valley, for instance — had no appreciable effect on tonnage. Neither did his elimination of the fifty-cent-per-ton wharfage charge on export coal at Seward. Landis openhandedly entertained railbelt businessmen, but the goodwill evaporated in the absence of more substantial assistance. He did suggest reducing local rates 20 percent immediately. Work was not convinced by his assurance of increased tonnage and took no action. The rate recommendation could be excused on the ground of inexperience, but after January 1924, Landis knew that the railroad faced a serious "backhaul" problem. "Our traffic on this line is practically all loads for certain kinds of cars one way, and empty back," Trainmaster Cunningham informed him.[9] The harsh truth was that the country produced virtually nothing to haul in the boxcars returning to Seward. Except for an occasional load for a coal car, there was nothing to put in the cars going from Anchorage back to the Moose Creek coal mines. Statistics told the story: in 1923 loaded freight car miles were 1,340,110; empty car miles a huge 731,651.

Landis' efforts to increase revenues and reduce expenses through improved practices did have some useful results. He forced station agents to make the proper demurrage charges for cars parked on company sidings, ending what amounted to subsidies for a few Alaska businesses. He enforced more careful inspection and payment on tie contracts. But none of these or other changes made much money for the railroad. His recommendations for a 40 percent wage increase and for reopening the Anchorage commissary were panicky reactions to a threatened strike in May 1924. Perhaps they would have won labor's temporary allegiance, but they certainly would have undermined the economy drive. Landis' immediate call for new equipment was understandable in view of the patchwork locomotive boiler maintenance of past years, the relatively few passenger cars, and the condition of the riverboat *Davis*. The new equipment would not have interfered with his longer-range plans for an appropriation-free 1926.

Landis really wanted economy, nothing more. He got results — a $608,311.66 reduction in expenses during fiscal year 1924 compared with the previous fiscal year. He also begot opposition to his reductions and soon turned to firing for reasons for policy as well as economy. One of the first to be discharged over policy was the bridge engineer, who vigorously protested Landis' eliminating his maintenance funds and cancelling his requisitions for replacement materials. "There is a serious condition to be faced," the bridge engineer warned, predicting "disaster" if the funds were not restored.[10] Shortly after he issued his warning, the bridge engineer was relieved of his job. Landis continued to press his economy drive. His curt memoranda, his egotism, his arbitrary firings, and his attempt to build an organization loyal to himself, plunged his labor relations toward disaster.

Landis might have fired more managerial people sooner had it not been for the restraining presence of the policy committee. Work established this curious organization on October 30, 1923, a month after he appointed Landis to be general manager. He named Governor Scott C. Bone chairman, and as members Landis, Burton H. Barndollar, the railroad's examiner of accounts, and John C. Gotwals, who stayed on for a time at the post of chief engineer. Ostensibly the committee was to act somewhat as a board of directors, "to strengthen the hands of the General Manager and contribute in fullest measure possible to the successful administration and operation" of the railroad.[11] Yet, it had no real role, for, as Barndollar wrote, Work was responsible for major policy, while Landis made up the policies necessary to daily operation. The committee had no financial powers or other authority. Further, Work compromised Landis' control over his own subordinates. By appointing Barndollar and Gotwals he made two key men, the railroad's operating and financial chiefs, responsible to himself. Work understood institutional organization and would not have violated its principles unintentionally. Probably he never fully trusted Landis and intended for the two old Alaska hands and the governor to keep an eye on him.

The policy committee met from time to time and considered agendas which Landis submitted in advance. Usually it accepted his advice, but the relationship between the general manager and his committee soon was only superficially cordial. Landis' December recommendation for rate reductions and his later request to reopen the Anchorage commissary contravened committee decisions. By mid-March Bone was questioning the committee's value. Although he agreed with Landis' objectives, Bone wrote to Work, the committee was without authority in the "present circumstances"[12] and should be dissolved to save its members from criticism. Work's vigorous reply directed the committee to stay on the job, hold regular meetings, and send minutes and reports to him. At about the same time, Work, the former postmaster general, borrowed trustworthy inspectors from his old department and sent them to Alaska to investigate Landis. Their report confirmed a growing demoralization, although their investigation had a positive effect. It caused Landis to loosen up his maintenance budget and spend some money on the roadbed.

Landis forced the crisis at the end of June when he fired three department heads without notice. The most flagrant dismissal was of the capable trainmaster, J. T. Cunningham. Landis replaced Cunningham with his chief clerk and factotum, one E. Van Gundy. He could not relieve Gotwals and Barndollar, protected as they were by their appointments to the policy committee. The new careers of Van Gundy and the other replacements were destined to be brief. As soon as Landis issued his dismissal circulars, Barndollar wired the news to Work. The secretary immediately ordered the general manager to restore the dismissed men and then to "make no changes in personnel until authorized by me." Landis returned Cunningham and the others to duty amid acclaim for Work's prompt action. "Employees had reached breaking point," the usually calm and cautious Barndollar wired Bone.[13] But Landis refused to follow the literal meaning of the secretary's telegram. Instead, he began an orgy of firing, discharging lower-level employees in droves. Section gangs normally six or seven men strong were cut to two or three. The shock was so great that even after Landis' departure, section foremen were afraid to ask for new men for fear of their own jobs.

The telegrams from Bone to Work and from Barndollar to both men assumed an edge of panic. On July 5 Barndollar asked Bone to take charge of the railroad, but the governor had already recommended to Work that a full-time civilian employee be placed in control. On the seventh Work resolved the crisis. He appointed Noel W. Smith, a veteran executive with the Pennsylvania Railroad, to be "Special Assistant to the Secretary of the Interior." He told Smith to get to the bottom of the trouble and to recommend the necessary changes. Landis continued his frenzied firings while Smith traveled toward his new assignment. It was denouement for Landis after Smith arrived at Seward on July 27. The special assistant ran the railroad through Landis for one month, hoping that the general manager, repudiated by his superiors and his subordinates, would do the graceful thing and resign. Landis stubbornly clung to his job. Smith assumed active charge on August 26, directing department heads to report to himself. He gave Landis a humiliating order "to perform such duties as may be assigned."[14] Two days later the general manager sent his resignation to the secretary of the interior.

Whatever his private feelings, the public Lee Landis remained brash, assertive, and less than candid to the end. When he arrived in Seattle, he denied rumors of mismanagement, denied that he had organized "wild parties," denied that he had resigned. He had asked for a leave of absence, he said, and was on his way to a vacation in Texas. He blamed everything on former employees and Alaska businessmen "unwilling to face the railroad's lower post-construction expenditures." The railroad's condition "should require no apologies whatever," he said, "and I'm not here to make any."[15] His resignation was effective November 10, 1924.

Alaska Railroad executives hoped that sublime scenery would attract tourists, but the railroad's tourist promotion was a breakeven business at best until after World War II. Here a passenger train grinds through the Loop, May 1949. *The Alaska Railroad*

Mount McKinley, "Denali," from mile 228. *The Alaska Railroad*

A tourist party of the 1920s reboards after a stop in the Loop District. *Alaska Historical Library*

Tourists in the Loop District, May 1949. *The Alaska Railroad*

Brill car and trailer at McKinley Park station, late 1930s. The bus belonged to the Mt. McKinley Park Tourist and Transportation Company, a private concern. *The Alaska Railroad*

Passenger train at McKinley Park, July 1938. *The Alaska Railroad*

A tour party views the Healy River coal veins, Suntrana, 1924. *The Alaska Railroad*

A tourist special arrives at Fairbanks, late 1920s.
Charles Bunnell Collection, University of Alaska Archives

An auto tourist party at Fairbanks in the 1920s.
Reuel Griffin Collection, University of Alaska Archives

Mile 18 on the Richardson Highway, about 1924. An auto tourist fleet drawn up to a typical roadhouse. Auto tourist companies on the Richardson from Valdez to Fairbanks both cooperated and competed with The Alaska Railroad. *The Alaska Railroad*

Noel Smith to the Rescue

Noel Smith came to The Alaska Railroad intending to stay for a few months. He remained four years. During that time he lifted the organization out of near-chaos, forged an operating railroad, and established many of the policies usually associated with his successor, Otto F. Ohlson. Smith's practices emerged from his thirty-one years' experience on the Pennsylvania System. His political and economic conservatism was leavened, usually, by reasonableness and sincerity. The grey-haired, bespectacled Smith could be slyly humorous, but he rarely unbent to his managerial subordinates. They found him a dignified, reserved, and dedicated railroad man. The train and enginemen thought of him, with some justification, as an erratic, arbitrary stuffed shirt. Labor relations were Noel Smith's Achilles heel. Yet, he inspired so much confidence in Secretary of the Interior Hubert Work that Work rarely overruled Smith's recommendations.

Smith's assumptions about the railroad and its territory helped to shape the line's destiny. First, he acknowledged the secretary of the interior's right to set policy and prescribe the limits of the general manager's freedom of action. For a general manager to attempt to circumvent or evade the secretary's policies and restraints was folly, because without the mutual trust and cooperation of secretary and general manager there could be no real improvement in the railroad's condition. Second, he followed a policy of strict economy. It would be wrong to interpret his attitude as mere parsimony, for Smith was eager to spend money on permanent improvements. His "estimate for completion" was a staggering $11,878,781.30 to be spent on new engines, rolling stock, bridges, and betterments in roadbed, yards, and appliances. To his mind such expenditures were true savings because they reduced maintenance costs.

Third, Smith believed that The Alaska Railroad should not subsidize territorial economic development. He opposed, not always successfully, the practice of spur-building to prospect mines. He reluctantly approved other subsidies, such as guaranteeing the payroll of a private firm in case of immediate, direct benefit to the operation or maintenance of the railroad. Assistance to tie contractors, themselves chronically underfinanced, was such an instance. Certainly Smith was not hostile to development. He offered special rates on mining machinery and local products and was sympathetic to development schemes involving reindeer, birch timber, and metal ores. He refused his enthusiasm to promoters who were "inexperienced" and "more or less visionary."[1] He argued that The Alaska Railroad, by operating at a heavy deficit, was already funneling a sizeable, indirect federal subsidy into the territory. The territory's businessmen should acknowledge that fact. They should cease badgering the railroad for rate reductions. "I think you will agree with me," he wrote to W. F. Thompson of the *Fairbanks Daily News-Miner*, "no country can be really prosperous or make substantial progress if it does not pay its transportation costs."[2]

Fourth, as a corollary to the third proposition, Smith was less interested in explosive economic growth that would produce a burst of tonnage than he was in modest, but sure, development. For instance, the Fairbanks Exploration Company's shipments of machinery and pipe for its large gold dredging operations briefly increased the railroad's tonnage and revenues. They also increased operating expenses and bred difficulties such as derailments of overburdened narrow gauge cars on the Chatanika branch. When the shipments were completed and tonnage declined, Smith had to explain to the secretary of the interior. It was better to have the less spectacular, but steadier, revenue from maintenance and subsistence items for power plant, dredges, and crews.

Fifth, Smith was firmly convinced that, so long as he remained at the head of the road, he should make the basic decisions, subject only to Interior Department policies. He resented real or imagined interference, especially from trainmen. His hostility was a compound of his feelings of insecurity and administrative isolation, his doubts about the abilities of many administrative subordinates, and his archaic attitude toward labor relations. So Smith forged a tightly centralized organization with himself in control. The effect on the rather loosely joined railroad might have been stifling. It was not. For all his dignity and reserve, Smith asked for advice, learned quickly, developed real respect for the capabilities of some department heads, and retreated when proven wrong.

Of course, Smith would not have survived in his job had most of his ideas diverged from those of the Coolidge administration. In President Coolidge's view, Alaska was an economically sluggish place where one white person in eleven battened on the federal payroll, while most of the other ten coveted a government job. More than enough federal money went there as it was. Neither Alaska's prospects nor the quality of its population justified an increase. Smith repeatedly urged larger appropriations for rebuilding the railroad. The general manager had to live with a different philosophy of federal spending.

The relationship between Smith and his superior, Work, set the frame for developments on the railroad. The secretary supervised Smith more closely than he had Landis. He required a weekly "Friday letter" from Smith in addition to the regular monthly and annual reports. In the Friday letters the general manager set down his candid judgments on men and events within and without his organization, along with routine operating and maintenance information. Work acknowledged many Friday letters, often routinely, sometimes with suggestions and encouragement. On February 5, 1925, the secretary approved a detailed definition of responsibilities between himself and Smith. Under the terms of this statement, Work required his approval for policy changes, construction projects over $10,000, changes in train service, appointments to jobs paying $200 per month or more, raises of over $300 per year, and significant rate changes, among other matters. In an emergency the railroad head could take action and inform the secretary later.

At the same time that Work drew his lines of control more tightly, he often reassured Smith of his support. "Your administrative actions up there have given me the greatest confidence," he wrote in October 1924. On December 19 he appointed Smith general manager, which office the railroader had filled in fact since late August. The following summer, when rumors circulated that Smith might return to the Pennsylvania Railroad, Work urged him to "give it out that you have been asked to continue" to "quiet those malcontents." Still later, when Smith and the head of the railroad hospital had a policy disagreement, Work wrote: "Supremacy must lie with one, and I cast my vote for you."[3]

Closing the port at Anchorage was one of Smith's earliest, most controversial decisions. It required less than Work's active support, but the secretary did assent to the closing in the face of local pressure to keep it open. The Anchorage dock was one of several costly millstones hanging from the necks of The Alaska Railroad's managers. It chafed the managers, too, because the railroad lost money—a net $28,600 per year by its own estimate — to steamships moving freight to Anchorage. During the open season of some seven months, the steamship companies hauled certain freight to the Cook Inlet port more cheaply than the railroad could carry it from Seward over heavy grades. Even with their high local rates to Anchorage, the steamers could better the through rates from Seward, for the through rates were set to compensate the railroad for its difficult haul over Kenai Peninsula. More galling to the railroad managers was the fact that they maintained the dock and dock forces for steamship use. The railroad received wharfage and transfer fees which more than paid expenses, but they were much less than the potential income of the line haul from Seward. The obvious move was to close the Anchorage dock to "all water traffic" and force all freight over the "water and rail" route from Resurrection Bay.

The simple solution cut across conflicting interests and was bound to appear stupid or venal to somebody. Moreover, the solution was simple but its implementation was not. Smith and J. T. Cunningham, the superintendent of transportation, were well aware of the interests affected and of the complexities involved. They were bound to consider but one interest, the interest of Congress and the Interior Department in increasing the railroad's net earnings and reducing its deficit. They intended to damage other interests as little as possible and showed as much concern for them as they could, consistent with shifting the freight from "all water" to "water and rail."

Smith overrode the desires of Anchorage businessmen and consumers when he decided to close the port, for there was no doubt that freight costs to the Anchorage public would rise. Cunningham estimated the increase at $5,000 annually, no small sum at mid-1920s price levels for a community of two thousand. According to his figures, the extra charge would be no more than ½ cent per item on canned goods — cold comfort to the housewife who bought hundreds of cans per year. The Cunningham calculations probably were too high by about 25 percent. They were based on the average differences of 57 percent between freight charges per ton on the weight/measurement system *versus* the straight weight basis, and not on a re-billing of actual shipments to Anchorage via "all water." A re-billing would have shown a lower percentage via "all water" and weight/measurement. The Anchorage merchants shipped most light, bulky items — expensive via steamship — by "water and rail" on a straight weight basis. They shipped heavy items and those few commodities which the steamships carried on a straight weight basis by "all water." These tactics reduced the percentage of expensive "measurement tons" via steamship substantially below Cunningham's calculations. Cunningham accepted the higher percentage because it gave him a dual advantage. He artificially inflated both the costs of steamship freight to Anchorage and of the anticipated rail revenue, thus strengthening the arguments for closing the port. At the same time, he falsely inflated the new freight costs to Anchorage, but that was an unavoidable consequence of his overly optimistic revenue projection. The true costs brought no joy to Anchorage in any event.

At the same time that he closed the dock, Smith made some overtures to the Anchorage interests. Special commodity rates were the most important. The least satisfactory, from the Anchorage viewpoint, was his effort to establish a community of interest between the railroad and the town. Cunningham assembled figures to show that the railroad distributed about $110,000 each month at Anchorage in wages and purchases, receiving but $7,700 monthly in freight and passenger revenues. Yearly steamship outlays at Anchorage, including wages and purchases by crews, were about $7,000, while the steamers earned well over ten times their expenses — $95,287.57 during fiscal year 1924. Anchorage's duty was clear: it should support the railroad, the economic pillar of the community. What was clear to Smith and Cunningham remained opaque to the Anchorage merchants. They told a railroad agent who interviewed them that savings on freight rates went to development or other good uses. Any increase in the railroad forces needed to haul Anchorage's freight from Seward would benefit mostly the railroad commissary.

Some of Smith's actions were more soothing. He ordered the existing dock maintained "in reasonable physical condition,"[4] even though no railroad employees would be working there. The dock would be available in case large shipments of coal, ore, or other heavy commodities seemed likely during the open season. It would be ready if freaks of weather or accidents blocked the railroad south of Anchorage for an extended period. Anyone who wished to use the dock could do so provided he paid all of the costs involved, including dockage, warehouse, and switching charges, and employed his own forces to handle the freight. Later, in the spring of 1927, Smith and the Anchorage City Council agreed to share the costs of a supplementary city dock at the mouth of Ship Creek for small boats trading in the Cook Inlet area. This additional dock was completed in the fall, but the council disapproved of its construction and refused to pay.

Smith made his decision to close the port in the autumn of 1924. He accepted Cunningham's analysis, already discussed, in favor of diverting the traffic via Seward. To strengthen his position still more, he instructed Cunningham to charge depreciation against the dock revenues, making the dock the only railroad facility thus burdened. Depreciation turned what would have been a $3,133.64 credit into a loss of $2,116.36. Rates and related matters formed the core of the closure. The railroad and steamship companies agreed that rates to Anchorage via Seward would have to be lowered, but no consensus was reached about how the reductions should be shared. At a series of conferences in Seattle during early 1925, Cunningham (joined later by Smith) and the traffic managers of the steamship lines plucked agreement from the welter of special interests. Basically, the water lines abandoned their higher Anchorage rates and accepted lower divisions on all but the first four classes of freight as far north as Wasilla. They increased their divisions on the first four classes, but joined with the railroad on new low commodity rates on merchandise traditionally cheaper by water, including building paper, newsprint, explosives, and cement. The railroad covered selected rate reductions and the commodity rates with general increases in its class rates.

Smith was wise to close the Anchorage dock. It was expensive to maintain even though it produced a modest surplus. The railroad received far less revenue from dock fees and charges than it did from a train haul on the same tonnage. Smith reasonably contended that the dock was maintained largely for the convenience of the steamship companies. He was trapped by the transportation illogic of the long and difficult track from Seward, so vulnerable to "short haul" by ship. The possibility of a better escape, a port on Portage Bay (Passage Canal) to bypass the line through the rugged Kenai Peninsula, fascinated him. Unfortunately, that route was not an immediately available solution. Under the circumstances, Smith acted in the best manner he could to protect his railroad's interests.

Smith was several months free of the port negotiations when another relationship between railroad and steamships underwent a series of changes. A contract with the steamship companies for handling railroad freight and passengers had been part of that relationship since 1920. In November 1922, when the Alaskan Engineering Commission advertised for bids on ocean transportation for 1923, it offered an exclusive contract in hopes of a response from some company new to the Alaska trade. No such bid materialized, despite assurances from territorial officials that it would. As usual, the only bid was a joint one submitted by Alaska Steam and the Admiral Line. After extended negotiations, in February 1923 the railroad and the steamer lines agreed on $12.50 a ton weight/measurement for most railroad freight, 50 cents below the 1922 level. The charges were the same to Seward or Anchorage, in contrast to the commercial rates. The companies continued the 25 percent rate reduction for railroad employees and reduced their through rate divisions to Wasilla and stations north. In return, the companies demanded the exclusive right to ship all railroad freight. To this end the contract provided for the routing of all railroad freight via Puget Sound and prevented the railroad from purchasing material at "delivered in Alaska" prices. The solicitor of the Interior Department objected to such a deviation from government practice, but the steamship companies demanded the exclusive arrangement as the price for their concessions. Another clause prevented the railroad from sharing fully in special reductions of commercial rates. With all its disadvantages, government officials admitted that the contract offered superior service at less cost than any other available means. Through November 1923, the arrangement saved the railroad $53,578.81 from commercial rates.

Contract negotiations in 1923 and 1924 reflected further changes in the railroad's status and its relations with the steamer lines. The companies objected to continuing the contract at all, principally because the railroad was no longer in the construction stage. As an operating railroad it should pay full tariff rates, they argued. After heavy pressure from the Interdepartmental Alaska Traffic Board, formed to rationalize government shipping to the territory, the companies agreed to a rate of ten dollars per ton on railroad equipment. In return, they demanded an exclusive contract and full rates on most commissary supplies. Both General Manager Landis and C. E. Dole, chairman of the traffic committee, considered the agreement a bargain.

This was the immediate background of the 1924 contract in effect when Noel Smith took charge of The Alaska Railroad. Burton K. Wheeler, Robert M. LaFollett's Progressive party running mate in 1924, attacked the agreement during a Seattle speech late in the campaign. Wheeler's attack probably did not influence Smith because the politician railed against "collusion"[5] with the steamship companies, making charges identical to those of James Wickersham and John Ballaine, who was the Progressive party campaign manager in Washington state. Rather, Smith disliked the exclusive clause preventing shipments of opportunity on other vessels. He did extend the contract through 1925. Late in that year he wrote to John H. Bunch, Alaska Steam's traffic manager, that the railroad would insist upon the right to move freight on government ships. Bunch held firmly for an exclusive contract. Smith then let the agreement lapse at the end of 1925.

Two decisions, one by the attorney general's office, the other by the comptroller general, also affected rail-steamer relationships. In June 1924 the attorney general ruled against the railroad's giving out free passes to officers of other transportation lines. According to the ruling, the enabling act of 1914 did not grant to the government line the right to distribute passes, a right enjoyed by privately owned railroads. The decision worked a hardship on employees of The Alaska Railroad, who had been using their reciprocally granted passes on transcontinental lines. It served as an excuse for the steamship companies to refuse to renew their 25 percent passenger discounts. Even after Congress, heeding the pleas of Smith and Work, restored the annual passes, the companies insisted on Alaska railroaders paying full fare.

The next year the comptroller general issued a ruling in effect voiding part of the last, 1925 rail-steamer freight contract. The comptroller general held that payment for any shipment of the railroad's freight beyond Seward would be based on the steamship's division of the through rate. Ever since the railroad project began, its "company" freight had moved on the steamer's local, or port-to-port, weight/measurement rates. Even after the joint through, straight-weight basis was adopted in 1922, the water shipments of railroad freight continued on the contract local rates, which were frequently higher. It was unfair to ask the railroad to pay a high local rate to steamship companies on goods moving beyond Seward if the steamer proportion of the through rate were less. On the other hand, if the railroad could choose between Seward and an inland destination, it would bill its shipments to take advantage of the lowest rate, depending upon the commodity. That is, the railroad would ship either via local rate to Seward, or by the steamer division of the through rate to some other station, whichever was cheaper. Because the railroad could use most of what it shipped at many points along its line, it would be difficult for the steamship companies to dispute the billing. In any case, after the expiration of the 1925 rail-steamer contract, the steamship companies could not force the railroad to ship on local rates. The railroad would be obligated, in the interests of its own operating economy, to use selective billing.

Other government agencies might lack the railroad's knowledge of the lowest rate on each commodity. However, the comptroller general's ruling embraced them as well. It insisted that all government freight bills be settled for the lesser charge irrespective of the destination of a shipment. The comptroller general, in other words, demanded an advantage for government agencies not available to commercial shippers — to enjoy the lowest rate regardless of destination. Both findings cost the steamer lines money. The first, concerning the railroad, was reasonable, but federal payment of the lowest rate under all circumstances was arbitrary and unfair. The Alaska Line refused at first to accept the comptroller general's settlements, but when he stood firm, the line relented on April 4, 1927. Smith's position throughout was that the railroad should enjoy the lowest rate open to any other shipper. Steamship executives who came to him for sympathy found little comfort in his attitude.

Despite differences and protracted negotiations, both Smith and Bunch affirmed the cordiality of their relationship. The changes in that relationship were the marks of the railroad's growth. They reflected, too, the changing expectations of Congress and the executive. Congressional threats to curtail or cease the railroad's operations worried Smith. Perhaps they worried him too much, for there was no real threat of closing the railroad. Congressional rhetoric was spirited but superficial: "Pull up the rails and make a highway of it," snorted Congressman Arthur M. Free during a Seattle interview in late August 1925.[6] Free, a California representative, had visited the territory as a member of the committee on the merchant marine and fisheries. His knowledge of matters maritime failed him in matters terrestrial. Unfortunately for his reputation as an analyst, Free argued that the railroad served a mere 5,000 persons and that Alaska coal was of poor quality. The first statement was not true and the second required some qualification. His blast touched off a furor within Alaska and outside of it. Editorials and statements in support of the railroad and Alaska's promising future filled newspaper columns. An October meeting of the Seattle Chamber of Commerce cheered a satirical "campaign speech" by a character representing Free, who was made to say, "The Alaska Railroad is no good to California, let's tear it up." Work reassured Smith that Free's ideas "may be dismissed from discussion," and Smith himself told the press that they "should not be taken seriously."[7]

In the aftermath of the Free episode, Smith wrote out a long analysis for Work, speculating on the options to the current operations: abandoning all or part of the railroad, converting a portion of the right-of-way to a truck highway, ceasing to run during the winter, and so on. It was easy enough to point out the absurdities in Free's arguments. Part-year operation would save rail expenditures but would increase retail prices and inventories. A highway would be extremely expensive to build and maintain, and trucking would be costly. The railroad had been formally completed for but two years, scarcely sufficient time for a true test of its merits. Smith recommended continuing the through, year-round operation, and there was no doubt about Work's accepting that recommendation.

Yet, Smith was worried and disconsolate. Free's attack was serious enough as a symptom of Congress' displeasure with railroad deficits. Worse, Work trimmed his sails to congressional breezes and requested less than Smith wished for permanent improvements. Smith saw the railroad on a treadmill of high maintenance charges forced on it by temporary wooden construction replaced with more cheap, temporary construction. He wanted funds for filling trestles, building steel bridges, and ballasting. He argued time and again that money spent on permanent improvements reduced maintenance costs. In the long run, permanent improvements were the only way to insure economy, safe operation, and dependable service on The Alaska Railroad. Not a visionary or an extravagant man, Smith maintained that all he wished for was a sound railroad. The traffic, he admitted, would not justify building to the standards of a first class line. A private railroad would have sold bonds for funds to improve its facilities, while Smith had to appeal to stubborn appropriations committees. The congressmen usually questioned the general manager fairly, if closely, but they were unwilling to appropriate much money for a railroad already losing one million dollars and more each year. It was understandably difficult for them to grasp the argument that an enterprise deeply in the red would eventually improve if it substantially increased its deficits for the next several years. Central Alaska's narrow, modest economic advance, on which the railroad's financial improvement really depended, did nothing for Smith's case. When Work refused to support him, Smith was doomed to small capital expenditures. It was one of the few issues seriously dividing the two men.

The railroad's relationships with other governmental officials also were strained at times. The comptroller general, John R. McCarl, was the most exasperating appointed public official with whom the railroad had to deal. Smith accused McCarl of fiscal policy-making through his decisions. His charge was well founded, for McCarl injected himself into an extraordinary number of the railroad's financial dealings. Not only did he determine whether government shippers would pay local or through steamship rates, he also stopped other government agencies in Alaska from shipping their freight free over the railroad after June 30, 1926. Those two decisions may have been unwarranted meddling, but they improved the railroad's financial picture.

Smith found other decisions less appealing. When the comptroller general required all agency officials to purchase railroad tickets under most circumstances, deputy marshals stopped riding trains unless they were traveling to serve a warrant or traveling with a prisoner. As a result, bootlegging throve along the right-of-way. The change irritated Smith, but it could be defended in the name of fiscal and administrative integrity. Other decisions were simply literal and petty. The comptroller general's office insisted on following the letter of purchasing regulations even when the regulations made it difficult to buy the employees' preferred brands of food for the commissaries. The comptroller general held up the railroad's payment to the J. G. Brill Company for a service specialist who accompanied the first Brill gasoline car on its trial runs in Alaska. He insisted that the arrangement was not in the contract and that the specialist had performed the duties of the general manager. The railroad replied that the specialist had been retained because the car had been damaged in disassembly for shipment. His check on its performance was of great value. Any notion that he was performing the duties of the general manager was preposterous. The General Accounting Office relented after three months of argument. In another instance the comptroller general refused to allow payment for rubber boots for an emergency crew even though the men could not have been hired unless the boots had been provided. Special legislation was necessary in this case and in several similar instances. Finally, the comptroller general's office insisted upon certified authority that all who signed contracts on behalf of the railroad be authorized to do so. The railroad signed large numbers of contracts at several locations and at various administrative levels with ever-changing personnel. Meeting the comptroller general's demands required heavy paperwork from the railroad's accounting office.

Smith's other serious quarrel with federal action arose when the army withdrew its detachment of troops from the barracks in the railroad yards. The company from the 7th Infantry Brigade had guarded the yards since construction days. On December 4, 1926, the troops assembled at the barracks for the last time. Smith opposed their removal and was especially anxious because they left during one of his periodic crises with labor. His objections were unavailing. The Anchorage removal was part of a determined War Department policy to abandon most of the posts and barracks in Alaska.

Relationships with other federal agencies improved over those of previous railroad administrations. Smith, no empire builder, so evidently sincere in his dealings with other arms of the government, inspired little jealousy. The general manager wished for the railroad to give maximum service at fair compensation. At the same time, he was anxious to keep it out of new activities such as general fire fighting, for which it lacked a specific appropriation. In general, discussions with the Post Office over mail contract rates, with the Forest Service over fire prevention, and with the United States marshals over bootlegging, were carried on without acrimony.

The railroad maintained its multitude of relationships in Alaska and made many contributions to the territory during Smith's tenure. He supported, as had the A. E. C. and Landis before him, a project to develop a power site on the Eklutna River near Anchorage. The railroad and Anchorage would have to be the principal customers of any such project. Smith was willing to keep the railroad's aging generators in emergency reserve should hydroelectricity fail. Anchorage opted for hydroelectricity, and the power station was built. In another power matter, the railroad reassumed operation of the Nenana power plant on December 1, 1925. The railroad had leased the plant to Nenana to 1922, conforming to the policy of placing federal operations in other hands whenever possible. But the dwindling town failed to make the operation a financial success.

The Alaska Railroad played a critical role during the famed diphtheria epidemic at Nome in January and February 1925. Public attention riveted on the dog team relay dash carrying the antitoxin — man and malemute racing against time through the frozen North. The contributions of others were less well known. Dan Sutherland, the territorial delegate, received word of the epidemic at Washington, D.C. He requested help from Smith, who was also at Washington. Smith wired the purchasing agent in Seattle to telegraph the chief surgeon at Anchorage, who was in turn instructed to place diphtheria serum on board the train for Nenana. The antitoxin arrived at Nenana the next day, on January 27, and was transferred to the dog team.

As part of its larger concern for the territory, the railroad assisted in conservation efforts. In February 1927 Smith secured an executive order protecting beaver and muskrat at certain locations along the right-of-way. He wished for rail travelers to see the animals. Beaver and muskrat thus protected would provide breeding stock for other areas depleted by overtrapping. The same order secured a small wildlife refuge around the Curry Hotel. A year later the railroad hauled a group of bison from Seward to Fairbanks for the Alaska Game Commission. Smith waived freight charges on the shipment.

Important as these external relationships were, however, Smith considered them of less moment than the railroad's internal crises. The labor situation was the worst of them. Except for the strikes and agitations of the early years, The Alaska Railroad had been relatively untroubled by serious labor disputes. In general, employment practices were those of private railroads, not those of other government agencies. Neither operating nor clerical employees had Civil Service status. On April 1, 1920, the railroad and its trainmen and enginemen reached an agreement governing pay rates and operating rules. Labor's position eroded after that. The A. E. C. cut wages some 10 percent in the spring of 1922. The railroad also began charging men for overnight quarters formerly occupied for free. Steese, then Landis, had insisted on uniforms and improved performance with no increase in pay. Some prices had advanced. The reduced steamship fare was canceled in 1924. Working out these accumulated grievances would have tried the patience of a general manager well disposed toward labor. Noel Smith was not well disposed.

Smith's view, that management should run the railroad with a free hand, clashed with twentieth century realities and with the aspirations of his operating employees. Within a few months of his arrival at Anchorage, the employee representatives asked for a wage increase. They protested the firing of a telegrapher for, as they alleged, union activity. Smith thought a strike was likely and asked the War Department's cooperation in alerting the troops at Anchorage. There was no strike, no threat to government property. Smith, Work, and representatives of the railroad brotherhoods reached their first settlement at Washington during the winter of 1924-25. The January 1925 agreements granted a pay increase and unionization. Men in the train and engine service and telegraphers were organized into the Brotherhood of Railroad Trainmen, the Brotherhood of Locomotive Firemen and Enginemen, the Order of Railway Conductors, and the Order of Railroad Telegraphers. The railroad also agreed to a variant of the dual system of compensation for the train and engine service used on most railroads in the United States. Smith did not record what he thought of all this, but there is little doubt that he went along under orders from Work.

The general manager was not long in implementing his views on close management control. Shortly after returning from Washington, he refused to increase the wages of employees in the mechanical and stores departments. In June 1925 he charged employees with discussing railroad matters "around the streets of Anchorage." He notified department heads that any employee found "giving out information of a confidential nature, or with malicious intent" would be "summarily dismissed from the service."[8] In March 1926 he instructed his department heads to check closely on the planned outside business ventures of all employees. Smith wished to make certain that the proposed businesses would not interfere with railroad work and that employees would not have a competitive advantage because of their connection with the railroad. The general manager's requirements were more strict than those of the Interior Department, which required only that outside occupations not interfere with the government job. Smith did not wish to force employees away from outside work, but his increased restrictions were a greater handicap to outside employment.

The men in the train and engine service fought back. Their leaders first tried to force Smith's removal and his replacement by Cunningham, the superintendent of transportation. Their tactic failed but caused Smith to suspect Cunningham of complicity with the men and to undervalue his considerable abilities for a time. No evidence existed then, or later, that Cunningham had lent himself to the scheme. Next, the local representatives of the brotherhoods complained frequently of management violations of the new work rules. The representatives did expect strict adherence to the unfamiliar and often complex rules, and their demands in this instance carried the overtones of harassment. On the other hand, management sometimes followed its own notions of fairness and logic in job assignments. Neither side was willing to see the other's viewpoint. If the local brotherhoods continued in their attitudes, Smith wrote to Work, "it will be necessary for me to take a very definite stand and simply tell these train service men, in The Alaska Railroad, what they will have and what they will not have."[9]

While attitudes hardened, Smith's nervousness and resentment approached paranoia. He placed slips of paper in his desk drawers to learn whether they had been opened in his absence. On at least one occasion he feared for his life and asked his driver, J. J. Delaney, to spend the night at his house. The men who manned the trains were liable to feel Smith's wrath whenever he rode. Smith rightly resented what he called "slack railroading,"[10] but his corrective actions were extreme. Once he swooped down on a conductor who had pulled out of a station two minutes early and gave him a tongue lashing. He suspended an engineer who ran five minutes late into Anchorage from Curry, after Smith had sent word forward that the train must arrive on time. Under pressure, the poor engineer had run fast, then slow, in an effort to make his time exactly. "He puttered along," Smith replied when the local representative submitted a grievance.[11]

Smith's more extreme suspicions were unjustified, but it was certainly true that the men were trying to remove him. Their most articulate leader, Conductor John J. C. Moore, was a formidable antagonist. Moore, a burly, bold, and intelligent man, was a match for Smith in verbal encounters. In November 1926 Moore and the other leaders wrote a letter to Smith denouncing him and all his works. The letter contained some misstatements of fact, for instance, that Smith had closed the mess houses. Even so, the heavy criticism, coming at a time when Smith was in Washington appearing before appropriations committees, shook the general manager badly. A few months later the Anchorage representative introduced a railroad safety bill in the territorial house. Its requirements exceeded Interstate Commerce Commission standards in several instances and held the general manager personally liable for defects. Governor George A. Parks and other representatives saw to it that the bill never emerged from committee. Moore and his associates denied any knowledge of the bill, but its timing and wording belied their claims of coincidence.

In May 1927 Smith and Moore faced each other in a bitter meeting of the grievance committee. Evidently Work had instructed Smith to smooth over the quarrel. But Smith was too aggrieved to be conciliatory at first. He forced Moore to retract some statements in his letter, trading insults with him all the while. When it finally came, Smith's lame effort to placate the heavyset conductor failed completely. The meeting dissolved in recriminations, and the labor situation continued to deteriorate. Work dispatched an inspector who investigated both sides. On August 4 he recommended Moore's removal. Smith promptly fired Moore. A few weeks later, again on the investigator's recommendation, he relieved two other men. When the men protested that Smith's actions were a violation of the 1925 working agreement, Smith declared that the secretary of the interior (or his representative) could remove anyone at any time. Any work rules with the government were necessarily "in the nature of a gentlemen's agreement."[12] After the firings, some of the trainmen fanned out over Anchorage, collecting gossip or damaging information about Smith or anyone else in management. Turning on their erstwhile friend Cunningham, they falsely accused him of draft dodging in the World War. The discharged men appealed to Work, who ordered their reinstatement. They returned to duty November 17, but their claims for back pay were disallowed. Work's motives were not recorded, but he may have wished to avoid trouble with the national railroad brotherhoods and to require Smith to cooperate with local labor leaders.

Ever since the wage increase of 1925, the men in the train and engine service had demanded another. Smith was unimpressed. He countered labor's persistent claim that wages should be significantly higher than those paid in the Pacific Northwest with a showing that men on The Alaska Railroad made more money than those on the Copper River & Northwestern. Work, always more sympathetic, granted an increase effective February 1, 1928. Smith and the operating forces closed their association in an atmosphere of mistrust, despite union recognition for the crews and two wage increases. Besides, in 1926 employees won the right, by executive order, to hold local offices. The next year another executive order established a Saturday half-holiday for clerical employees. Ironically for both the general manager and the men, labor had gained more during Smith's four years than it had in any other comparable peacetime period.

The second internal crisis of the Smith years concerned the purchasing department at Seattle. The nub of the issue was whether the purchasing department was subordinate to the headquarters, much as any other department, or whether it was obliged to balance orders from Anchorage against government purchasing specifications, past policies, and on-the-spot judgement. Some friction between a headquarters and a department so separated in space and time could be expected. Complaints from Anchorage exceeded the expected. Storekeepers and general managers complained of produce inferior to that consigned to retail merchants, of orders incorrectly filled, and of low-grade goods. During construction days, Mears once became so exasperated that he charged the purchasing department with harboring "disloyal" employees.[13] In fairness to the department, Anchorage did not always appreciate the problems and requirements. The difficulty was rooted in the transition from construction to operation.

In the engineering commission days supplies flowed heavily. Many purchasers were for standard items requiring little or no inspection. Most equipment sailed directly from Panama. The purchasing agent, C. E. Dole, had been with the commission from the beginning and was an old Panama Railroad hand. Over the years he had become entrenched in a routine of buying, hiring, and handling a variety of tasks for the railroad in Seattle. While Dole was burrowing into his routine, the situation in Alaska was rapidly changing. With the passing of heavy construction, the percentage of perishable commissary items, small equipment, and finished goods increased. In several instances these materials did not receive an adequate inspection. The overall reduction in purchases, coupled with increased stress on economy and efficiency, demanded new attitudes and systems. But Dole, though he was dissatisfied with his light work load, refused to accept additional duties or to reorganize his staff. Consolidation of the purchasing departments of the railroad and the Bureau of Education activities in Alaska, accompanied by force reductions, encouraged greater efficiency. Dole's salary and responsibilities were reduced. Under the circumstances, he elected to retire, so his office was abolished to enable him to draw his pension. Dole retired on April 1, 1926.

Alas, there was little immediate improvement in service. The railroad's experience with hams for the commissary and mess houses illustrates the problem. Both the men on the section gangs and the commissary purchasers overwhelmingly preferred Swift's hams to all others. The superiority of Swift's had to do with curing and trimming processes which kept the meat well through climatic changes and long storage. Swift's cost more than other hams, but reduced waste made the actual expense lower. Jacob R. Ummel, the new office manager of the purchasing department, argued that some positive showing as to Swift's superiority had to be made in order to satisfy the comptroller general, or the General Accounting Office would object to the sale. To Ummel, ham was ham. As he saw it, "the personal preference feature should be disregarded,"[14] and employees should be required to purchase ham from the lowest bidder. Smith replied that the section gangs and others were paying for their hams and therefore should be given the brand of their choice. He cited the need to maintain morale and reduce labor turnover in remote section camps. Furthermore, he wrote, the railroad added 20 percent to the landed cost of its supplies, more than making up any paper loss on the 10 percent of ham consumed at fixed prices per meal at the Curry Hotel, mess houses, and boarding cars. To settle the matter Smith suggested a baking test to discover the relative weight loss of each ham in cooking. Another brand finished first in the test despite Smith's confidence in Swift's. When he inquired how the hams had been selected, Ummel replied that the contractors had furnished samples on request. Neither Smith nor Ummel was satisfied with the arrangement, so another test was made. This time the Swift's ham showed the smallest percentage of loss, but it was not significant enough to overcome Swift's higher price. Smith resolved the dilemma by requiring Ummel to award bids on certain items in accordance with the general manager's instructions, after the bids had been forwarded to Anchorage. Payment for the items would be made from Anchorage as well.

Difficulties continued between Anchorage and Seattle, nor did they end with the Smith administration. The differences were not matters of personality. The purchasing department continued to ship some items not in accordance with specifications. Storekeeper Dewey W. Metzdorf continued to complain of the quality of his fruit and to harbor suspicions that wholesalers were unloading inferior merchandise on the purchasing department. Nevertheless, the relationship between Anchorage and Seattle had improved. Ummel had convinced Smith that he and his staff were "trying to do the right thing."[15]

Though Smith battled manfully against these and other administrative nettles, operation and maintenance remained the railroad's heartbeat. The river service presented operating challenges all its own. Unlike the train service, the weather controlled travel, with the number of trips depending on the dates of "breakup" and "freeze-up." Freight traffic was heavy at the opening of navigation, when accumulated freight for river points bulged the Nenana warehouse. It was heavy again near the season's close, when canned goods and grains arrived to supply the downriver villages through the winter.

Smith, as had Mears before him, wished to embrace the entire Yukon with the River Boat Service. Instead of boats merely running downriver from Nenana 723 miles to Holy Cross, with occasional runs up tributaries as business offered, he envisioned them sweeping the river from its mouth to Eagle, six miles due west of the border with Yukon Territory. He and his staff actively planned an expanded service on the lower river during the fall and winter of 1924. Alaska newspapers bristled with rumors that the railroad's boats were going on the upper river (above Tanana). Several obstacles, however, combined against Smith's plans. Work never warmed to them. Congress refused requests for another, necessary boat, and it was not until 1927 that the railroad was able to purchase the old steamer *Alice* from the Alaska Yukon Navigation Company to replace the dilapidated *Davis*. Cunningham warned against expanding operations with only marginally adequate equipment.

The Alaska Railroad operations on the upper river probably would have ended the Canadian service altogether and would have unstitched the carefully patched relations with the White Pass line. Superior service from the "White Pass boats" in 1925, together with amicable rate negotiations between the two railroads, virtually closed the subject. As for the lower river operations from Holy Cross to the river's mouth, it would have been difficult to handle them simply as an extension of the Nenana-to-Holy Cross service. The rates increased downriver from Nenana and upriver from the mouth to the exchange point at Holy Cross. Therefore, The Alaska Railroad's boats, continuing downriver, would be hauling freight in many instances more expensively than the boats of the Northern Commercial Company operating upstream. The disparity would increase as the downriver Alaska Railroad boats approached the Yukon Delta. The only solution would have been to maintain service from St. Michael or to interchange with a private seagoing boat inside the bar at the river's mouth.

The solution could have been managed, but it would have forced rate adjustments up and down the Yukon. In addition, it would have meant taking the mail contract from the Northern Commercial Company. The government's putting private enterprise out of business in that fashion almost certainly would have been considered bad form in Congress. Smith did extend the service to Marshall, 858 miles from Nenana, in 1926. In 1928 the Northern Commercial Company added a new boat, significantly upgrading its service.

The River Boat Service carried a modest tonnage, from a low of 3,125 in fiscal year 1925 to a high of almost 3,826 in fiscal year 1928, Smith's last full year as general manager. The improvement reflected increased mining and prospecting in the interior. Passenger traffic varied from a low of 721 in 1927 to 892 in 1928. Service between Nenana and Holy Cross was weekly, with a semi-weekly service to Marshall. During most navigation seasons, about eighteen Nenana-Holy Cross round trips were possible. The river operation steadily lost money — more than $22,000 in 1926. The deficit was more than $27,000 in 1927, a decline in tonnage and passengers and a rise in operating costs cancelling a rate increase. In 1928 the service showed a small surplus — $6,499.21 — for the first time. The losses were but a tiny part of a greater annual deficit and were justified by the railroad's commitment to development. Without the little stern-wheelers, the miners, prospectors, woodchoppers, trappers, and others along the great river would have found it difficult or impossible to keep a foothold in the wilderness. A private operation probably would have reduced the service or insisted upon an increased mail contract, or both. The River Boat Service helped to keep the remote interior communities alive.

Smith bore down heavily on the high costs of rail maintenance and operation. At times his subordinates must have thought that his concern for economy and efficiency had become an obsession, but he consistently urged true economy instead of a mere favorable showing on the balance sheet. He studied ways to reduce the work force yet keep up standards of efficiency, maintenance, and safety. From 1924 to 1928 he reduced the average number of employees from 1,056 to 934. Always eager to spend money in order to save it, Smith plumped for right-of-way improvements. Congress never gave him enough to fill all the rickety trestles, or conquer the slide conditions in the Nenana Canyon, or raise all the grade high enough above swampy soil to eliminate frost heaves. Through 1928 the federal legislature granted him less than $2,500,000 of the almost $12,000,000 he had estimated to be required for completion of the line. Yet, he was able to widen many cuts, bank fills, and rebuild bridges. In 1925 the high, wobbling, curving trestle over the Eagle River was rebuilt into four steel spans. Steel and fills replaced wood at many other locations. By 1927 Smith could point to a significant accomplishment — reducing the "wooden railroad" from 17.2 miles to 13.7 miles of track and bridges resting on wood.

For all of Smith's attention to betterments, the overall condition of the roadbed improved but little. Snowslides, including one that blocked the line from Seward for two weeks in 1925, continued to bedevil track maintenance crews. Replacing rotted pilings diverted men and money from permanent construction. Even so, the wood was deteriorating more rapidly than it could be replaced. With each year's frost heaves, miles of track were bent and twisted beyond straightening, yet were left in place for lack of funds. Slow orders often substituted for the scrapping of damaged track.

In the interest of long-range economy, Smith purchased new and secondhand equipment to replace wheezing Panama engines and dilapidated rolling stock. He ordered engines, plows, and other heavy equipment overhauled for more efficient operation. The Anchorage shops built speeders, hot cars, automobile cars, and other specialized equipment to improve service. Smith believed that the Brill 75 gasoline car bought in 1926 was an important addition. The big, fast Brill held forty-eight people and contained a sixteen-foot baggage compartment. It performed so well that it substituted for one of the summertime, three-a-week steam trains. Other equipment improvements included gasoline section cars to replace the physically tiring, hand-operated models. Smith reduced the railroad's responsibilities and increased its income by selling many of the houses and cottages built during construction days. To cut inventories and make a little more money, he began cleaning up and selling scrap. He leased the Anchorage dock warehouse to a cannery which shipped over one thousand tons of salmon to Seattle via rail-and-water during fiscal year 1928. He was always ready to figure special rates on any local products showing a promise of added income.

Service, except for some improvements in cars, was not much changed from the last days of the A. E. C. During the summer months three mixed trains per week ran between Seward and Fairbanks. Two round trips each week were standard for the rest of the year, with adjustments to meet the demands of heavier or lighter tonnage. The Chatanika and Chickaloon branches each carried two round trips per week, with extra trips as tonnage required. On the Chickaloon branch, trips beyond Sutton were reduced to one per month.

The Alaska Railroad began to make a better financial showing during the late 1920s. An improving balance sheet was not necessarily the only, or even the most important, criterion for its success. In congressional and administrative eyes, however, reduction of the annual deficit mattered above all else. Had the financial picture not improved, Smith almost certainly would have been removed. The improvement was due less to Smith's labors, necessary as they were, than to new activity in gold mining. The operations of the Fairbanks Exploration Company were the most important. The "F. E." company shipped materials for a power plant at Fairbanks, for dredges on nearby creeks, and for water-carrying ditches totaling over eighty miles. The shipments more than offset sharp reductions in Mayo ore from Yukon Territory.

Revenues rose steadily. The combined income in fiscal year 1925 was $797,439.82. In 1926 it rose to $994,354.60 and jumped to $1,260,029.41 in 1927. In 1928 it rose again, to $1,354,939.44. The annual deficit, that crucial figure, fell from $1,673,997.73 in 1925 to $840,890.93 in 1928. Expressed as an operating ratio, the 1928 record was 159.32, still staggeringly high. Nevertheless, it was a good showing. As Smith remarked, expenses tended to rise with revenues because operations increased with income. He had held down expenses. In December 1927 the balance sheet, for the first time, showed a surplus. The railroad's detractors never tired of pointing out that the deficit was merely an income-and-outgo statement; the railroad paid no interest on investment, it maintained no sinking fund. What they did not mention was that, like most federal agencies, the line carried no insurance. Any serious loss had to be met from current revenues. When the engine house and power plant at Curry went up in explosion and flames on July 18, 1926, they were rebuilt from congressional appropriations and charged to the deficit.

Smith left the railroad in the summer of 1928 to return to the Pennsylvania System. He had made an enviable record in every area except labor relations. He had saved the railroad as an institution by bringing order out of administrative chaos and demoralization. Closing the Anchorage dock helped to improve the line's financial situation. In his appearances before congressional committees and in his statements to Secretary Work, he was almost always the model of the responsible railroader. He lost some battles, most notably those for increased improvements appropriations and for control of the trainmen who, in spite of both Smith and themselves, made remarkable gains during his tenure. Most important, he had laid the foundation and marked the direction of the railroad's development for the next ten years.

Passenger train near Moose Pass in the Kenai Peninsula, about 1950. *The Alaska Railroad*

At Moose Pass, July 11, 1948. *The Alaska Railroad*

Crossing a trestle in the Loop Area, 1948. *The Alaska Railroad*

Emerging from a tunnel in the Loop Area, 1938. *The Alaska Railroad*

A double burden passenger train, northbound on a Loop trestle, April 14, 1941. *The Alaska Railroad*

Head-on collision, October 19, 1943, about two miles south of Anchorage station. *The Alaska Railroad*

A train crosses Ship Creek on its way north from Anchorage. The railroad hospital is at the extreme left. About 1924. *The Alaska Railroad*

A passenger train at Anchorage station in the late 1920s. *Alaska Historical Library*

No. 551 at the new station and office building, May 31, 1949. *The Alaska Railroad*

A freight steams across the Knik River bridge, August 3, 1948. *The Alaska Railroad*

A wooden, open platform coach at Wasilla, 1925. *The Alaska Railroad*

At Broad Pass. *Eugene McCracken Collection, University of Alaska Archives*

B & B No. 7 Outfit at Windy Creek, December 1925. The tripod telephone poles in the foreground were once a railbelt trademark. *Charles Bunnell Collection, University of Alaska Archives*

Brill car at McKinley Park station about 1930. *Alaska Historical Library*

Passenger train at McKinley Park station about 1930. *Alaska Historical Library*

Coaling at Nenana. No. 556 now rests in an Anchorage park. *The Alaska Railroad*

No. 557, the last operating steam engine in Alaska, now privately owned, pulls a train through flood waters at Nenana, June 1962. *The Alaska Railroad*

No. 901 with a freight train at Saulich, 19 miles from Fairbanks, September 9, 1949. *The Alaska Railroad*

The "Toonerville Trolley" gas car, providing service between Fairbanks and the Alaska Agricultural College and School of Mines, later the University of Alaska, at College. The College station is three miles west of Fairbanks. This service, a victim of improving busses and taxis, was discontinued in 1931. *Charles Bunnell Collection, University of Alaska Archives*

Railcar at College station, late 1920s. The inner rail carried the narrow gauge trains of the Chatanika Branch to Happy station, mile 465, where the narrow gauge swung north to Chatanika, 39 miles from Fairbanks. Narrow gauge service was discontinued in 1930 and the narrow gauge rails removed in 1931. *Charles Bunnell Collection, University of Alaska Archives*

Railcar at the Fairbanks station, possibly the "Toonerville Trolley." *Lulu Fairbanks Collection, University of Alaska Archives*

No. 620 pulls in at College station. *Otto Geist Collection, University of Alaska Archives*

Waiting at the College station, late 1930s or early 1940s. *Otto Geist Collection, University of Alaska Archives*

Brill car at the Fairbanks station, with inner, narrow gauge rail in place. At this time The Alaska Railroad operated two Brills of the same general appearance. The M-107, shown here, was placed in service in 1926, seated 48, weighed 62,100 pounds, and was over 57 feet long. It was powered by a six cylinder gasoline engine. In 1927 the railroad acquired another Brill, a gas-electric model seating 26, but having a larger baggage compartment and capable of pulling a trailer with a seating capacity of 60. *Charles Bunnell Collection, University of Alaska Archives*

Brill at Fairbanks about 1930 with a tourist or excursion party. *Historical Photograph Collection, University of Alaska Archives*

Railcar at Fairbanks about 1930. *Mike Erceg Collection, University of Alaska Archives*

A crane and grab bucket coaled engines at Fairbanks, typical of the primitive conditions at the yards of the northern terminus even after World War II. *The Anchorage Historical and Fine Arts Museum*

Ohlson and a government geologist survey the scene. *The Alaska Railroad*

Otto Ohlson and His Era

Otto F. Ohlson was a tenacious man. For more than seventeen years he managed The Alaska Railroad, controlling it closely and becoming inseparably identified with it in some minds, including, occasionally, his own. For a generation and more after he left the road, Ohlson remained a vivid memory to those who had lived along the railbelt during his tenure. Unfortunately, the later recollections of those who loved, and those who loathed him are of a querulous, hypersensitive old widower bedeviled by failing health, labor troubles, and the strains of a war that his railroad was not built to bear. He had not always been so cantankerous.

Ohlson was a native Swede and a lifelong railroad man. Born in 1870, he became a telegrapher in Sweden while still in his teens. Combining his occupation with wanderlust and a taste for adventure, he served as a railroad telegrapher in South America and East India before joining the Pennsylvania System in 1893. He rose to be the assistant passenger trainmaster but left the Pennsylvania in 1901 for the Northern Pacific. Early in 1918 he entered the army and saw service as the general superintendent of United States railroads in France. In December 1919 he was back at the Northern Pacific, continuing a rise that brought him to the head of the Lake Superior Division in August 1927. About the same time, he came to the attention of a government official, possibly even of the vacationing Calvin Coolidge. Ohlson was capable, his Republican politics were right, and Alaska could not faze him.

Ohlson was fifty-eight years old when he arrived at Seward in mid-August 1928. Alaskans, in deference to his reserve lieutenant-colonelcy, soon called him "Colonel" Ohlson. A paunchy man with a prominent nose, he sported a thin mustache, cigars, and natty, sometimes flamboyant, dress. During a 1936 newspaper interview in Seattle he wore "a hunter's green suit, emerald-green socks, shirt with nile-green stripes, olive green tie, bottle-green hat and grass-green handkerchief."[1] Although he possessed considerable bluff charm, the colonel could use words with a bite. The manager of the Kennecott Copper Corporation left himself open for one such assault when he offered some surplus fire brick to the railroad at an inflated price. "I thought that all the Jews had left Alaska, but apparently they have not," Ohlson shot back.[2] No bigot, Ohlson intended a personal, not a religious, slur. His standards of fiscal responsibility were high. Cautious with the railroad's money, he was generous with his own, especially if the recipient were a farmer who showed some promise. He was the victim of rumors about alleged mining interests along the railroad and irregularities in the use of railroad equipment at the mines. No one ever advanced any proof of either the mining interests or the irregularities. Ohlson made no secret of his part ownership of a mine near Platinum, but Platinum was hundreds of miles from the railroad on the shores of Goodnews Bay.

The heavyset general manager was much more than a loud dresser who flashed a platinum nugget. He was personable, he was fair to his men, and he worked hard and well. He was a familiar sight "out on the line" in his Dodge

195

railmobile. Merely dictating and signing his massive correspondence would have made a day's work for most men. He threw himself into promoting and developing Alaska and drumming up traffic for the railroad. He mastered, and often interfered in, the details of operation. He did it all with exuberance and style in contrast to Smith's unspectacular, dutiful performance.

Despite the dissimilarities between the two men, in several ways Ohlson's administration represented continuity, not change. He agreed with Smith's ideas of loyalty to the secretary of the interior, strict economy, and one-man control of the railroad. He pressed further with them, just as he was more willing to involve the railroad in development and to generate traffic — almost any traffic — for its own sake. Only once, and then in his later years, did Ohlson try to circumvent the secretary of the interior. At other times he was an especially loyal man who labored to execute policies even when he disagreed with them. In 1933, after suspicious Harold L. Ickes assumed the secretaryship, he dispatched a friend to Alaska to check up on Ohlson. The report from Harold L. Snell, whom Ickes had appointed to be the railroad's agent at Chicago, was an unqualified endorsement. Ohlson, Snell wrote, "would relentlessly carry out orders," a judgment that stood the test of time.[3]

An incident of Ohlson's early years demonstrated his concern for economy and for employee loyalty. When he arrived, he found the inventory of supplies and equipment over $1 million, an amount he considered excessive by more than half. He gave orders to cut inventory by $45,000 per month, allowing for a monthly inventory of $50,000. This reduction was to be in effect until stocks reached the $500,000 level. He further explained to the Seattle purchasing agent that the commissary department and cold storage plant soon would be leased; therefore, no large commissary orders could be expected. In February 1929 the stores department ordered a modest 5,000 pounds of beef. The purchasing agent misread the order and shipped 25,000 pounds — twelve and one-half tons — of beef. Ohlson angrily attempted to remove the purchasing agent, not only for the overshipment of beef, but also because orders under his care had been a source of past friction between Anchorage and Seattle. Ohlson failed. He was unable to fire the purchasing agent because Secretary Ray Lyman Wilbur ruled that the Seattle office had become directly responsible to the Interior Department under the 1926 reorganization. Ohlson did agree to another reorganization and consolidation of the Seattle office to include most of the federal agencies shipping to Alaska. The reorganization and other economies saved money for the railroad over the next several years.

Ohlson's handling of the policy committee illustrates his drive for exclusive local control of his line. Back in December 1927, Work had resuscitated the committee, ordering it to meet at the call of the territorial governor, who was to submit an annual report. Work was looking ahead to his own resignation and to the departure of Smith, who had asked to be relieved. The committee had been useful during the Landis crisis of 1924. It might be useful again. Governor Parks held a routine meeting before Smith's departure. Two months after he arrived in Alaska, Ohlson called a meeting of the committee. Committee member Benjamin D. Stewart, supervising mining engineer of the Geological Survey, offered suggestions and recommendations on almost every topic. At one point Ohlson was asked to send out no information about mining along the railbelt without Stewart's prior approval. Ohlson bore Stewart's remarks patiently, but he held no more committee meetings. For a time he continued Smith's practice of consulting with the governor about railroad matters. Even these written consultations ceased during Ohlson's first year. Thereafter he welcomed advice only when he sought it.

Ohlson's decision to close the Chatanika branch was a major decision in the realm of operating economy and service. Formerly the privately owned Tanana Valley road, the branch was rebuilt after its purchase by the A. E. C. in 1917. The rebuilding kept the little thirty-nine-mile line in a condition barely adequate to its modest traffic to and from the mining camps. Over the years, crews had ballasted and raised the track in swampy places and had improved some cuts and fills. Nevertheless, the road remained in pioneer condition. Rotting wooden trestles usually were replaced with wood. The little trains still climbed over the tortuous switchback northeast of Fox. They still crossed a divide one thousand feet above Fairbanks. They still wound around the contours of the high hills between Goldstream Creek and Chatanika River. Each year they lost more business to busses and trucks on the Steese

Highway and its branch roads.

In 1928 Smith had considered closing the Chatanika branch during the winter, when expenses increased. The Fairbanks Exploration Company had completed its heavy materials shipments over the line and revenues were "practically nil."[4] Smith took no action, but the next year Ohlson announced a three-month suspension. In September 1929 he told residents of the creeks that the trains would not operate for the first quarter of 1930. He had reckoned without the Alaska Road Commission, which was unwilling to keep the roads open during that time. The road commission's refusal, coupled with a petition carrying 122 signatures against the suspension, persuaded Ohlson to rescind his order. The general manager insisted upon a condition. Either the dwellers north of Fairbanks would give all possible business to the branch the year around, or he would close the little railroad forever. When springtime came the mining communities returned to busses and trucks. The railroad continued in its losing ways, rolling up a $44,799 deficit during the twelve months ending in March 1930. Ohlson, in his request to shut down the branch, wired Secretary Wilbur, "The highway is the people's choice."[5] Obviously the creeks' residents preferred the freedom of personal automobiles and daily bus and truck service to the railroad's bi-weekly schedule.

Ohlson made the only decision he could have made. Closing the branch during the winter months was no solution. It would have saved on the heavy expenses of maintaining and operating the road in the depths of an interior Alaska winter, but wintertime was the season when creek residents depended most upon the line. Had he considered only public service, Ohlson would have operated the line in winter and closed it during the summer. He could not consider public service alone. Congressional exasperation with heavy deficits was growing. Even as Ohlson worked out the last details of the closing, a special Senate committee planned a trip northward to investigate his railroad. He could not accept the argument of creek residents: that because the railroad as a whole lost money, the Chatanika branch should not be singled out for abandonment.

Ohlson might have defended the narrow gauge if its losses had approximated those of the railroad as a whole. They did not. During fiscal year 1929, The Alaska Railroad had operating revenues of $1,165,910.50 and operating expenses of $2,090,212.50. That is, the railroad spent about two dollars to earn each dollar. The Chatanika branch earned $17,377 but spent $62,096 during a comparable period. The branch, then, cost almost four dollars for each dollar of income. Finally, the character of the branch's traffic was unstable. Scarcely any outbound freight moved on the branch line. Much of the inbound tonnage was mining company fuel. All fuel — coal, gasoline, and oil — was unloaded from standard gauge cars at Fairbanks and reloaded on board narrow gauge cars. It was trucked from the branch stations to dredges and mines sometimes several miles away. The companies could make the entire haul just as conveniently by truck, Ohlson believed. The companies admitted that they could, even though their costs would increase slightly.

Late in May 1930, after receiving Wilbur's concurrence, the colonel announced that he would close the Chatanika branch on July 1. He worked to convince the Alaska Road Commission that it should maintain the Steese Highway and some of its branch roads during the winter. His unequivocal order helped. He also suggested to the Fairbanks Commercial Club and to Governor Parks that they put pressure on the road commission. Exceptionally heavy rains in June turned stretches of the Steese Highway into bogs and underscored the importance of keeping the gravel road in good condition. Ohlson rescinded his closing order for the duration of the emergency.

On July 7 Ohlson, Parks, and Major Malcom Elliott, the commission president, met at Fairbanks to discuss the road situation. Parks assured the meeting that the territory had allocated its funds for the year. It could not lend assistance either by helping to maintain the Steese or by taking over a portion of the narrow gauge right-of-way. Ohlson refused Elliott's request to share the estimated $10,000 to $15,000 required to keep two branch roads open. He did agree to loan a clamshell to the commission to aid in the work of filling and grading. Elliott agreed to maintain the Steese year-round and later accepted Ohlson's offer of the clamshell for the branch roads. The general manager then ordered the trains stopped on August 1.

The month-long pause in closing the narrow

gauge allowed Ohlson time for analyzing a second petition against closure. One hundred and fourteen people signed the petition, but the railroad's special investigator found twenty who lived in Fairbanks, not out on the creeks. Fewer than half had shipped merchandise over the branch in fiscal year 1930. Only twenty-three had shipped more than one ton during the year. Many who had listed their occupations as "miner" or "prospector" had neither mined nor prospected for several years. The investigator talked with several signers, all of whom save two were willing to see the narrow gauge abandoned if the roads were improved. A farmer and his wife who had no outlet but the railroad were the only exceptions. Ohlson also ran an eleven-day check on tonnage moving via rail and road. From June 25 through July 5 the railroad hauled a little more than 17 tons, while the trucking companies carried over 246 tons that could have been handled by the branch line. Shippers via truck included the Fairbanks Exploration Company, the Northern Commercial Company, and the Standard Oil Company. The actions of these and other large companies sealed the fate of the branch. After the trains stopped running, Ohlson kept the tracks in place to guard against maintenance failures on the roads and exorbitant trucking charges. He ordered the tracks removed during the summer of 1931. Most of the steel and rolling stock was gathered up and sold.

The railroad wanted by so few was quickly forgotten by many. Occasional reminders persisted in the Fairbanks area. The hulk of a narrow gauge engine rested at the site of the Alaska Centennial Exposition. A few stacks of ties slowly rotted along the banks of Goldstream Creek. Travelers along Elliott Highway could glimpse sections of the right-of-way, a brushy overgrowth tracing its path through the surrounding forest of spruce and birch.

Congress applied heavy pressure for further drastic economies. In August 1931, just after Ohlson closed the Chatanika branch, the Special Select Committee on Investigation of The Alaska Railroad arrived in the territory. The senators were frankly dubious. Their report was critical of the railroad's management and skeptical about its economic future. The rate increases and reductions in service that followed its recommendations marked the greatest degree of congressional control since construction days. The Howell Committee, as it was called after its chairman, has been criticized for the superficiality of its investigation and the severity of its recommendations. There was much about the report to criticize. Senator Robert B. Howell used it to vent a prejudice. Because no significant development had taken place along the railbelt, he argued, the line's success or failure should be judged by profit-and-loss alone. Furthermore, he misinterpreted contracts, unfairly criticized the railroad's debt policy, and snidely remarked on the competence of some employees. The report of the examiner charged with investigating the railroad's bookkeeping is the condescending statement of a big-time expert who was in the provinces to show the rubes how it was done.

The committee's merits overshadowed the weaknesses in its report. Howell himself was not the least of the strengths. The senator, born in Michigan, graduated from the United States Naval Academy in 1885. Three years later he went to Omaha, where he established himself as an engineer and a champion of public utilities. He served in city and state engineering positions and on various water boards, meanwhile building a following within the Republican party. Elected to the Senate from Nebraska in 1922, he was re-elected in 1928. Howell's colleagues liked him and respected his analytical ability.

Howell understood the railroad as well as any senator, and better than most. His prejudice against its losses and his mistakes in detail detracted little from his comprehension. His experience with the railroad dated from 1923, when he traveled with the congressional party. From that time forward he argued against continued operation between Nenana and Fairbanks, including the Chatanika branch, and between Anchorage and Seward. The Seward-Anchorage line was disproportionately expensive to operate, he said, therefore it should be abandoned. Anchorage could be fashioned into a port to replace Seward for most of the year. Alaskans could import a years' necessities during the nine months that Anchorage was open to navigation. Nenana, an interior river landing, was a less expensive terminal than Fairbanks, another fifty miles inland.

The senator looked upon Fairbanks' economic revival with a jaundiced eye. It was based, he told the Senate in February 1928, on the corporate gold dredge mining which frequently followed the exhaustion of rich, easily worked placers.

Instead of scenes of renewed activity, Howell saw "the mechanical vulture" coming "to pick the bones of these exhausted placers. They are setting up dredges for the final feast. They are not building up an industry. Their activity means that the dream is all but over, the end of the rainbow is at hand."[6] The Chatanika branch, he claimed, operated at a loss solely to benefit the United States Smelting, Refining, and Mining Company interests, whose Fairbanks Exploration Company was shipping in dredges for that "final feast." The senator's judgment was unduly pessimistic and harsh, but he did expose the narrow foundations of the Fairbanks economy.

The Senate was unwilling to follow Howell to his conclusions. It decisively defeated his amendment to block funds for operating the Chatanika branch, fifty-six votes to seventeen. On an unrecorded vote, it refused his second amendment — to spend none of the $400,000 budgeted for capital improvements to aid the Seward-Anchorage line. The senator made his mark despite the votes. He had a demonstrated grasp of the railroad's engineering problems. He knew something about the central Alaska economy. He understood the rudiments of railroad accounting. His reckoning of the tiny population served by the railroad — a mere 5,000 souls — stood unrefuted. However, he still did not introduce a resolution for an investigation. The next year the railroad's annual deficit began to rise, reversing a downward trend. Two years later, on June 23, 1930, Howell proposed an investigation of the railroad's "operation, economic situation, and prospects."[7] Eight days later, the committee to audit and control the Senate's contingent expenses favorably reported his resolution. It passed on the spot, without recorded discussion. For committee members Howell chose two western colleagues, John B. Kendrick of Wyoming and John Thomas of Idaho.

The senators bolstered their committee with Chairman Frank McManamy of the Interstate Commerce Commission and an I. C. C. examiner whose job was to comb the railroad's accounts. They worked hard in Alaska, convening twenty-two times during twelve August days to hear fifty-six witnesses. They conducted informal investigations when the committee was not in session. They struggled through the usual rounds of banquets and speechmaking. Howell spoke his mind during his visit, but he talked past his listeners. Most railbelt commentators interpreted his criticisms of Alaska as strictures against the management of the railroad and federal policy in the territory. Not surprisingly, Howell's report stunned central Alaska. Howell recommended a 66⅔ percent increase in passenger revenue and a freight increase hefty enough to insure 50 percent more revenue. Alaskans would have been more shocked had Ohlson not leaked an advance warning of the increases, enabling shippers to order supplies at the old rates. The report called for a reduction of 100,000 train miles below fiscal year 1930, for efficiency and economy, and for continuous congressional surveillance.

In justification of his demand for rate increases, the senator compared The Alaska Railroad's passenger fare of six cents per mile with the Copper River's twelve cents and the White Pass' twenty cents. He recalled that the first freight rates had been set at 100 percent of the rates in the Pacific Northwest. Increases to railroads "outside" and decreases in Alaska had brought charges on the federal line to 30 percent above Pacific Northwest rates. The convergence had occurred despite The Alaska Railroad's continuing deficits. A difficult climate, an underdeveloped country, a population of less than 8,400 within fifty miles each side of the railroad, and insignificant outbound traffic contributed to the problem. Howell calculated the freight business at the equivalent of 102 round-trip trains of less than nine cars each during fiscal year 1930. The passenger traffic was the equivalent of 176 trains carrying under twenty-two passengers per trip. Ohlson and his assistants refuted several of Howells' contentions, but they did not challenge his statements of traffic equivalents.

Howell reiterated his view of the railroad as a public utility. The line should not lose money, it should vindicate public ownership through competent management and a fair return on its $70 million investment. But it had never met its operating expenses. To Alaskans who argued for the railroad as an instrument of development, Howell retorted that the decade's increase in railbelt population had cost the railroad $800,000 in deficits for each 100 persons, "a vast generosity with indeed small results." He could have mentioned that Alaskan's definition of the railroad's role had changed, too. From arguing that the completed rails would bring development in their wake, they had shifted to the more dubious and vulnerable assertion that Congress had expected prolonged deficits to be the price of development. On the other hand, Howell discounted development more than he should have. He noted that if Alaska farmers reversed their economic decline, the increased farmer demand for supplies merely would balance the railroad's losses from reduced food imports. Therefore, "the development of agriculture would neither advantage or disadvantage the railroad." Howell's myopic concentration on profit-and-loss blinded him to the wording of the 1914 enabling act. The legislation had directed the location of a railroad "so as best to aid in the development of the agricultural and mineral or other resources of Alaska."[8]

Howell's report was one of the few government documents to evaluate Alaska's coal realistically. The lignite in the Healy area, Howell noted, was largely confined to the interior market. The Matanuska Valley coal was friable, lay in folded beds, and was difficult to mine. Permits had been issued for the development of potentially rich anthracite mines at the valley's upper end, but little activity occurred on the ground. British Columbia coal dominated the Alaska market beyond the railbelt, despite the railroad's low export rate. Howell acknowledged Alaskan visions of new metal mines, reindeer herds, and birch mills springing up along the right-of-way. At their best, those new development schemes, other than large-scale gold mining, were in the preliminary planning stages.

The senator was on less firm ground when he attacked the railroad's relationships with private business and Alaska towns. Before his trip, Howell had developed a populistic malice toward the Fairbanks Exploration Company and its parent firm, United States Smelting, Refining, and Mining. His claim that low rates on the deficit-ridden Chatanika branch subsidized the shipment of the "F. E." company's dredge components may have been true, but it overlooked several facts. The railroad received a full line haul on dredges. Declining revenues in fiscal year 1929 were traceable in part to the lack of heavy dredge shipments during the year. The railroad received a 112-mile haul for coal consumed in the company's power plant at the north edge of the Fairbanks yards. If Ohlson's eleven-day check would serve as a guide, Fairbanks Exploration shipped little else than heavy pieces and fuel over the Chatanika branch. Like other shippers, it preferred the Steese Highway. Howell was shocked to find the "F. E." company mining the abandoned Chatanika branch right-of-way without compensation to the government. Had he inquired, he would have discovered that the claims had been located before the narrow gauge was built and that the railroad enjoyed only surface rights.

With equal bitterness and intemperance, the senator attacked the railroad's agreement with the Anchorage Light and Power Company. It was correct, as Howell remarked, that prior to 1929 the railroad sold power to the town of Anchorage for a profit. It was also correct that the railroad abandoned this profitable enterprise in 1929, when the Anchorage Light and Power Company completed its hydroelectric plant. Howell said, correctly, that the railroad purchased power from the company while at the same time it operated its generators as a central heating plant for the railroad yards at an absurdly excessive cost. Howell was grossly unfair, however, to charge Ohlson and his staff with behavior which would have been criminal had it not smacked of naivete.

Since the early 1920s, a group of Anchorage businessmen had labored to find the capital for a hydroelectric station at Eklutna, twenty-seven miles north of Anchorage. The railroad's management urged them on, Smith promising the group that the railroad would buy power from the plant when it was established. A long-standing Interior Department policy of encouraging private business in Alaska stood behind Smith's promise. The colonel signed a contract with the Anchorage firm on August 31, 1929. Both Anchorage and The Alaska Railroad benefited from the new contract. Anchorage's power supply was more assured because the railroad had sold only surplus power to the town. The railroad's aging generators, while adequate to the railroad's needs and those of the Anchorage community, would have required replacement at some future time. The company sold power to the railroad at four cents per kilowatt-hour, or almost a penny per KWH less than the railroad could produce its own electricity. The company also made low rates to users in Anchorage. Howell harped on the loss of some $50,000 a year in railroad revenues. He dwelt on charges to residential customers as low as 2½ cents per kilowatt-hour, citing the wholesale price and not the retail 3½ cents per KWH actually charged to consumers. The charges were designed to spur the sale of electric appliances. Howell was uninterested in the reduced electric bills, the greatly increased use of electric kitchen appliances, and other benefits to Anchorage.

The outraged senator ordered Ohlson to negotiate a rate of three cents per KWH or lower. If the power company refused, Howell told Ohlson, the railroad was to resume its own power production. The colonel was delighted to force a reduction in rates even further below the railroad's cost of production. The company depended upon the railroad's consumption and could not afford to refuse. Ohlson and the company agreed on a sliding scale of rates that brought the effective rate down to three cents per KWH. The new scale became effective on April 1, 1931, after the railroad had installed additional electric pumps and stokers at the Anchorage shops.

Howell accurately accused the railroad of extravagance in only one comparatively minor circumstance. During the winter of 1929-30, the railroad power plant heated the railroad buildings at an excessive cost. The following spring workmen dug down to the steam pipes. They found leaks and poor insulation. Ohlson arranged to heat each building with coal stoves, thus correcting the condition before the Howell committee arrived at Anchorage.

The Howell report made other misrepresentations regarding the Anchorage telephone system, the railroad's accounts receivable, and the Nenana power plant. The examiner's report, appended to Howell's, was critical of several details of the railroad's bookkeeping. In general, however, the examiner was well enough satisfied with the railroad's accounts. The management, piqued, answered many of Howell's statements and answered them well. Barndollar's refutation of the examiner showed that most of his criticisms were entirely matters of judgment. Yet, Howell carried the field. He had been to Alaska, and he had gathered facts. The railroad's accountants were hard pressed to feed his voracious appetite for information. The senator had his basic ideas straight. The railroad had lost money, was losing more, and its revenue was declining. The railroad had not fulfilled its dreams for Alaska's economy, and it was doubtful that it would do so in the near future. Moreover, Howell retreated from some of his positions. Abandoning his efforts to shrink the road to an Anchorage-Nenana line, he explicitly recommended continued operation. He accepted the prospect of a $500,000 deficit for fiscal year 1932, in contrast to his earlier statements that losses must cease. He requested $250,000 for an investigation of resources that would increase the railroad's traffic. An identical amount was to go for capital improvement. The $250,000 capital improvements request was not generous, but it was as much as Smith had received in some years and as much as could be expected, considering the deepening depression.

The Hoover administration was forced to accept the Howell committee's findings even before the committee's report was published. Howell, Kendrick, and Thomas called on Secretary Wilbur and told him that Congress would decide the rate policies. The committee was violating the 1914 act, which gave rate-making power to the president, but Wilbur wisely surrendered to the senators. The winter of 1930-31, with its worldwide political and financial crises, was no time for a showdown over The Alaska Railroad. Wilbur wrote out his capitulation on January 3, 1931. He would increase passenger rates from six cents to ten cents a mile and raise freight charges by an average 50 percent or more. A loss of business would follow, of course, but the net increase would cut the deficit to about $500,000. Wilbur was skeptical of the new policy, but he promised to give it a "full and fair trial."[9]

Ohlson set to work revising the rates and sent the new tariff to the printer early in March 1932. He and his staff made few across-the-board increases. Instead, they considered prevailing rates, competitive situations, and the characteristics of commodities in boosting freight charges about 100 percent above the Western Classification. Fuels — heavy, bulky, unlikely freight for most competitors — could stand large increases. Coal rates jumped 75 percent; rates on gasoline and oil, 80 percent. The colonel hiked other charges from 32 to 67 percent, with local tariffs in general taking larger increases than joint through rates. Special charges for crane service, storage, demurrage, and the like increased 50 percent.

The railroad's traffic experts could not boost rates by the same proportion on the Yukon

River. That territory was competitive with shipments via St. Michael and the river's mouth as well as by Nenana. Although Alaska Steam and the Admiral Line agreed to stay off the Yukon, Ohlson had no influence over small operators that had no ties to the railroad. Nor could he prevent the large steamship companies from accepting competitive cargoes to St. Michael for transfer to the river. A substantial water rate increase would have cost the railroad much of its steamboat patronage. Unfortunately for Ohlson, the revised less-than-carload rates were higher on the northern stretches of the railroad than they were on the Yukon. Merchants north of Honolulu (mile 289) were certain to criticize the line for charging more for goods hauled a few hundred miles than for the same merchandise carried to Nenana (mile 412), unloaded, reloaded on stern-wheelers, and landed far down the river. Ohlson solved the problem by raising the riverboat less-than-carload charges and lowering the comparatively high water carload rates.

Expressed in dollars, most increases were sharp. Some were staggering. First class through rates to Fairbanks rose from $78.80 to $119.00 per ton. The fourth class rate, an approximate average of all freight charges, climbed from $49.60 to $72.00. Commodity rates shot up: canned goods to Anchorage, from $24.00 to $37.40; carloads of cement to Fairbanks, from $24.20 to $32.80; and sugar to Anchorage, from $20.00 to $31.00. Coal from Healy to Fairbanks, formerly assessed at $1.50 per ton, was now $2.75.

President Charles Bunnell of the Alaska Agricultural College and School of Mines supplied the Fairbanks Chamber of Commerce with concrete examples of the new charges. Cement worth $1,272.48 was assessed an additional $3,318.77 from Seattle. A shipment of 161,000 pounds of lumber from a Ketchikan mill cost $1,932.00 in freight, while the mill received $1,800.66. Railbelt residents did not wait for Bunnell's horror stories. In late November 1930, the Fairbanks Chamber protested against possible increases. That same month Republican James Wickersham narrowly won a hard-fought race for the delegate's seat in Congress. He attributed his opponent's strength partly to "the action of the Senatorial Committee along the railroad, where I lost almost every precinct."[10] The committee's published recommendations inspired another wave of protest. Still more objections flowed in after the new rates went into effect during March and April 1931. In the main, their objections rehashed old arguments against rate increases.

Beginning with the summer of 1931, Alaska merchants and travelers threw as much freight and passenger business as possible to the railroad's competition. Busses and trucks on the Richardson Highway, gasoline boats from Seattle to Cook Inlet, and airplanes claimed more and more tourists, business travelers, and high-value freight. Steamers to St. Michael carried fuel. Competition and the mounting effects of the Great Depression combined to depress revenues far below the Howell committee's expectations. Rail passenger revenue had been falling since 1928 and stood at $200,431 for fiscal year 1930. Ohlson carefully, conservatively predicted an increase of $136,604.73 for the twelve months after March 20, 1931, when the new rates became effective. Instead, passenger revenue for fiscal year 1931 dropped to $191,475, though it crept up slightly to $191,873 in fiscal year 1932. In December 1932 Ohlson made the first in a series of rate reductions, cutting passenger fares back to six cents per mile. As if to mock his action, passenger revenue plunged to $121,119 in 1933, a lesser total than the increase he had predicted two years before. Freight revenues rose from $688,440 in 1931 to $906,123 in 1932 then fell back slightly to $890,248 in 1933. The figures concealed a net loss of revenue tonnage, from 101,470 in 1931 to 97,479 in 1933. Ohlson's selective rate reductions begun early in the latter year probably helped to ease the decline.

The Howell committee's rate policies were an unqualified failure by the time the senator died in March 1933. Total rail and water revenues had risen less than $73,000 from 1930, Howell's base year, to 1933, the last fiscal year of his personal influence. The sum was far, far short of Howell's demanded $500,000 increase and Ohlson's carefully estimated $476,382.15. Yet, Howell had succeeded in his basic purpose — to reduce deficit spending. The credit, however, should go to Ohlson.

The colonel did not need to be told that his job future depended on his ability to slash expenses. He set to work with energy, determination, and, sometimes, ruthlessness. His inventory reduction program has been mentioned. Closing the

Chatanika branch helped to reduce costs. A "get-tough" policy on hospital admissions saved money. The policy continued even though an Anchorage resident, denied admission, died aboard ship en route to Seattle for treatment. The foundry was closed and castings ordered from "outside." When revenues began to drop in the summer of 1930, Ohlson cut his forces. The average number of employees in fiscal year 1931 was 671, down 263 from Smith's last year. In 1933 the line averaged a mere 650 employees.

Contracting out or abandoning some functions saved still more. Beginning May 15, 1929, the Northern Commercial Company assumed the railroad's mess house, commissary, and cold storage operations. The private operation, Ohlson predicted, would not only reduce expenses, it would also raise revenues because the company would pay freight charges on its supplies. During fiscal year 1931, the railroad stopped producing light, heat, and power at Nenana. It decentralized its heating and purchased power from a private concern, as it had done in Anchorage. On October 1, 1932, the colonel turned the Anchorage city telegraph office over to the Signal Corps. He was not dogmatic about divesting the railroad of its various operations. In the case of the Anchorage terminal water supply, he decided that the railroad could furnish its own at less cost than by purchase from the city. He ordered a pump installed in Ship Creek near the Alaskan Engineering Commission's original water pipes. On March 2, 1933, the railroad once more supplied its own water.

Ohlson found other ways to save. He consolidated sections and discontinued stations. He bought used rolling stock, replacing wooden coaches and broken-down cars while saving 50 percent on the price of new equipment. The Howell committee, plus declining revenues, forced cutbacks in train operations. The thrice-weekly summer service of fiscal year 1930 was reduced to two round trips per week over much of the line. Winter service suffered reductions. On December 1, 1931, the railroad suspended its gas car service from Fairbanks to the territorial college. The service had operated during each academic year since the college opened in 1922, running the three miles from Fairbanks station to the foot of the college hill several times a day. It was a service in fact as well as name, for revenues rarely equalled expenses. For years it did a good winter business, but improving roads and equipment enabled bus operators to provide year-round service to the door of the main academic building. When colder weather reduced revenues instead of increasing them, there was nothing to do but pull the cars off the run. Curtailments such as these reduced train mileage from 262,651 in fiscal year 1930 to 173,220 the next year. Mileage for fiscal year 1932 — 148,819 — more than met Howell's requirement for a 100,000-mile reduction from fiscal year 1930. Train miles during fiscal year 1933 totaled only 90,727.

Ohlson claimed his reward in the rapid drop in deficits during the early 1930s. In fiscal year 1930 the railroad ran $1,213,155.78 in the red. Losses in 1931 were $577,474.24; in 1932, $401,123.92; and in 1933, a mere $257,083.73. The 1932 and 1933 accounts were in even better condition than the figures indicated, because congressional appropriations for resource investigation were charged to operating expenses. Appropriations against the $250,000 which the senator had secured for that purpose were $65,183.17 in 1932 and $102,962.17 in 1933. Little wonder that Howell acquiesced in the rate decreases. Ohlson took justifiable pride in the way he stanched the flow of red ink. In his summary of the 1932 annual report, he "safely" predicted that his railroad would be "self-sustaining" after five more years.[11] He would have been a true prophet except that a maritime strike during fiscal year 1937 forced him to operate ocean ships at a loss. The next year the railroad turned a surplus, and never again did Ohlson have to ask Congress for money to meet the expenses of maintenance and operation.

After economy, improving the roadbed was the general manager's primary concern. There was a lot to improve. Much of the track north of the Nenana River canyon rested on low, swampy ground. Ohlson began a determined program of track raising, ballasting, and bank widening. He hoped to lift the roadbed high enough to avoid sags and frost heaves, but settling continued to be a problem. Elsewhere, the maintenance-of-way-gangs filled more wooden trestles, installed concrete culverts, and replaced sharp curves with new roadbed.

By the beginning of 1933, Ohlson had managed The Alaska Railroad for over four years. In that time he had earned a reputation as a tough, but fair-minded, man. He had no important enemies. In 1929 John Rustgard, Alaska's attorney general, denounced ocean and joint freight rates in a tirade reminiscent of his earlier charges. The general manager easily rode out Rustgard's attack. The same year, the Seward Chamber of Commerce publicly praised Ohlson's "efficiency and skill."[12] Petitions against closing the Chatanika branch, or the Howell committee's rate program, did not blame Ohlson; covering letters to him were polite. In 1931 the *Seward Daily Gateway* lauded his "outstanding achievement" and "the soundness of his judgment in pioneer railroad management."[13] Men in Washington, D. C. were equally impressed. Edward T. Taylor, chairman of the House Appropriations Committee, assured Ohlson of the committee's "kindliest feelings" for his management, and Secretary Wilbur exclaimed, "I think he is one of the big finds."[14] Ohlson's extraordinary record merited all the notice it received.

A late photograph of Ohlson, but his indomitable character still shows through. *The Alaska Railroad*

Otto F. Ohlson, third and most effective General Manager of The Alaska Railroad, served from 1928 to 1945. Here he and his Dodge railmobile pose in front of the railroad's Curry Hotel, a stop for tourists and trainmen. *The Alaska Railroad*

William C. Edes. *The Alaska Railroad*

Thomas Riggs, left, in charge at Fairbanks and Nenana, and Frederick Mears, who supervised the Anchorage area. *The Alaska Railroad*

The members of the Alaskan Engineering Commission, in an uncharacteristic formal pose, probably shortly after their appointment in 1914. From left to right, Frederick Mears, William C. Edes, chairman, and Thomas Riggs. Riggs resigned in 1918 when President Wilson appointed him governor of Alaska. Ill health forced Edes' retirement in 1919. Mears resigned in 1918 to go to France as colonel of the 31st Engineers, but returned in 1919 to become chairman of the commission, replacing Edes. Mears remained chairman until 1923, almost to the formal close of the construction phase. *National Archives*

By Land, Sea, or Air?

Throughout the thirties Otto Ohlson fought competing trucks, busses, boats, and airplanes. The tough Swede faced most of his competition during the summer months only. In winter, ice pans large enough to crush a hull choked Cook Inlet, and snow drifted over great stretches of the Richardson Highway from Valdez to Fairbanks. No boats or trucks could move. When the Yukon froze fast, it halted competitive shipments upriver from its mouth, just as it stopped downriver movements by the railroad's River Boat Service. Only a small air passenger business continued through the winter.

The competition hauled almost entirely high-value perishables, first class freight, and passengers, including tourists. Competitors began sailing and driving in earnest during 1931, after the drastic "Howell committee" rate increases. They continued despite Ohlson's harassment of Heinie Berger, Ohlson's chief competitor by boat, despite the railroad's low summertime competitive tariffs, despite a system of licensing and tolls on the Richardson Highway. They continued with hearty emotional and financial support from central Alaskans. As competition continued, its emotional content expanded until motorship captains and truckers were the heroes, Ohlson and his railroad the villains, of Alaska transportation.

Ohlson carried the fight to the trucks, but he was a victim of geography. The port of Valdez lay tucked into the northeast corner of Prince William Sound, a one-half-day sail from Seward, some 140 air line miles to the southwest. The steamers touched at Valdez before sailing to Seward, so the truckers had a head start. On a typical Thursday they were toiling up the steep grades of the Chugach Mountains in their two-ton trucks, while the steamer was still threading its way through the straits toward Seward. While the steamer was swinging cargo onto the Seward dock early Friday morning, the tired, dusty truckers were highballing through the Tanana Valley toward Fairbanks. On Saturday the freight train was well up the line, but in Fairbanks, grocers were unloading fruits and vegetables from the trucks. On Sunday night the freight steamed into the northern terminal. Those grocers who shipped by rail then set their goods out for sale on Monday morning. All this made the advantages of trucking embarrassingly evident. Grocers who operated trucks received their perishables in time for Saturday's sale. Grocers who shipped by rail received their goods — carried on the same steamer — two days later.

More than geography hampered Ohlson's battle against the trucks. Through the thirties the transportation companies purchased larger trucks, truckers began icing their perishable loads, and more powerful trucks appeared. The Alaska Road Commission slowly but steadily filled bridges, straightened curves, and raised roadbeds on the "trail" — officially the Richardson Highway. By the end of the decade, a lucky trucker could make the Valdez-Fairbanks distance in twelve to fourteen hours. If he were not so lucky — high water at fords, soft spots in the road, or breakdowns could interfere — he pulled into Fairbanks twenty-four hours or more after leaving Valdez.

Bus competition developed in threatening

proportions at about the time trucks began hauling in earnest. Before the 1931 rail fare increase, one substantial bus operator, the Richardson Highway Transportation Company, met the Copper River & Northwestern at Chitina, on a branch of the Richardson Highway. Most of the Chitina-Fairbanks summertime travelers were tourists. Twelve-cents-per-mile fares on the CR & NW discouraged most Fairbanks residents from taking that route "outside"; however, a few paying passengers in private cars and trucks traveled the Fairbanks-Valdez distance. The Richardson Highway Transportation Company also carried passengers over the length of the highway in its busses and big cars. Neither Smith nor Ohlson felt threatened by such traffic. Both of them cooperated with the Richardson Highway Transportation Company in promoting the "Golden Belt Tour."

In 1931 the railroad's passenger fare rose from six to ten cents per mile, the rate demanded by the Howell committee. The price of a one-way ticket, Seward to Fairbanks, jumped from $28.23 to $47.05. The Richardson Highway Transportation Company maintained a rate of fifty-five dollars during 1931, but other highway carriers undercut the fifty-five-dollar fare. As an official of the transportation company phrased it, "every Tom, Dick and Harry that had a car and was not using it for something else, started hauling passengers for Valdez for whatever he could get out of it."[1] In 1932 the established company struck back, lowering rates until a happy tourist or interior resident could travel to the coast for ten dollars. By early July the highway fare had climbed to twenty-five dollars, still well below the railroad's price. The heavy passenger competition among carriers on the Richardson made the situation that much worse for Ohlson. From fiscal year 1931 to fiscal year 1932, his main line lost 4,650 riders. Part of the loss could be charged to the steadily shrinking local travel, another part to declining tourism. From one third to one half should be imputed to growing highway travel. On June 30, 1932, the train from Fairbanks carried five passengers to Seward, while more than forty through travelers used the highway.

Ohlson's railroad lost, by his estimate, some $70,000 in 1932 to passenger and freight diversions over the Richardson. His estimate, when checked against the railroad's rate division on diverted tonnage, excluding tonnage rerouted during blockades on the railroad, seems to be correct. Rates, tonnage, and passengers on the highway varied during the decade, as did the railroad's competitive rates. These changes appear to have been mutually cancelling, leaving the railroad's average annual loss at about $70,000. Assuming that the tonnage and passengers could have traveled over the railroad at only a modest increase in handling expenses, Ohlson would have enjoyed at least $40,000 more net revenue each year. Another $40,000 would have cut the deficit by one tenth in 1932, by one half in 1935. Forty thousand dollars would have wiped away the red ink in 1936 and 1939 and would have staunched it considerably in 1937 and 1938. Ohlson well knew that his job depended on his continuing good performance with profit-and-loss. Any addtion to the net revenue was worth fighting for.

To carry the war to the truckers, Ohlson improved service, lowered rates during the competitive season, cut passenger fares, launched a propaganda campaign, and even attempted a little subversion. None of it was very effective. A look at his tactics against the backdrop of circumstances shows why. Beginning in the 1932 summer season, the railroad halted one of its semiweekly passenger steam trains at Anchorage and shifted perishables and through passengers to a Brill gasoline car. The Brill ran on to Fairbanks, omitting the overnight stop at Curry. Fresh fruits and vegetables then arrived at the northern terminal one day ahead of the regular schedule. Later, a Brill car met the ships at Seward and raced perishables through to Fairbanks in twenty hours. In 1939 the Alaska Steamship Company adjusted its schedule so that every other ship called first at Seward, then at Valdez. Probably Alaska Steam capitulated to pressure from Ohlson, reinforced by Secretary Ickes' antagonism toward the company. Ickes held Alaska Steam in low regard from the time it failed to maintain its schedule during his 1938 visit to the territory.

Ohlson's schedule juggling merely emphasized the railroad's inescapable geographic difficulty. Ohlson's line was 470 miles long, the highway, 371. Before the steamship route change, the trucks from Valdez always enjoyed a half-day's head start. Even when the trucks took a full day, they still arrived eight hours ahead of the Brill car. After the steamer change, the railroad held a similar advantage over the trucks on alternate shipments. But it achieved parity only late in the decade. Anyway, roughly equal elapsed time was not enough by itself to persuade shippers to abandon the trucks.

Ohlson believed that lower rates would restore most of the summer traffic to the railroad, reducing truck hauling to a marginal operation. He was wrong. A few trucks owned or financed by grocers were moving perishables into Fairbanks before the 1931 rate increase. The rate hike was spectacular — slightly over 70 percent — but increased trucking was more than a matter of simple cause and effect. And it certainly did not follow that rate reductions would defeat the trucks or the busses. Ohlson recommended reductions on competitive traffic in the summer of 1932, when the situation became serious. With Wilbur's permission, he restored the six-cent passenger rate in December of that year. He reduced the rate on perishables for the summer of 1933 to $4.75 per hundred pounds, compared with a year-round $4.99 rate under the tariff of 1925. At the end of the summer season, of course, the rate reverted to seven dollars, the charge under the 1931 "Howell committee" tariff. In 1933 he established special commodity rates on sugar and poultry and lowered various terminal charges. Each spring he reissued the special tariffs. Neither these seasonal adjustments nor a reduction of local rates in 1935 helped the competitive situation. Tolls levied on truck tonnage, not lower rates, forced a temporary decline in through highway traffic from 734 tons in 1934 to 304 tons in 1935. In 1938 the truckers moved 2,165 tons, and the standard passenger fare on the highway was $15.00 compared to the railroad's $28.23. "Any rate reduction made by the Railroad is promptly met with corresponding reductions by the truck operators," Ohlson confessed.[2]

There were plenty of noneconomic reasons for Fairbanks residents to support the truckers, however. One was the advantage in time. When Cunningham interviewed three grocers in 1931, only one of them claimed a saving in cost by shipping over the highway. They were much more interested in better service. Even after Ohlson equalized the time in transit, other considerations kept the trucks and busses rolling. Fairbanks residents knew that the railroad's improved summer service resulted from competition, not from Ohlson's charity. If they deserted the truckers, Ohlson might abandon the summertime Brill car, leaving fresh fruits and vegetables to the slower freight and passenger trains. Competition, not Ohlson's kindness had reduced rail rates. If trucking ceased, the competitive rates would not be reissued, and the general level of rates might rise. In 1946 one of the truckers declared that "merchants are giving us the business only because they feel in that way they are holding the freight rates down."[3]

Because truck operators hauled at rates scarcely higher than the railroad's division of the through rate from Seward to Fairbanks, they probably made no more than drivers' wages. Camaraderie, popular support, private subsidies, and adventure kept them rolling. The truckers fought federally imposed tolls to the applause of Fairbanks residents. Alaskans financed the trucking ventures, for rarely did such a happy combination of principle and potential gain present itself. Grocers, a warehousing and transfer firm at Valdez, and others gladly carried notes on the trucks. The drivers saw themselves, with some justification, as beleaguered knights of the highway.

The rigors of the "trail" supplied the adventure. The narrow roadbed, washouts, weak bridges, construction activity — all were obstacles. Melting snows on hill and mountainside added another — swollen streams during late summer. Bridges were few, and many creeks had to be forded. Crossing a swift stream filled with rolling boulders required icy nerve. To prepare for fording, the driver pulled a special canvas tarpaulin from the truck. He spread part of it over the grille, hood, windshield, and cab top, pulled the bottom part under the oil pan, and tied the "tarp" together at the back of the cab. Then he threw the truck in gear and, standing on the running board, one foot jammed against the accelerator, one hand gripping the wheel, he plunged his load into the roaring water. Sometimes he made it, sometimes not. If not, he lost his load, a loss the shipper had to bear.

While Ohlson tried cutting his schedules and rates, he also propagandized. His propaganda struck a basic truth. As he told a meeting of Fairbanks merchants early in 1932, the railroad ran the year around. The railroad ran while trucks crashed through bridges or mired in turbulent streams. It ran when heavy rains made the Richardson an impassable quagmire. When the snow stood ten feet deep in Thompson Pass out of Valdez, the railroad ran. Ohlson's line spent "between one and two million dollars annually in the territory," the railroad maintained an expensive wintertime operation, the railroad was built to develop Alaska and was essential to development. Ohlson criticized merchants who were "patronizing temporary fair-weather competitors of the railroad that did not contribute to the upkeep of Fairbanks."[4]

None of it made much difference to potential shippers. "No appeal to shippers to patronize the railroad in the summer because it is their friend in need in the winter will be effective if it is cheaper to ship another way," was one judgment.[5] Almost every grocer in Fairbanks shipped by truck at one time or another. Other merchants took advantage of the truckers' willingness to haul almost any freight at rates that would meet expenses. The truck rate was about fifty dollars per ton from Valdez to Fairbanks, although a new operator might solicit some business for less. But not often: fraternal feelings, plus the chance of vigilante action against mavericks, maintained a rough rate stability on the highway.

Ohlson tried to discourage highway competition by methods high-handed and by methods devious. During the summer months he maintained a close check on highway traffic: tonnage, shippers, and carriers. No evidence of railroad discrimination against highway shippers exists. The mere noting of competitive traffic, however, opened the possibility of petty slights against merchants who shifted from railroad to highway each spring. In March 1932 the general manager privately urged moving the federal court from Valdez as the "most expedient and effective way" to defeat truck competition. If the court were moved, Ohlson argued, Alaska Steam would "not call at the port of Valdez on the northbound trip, which will eliminate the truck competition entirely." Then, he suggested, the Richardson Highway could be abandoned south of the branch to Chitina, "which would effect a considerable reduction in Alaska Road Commission expenditures in Alaska" and close the Valdez gateway.[6] In May, Ohlson denied that he had used his influence to curtail the Richardson Highway maintenance appropriation, "because we all know that the Richardson Highway is badly needed for transportation purposes."[7] Ohlson's denial may have been technically correct, but it was not in the spirit of his private suggestion to close the south end of the highway.

If Ohlson arranged for other agencies to disrupt truck movements, he kept the plans out of his surviving correspondence. At least one trucker, John E. Clark, was convinced that the road commission did Ohlson's bidding. Work crews sometimes tore up the highway ostensibly for repairs, actually to make it impassable to trucks, he believed. Clark maintained that Ohlson inspired the territorial police to harass truckers. Whether Ohlson actually wielded such influence in the bitter contest was less important than Clark's conviction that he did. One day when Clark was steering his truck north toward Fairbanks, he spotted a car stuck along the road. He stopped, intending to fasten his chain to the car and pull it out of the mud, a service the truckers often rendered to stranded motorists. As he reached for his towing chain, a stocky figure detached itself from the mired car. "I'm Colonel Ohlson," the motorist said.[8] Without a word, Clark tossed the chain back inside, slammed his cab door shut, and threw his truck into gear.

Ohlson threatened the Richardson Highway Transportation Company with the loss of the railroad's cooperation in promoting the Golden Belt Tour in 1932, when the company planned to introduce trucks, and again in 1936, when the highway carrier dropped its Valdez-Fairbanks passenger fare to the prevailing fifteen dollars. On the first occasion the Alaska Steamship Company protested the general manager's threat. The steamer line had invested in the highway carrier. It also expressed concern over the future of the Golden Belt Tour. No direct evidence indicates that Ohlson carried out his threats, but in any case, they had no more effect than his other tactics. The Richardson Highway Transportation Company and the other freight and passenger carriers continued to run.

Ohlson's final hope was a toll on highway tonnage. He opposed the idea at first, accepting it only as a last resort. With good reason, Ohlson hesitated before approving the tolls. The Interior Department derived its authority to collect tolls from an act of Congress approved June 30, 1932. The law transferred the Alaska Road Commission from the War Department to the Interior Department and established highway rules. The transfer was consistent with the War Department's steady withdrawal from Alaska. It recognized the desirability of coordinating transportation routes under one head. Up to 1932 no formal regulations governed the speed, weight, and type of vehicle on the "trail." Regulations were needed to protect the highway during the soggy "breakup" season against ever more powerful and heavier cars, busses, and trucks.

So far, the act would seem entirely constructive and innocent of purpose, but it contained potential dynamite in its provisions empowering the Secretary of the Interior to collect tolls on highway traffic. In plain fact the act intended to penalize the highway carriers who were competing with the railroad. Otherwise, a department official noted, "it is evident that if no restrictions are placed upon highway carriers, the railroad would soon be unable to justify its existence."[9] The situation was not really so bleak, for the railroad could be justified by its year-round operation or by its development role. Yet, the statement was close enough to the truth to be uncomfortable. In its official explanations, the Interior Department preferred the "competition" argument, which Secretary Harold L. Ickes stated trenchantly after the tolls became law: "I didn't see any validity in the argument that the United States Government ought to maintain a highway to compete with its own railroad."[10] The difficulty was that tolls were not a logical response to competition. One way to deal with competition would have been to limit travel to standard passenger cars and small trucks. Or the department could have closed the road. Either action would have brought howls of protest. The department appeared to be attempting indirectly what it dared not do openly. At the same time, it was imposing new levies on the population of a struggling frontier land.

Ohlson stated the problem with refreshing candor. In his opinion, the department could take three effective courses of action. It could sharply reduce rates on the railroad. It could close the highway below the Chitina branch. It could arrange weight limits and fees to eliminate the large trucks carrying bulky perishables, and the large passenger busses. Or it could do all three. Tolls might burden highway carriers but would not force them out of business, he argued, unless they were confiscatory. Since confiscatory tolls would mobilize public opinion against the government, the department gave Ohlson half a loaf. He was allowed to reduce rates. Ohlson came to understand, however, that he would have to lower rates to ruinous levels before his competitors would surrender. The department imposed weight limitations, but only enough to protect the "trail" from heavy loads. Stricter limits would have restored traffic that rightfully belonged to the railroad, Ohlson believed. He pointed to his native Sweden, that "hardheaded and practical nation," which had banned trucks and busses on its highways.[11] He was unwilling to admit what others foresaw — that severe weight restrictions would have outraged Alaskans just as much as confiscatory tolls.

Bound as it was by its regard for public opinion, the department could do only so much as public opinion would tolerate. That was little indeed. The first tolls were not tolls in the usual sense, but were license fees levied on all vehicles according to their purpose and capacity. The uniform fees were imposed without regard for the distance the vehicle traveled on the "trail," nor for the number of times it used the road. Most truckers refused to pay. The department could do nothing about it, because the law failed to provide penalties for violators. This legislative oversight was acutely embarrassing. One anguished homesteader wrote to Ickes that truckers who ignored the fee "laugh at you and your regulation and at us, the poor *saps* who did pay it."[12] The provisions regarding weight, safety, and speed were equally unenforceable.

Ohlson proposed to find a way out. He and Ike P. Taylor, chief engineer of the Alaska Road Commission, emerged from a conference at Washington early in 1935 with a scheme for striking at the truckers where they could be hurt. Their plan was simplicity itself. At the village of McCarty, now Big Delta, the road commission operated a ferry across the Tanana. Ohlson and Taylor recommended collecting a toll of 2½ cents per ton-mile at the ferry. The rate for one ton going the full distance was $9.27, a charge which, they believed, would return some traffic to the railroad. Of course, the truckers could refuse to pay. They could not be prosecuted for nonpayment. But they would not cross the river until they paid.

For a while the new system seemed to work. The truckers did not evade the toll station seventy-three miles southwest of Fairbanks, for there was no way to avoid crossing the water. Highway tonnage slipped during the summer of 1935. But Ohlson's hopes were short lived. With financial

211

assistance from interested parties in Fairbanks and Valdez, the truckers soon regained their lost tonnage. By 1939 the trucking business was booming. Confident of public support, the truckers were prepared to evade the tolls by subterfuge if possible, by force if necessary. In September a trucker briefly blocked the highway, touching off a flurry of suits and countersuits. The next year the truck drivers sometimes unloaded their trucks at the river, shipping their loads across on a motorized, homemade scow defiantly waving a skull-and-crossbones flag. Then they boarded the ferry in their empty trucks, paid a one-dollar fee, and reloaded when they reached the north bank. In October 1940 a group of truckers went even further. They broke the chain locking the ferry, using the vessel without paying a toll. The marshal at Fairbanks dispatched a deputy to the scene, first instructing him not to load his shotgun. The next group of truckers knew about the unloaded gun. They swaggered up to the deputy, wrenched the useless gun from his hands, and locked him in the scale house while they moved ten loads across on the ferry. All this ocurred to the ecstatic applause of Fairbanksans. Juries would not convict on the most solid evidence of toll evasion. A grand jury refused to indict the truckers who assaulted the deputy marshal.

Obviously the tolls encouraged lawbreaking without shifting the freight from truck to railroad. Public opinion, as the Fairbanks newspaper remarked, was "bitterly against the present toll."[13] By the summer of 1942 there was no doubt that the tolls only added to the cost of supplies and equipment for federal wartime projects. Ohlson had all he could manage in moving an unprecedented volume of military freight and in keeping his railroad from buckling under its weight. The small amount of truck cargo destined for Fairbanks civilians no longer mattered. On July 15 Ickes removed the tolls. They were never restored.

Ohlson's motive from first to last was to recapture high-value freight for the railroad, in order to strengthen his line financially. He regarded the tolls themselves as makeshift, useful only because all other tactics had failed. But he always fought to win, and he never pretended anything else. "If any of these people were placed in my position they would resort to the same tactics that I have used," the general manager wrote of his detractors.[14] Truly, Ohlson had to fight. For interior Alaskans to enjoy the best service and transportation rates, it was a fight he had to lose. His efforts only made his competitors more determined. The memory of the railroad's indifferent service on perishables in the days before competition, plus Ohlson's war on the trucks, brought citizens and financial backers to the side of the highway carriers.

While trucks rolled along the Richardson, motor vessels from Seattle ran to Anchorage in the summer, forcing Ohlson to face a competitive situation in his own backyard. The railroad's principal competitor was Heinie Berger, a Seattle resident who for several years operated a passenger and freight boat service for communities on the shores of Cook Inlet. The Alaska legislature subsidized Berger's shipping service, but withdrew its subvention about the time of the railroad's drastic rate increases. Circumstance, plus interest and possibly some financial assistance from a few Anchorage merchants, prompted Berger to begin shipping from Seattle to Anchorage. Berger's motor vessel *Discoverer* carried from 70 to 118 tons of freight and a few passengers per trip, each trip usually being scheduled once a month during the navigation season. The season varied with the weather, beginning in March or April and ending in October or November. Berger owned other ships, but they usually ran in Cook Inlet only, or to Bering Sea ports. Berger was Ohlson's chief gadfly, but he was not alone. One or two other ships regularly plied the Seattle-Anchorage run. Occasionally a steamer or motor ship would sail into the harbor with merchandise that was either ordered by Anchorage residents or that was for sale at cut-rate prices to the public at large. Water competition cost the railroad some $15,000 each year. To those who accused Ohlson of straining at gnats in his effort to suppress the water trade, the general manager had a compelling reply. Large motor ships, he reasoned, would join the competitive fleet if the railroad could not stamp out the small ships. Events proved him right.

Ohlson tried cutting rates as he had done against highway competition. He matched Berger's rate, twenty-two dollars per ton including Seattle wharfage charges, after pressuring a cost-conscious Alaska Steam to join the railroad in reductions. Berger continued to haul fresh fruits and vegetables, flour, feed, iron and steel, automobiles, and other commodities. From time to time Ohlson lengthened his list of competitive goods. He gained little by it. Berger dropped his rate still lower because he could afford to do so. He was a tough competitor: he sailed directly from Seattle, while Alaska Steam's vessels called at several ports before meeting the railroad at Seward. Everything carried on the steamers had to be transferred, increasing the spoilage of fresh fruits and vegetables. Berger sailed only when he collected sufficient cargo. He scheduled his maintenance and routine repairs in Seattle, where costs were lower. During the winter he berthed his small fleet in Puget Sound, avoiding high wintertime operating costs.

Berger cost Ohlson money, but the General Accounting Office cost him still more. In a decision that boggled the minds of the railroad's executives, it ordered the railroad and Alaska Steam to forward freight for government agencies north of Anchorage at the competitive rate plus the local rail rate, if that charge were lower than the established joint through rate. The comptroller general based his decision on a narrow construction of laws and decisions holding that, in general, a through rate could not be higher than the sum of the local rates. The regular through rate was higher than the competitive rate plus the local rail rate to stations north of Anchorage. Therefore, the comptroller general ordered both railroad and steamship to refund the difference between the regular and competitive rates from the summer of 1935 to the date of his decision in June 1936. The comptroller general's quest for federal economy was understandable, even if misguided when seen in the light of the railroad's competitive difficulties. But that worthy official went further in his myopic quest for economy. He ordered government freight forwarded at the lowest rate the year around. This meant that federal agencies enjoyed competitive rates in February, when Cook Inlet filled with ice and competitive tariffs were not in effect. Ohlson protested this unwarranted interference in transportation policy, but to no avail.

Ohlson's propaganda had as slight an impact on the motor ships as it did on the trucks. Most of his arguments were well-worn, but he did play one new variation of his support-the-railroad theme. Merchants who shipped by boat failed to lower their prices to customers, he maintained. The general manager's contention probably was correct concerning canned goods and building materials, but he neglected to add that the grocers shipped fresher seasonal fruits and vegetables more cheaply by boat than they could by steamer and railroad. The Alaska Railroad Employees' Association paralleled Ohlson's propaganda with its own — a gesture weakened by railroad employee purchases of various commodities from the boats.

Boycotts were somewhat more effective. In 1934 an Employees' Association boycott forced the National Grocery Company, a Seattle wholesaler, to ship by steamer and railroad unless the company's Anchorage customers specified all-water shipment. Ohlson ordered checks on cargo moving over all the docks in the terminal reserve. Whenever he could retaliate against businesses shipping via boat, he did. In 1934 a grocer asked to buy a steer from the railroad. "You expect me to patronize the Railroad and I am glad to do so but I need a little cooperation also," the grocer announced. "You must be somewhat of a jester," Ohlson shot back, "as we know it is a fact that you had some fifteen tons of groceries shipped in via the Steamer [sic] DISCOVERER on her last trip."[15] Ohlson's answer was no.

Four years later a cannery operator shipped a cargo in one of his own boats, ostensibly for his cannery but actually destined for several businesses and individuals in and around Anchorage. He moved the freight over his cannery's dock, a dock leased from the railroad. Ohlson called the cannery operator on the carpet. In 1939 Cunningham caught Berger at conniving to conceal the true weight of newsprint shipments to the *Anchorage Daily Times*. Berger provided the railroad with a false cargo list but by accident attached a second cargo list made up for a local transfer company. The transfer company's list showed 2½ tons more freight for the newspaper than did the railroad's list. Ohlson quickly hit the newspaper where he could hurt it. He cut off all railroad advertising in the *Times* for one and one-half months until he and the newspaper reached an understanding. The general manager proved to be a tough infighter in these encounters, but his opportunities for retribution were too infrequent to affect the competitive situation very much.

The railroad's major advantage lay in its control of the waterfront. When Berger or other ship captains wished to use the railroad's "ocean dock" north across the mouth of Ship Creek from Anchorage, Ohlson insisted on collecting wharfage charges. Berger refused to pay. Ohlson sued and collected. In the meantime, Berger acquired a new *Discoverer* and again refused to pay on the grounds that the court decision applied only to his previous boat. Ohlson could have chased the determined captain from the dock, but his action "would have resulted in much inconvenience to travelers, and persons shipping to and from points on Cook Inlet, and would have done harm to local commercial interests."[16] In 1933 Ohlson successfully appealed to the Post Office Department to withhold from Berger's mail contract an amount equal to the wharfage owed. Thereafter, Berger unloaded some of his cargo at the "city dock," south of Ship Creek and under the bluffs of Anchorage. Whenever the thirty-five-foot tides were contrary, he lightered his goods ashore on scows. To stimulate the area economy, the railroad allowed Cook Inlet products and merchandise consigned to Cook Inlet or Knik Arm points to land free of charge. Berger therefore unloaded at the ocean dock whenever he carried Cook Inlet products or cargo too valuable to risk. In the latter instances he paid the railroad's wharfage charges.

The city dock and two or three cannery docks, as well as the ocean dock, were in the railroad's terminal reserve. Ohlson could regulate the use of all of them, and he did so just enough to harass Berger, but not enough to force a showdown with him. He inserted clauses in cannery contracts obliging the canneries to deny their docks to boats in the Seattle trade, on pain of forfeiture. He allowed Berger to use the city dock and to operate scows for several years. So long as Berger's business remained relatively small, Ohlson contented himself with inconveniencing the doughty boat captain. Ohlson abruptly changed his attitude when Berger constructed the *Lake Francis*, a vessel capable of carrying one thousand tons.

Ohlson forced a showdown over the big boat. He decided to collect wharfage charges on all of Berger's shipments whenever they landed in the terminal reserve. Surely he knew that forcing Berger to pay wharfage over the city dock would destroy whatever goodwill remained toward Ohlson in Anchorage. His alternative was to see all of the summer's perishable freight, and much else besides, travel on Berger's capacious new vessel. Ohlson did not have long to wait. Early in 1938 Berger completed his boat, landed the contract for shipping the building materials for a new school in Anchorage, and improved the city dock at his own expense. On May 25 he was unloading from a barge alongside the city dock when a switching crew drew a string of coal cars across the road leading from the dock to town. Berger protested, but the coal cars stayed put until he paid his wharfage. He then secured a temporary injunction from the district court at Valdez. The case was in litigation for more than three years before it went against the boat captain. During that time Berger occasionally unloaded cargos wharfage-free at the city dock.

Throughout their legal jousting, Berger sought to stop Ohlson from collecting wharfage again. The general manager had permitted boats to land at the city dock without wharfage payment, therefore, he was bound by his past actions. To this Ohlson replied that the city dock was within the terminal reserve; thus, the railroad could respond as it chose to developing competitive conditions. The district judge at Valdez accepted the railroad's reasoning when, on September 30, 1939, he denied Berger a permanent injunction. In denying Berger's motion for a rehearing, the Ninth Circuit Court of Appeals affirmed the railroad's right to close the city dock, while it refused to rule on Ohlson's authority to block the road from the dock or to demand wharfage. Because wharfage payment was the condition on which Ohlson opened the dock, nothing else mattered much. The circuit court reached its decision August 4, 1941, and soon after, Ohlson moved to collect the wharfage payments which he had suspended during the litigation.

Berger and the railroad executives remained on good terms during their legal battle. They all recognized that the general manager had no choice but to make the boating operations as expensive as he could. World War II made the question of competition a moot one soon enough. In any event, Ohlson could not stop the boats.

The general manager struggled with waterborne competition of a different sort at the far end of his transportation line — the lower Yukon. The crux of his situation was this: goods could not be hauled via Seward to the lower Yukon as cheaply as they could be carried by steamer from Seattle to Marshall village, the transfer point on the lower river. Competitive exigencies forced an unreal rate structure on the railroad's river service. In 1931 The Alaska Railroad charged $5.62 to ship 100 pounds of first-class goods from Seattle to Nenana, transfer them to a stern-wheeler, and send them downstream 858 miles to Marshall. The same 100 pounds cost $5.95 in Fairbanks, or 33 cents more for an easy fifty-eight-mile rail haul from Nenana.

The rates were not just absurd, they were frozen as fast as the Yukon in January. If Ohlson raised them he would invite the Northern Commercial Company, the regular carrier from the river's mouth to Marshall, to compete for traffic upriver. If the "N. C. Co." moved above Marshall, independent merchants who competed with Northern Commercial's stores might be forced into shipping exclusively with their competitor. Upriver merchants and missionaries, some of whom already owned river boats, would be tempted into more frequent trips downriver to Marshall to buy their freight and haul it back upstream. All of it would spell pure loss for the railroad's steamers chuffing down from Nenana.

It would have been just as disastrous to reduce rates. If independent merchants from Northern Commercial's preserve began running boats upriver to take advantage of lower rates at the connecting point, the company could raise a cry of unfair federal competition with private enterprise. Lower boat rates would almost certainly produce howls in Fairbanks, where merchants already paid more freight than other customers hundreds of miles downriver. Abandoning the service and the people along the Tanana and Yukon rivers was out of the question. It was a bad situation all around, but its certainties were much preferred to the imponderables of a new arrangement. Ohlson left the rates alone. He confined himself to solicitous concern for shipper's welfare, which was no substitute for lower rates. By 1945, 62 percent of the railroad's river tonnage was gasoline, oil, and coal. Much high-value freight took the all-water route.

The railroad's inflexible river rates, combined with its vulnerability elsewhere, led Ohlson to be unusually gentle with his Yukon competitors. When the Lomen family of reindeer fame sought Yukon business for its steamship line, Ohlson merely hoped that Ralph Lomen would not be "too active in his solicitations for competitive Yukon River business."[17] After the Lomens refused to shift their reindeer herding to the railbelt, however, Ohlson raised no objection to a rate war against them. Alaska Steam and Northern Commercial cut their rates in 1934 in the hope of driving out the Lomens and their connecting carrier on the river — the Day Navigation Company.

Ohlson had reason to believe that the "N. C. Co." was already rate-cutting on the Yukon, but his situation was too precarious for a protest. The stocky Swede could not afford to alienate a volume rail shipper over a quarrel at the far end of the boat line. His appeasement of Northern Commercial was so uncharacteristic as to be inexplicable without reference to the overall competitive situation. When the company protested against paying express rates for a shipment of toys arriving at its Fairbanks store after Christmas 1936, Ohlson supported the protest. "The reason for making this appeal," he told the express company, "is that the Northern Commercial Company has, ever since the Richardson Highway competition sprang up several years ago, consistently patronized the Railroad and the Express Company and never shipped anything over the Highway."[18] Ohlson's statement was not true and he knew it. Northern Commercial had shipped over the highway before and it would again. But Ohlson was less worried about what the "N. C. Co." had done than what it might do. It could beat him on the Yukon if it so wished. It could shift its Fairbanks tonnage to the trucks during the summer season on the "trail." And it could ship a lot of its Anchorage merchandise with Heinie Berger. Better for Ohlson to overlook a few transgressions than to war on so resourceful a company.

The most significant of the general manager's minor competitive skirmishes was with Alaska's burgeoning airplane companies. Ohlson gave airplanes their due as the only rapid way to conquer Alaska's vast wasteland. He hoped that flights from Fairbanks and other points would open up new areas to prospecting. If airplanes carried a few passengers who might have traveled by rail, there were compensations. The railroad hauled aviation gasoline, oil, and aircraft parts, and planes flew passengers to and from the line itself.

From 1930 on, Ohlson had to face more serious aircraft inroads on his passenger business. The airplane companies compensated with optimism and aggressiveness for what they lacked in size. Expanding air networks, new airfields along the railbelt, and the construction of major airports at Anchorage and Fairbanks boded ill for the railroad. By the early 1930s, the planes were carrying some cargo. After the railroad raised its passenger rates, the pilots slashed theirs to bring the competing fares within a few dollars of one another. Even though the rates over the Richardson Highway were substantially lower than the railroad's rates, the dauntless pilots flew passengers and perishables to Fairbanks from Cordova and Valdez. Only bad weather prevented the planes from becoming a serious threat in season and out.

Ohlson could do very little about his air competitors other than refuse to reduce rates on their supplies. In 1934 he did cut the rate on disassembled aircraft to prevent the airplane companies from assembling their craft at Seward and flying them to the interior. Only rarely could he retaliate as when, in 1940, he ordered a taxi driver off the Seward dock for soliciting airplane passenger business. In general, he had to rely on high air transport costs and bad weather to keep the competition down.

The story in the air was much the same as on the ground or in the water. Ohlson could worry and harass his competitors, occasionally he could strike them a telling blow. But he was too bound by geography, policy, and economic exigencies to defeat them. Competition undermined Ohlson's popularity, wounded his psyche, and hurt the railroad's standing in the territory while, paradoxically, it improved rail service and reduced rail rates. Competition was a fault line separating Alaskan desires and federal transportation policy. After competition developed, fewer Alaskans could accept the statement that the interests of the Territory of Alaska and The Alaska Railroad were identical.

No. 702, completed by Baldwin in 1927 and placed in service in March of that year, pulls a freight in June 1945. The Mikado type 2-8-2 was intended to beef up the motive power of the aging, Mogul-dominated locomotive fleet. *The Alaska Railroad*

No. 502, a 2-8-0 Consolidation, built by Lima for the War Department and placed in service June 1942. *The Alaska Railroad*

A 300-series engine arrives at Whittier. The 300s were used in yard service. *The Alaska Railroad*

No. 315, built by Lima in 1944. *The Alaska Railroad*

No. 312, 0-6-0 with 40,000 tractive power, at Whittier, May 5, 1948. *The Alaska Railroad*

No. 751, placed in service May 26, 1942. A MacArthur type, renamed when the Mikado went out of fashion in World War II. *The Alaska Railroad*

The 901, a 4-6-2 Pacific type, was built by Baldwin in 1940 and placed in service March 1941. *Eugene McCracken Collection, University of Alaska Archives*

No. 557, a Consolidation type built by Baldwin in 1943 and sold for scrap in 1965, was rescued and is now privately owned. It was photographed in June 1959 and refurbished for a trip from Anchorage to Whittier sponsored by the California-Nevada Railroad Historical Society. *The Alaska Railroad*

The beginning of the end for the Age of Steam: diesel No. 1000 rests in its protective cocoon after unloading at Whittier, 1944. Placed in service June 1944. *The Alaska Railroad*

No. 1001, twin of the 1000 and like it, built by the American Locomotive Company, strikes a pose at Whittier with two tired Panama relics, 1944. *The Alaska Railroad*

Newer Brills, the 212 against a spectacular backdrop at Palmer. From the founding of the Matanuska Valley Colony in 1935 and for many years thereafter the railroad operated an Anchorage-Palmer railbus service. *The Alaska Railroad*

No. 213 nosing out of the Anchorage Roundhouse. *The Alaska Railroad*

Brill No. 216, the "Tanana." *The Alaska Railroad*

Old Business Car B-1 about 1930. This car was a fixture on The Alaska Railroad for many years. It survived World War II only to be denounced for its incommodiousness in the first postwar report on the railroad's present condition and future prospects. *The Alaska Railroad*

Hart convertible car, in service during the construction days. *The Alaska Railroad*

A wooden flatcar of the type in service from the beginning of construction until after World War II. *The Alaska Railroad*

An Alaskan Engineering Commission tank car in the Anchorage yards. *The Alaska Railroad*

Dump cars, 1919. *The Alaska Railroad*

An Alaska Railroad coal car. *The Alaska Railroad*

Handcars were common in the construction days but were phased out beginning in the 1920s. *The Alaska Railroad*

Goodbye, Red Ink

Ohlson intervened dramatically during two bitter maritime strikes, once in 1934, and again in 1936. His mediation moved relief ships to Alaska, averting hardship or worse in the territory. His superb performances brightened a reputation rapidly losing luster along the railbelt. They were more than personal triumphs in a later general managership largely bereft of them, for they helped to secure Ohlson's tenure under Interior Secretary Ickes.

The Pacific coast longshoremen's strike of 1934 began on May 9 over wages. Violence became the norm in Seattle after the steamship lines hired strikebreakers. On May 12 an angry mob of strikers smashed through the lightly manned police lines and beat non-union laborers. The strikers' tactic effectively paralyzed shipping. As the situation deteriorated into shootings and beatings involving pro- and anti-union elements alike, the threat to Alaska grew. Towns in the territory located on year-round transportation lines were stocked with five or six weeks' worth of staple foods. When food supplies were exhausted, the horrors of starvation and social chaos would become real. The strike ran on while Alaska Steam appealed to the mayor of Seattle and the governor of Washington for guards to protect Alaska-bound shipping. They refused. A week slipped by before Alaska Steam's vice-president wired Ohlson, asking his "help in getting us protection needed to load ships."[1]

To his credit, Ohlson refused to be stampeded by visions of doom, or by wires from Alaska Steam. His May 15 telegram to Ickes merely mentioned delays to railroad shipments, mail, and mining equipment. Later he ordered the railroad's material moved on the *North Star,* sailing on May 29. On June 2 he asked Ickes for permission to fly to Seattle, lease two steamers, and arrange for regular sailings to Alaska under the railroad's auspices.

For a time it seemed that Ohlson's request would be unnecessary. On June 8 Alaska Steam reached an understanding with the longshoremen and other maritime unions for relief sailings to Alaska. Two steamers left Seattle laden with merchandise for the territory. On the twentieth of July, Seattle's mayor bid for control of the docks by directing a police tear gas charge against a picket line. After scattering the strikers, the mayor set up armed guards to supervise non-union loading. The angry longshoremen walked away from Alaska Steam's vessels with a vow not to return until the mayor dropped his law-and-order stance and removed his police guards.

With the crisis renewed, President Roosevelt invoked the 1914 enabling act authorizing The Alaska Railroad to charter ships for the Alaska run. On July 2 Ickes ordered Ohlson to fly to Seattle, then a noteworthy action in itself, and negotiate charters. When he arrived in Seattle two days later, the general manager discovered that the maritime unions and the Alaska Steamship Company had agreed to load and unload the company's vessels at Tacoma. Ohlson urged the unions to operate from Seattle because "only a very small percentage of the Alaska tonnage originates at Tacoma [and] I felt that the added mileage transporting freight. . .from Seattle to

Tacoma...thirty-five miles would increase transportation costs which in the end are always absorbed by the consumer." The unions stood fast by their decision not to work at Seattle until the mayor disbanded his armed guards at the dock. Ohlson interviewed the mayor, pressing him to call off his guards. The mayor refused. Ohlson then approved the Tacoma operation with the warning, he informed Ickes, "that if the service was interrupted and not continuous that I would act upon instructions that I had received from you to charter ships in order to insure continuous and dependable service to the Territory of Alaska."[2]

July 7 saw the first sailings under the new arrangement. Ohlson was well satisfied with the solution. Chartering ships in the face of the special Alaska relief agreement would have meant hiring new crews and loading under the protection of troops. Ohlson had no more trouble with Puget Sound shipping, but while he was in Seattle checking the Alaska sailings, the ship's longshoremen at Seward struck on July 14 for higher pay. Cunningham persuaded them to return to work by placing them under the railroad, which paid its dock workers more than the steamship company did. He charged the difference to the ships. Secretary Ickes was delighted with Ohlson's work. "I desire to felicitate you upon the efforts you have put forth," he congratulated the general manager.[3] On August 2 regular shipping from Seattle resumed under a labor-management truce.

The 1936-37 maritime strike was the true test of Ohlson's mettle. In 1936 he did what he had threatened to do in 1934 — charter and operate steamships to Alaska. Unfortunately, Ohlson marred his own performance in a fit of pique over truck and water competition. The trouble began in the fall of 1936, when labor unrest and brief work stoppages in Seattle presaged a major strike. Early in October Ohlson prepared a detailed plan for curtailing rail operations and maintenance, reducing the line to emergency service for the strike's duration. By itself the plan was an intelligent improvement over the catch-as-can rail service, with its frequent train annulments, during the 1934 strike.

Ohlson's justification for suspension was another matter. His defense, as given to the Anchorage Chamber of Commerce, was representative of his replies to critics. "The Alaska Railroad is a business and not a charity institution and cannot obligate expenditures beyond its available funds," he declared. "Had the merchants in Anchorage and elsewhere in the rail belt patronized the railroad instead of its competitors...it could have operated through this emergency but under present conditions it cannot without a deficiency appropriation."[4] With all respect to Ohlson, his remarks were silly. Had the railroad faced no competition and assumed greater profit, Ohlson would have spent the money on improvements. He would not have left funds lying around waiting to be spent during maritime strikes. The emergency demanded Ohlson's waiving the usual profit and loss considerations, as he did later when the railroad undertook steamship operations. His manner raised a storm of protests and angry calls for his resignation. His outrageous justifications obscured his stated willingness to operate emergency trains and to inaugurate steamship service whenever food supplies reached dangerously low levels.

The strike began on October 29 while Ohlson was in Washington. Cunningham curtailed operations, modifying Ohlson's plan to allow for some additional maintenance work and fuel shipments. He acted against the backdrop of protests over the railroad's closing. The local protests were unavailing, but the Post Office Department saved train service for the railbelt when it arranged for Alaska mail shipments on Canadian steamers and Coast Guard vessels. On November 6 Ohlson authorized a weekly mixed train connecting with the mail ship at Seward and running to Fairbanks. Skeleton section crews and minimum forces elsewhere kept the line open.

Still the strike wore on. When labor and management showed no signs of reaching an interim agreement, President Roosevelt on November 17 again invoked The Alaska Railroad's authority to operate steamships to Alaska. On November 20 Ohlson arrived in San Francisco by air. He met with the maritime union leaders to gain their cooperation in the loading and manning of ships under charter to the railroad. He presented an assessment of food stocks in the railbelt, revealing that Central Alaskans would exhaust their supplies of fruit, vegetables, meat, and dairy products within two to four weeks. Tough, combative Harry Bridges of the International Longshoremen's Association disputed Ohlson's figures, but "after some discussion" the meeting accepted the general manager's evaluation.⁵ On other issues the unions were not so pliant. They asked for an agreement granting all of their strike demands and requiring Ohlson to charter ships from firms not involved in the strike. Ohlson countered with an offer to grant prestrike wages, hours, and working conditions. The union men replied that they would have to think about it.

Alaska Steam was just as cool to Ohlson's advances. The company refused his request to withdraw from the steamship owners' association and reach a separate understanding with the unions regarding the Alaska run. In between conferences Ohlson searched for ships. He discovered the cannery ship *Arctic*, available except for the load of salmon in its hold. Then he returned to the maritime unions' representatives and forged wage agreements. The agreements boiled down to granting the seamen the higher, temporary-service pay they earned aboard seasonal cannery vessels and granting the longshoremen a wage increase conceded by the ship owners prior to the strike.

After supervising inventories and other preliminary work, Ohlson went from San Francisco to Seattle, where he found about ten thousand tons awaiting shipment to Alaska. Moreover, Western Alaskans were clamoring for passenger service to Seattle. So he chartered the *General W. C. Gorgas*, another cannery ship, with a 4,500-ton capacity and space for 288 passengers. Finally, he ordered the Bureau of Indian Affairs motorships *Boxer* and *North Star* reconditioned at the railroad's expense, the first for auxiliary service between southeastern Alaska and Seward, the second for the southeastern Alaska run. In parallel negotiations with the Post Office Department, he arranged for mail shipments on the vessels that he had pressed into service.

Ohlson at first planned only one sailing each for the *Arctic* and the *Gorgas*, but the strike dragged on beyond the early January settlement that he had predicted. To keep Alaska supplied, he ordered the *Gorgas* to make a second trip. On February 5 the embattled unions and ship owners at last composed their differences. The railroad's emergency service, which had begun with the *Boxer's* first sailing December 6, ended on February 9 when the *Gorgas* dropped anchor in Elliott Bay.

Once again Ohlson had placed his flair for negotiation and improvisation in the service of Alaska. On short notice he had assembled a shipping fleet, seamen, stewards, dock forces, and the organization required for ticket sales, collections, and freight handling. Error and confusion were apparent, too, however. Ships bypassed ports because of storms or misunderstandings. At least one ship was overmanned. Heavy expenses ran what would have been the railroad's first yearly surplus into a deficit of over $172,000. Alaskans who had expected regular service bombarded Governor John W. Troy with complaints. When building materials ran out in Juneau during the strike's final week, Troy himself verged on hysteria.

The difficulties could not be charged to Ohlson. An improvised organization was especially prone to error. Ship charters were expensive, and repairs to the *North Star* were unexpectedly costly. Alaska offered little southbound freight revenue during the wintertime. Ohlson's critics, who anticipated business-as-usual, forgot that Ohlson was providing an emergency service, not a substitute for Alaska Steam's regular sailings. J. R. Ummel of the Seattle purchasing department believed that stories of food shortages in southeastern Alaska were deliberately manufactured to stampede the railroad into establishing regular service. In the midst of an outcry over the supposed scarcity of meat in the Northland, his forces had to load thirty tons of hay to fill the cold storage space on the *North Star*. Despite the criticism, Ohlson's labors were also recognized and praised. The *Seward Gateway*, no friend of the general manager's, headed its approving editorial "Alaska Grateful." The Tacoma Chamber of Commerce considered Ohlson's labors "wonderfully successful under the circumstances."⁶ Ickes was so impressed by Ohlson's abilities that in December 1936 he sent the charming, forceful Swede to strikebound Hawaii with orders to reach a temporary maritime settlement.

The Alaska Railroad's normal maritime relationships had no happy ending. Ohlson and Alaska Steam's executives fought a running battle over the quality of the water line's service. The general manager complained of ships arriving "anywhere from twelve to forty eight hours late" at Seward. He railed against the steamship company's loading freight on board passenger ships at cannery docks. He accused Alaska Steam of failing to educate territorial businessmen and their suppliers into building up wintertime inventories.

"During the last tourist season," he wrote in 1938, "The Alaska Railroad lost thousands of dollars by increased operating expenses due to delayed boats and loss of revenue at Curry Hotel."[7]

The irascible Ohlson little appreciated Alaska Steam's difficulties. Its obligations were not only to tourists and to The Alaska Railroad. Large-scale miners, merchants, and canneries of all sizes experienced unpredictable business fluctuations. Stocking inventories in anticipation of new gold discoveries, heavy fish runs, or other unforeseeable events would have been extravagant and possibly futile. Ohlson, who relentlessly reduced his railroad's inventory when he arrived in Alaska, was inconsistent in expecting other enterprises to carry expensive surplus stocks. Alaska Steam well knew that large operators could charter their own vessels if it failed to deliver badly needed equipment and supplies on fast passenger ships. Small canneries deserved careful attention because of their greater dependence on the steamer line.

During normal times, the Alaska Steamship Company might have kept its ships reasonably close to schedule. The 1930s were not normal times in Alaska transportation. When the Pacific Steamship Company withdrew from the Alaska run in 1933, Alaska Steam was left in the lucrative but burdensome position of being the principal water carrier to the territory. While the Great Depression ravaged other lands, Alaska enjoyed a solid prosperity based on corporate gold mining in the interior and unprecedented salmon packs along the coast. Alaska Steam strained to stay abreast of the boom, expanding from nineteen ships in 1935 to twenty-two at the close of 1939. But the salmon packs of the mid-thirties averaged almost seven million cases annually compared with typical packs of about four million during the interwar years. Heavy runs late in the fishing season overlapped the peak of tourist travel in 1936 and 1938, snaring the steamship company in a net of conflicting obligations.

When cantankerous Secretary Ickes suffered delays during his 1938 travels on one of Alaska Steam's vessels, he angrily authorized Ohlson to seek passenger connections with another water carrier. Despite his threat to do so, Ohlson never intended to induce another steamship line to make regular connections at Seward. He understood the problems in competing for the railbelt's limited freight and passenger business. Over the years he consistently refused to join occasional shippers in the lower joint through rates. The Alaska Line, he claimed, offered adequate service on regular schedules and should enjoy some protection. But he leapt at the chance to pressure Alaska Steam. Probably he wrung a concession from the water carrier under the threat of encouraging competition, for in 1939 Alaska Steam made Seward its first westward stop on alternate sailings.

Ohlson was on firmer ground when he criticized the loading and handling practices of the Alaska Steamship Company. The company paid only modest attention to organizing its loads for the most efficient dockside handling. It was handicapped by the shippers' habit of dribbling in small tonnages to each of Alaska's little ports until just before sailing, when they dumped in larger shipments. With all allowances made, the water line could have done a better job. Ohlson fumed over a 1934 shipment of railroad cars so ineptly loaded that they could not be unloaded by the ship's boom. Two cranes, one of which had to be ordered from Anchorage, were required to unload the cars. After much preliminary pulling and hauling in the ship's hold, the unloading was finally completed. Better coordination and, after 1937, increased railroad responsibility for dock work, helped to mitigate unloading difficulties. Some loading problems remained. In 1941 Fairbanks merchants complained of spoiled fruits and vegetables arriving on the railroad but praised the quality of perishables trucked in from Valdez. Cunningham guessed that Alaska Steam stowed perishables for Valdez in the cool room and placed Seward shipments elsewhere until the Valdez merchandize was unloaded. A sharp protest from the railroad corrected the situation.

The water carrier had some grievances, too. The railroad may have dawdled with unloading at times, for its equipment was limited. In 1934 Alaska Steam vigorously protested the railroad's use of the government vessels *Boxer* and *North Star,* claiming a loss of $100,000 annually from the competition. Whatever the precise loss to Alaska Steam, Ohlson did ship via the *Boxer* and the *North Star.* But both vessels usually were busy with cargoes to Alaska's western coast during the open season. For most of the balance of the year they were docked in Puget Sound. Ohlson only rarely arranged for large shipments on the government vessels, such as a 1933 movement of creosoted ties from Seattle to Seward.

Ohlson's growing petulance was itself a source of discord. Frederick Mears, Noel Smith, even Ohlson in his earlier years, bore delays and errors without rancor. Alaska Steam could not complain about the situation, not to Ohlson at least, but its managers recognized that they would never appease the acerbic general manager without sacrificing other interests to his. They suffered his denunciations, offering explanations and improvements when they could, as the uneasy marriage of railroad and water line entered its third decade.

As they did with the water carriers, Ohlson's relationships within Alaska deteriorated during the 1930s. The general manager's unpopularity grew despite the railroad's improving service. His irascibility and petulance increasingly masked his geniality, contributing to the discord. His battles against competitors and his tie importing were necessary from his viewpoint, but they hurt him personally. So did the faded hopes for mineral, reindeer, and timber development. By 1936 the federal government's Matanuska Valley colonization project on which he had staked so much appeared to have a bleak future. During the year, Ohlson talked of resigning, and he could have retired then with his colorful reputation largely intact. Angry cries for that resignation came after he announced his plans to suspend service on the eve of the 1936-37 maritime strike. The territorial delegate, hard-working, self-righteous Anthony Dimond, sought Ohlson's removal in a bitter statement. Dimond was not alone, but his and the others' demands had the opposite effect. Ohlson replied by changing his mind. Though he was well past his sixty-sixth birthday he said: "I plan to continue indefinitely."[8] In the spring of 1939, Mrs. Ohlson suffered a fatal heart attack while she was in Chicago for medical treatment. Thereafter, Ohlson's life and his work were one.

The complaints of railbelt residents against the railroad centered on favoritism, discourtesy, negligence, high rates, and overcharging. A great many of the complaints were unspecific. Whenever anyone made a specific complaint, whether to the Anchorage office, to the Department of the Interior or another department, or to a congressman or senator, a prompt, full investigation followed. If the railroad or one of its employees were at fault, Ohlson ordered a correction.

First among the many reasons for unwarranted criticism and complaint was Ohlson's rigid impartiality. At Anchorage in 1936 a wholesale grocery owned by railroad employees offered quality perishables at less cost than the established grocers. The stores department purchased from the employee-owned firm. When a grocer complained, Ohlson stood his ground, presenting a list of comparative prices to support his stand. Second, most claimants believed in the absolute justice of their claims. Anything less than a full settlement would not have been enough. Even drastic action could be less than wholly pleasing. The Wasilla woman who complained of the local agent's concern with "how he can be smarty and fresh with the various girls and women"[9] had the satisfaction of seeing him fired, but the firing failed to improve her five-pound tomato shipment which spoiled because of the agent's carelessness.

A third reason for the prevailing dissatisfaction lay with the railroad's inability to control Alaska Steam or any other carrier. Railbelt shippers whose goods could have been damaged at any point in their travels filed their claims with the railroad and held the railroad responsible for restitution. When, in 1935, the Alaska Line refused any longer to absorb Seward wharfage on through shipments, the added amounts appeared on statements from The Alaska Railroad. Ohlson's road took the blame for delays in mail service, wherever they might have occurred. Poor steamer-rail connections at Seward usually resulted from delays to the ships, but railbelt residents noticed only the train's delay in reaching their station.

Fourth, Central Alaskans displayed monumental indifference or impatience toward the railroad's problems and its contributions to the life of the territory. Ohlson approved hundreds of free movements for charitable, educational, or agricultural purposes. He authorized special low rates for noncommercial institutions. In 1938, for instance, he granted the carload rate on mining machinery to the University of Alaska on equipment for its new power plant. Members of organizations holding intra-Alaska conventions were given low round-trip fares. The beneficiaries of

Ohlson's consideration warmly thanked him, but special services built little permanent goodwill for the railroad.

Alaska residents continued their masochistic revelations of the high local freight rates without any appreciation for the railroad's high costs, difficult operating conditions, seasonality, and one-way haul. The Alaska Railroad's traffic density (the ton miles of revenue freight per mile of road) was a miniscule 56,200 in fiscal year 1939, its best year under peacetime conditions. Two "stateside" lines of similar length, the Duluth, South Shore and Atlantic, and the Bangor and Aroostook, enjoyed densities of 284,000 and 374,000 respectively. The general reduction of local rates in 1935 appeased few. Selective rate reductions to shippers with special competitive situations were equally unappreciated by the general public. Silence greeted the steady reduction of express charges during the thirties. There was no applause in 1936 when the railroad abolished its reduced passenger fares for large tour parties, although the change placed large tour parties on the same fare footing with the "little fellow." The very existence of cost factors and a rate structure seemed suspect. The Interior Department's Thoron Report of 1947, while critical of the railroad, complained of shippers who denounced the railroad's practices while ignoring its problems. Radical rate reductions would not generate significant traffic, nor would they cut costs dramatically, for "other costs and markups, aside from freight, contribute to high prices in Alaska."[10]

The railroad's relation to its home department was altered in structure if not in substance during the New Deal years. On May 29, 1934, an executive order grouped several of the Interior Department's activities in United States territories and islands under the new Division of Territories and Island Possessions. Ernest Gruening, a dynamic journalist and public servant, directed the division until he became Alaska's governor in 1939. Despite its impressive title, the division was small. Three people supervised Alaskan matters. Gruening himself or Ruth Hampton, the assistant director, handled correspondence with the railroad. On February 13, 1936, Ickes placed the railroad under the division, where administrative practice had lodged it already. In effect, Gruening filled the role of the assistant secretaries and administrative assistants who in years past had overseen the railroad's relationships with its department.

The fundamental change of the New Deal years diminished the railroad's development role. Ickes was uninterested in using federal subventions to develop the railbelt. He refused to funnel funds through the railroad to encourage the private exploitation of resources. In part, his reluctance was a function of the Great Depression and lessened business interest in central Alaska. Basically, however, the cautious and prudent Ickes believed in Alaskans doing for themselves. In his opinion, most Alaskans were imbued with the miner's reckless gambling psychology. Alaskans, Ickes thought, expected the federal government to acquiesce in their failure to tax themselves or their exportable wealth. They expected the federal government to construct vast public works "while they continue exploring every crack and crevice for precious metal which will make them rich and enable them to go back to the United States to live in luxury."[11]

Ickes' attitude belied the stereotype of New Deal interventionism and prodigal spending. Had he wished to make The Alaska Railroad a showcase of federal operation and an economic stimulant, he could have ordered Ohlson to scrap his aged rolling stock and buy new from moribund railroad equipment manufacturers. He could have arranged to pump large sums into maintaining and improving the roadbed and refurbishing the physical plant. Whether spending of that sort would have produced a reaction in Congress and jeopardized Ickes' reconstruction spending under the Public Works Administration is not the point. Ickes believed in spending on productive public works that would enhance the value of the national estate — except where Alaska was concerned. In his opinion, the federal government should wait until Alaskans shed their speculative psychology before it undertook any new projects. The railroad received one allotment from Ickes under the Public Works Administration, in addition to a specific grant for McKinley Park hotel construction. The allotment was small and was used for miscellaneous purchases and improvements. Ickes' judgment contrasted sharply with the view of Ray Lyman Wilbur, Ickes' predecessor under the Hoover administration. Wilbur believed that federal encouragement to private enterprise would be the way, ultimately, to free the territory from federal dependence.

The secretary's policy reinforced Ohlson's reluctance to squander so much as one cent. The parsimonious Swede preferred a conservative improvement program, one that could be economically and carefully done during each summer's construction season. Besides, even the modest funds spent on capital improvements were, under the railroad's accounting, charged to the railroad's expenses. Heavy spending would have ballooned Ohlson's deficit and wrecked his plans for balancing outgo with income. Possibly it would have jeopardized his job. New Deal policy was a refuge for Ohlson after 1936, when experience failed his vision of broadly based territorial development.

Ohlson continued his cordial relationships with Congress. Almost every year he appeared before appropriations committee hearings, speaking candidly about the condition of his rolling stock and roadbed and about the need for improvements appropriations. On rare occasions he made misstatements of fact, such as his remark in 1938 that the railroad was continuing to purchase treated ties. Ohlson's errors before the committee appear to be the slips of an aging memory rather than deliberate deceptions. As a rule, congressmen treated the general manager courteously while trimming his funds below the recommendations of the Bureau of the Budget. The bureau's recommendations themselves were reductions from Ohlson's original estimates.

Supervising the operation and development of his railroad absorbed much of Ohlson's time and energy. Labor relations took a turn for the better during his general managership, even though he was strictly opposed to unlawful employee political participation, employees having a craft or skill competing with tradesmen in town, and the railroad's shops doing work for employees if it could be done by private concerns. He refused to allow employees who owned businesses to participate actively in the work or management of their firms. Ohlson was especially strict during the railroad's quarrel with Anchorage businessmen over their shipments by water. He ordered at least one of his executives to withdraw from his part ownership in an Anchorage grocery, a grocery outspoken in its defense of shipping via the railroad's competition. Some employees got away with violations of his restrictions, but when the violations were uncovered, Ohlson's orders to stop the forbidden practices came in no uncertain terms.

For all his strictness and occasional severity, Ohlson got along well with his employees until World War II. He tried to live by the letter and spirit of the operating employees' work rules established under the Smith general managership. Sometimes he reduced Cunningham's recommended penalties against trainmen for infractions of the rules. He upheld the right of furloughed employees to compete with established tradesmen. "We have numerous employees on The Alaska Railroad to whom we can offer but a few months work each year," he wrote to a complainant in 1936, "and we certainly would be without justification in insisting that they accept no other employment during the months in which we cannot make use of their services."[12] To Ohlson, the railroad's nonpartisanship in hiring, retention, and promotion was sacred. Qualifications and seniority governed the award of jobs in the clerical and operating forces. John W. Troy, Alaska's Democratic governor from 1933 to 1939, initiated or passed on applications or recommendations for The Alaska Railroad. Many were politically inspired. Ohlson accepted some qualified applicants whose recommendations came from the governor's office. For his part, Troy always recognized and reiterated the railroad's nonpartisan character.

Ohlson demonstrated his fairness in other ways. His announced policy was to maintain The Alaska Railroad's wages at 25 percent above the pay on the Northern Pacific. In fact, the wages ranged from 16 to 84 percent above the Northern Pacific's, depending upon the job classification, the year in question, and the calculation of various benefits. Most tasks on The Alaska Railroad paid about 27 to 48 percent more. Apprentices earned the greatest differential, with trainmen and skilled workmen receiving high wages but lower percentage increases over "stateside" pay. Line employees who purchased necessities from merchants received free billing, with only enough restrictions to prevent abuse or resale. The general manager was sympathetic toward employees' local political activity. An executive order of 1926 allowed them to seek and hold political offices until 1939, when the Hatch Act prohibited active involvement by federal employees. When Delegate Dimond introduced a bill permitting railroad employees to run for local political offices in Anchorage, Ohlson warmly

233

supported Dimond's proposal. "I would go even further and suggest that the Cities [sic] of Seward and Fairbanks also be included," he wrote. Railbelt municipal officials, Ohlson pointed out, received no pay and held their meetings in the evening. Railroad employees normally formed a "large portion" of the population of towns on the line, towns in which it was "generally hard to find suitable candidates for municipal offices."[13]

Ohlson sometimes advanced employee interests because he could support his working force while he smote his enemies. In 1935, Alaska railroaders complained of a new Interior Department policy restricting travel on the *Boxer* and *North Star* to federal employees on official business. Previously, any federal employee and his family could travel at cost on a space-available basis on either of the department's motorships. Ohlson pointed to the higher price of commercial transportation and its scarcity during the tourist season as reasons for modifying the new order. "If this restriction was issued because of complaint from the Alaska Steamship Company and for no other reason I do not hesitate to advise that this Company has not shown any disposition to cooperate with The Alaska Railroad, and I can see no reason why the Government should play into their hands," he wrote in a scorching memorandum.[14] Despite Ohlson's protest, the department reaffirmed its determination to be done with private passengers, excepting those from ports not served by commercial steamers.

Ohlson had better luck with extending commissary privileges to employees living in Anchorage. For many years he followed the policy of restricting commissary sales to line employees. Though several merchants began patronizing water competition in the early thirties, Ohlson continued the commissary restriction in deference to those Anchorage businessmen who shipped by rail. By 1938 he admitted "that practically all of the merchants patronize more or less the small boats that are operated in competition with the Railroad," and requested permission for employee purchase of subsistence items, tobacco, and work clothes through the commissary. The railroad's revenues would increase because it "would not only earn the revenue from the line haul of these commodities but in addition would make fifteen per cent above the landed cost."[15] The next year Ohlson received permission to open the commissary to Anchorage employees. Later he extended commissary privileges to retired employees, and during World War II he inaugurated a limited home delivery service.

The railroad's most persistent labor problems involved the conflict between federal labor legislation and the special status of the railroad's employees. Trainmen were not so easily brought under federal regulations because their dual payment system had evolved through railroad, not governmental, experience. In essence, the dual system called for train crews to be paid at straight time except in case of 1) work in excess of eight hours and a run of 100 miles or less, 2) exceptionally long runs, or 3) exceptionally slow runs longer than 100 miles. In other words, the trainmen's wage was in part a function of each day's work situation and not of overtime legislation uniformly applied.

Clerks and most workmen could benefit from the federal government's growing concern for its own employees through executive orders or special legislation recognizing the railroad's anomalous standing within the federal structure. Even clerks and non-operating employees were in an atypical situation, for the railroad as a transportation enterprise under the control of the president through the Interior Department was exempt from civil service or Interstate Commerce Commission regulations. In these curious circumstances, the railroad's employees fought to gain the advantages of federal employee status, and, at the same time, to retain the advantages peculiar to their jobs on The Alaska Railroad. Ohlson and the other federal officials followed no consistent line. Sometimes they were willing to spend extra money in meeting new obligations brought about by concessions to the work force. Sometimes they were not. Alaska's delegate to Congress from 1933 to 1945, Anthony Dimond, had little use for Ohlson, but he consistently supported the employees.

Two labor issues, leave and retirement benefits and the forty-hour week, generated the most heat. Employees secured their leave and retirement plans in 1936. They came in separate legislative packages, but they formed an indivisible issue for the employees. Sadly for them, Alaska Railroad workers originally had no retirement benefits. They were not in the classified civil service, therefore, President Wilson had excluded them from the retirement act covering civil servants. Other federal clerks retired with civil service pensions, but not the clerical employees of The Alaska Railroad. Trainmen on commercial railroads in the states enjoyed pension plans, but not the crews on Ohlson's trains.

Ohlson was sympathetic. "From time to time," he wrote, "employees have been retired from the service of the Railroad, without pension, involving hardship to them, when their service had been of such character and duration as to have made them eligible to pension if they had been employed by another railroad or another branch of the Government service."[16] More than 10 percent of the 449 employees on the payroll at the end of November 1931 were sixty years or older. Five of the forty-seven were in their seventies, while one was an octogenarian. Obviously, Ohlson was keeping on some oldsters because they had no dignified alternative to employment.

As early as his first year on the job, Ohlson was asking for an employee retirement plan on The Alaska Railroad. At first the Civil Service Commission flatly opposed extending retirement benefits to any federal employee not under civil service. By 1935 it had unbent to the point of permitting the railroad's employees to come under civil service retirement on the same terms as the other beneficiaries. The trainmen's representatives were cool to the concession. What they wanted was the earlier retirement age — sixty-two versus sixty-five or seventy — available to trainmen on the federally owned Panama Railroad Company, under the Canal Zone Retirement Act. The Civil Service Commission opposed granting a more liberal benefit under its own retirement scheme and creating another special retirement arrangement for Alaska Railroad employees, because a "policy of permitting various groups of Federal employees to set up separate retirement systems would tend to disintegrate the general retirement system."[17]

Ohlson understood his employees' desires, but he had to gauge the effect of the employer's contribution on his balance sheet. With Ickes' backing, he supported the less liberal, less expensive civil service plan. Placing employees under the civil service retirement plan did not mean putting them in the classified civil service. Ohlson adamantly opposed civil service for his railroad. The staff was too small, the job duties too varied, and changes in job assignments too frequent for civil service procedures to work smoothly, he maintained.

While the retirement bill moved along under Dimond's sponsorship, the trainmen worked for a more liberal leave policy. Trainmen were granted thirty days' sick leave per year, "practically the same working and leave agreements...as the railroad employees in the States have," according to Ohlson.[18] What they wanted was the additional thirty days' paid vacation granted to all monthly and annual salaried employees on The Alaska Railroad, and indeed to most federal employees in the territory. Dimond's draft legislation would have extended the liberal benefits to daily and hourly employees whom the railroad classed as "permanent," or unlikely to be laid off at the end of the summer season. Ohlson objected because of the increased expense, estimated at almost $85,500 per year, and because commercial railroad policies were not so generous. Congress was more concerned with eliminating the inequities among federal employees. In March 1936 it granted equal leave benefits to all employees of The Alaska Railroad.

Meanwhile, the retirement issue was coming to a head. Ohlson's role in the pre-passage maneuvering is obscure, but he probably suggested a compromise to Ickes. Under its terms, the trainmen and other operating employees received what they wanted — the more generous retirement insurance afforded the Panama Railroad employees — while clerical forces were to be taken under the civil service retirement. Ickes stood on the compromise. Dimond reluctantly accepted it rather than risk the probability of losing his bill from the Interior Department's determined opposition. The retirement bill passed in June 1936. In 1937 the railroad met the increased costs — about $100,000 — with a modest freight rate increase. A 1939 amendment brought the river boat employees under the act. An amendment which was passed the next year included the clerical forces because of the confusion arising from shifting individual employees from transportation jobs (covered under the 1936 act) to clerical work (covered under civil service retirement) and back again.

The battle for a forty-hour week paralleled the fight for retirement and liberalized leave. The battle began with congressional reductions in federal pay: the economy acts of 1932 and 1933. Together they lopped 15 percent from the pay level of June 1932. The railroad brotherhoods appealed to Ickes, asking him to request an opinion

235

from the comptroller general as to whether or not the economy acts applied to the transportation employees of The Alaska Railroad. Dimond joined the brotherhoods in arguing that The Alaska Railroad transportation employees' wages were fixed by the "stateside" wages prevailing in their trades, through a negotiation process embodied in agreements with the management. On November 27, 1933, Comptroller General McCarl issued his opinion: "The employees of the [sic] Alaska Railroad are rendering service in or under a branch of the Federal Government and are, therefore, subject to the percentage deductions required by the Economy Acts."[19]

Little else could have been expected from the close-fisted comptroller general, but his decision caught him in an inconsistency. "Does it not logically and, indeed, necessarily follow," Dimond asked Ickes, "that since these transportation employees of the [sic] Alaska Railroad are employees of the United States within the ordinary meaning of that term. . .they are entitled to the benefits heretofore conferred by law upon employees of the United States with respect to sick leave, annual leave with pay, and retirement insurance? All of these special benefits. . .have heretofore been denied transportation employees in the service of the [sic] Alaska Railroad."[20] Dimond urged Ickes to arrange for extending the benefits to Alaska Railroad trainmen. Ickes took no action. The delegate had to be content with watching the comptroller general hoist by his own parsimony. McCarl did not reverse his decision, but he did seize the first opportunity to wriggle out of his inconsistent position while reaffirming his devotion to federal scrimping.

In March 1934 Congress cancelled the economy acts effective in June. Further, it provided a forty-hour week for all wage earners, with time and a half for overtime. Ohlson had no choice but to apply the law to all hourly and straight-time employees, transportation employees included. Congress, however, made no appropriation for the estimated $200,000 or more per year needed to pay the new wages on The Alaska Railroad. The general manager had to be ruled by his budget. He asked Ickes to request the comptroller general to rule whether the forty-hour provisions applied to Alaska Railroad employees. As Ohlson surely expected, McCarl announced on July 13, 1934, that "railroad employees are regarded generally as a distinct class of personnel."[21] Therefore, the forty-hour and overtime provisions did not apply to them. Economy, not consistency, was McCarl's ruling passion. Railroad employees were the same as everyone else if that interpretation would save money for the government. A year after proclaiming their similarity, however, McCarl discovered them to be in a class by themselves. The comptroller general reversed his opinion because maintaining his original position would have cost the government more money under the new circumstances.

The railroad brotherhoods and the American Federation of Government Employees protested McCarl's decision. They fought a long and unsuccessful campaign, with Dimond's help, to win an amendment bringing Alaska Railroad employees within the 1934 act. They argued against the injustice of arbitrarily creating separate classes of federal workers. Ickes' rebuttal was, in essence, that Alaskan employees could not have their cake and eat it too. The wages of workers on The Alaska Railroad were fixed by local conditions and by payments for similar work elsewhere in the United States, not by federal employment practices. (The brotherhoods took the same position when they protested the 1932 and 1933 wage reductions.) Then too, no appropriations were made for the estimated increases required for overtime payments. In 1941 Ickes added the argument that bringing transportation employees under the law would require some of the railroad's departments to double the number of their employees. Of course, Ickes could have requested additional funds. He could have asked President Roosevelt to grant the pay increases under the authority vested in him by the original railroad act of 1914. Ohlson advised him to do neither. The general manager wished to maintain private railroading practices on his line, and he wanted to avoid asking Congress for a large appropriation which would be charged against earnings.

There was no "right" or "wrong" side to the pay issue. The railroad's employees could not be blamed for demanding the pay and working conditions of federal employees or those of other railroad workers, whichever would bring them the greater benefits. They saw nothing inconsistent in asking for a forty-hour week with overtime while accepting, in 1938, a 10 percent pay increase based on increases granted to workers on private railroads in the "states." Neither could

Ohlson be blamed for wishing to maintain traditional wage practices and a favorable balance sheet. The employees finally won their case in federal courts years after Ohlson's retirement.

Ohlson faced few other personnel or organizational problems, but the railroad hospital combined both. Shortly after his arrival, the general manager released the hospital's chief of staff and the surgeon because they drank too much. Soon he found reason to complain of their replacements. Despite the relatively good salaries and the opportunity to maintain some private practice, few physicians wanted to take on the railroad's medical labors. It was not until the spring of 1937 that Ohlson found an acceptable chief of staff. Meanwhile, the hospital chronically lost money. The aging frame building, a survival of the construction era, had seen many years of hard use. In 1936 a surprise inspection by the Anchorage fire chief, and subsequent "fire trap" headlines in the Anchorage newspaper, seriously embarrassed Ohlson. He railed against the hospital's chief of staff and the Anchorage Booster's Club, "composed of the town's half-baked youths," for instigating the inspection.[22] In this issue, despite his anger, he was definitely on the defensive.

In 1934 he began negotiations with the Sisters of Charity of the House of Providence to take over the railroad's patients. By 1937 the nursing order was ready with plans calling for a new hospital on the southwestern edge of town. As soon as the new Providence Hospital opened in 1939, Ohlson closed the railroad's facility to private patients. He kept the old hospital open to government patients because of the military buildup. In 1944 he ordered it converted into a dormitory, transferring the railroad's patients to Providence Hospital on a contract basis. The only other major organizational change occurred in 1934, when the railroad reassumed commissary operation at the expiration of the Northern Commercial Company's contract. Higher proposed commissary rates and the opportunity to make a small profit for the railroad on its own commissary operation influenced Ohlson's decision.

As always, operations, including construction and reconstruction, were at the core of the railroad's activity. By 1930 Ohlson was searching for a large, new, and necessarily expensive sternwheeler of proven design to replace the cramped, aging steamers *Jacobs* and *Alice*. He proceeded carefully because, as he explained to one of his riverboat captains, "we cannot experiment with anything on the Yukon River."[23] The possibility of trouble with diesel or diesel-electric engines and the impossibility of transferring a White Pass steamer to United States registry led him to write a contract for a traditional wood-burning, shallow-draft vessel. Built by a Seattle shipbuilding company at the Nenana ways, the *Nenana* was ready in the late spring of 1933. A big boat by Yukon River standards, she boasted a gross tonnage of 1,028, a length of 210 feet, and a passenger capacity of 52. By comparison, the doughty *Alice* was 110 feet long, carried 16 passengers, and was rated at 262 gross tons. Ohlson placed the *Nenana* on a semimonthly round trip from Nenana to Marshall. Formerly, the steamers sailed once-weekly to Holy Cross, semimonthly from Holy Cross to Marshall. River residents were satisfied with fewer sailings because of the *Nenana's* greater barging and carrying capacity. The general manager expected the new steamer to retire the rest of the river fleet, but he reckoned without increased business. Traffic rose so rapidly — from freight revenues of $36,826.30 in 1933 to $64,894.05 in 1937 — that the *Alice* was in "emergency service" for more than half as much time as the *Nenana's* regular sailings. Ohlson restored the *Alice* to full duty and a full crew in the summer of 1938.

New equipment for the railroad included heavier engines, steel passenger coaches, and steel freight cars. Most of Ohlson's early purchases were of used equipment, for they stretched his scarce dollars further. In fiscal year 1934 he bought new rolling stock with part of a $207,008 PWA grant, conforming to the New Deal's attempts at stimulating industrial recovery. Ohlson was proud of replacing all old wooden baggage, observation, and passenger cars "with modern steel cars." His pride was justified even though most of the passenger equipment was obsolete by the 1940s. And when he wrote of his all-steel rolling stock, he conveniently forgot his own business car, which was by 1947 "a wooden relic over 50 years old, heated with a coal stove."[24]

Improvement to the roadbed and structures continued apace, helped in 1934 and 1935 by a portion of the PWA grant. Year by year the maintenance-of-way forces widened cuts, reballasted track, banked fills, replaced wooden bridges with steel, and filled in trestles. Kenai

Peninsula stretches of the line, which Ohlson was accused of neglecting, were improved. In 1936 a line change bypassed two old snowsheds, and the next year the railroad's crews placed a new steel bridge in the Loop district. In 1938 and again in 1939 the railroad received unemployment relief funds totaling $378,800 to hire maintenance crewmen. In 1939 a dock extension at Seward and a spur line around Fairbanks, four and one-half miles to the army's new Ladd Field, were built in support of the military buildup.

Line problems remained. The spectacular but rickety trestles in the Loop district steadily deteriorated. Snowslides in winter and washouts in summer were ever-present possibilities at many points. The roadbed in Nenana Canyon, built on unstable earthen walls, demanded continuous reconstruction. Swampy spots north of the Alaska Range swallowed yards of fresh gravel each spring in the unending battle to stabilize the track. Some yard facilities were primitive by standards in the "states." Yet, by mid-1939 Ohlson had achieved his goal of building a railroad adequate to its traffic. Considering the restrictions imposed on him, his achievement was almost as great as the original construction itself.

With help from Alaska's economic revival, Ohlson did what no other head of the railroad had done — he put the line into the black. In fiscal year 1934 the railroad's deficit was $178,973.33. Ohlson chopped it by more than $100,000 the next year. In 1937 he would have turned a surplus of over $2,500 had it not been for a loss exceeding $174,500 on his emergency steamship operations. In 1938 he showed a surplus of $76,703.69. A special appropriation of $200,000 to replace a burned warehouse forced a deficit of $19,830.85 in 1939, inconsequential in view of the railroad's soaring income. Both freight and passenger revenues rose year by year from 1934 through 1939. Freight income increased from $1,009,357.32 to $1,716,941.68, and passenger revenue rose from $124,197.31 to $268,200.80. During the same years, freight tonnage climbed from 93,512 to 157,904, while the number of passengers increased from 15,824 to 27,436. The later thirties were good years for The Alaska Railroad. Nineteen-thirty-nine rang out on a railbelt in the midst of a military construction boom. More dramatic changes in the railroad's fortunes lay just ahead.

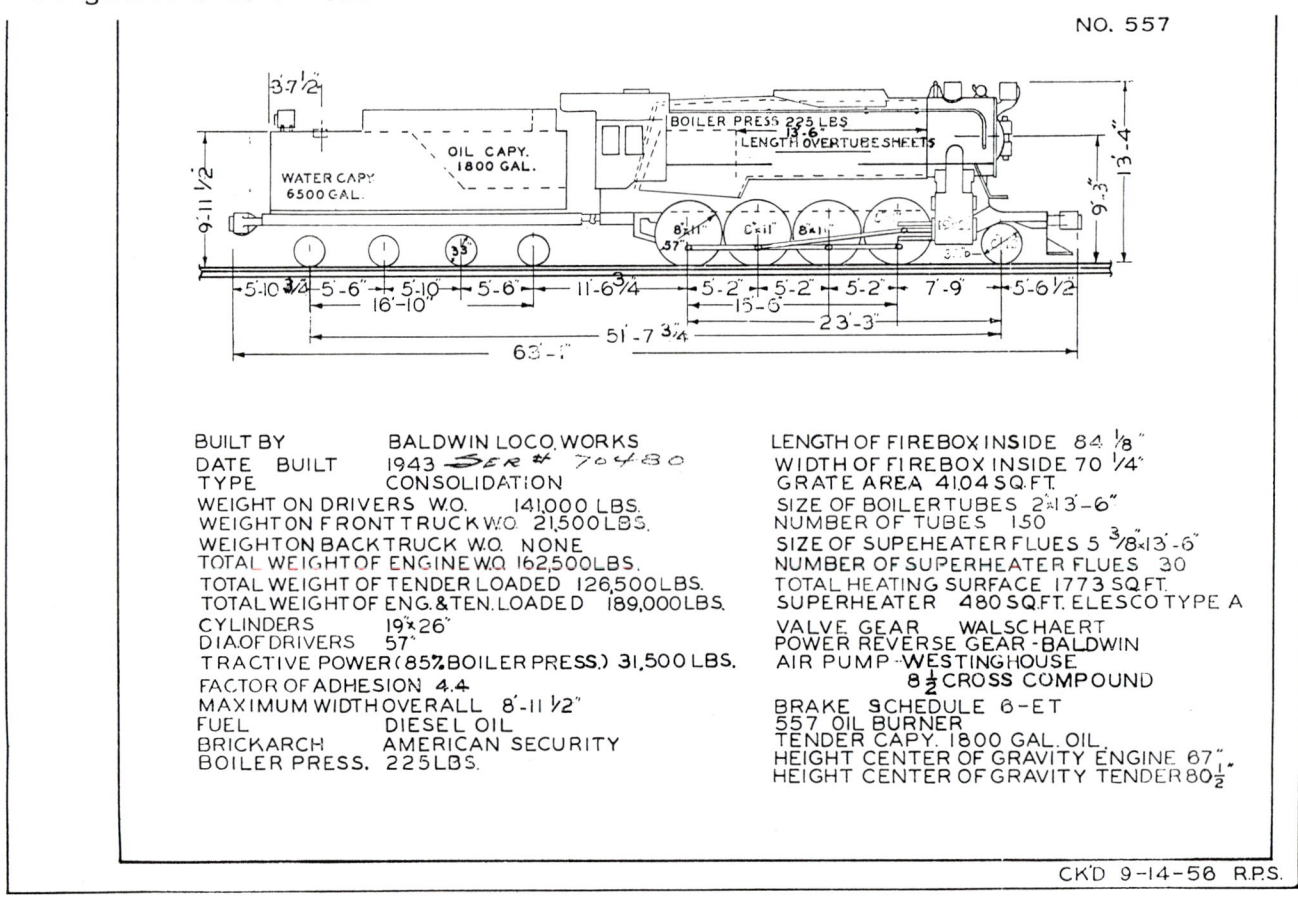

NO. 701, 702, 703 MIKADO TYPE

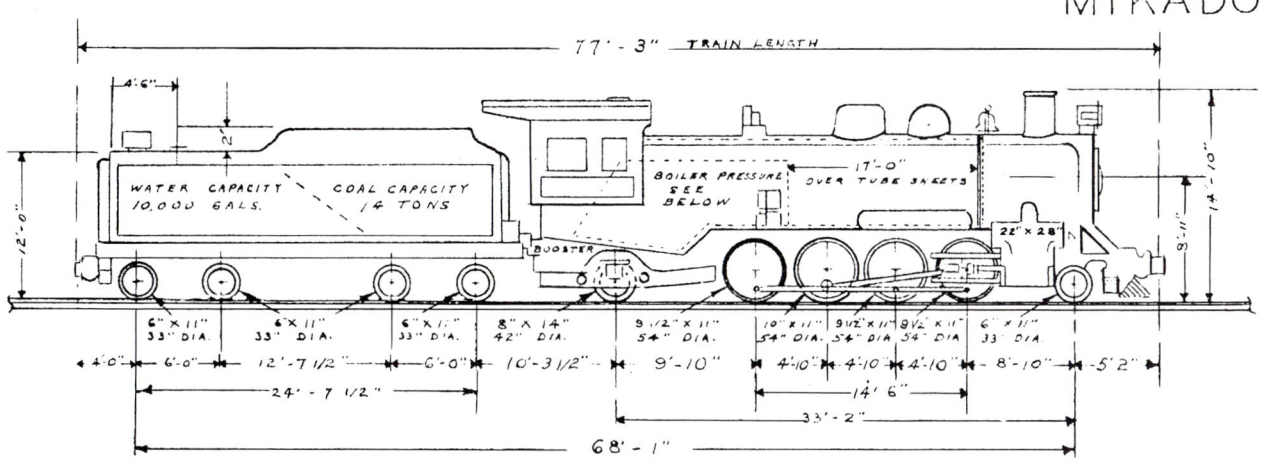

	NOS. 701-702	NO. 703		
BUILT BY - BALDWIN LOCO. WKS.			LENGTH OF FIREBOX INSIDE	115 1/8"
DATE BUILT	1927	1928	WIDTH OF FIREBOX INSIDE	72 1/4"
PURCHASED FROM - B.L.WORKS	NEW	NEW	GRATE AREA	57.7 SQ. FT.
PLACED IN SERVICE	1927	1928	SIZE OF BOILER TUBES	2" X 17'-0"
TOTAL WT. OF ENG. & TENDER	441680	441400	SIZE OF SUPERHEATER FLUES	5 3/8" X 17'-0"
TOTAL WT. OF ENG.	244400	244120	NO. OF SUPERHEATER FLUES	32
TOTAL WT. OF TENDER	197280	197280	TOTAL HEATING SURFACE	2718 SQ. FT.
WT. ON DRIVERS	172360	175680	SUPERHEATER	621 SQ. FT.
WT. ON FRONT TRUCK	23130	23130	VALVE GEAR	BAKER
WT. ON BACK TRUCK	45310	45310	POWER REVERSE GEAR	BALDWIN
CYLINDERS	22"X 28"	22"X 28"	ARCH TUBES	4
TRACT. POWER-LBS.(85% B.P.)	42600	44800	FACTOR OF ADHESION	5.44
BOILER PRESSURE LBS.	200	210	MAXIMUM WIDTH OVERALL	10'-5"
NUMBER OF BOILER TUBES	192	193		

SUPERHEATER	SCHMIDT TYPE "A"
AIR PUMP	ONE 8 1/2" CROSS COMPOUND
STOKER	SIMPLEX TYPE "B-K"
LOW WATER ALARM	BARCO TYPE "F-3A"
BRICK ARCH	AMERICAN SECURITY

Types of locomotives placed in service on The Alaska Railroad before the end of 1945. The 802 was added in 1942, the 901 in 1941, and the 902 in 1945. Numbers 1000 and 1001 were added in 1944 to help cope with ventilation problems in the tunnels of the Whittier Cut-off. *The Alaska Railroad*

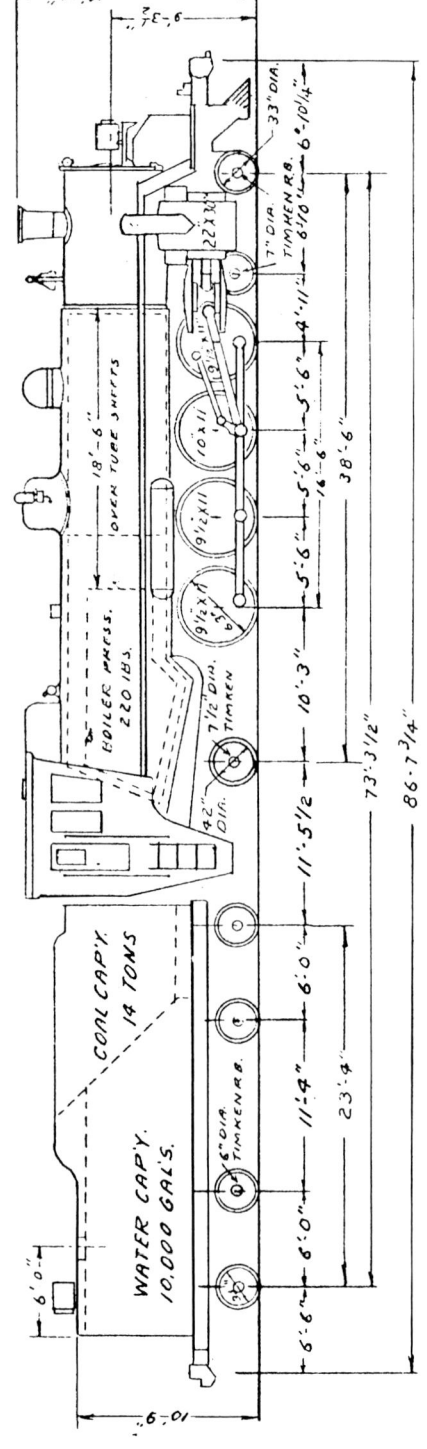

No. 802

COAL CAP'Y. 14 TONS
WATER CAP'Y. 10,000 GALS.
BOILER PRESS. 220 LBS.

BUILT BY - BALDWIN LOCO. WORKS
YEAR BUILT - 1942
TYPE - MOUNTAIN
WEIGHT ON DRIVERS, WORKING ORDER - 190,850 LBS.
WEIGHT ON FRONT TRUCK, WORKING ORDER - 43,700 LBS.
WEIGHT ON BACK TRUCK, WORKING ORDER - 38,750 LBS.
TOTAL WEIGHT OF ENG. WORKING ORDER - 273,300 LBS.
TOTAL WEIGHT OF TENDER LOADED - 200,300 LBS.
TOTAL WEIGHT OF ENG. & TENDER LOADED - 473,600 LBS.
CYLINDERS - 22"x30"
TRACTIVE POWER (85% BOILER PRESS.) 43,100 LBS.
FACTOR OF ADHESION - 4.4
MAXIMUM WIDTH OVERALL - 10'-10"
FUEL - BITUMINOUS COAL
BRICK ARCH - AMERICAN SECURITY.
THERMIC SYPHONS - 2

BOILER PRESS. - 220 LBS.
LENGTH OF FIREBOX INSIDE - 115 1/8"
WIDTH OF FIREBOX INSIDE - 78 1/8"
GRATE AREA - 62.5 SQ.FT.
SIZE OF BOILER TUBES - 2"x 18'-6"
NUMBER OF BOILER TUBES - 181
SIZE OF SUPERHEATER FLUES - 5 3/8"x 18'-6"
NUMBER OF SUPERHEATER FLUES - 32
TOTAL HEATING SURFACE - 2870 SQ.FT.
SUPERHEATER - 706 SQ.FT.
SUPERHEATER - TYPE "A"
STOKER - SIMPLEX TYPE "B.K."
LOW WATER ALARM - BARCO TYPE F-311
VALVE GEAR - BAKER
POWER REVERSE GEAR - FRANKLIN TYPE "E"
AIR PUMP 8 1/2" CROSS COMPOUND.

DEPARTMENT OF THE INTERIOR
THE ALASKA RAILROAD
OFFICE OF SUPT. M.P. & E.   ANCHORAGE, ALASKA

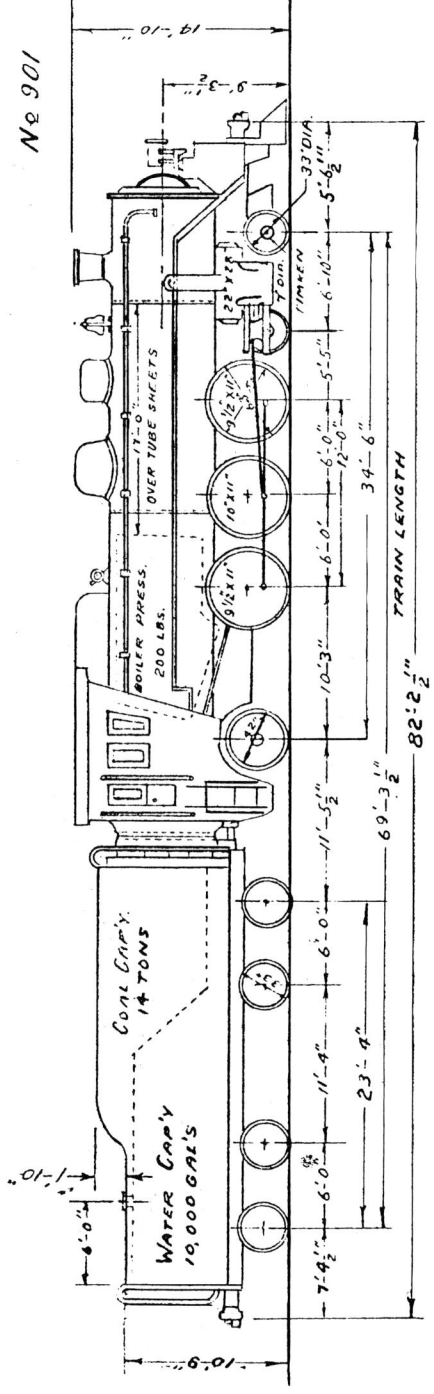

Built By - Baldwin Loco. Works
Year Built - 1941
Type - Pacific
Weight on Drivers Working Order - 156,200 lbs.
Weight on Front Truck Working Order - 52,200 lbs.
Weight on Back Truck Working Order - 40,600 lbs.
Total Weight of Eng. Working Order - 249,000 lbs.
Total Weight of Tender Loaded - 197,500 lbs.
Total Weight of Eng. & Tender Loaded 446,500 lbs.
Cylinders - 22" x 28"
Dia. of Drivers 63"
Tractive Power (85% Boiler Press.) 36,500 lbs.
Factor of Adhesion 4.27
Maximum Width Overall - 10'-10"
Fuel - Bituminous Coal
Brick Arch - American Security.
Thermic Syphons - 2

Boiler Pressure - 200 lbs
Length of Firebox Inside - 115 $\frac{1}{8}$ in
Width of Firebox Inside - 78 $\frac{1}{4}$"
Grate Area - 62.5 sq.ft.
Size of Boiler Tubes - 2" x 17'-0"
Number Of Boiler Tubes - 181
Size of Superheater Flues - 5 $\frac{3}{8}$" x 17'-0"
Number of Superheater Flues - 32
Total Heating Surface - 2660 sq.ft.
Superheater - 646 sq.ft.
Superheater - Elesco Type "A"
Stoker - Simplex Type "BK"
Low Water Alarm - Barco Type "3A"
Valve Gear - Baker
Power Reverse Gear - Franklin Type "E"
Air Pump - One 8 $\frac{1}{2}$" Cross Compound

DEPARTMENT OF THE INTERIOR
THE ALASKA RAILROAD
OFFICE OF SUPT. M.P.&E.   ANCHORAGE, ALASKA

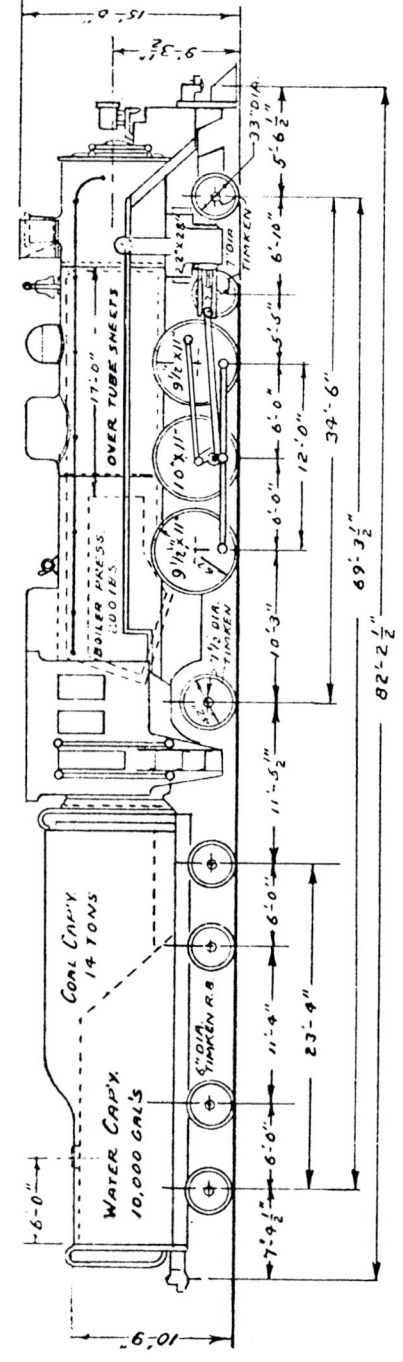

No. 902

BUILT BY - BALDWIN LOCO WORKS
YEAR BUILT - 1945
TYPE - PACIFIC
WEIGHT ON DRIVERS, WORKING ORDER - 156,200 LBS.
WEIGHT ON FRONT TRUCK, WORKING ORDER - 52,200 LBS.
WEIGHT ON BACK TRUCK, WORKING ORDER - 40,600 LBS
TOTAL WEIGHT OF ENG. WORKING ORDER - 249,000 LBS.
TOTAL WEIGHT OF TENDER LOADED - 197,500 LBS.
TOTAL WEIGHT OF ENG. & TENDER LOADED - 446,500 LBS.
CYLINDERS - 22" X 28"
DIA OF DRIVERS - 63"
TRACTIVE POWER (85% BOILER PRESS.) 36,500 LBS.
FACTOR OF ADHESION - 4.27
MAXIMUM WIDTH OVERALL - 10'-10"
FUEL - BITUMINOUS COAL
BRICK ARCH - AMERICAN SECURITY
THERMIC SYPHONS - 2

BOILER PRESSURE - 200 LBS.
LENGTH OF FIREBOX INSIDE - 115 1/4"
WIDTH OF FIREBOX INSIDE - 78 1/8"
GRATE AREA - 62.5 SQ.FT.
SIZE OF BOILER TUBES - 2" X 17'-0"
NUMBER OF BOILER TUBES - 181
SIZE OF SUPERHEATER FLUES - 5 3/8 X 17'-0"
NUMBER OF SUPERHEATER FLUES - 32
TOTAL HEATING SURFACE - 2660 SQ.FT.
SUPERHEATER - 646 SQ.FT.
SUPERHEATER - TYPE "A" SUPERHEATER Co.
STOKER - SIMPLEX TYPE B.K.
LOW WATER ALARM - CLEVELAND
VALVE GEAR - BAKER
POWER REVERSE GEAR - FRANKLIN TYPE "E"
AIR PUMP - ONE 8 1/2" CROSS COMPOUND.

DEPARTMENT OF THE INTERIOR
THE ALASKA RAILROAD
OFFICE OF SUPT, M.P. & E.   ANCHORAGE ALASKA

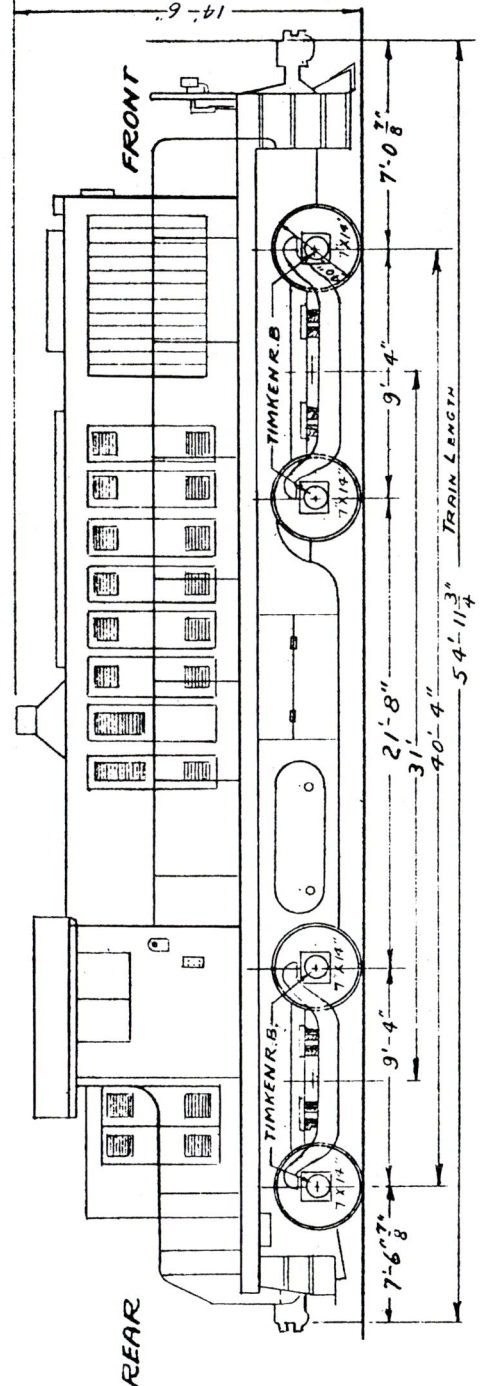

No. 1000 & 1001

REAR — FRONT

BUILT BY - AMERICAN LOCO. CO. 1944
TYPE - DIESEL ELECTRIC - 1000 H.P.
NOMINAL RUNNING SPEED - 740 R.P.M.
IDLING SPEED - 270 R.P.M.
WEIGHT IN WORKING ORDER - 244,800 LBS.
CYLINDERS - NUMBER SIX
CYLINDERS - DIA. & STROKE - 12½" x 13"
DIA. DRIVERS - 40"
TRACTIVE POWER - STARTING - 72,000 LBS.
TRACTIVE POWER - 10 M.P.H. - 30,000 LBS.
TRACTIVE POWER - 30 M.P.H. - 10,750 LBS.
MAXIMUM WIDTH OVERALL - 10'-0"
FUEL - STANDARD DIESEL
FUEL OIL TANK - 800 GAL. CAP'Y.
LUBRICATING OIL - 80 GAL. CAP'Y.
ENGINE COOLING SYSTEM - 240 GAL. CAP'Y.
SAND - 27 CU. FT.

BOILER WATER TANK - 800 GAL. CAP'Y.
WHEELS - STEEL TIRED.
JOURNAL BEARINGS - TIMKEN
BRAKE CYLINDERS - 8 (4-9"x 8" EACH TRUCK)
AIR BRAKE SCHEDULE - EL-14
2 - 250 H.P. MOTORS EACH TRUCK.
AIR COMPRESSOR - 2 STAGE - 228 CU. FT. PER MIN.
MAXIMUM AT FULL ENG. SPEED, 83 CU. FT. PER. MIN. AT
ENG. IDLING SPEED.
HEATER - VAPOR CAR HEATING Co. TYPE CFK-4160-2B
CAP'Y - 1600 LBS. PER HOUR.

DEPARTMENT OF THE INTERIOR
THE ALASKA RAILROAD
OFFICE OF SUPT. M P & E.   ANCHORAGE, ALASKA

Equipment used on The Alaska Railroad at various times from the construction days through 1945. *The Alaska Railroad*

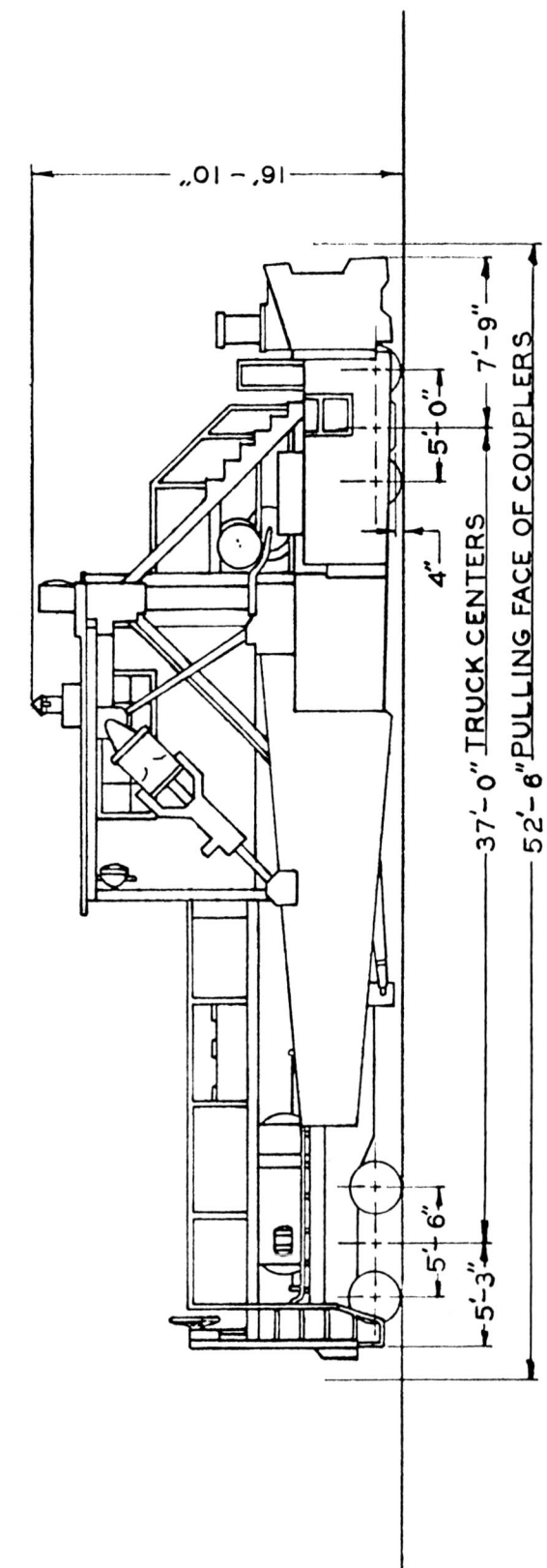

JORDAN SPREADERS, NO. 3, 4, 5 & 6

BUILT BY	O. F. JORDAN CO.
DATE BUILT	3-1929
REBUILT BY	
PURCHASED FROM	O. F. JORDAN CO.
PLACED IN SERVICE	
WHEELS	33"
TRUCKS	UNIT
AXLES	FRONT 6"x11", REAR 5¾"x10"
BEARINGS	FRICTION
UNDERFRAME	STEEL
LIGHTWEIGHT-LBS.	
CAPACITY-LBS.	
COUPLERS	TYPE-E 60 A.S.F.
YOKES	A.S.F.
AIRBRAKES	AB, 10"x12" CYL.
HANDBRAKES	POWER AJAX

GENERAL DIMENSIONS:
TRAIN LENGTH 52'-6"
MAX. HEIGHT 16'-10"
MAX. WIDTH OVER WINGS (WINGS IN) 10'-3"
PROJECTION OF OPEN WING FROM CTR. OF TRACK 20'-5"
SIZE OF WING 48"x20'-0"
VERTICAL ADJUSTMENT OF WINGS APPROX. 36"

A.L. 8-15-57

RUSSELL SNOW PLOW NO. 3

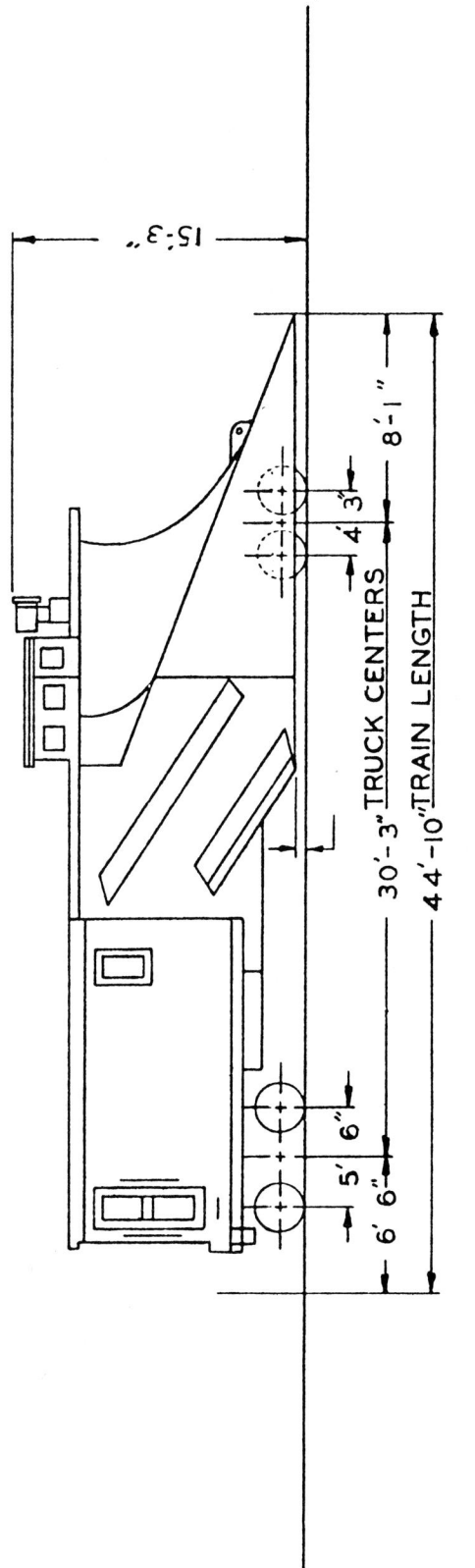

BUILT BY	RUSSELL SNOW PLOW CO.	
DATE BUILT	1944	
REBUILT BY		
PURCHASED FROM	RUSSELL SNOW PLOW CO.	
PLACED IN SERVICE	1945	
WHEELS	33"	
TRUCKS	UNIT	
AXLES	5"x9"	
BEARINGS	FRICTION	
UNDERFRAME	STEEL	
CAPACITY-LBS.	84,500	
COUPLER		
YOKE		
AIRBRAKES		
HANDBRAKES		

GENERAL DIMENSIONS:
TRAIN LENGTH   44'-10"
MAX. WIDTH   10'-4"
MAX. HEIGHT   15'-3"

NOTE: WINGS & FLANGERS OPERATED BY AIR FROM LOCOMOTIVE MAIN RESERVOIR & CONTROLLED FROM PILOT HOUSE ON PLOW.
WIDTH OF NOSE OF PLOW   9'-4"
WIDTH WINGS EXTENDED   16'-8"

A.L. 9-20-57

ROTARY Nº 2

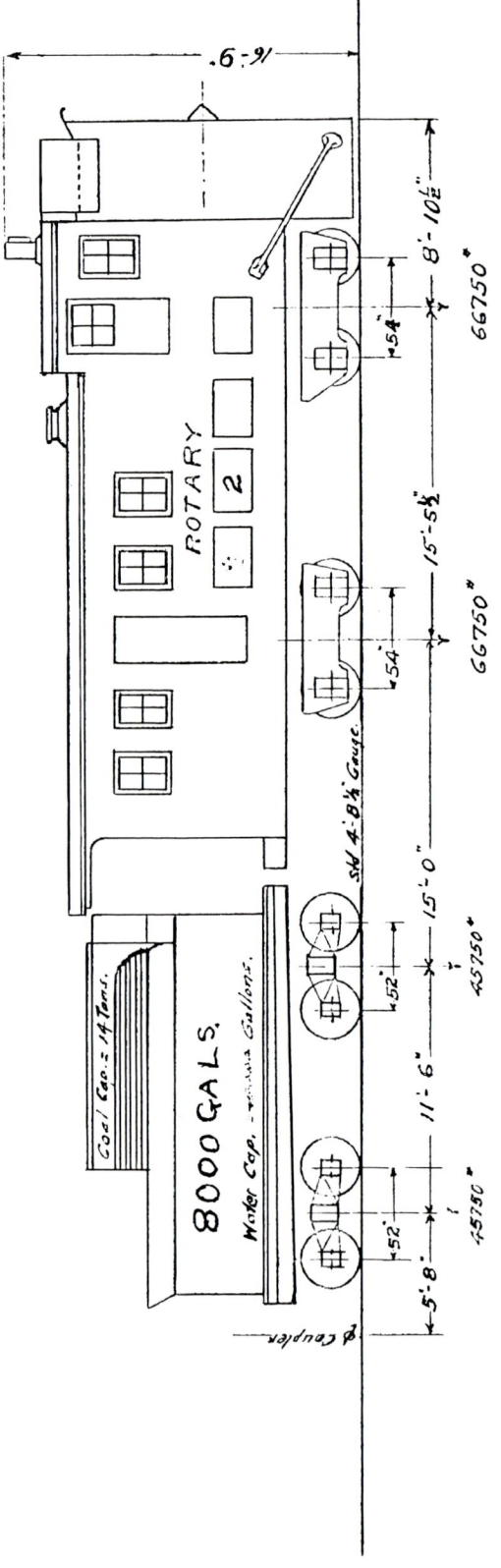

A.R.R. - ROTARY SNOW PLOW #2

"SPECIFICATIONS"

Rotary Snow Plow	#2
Purchased from	Colorado Midland Railroad.
Second Hand Equipment.	
Built by	Cooke Locomotive Co. Patterson N.J. Year 1900
Placed in Service	Anchorage 1919.
Estimated Life	15 Years.
Weight of Rotary	132,500 "
" Tender (Loaded)	91,500 "
" Rotary & Tender	225,000 "
Cylinders	18" x 26"
Valve Gear	Walschaert
Wheel Base (c.t.c. Trucks)	15'-5½"
Trucks	Structural Steel
Wheel Base of Trucks	4'-6"
Axles	7½ x 10" Journals.
Wheels	Eight 33" diam.
Plow Wheel Diam.	10'-0"
" Cutter	Rigid
Underframe	Steel.
House	Steel - Ceiled inside with wood.

Maximum length Rotary & Tender - 56'-6"
Maximum Width - 11'-10" CUT.
" Height - 16'-6"
Length of Rotary - 35'-2"
Tender - 8 wheel, Steel underframe, Sq. End Tank.
Coal Capacity - 14 Tons.
Water Capacity - 4000 Gallons.
BOILER-
Working Pressure - 160 Lbs.
Heating Surface - 1520 Sq.Ft.
Length of Boiler - 21'-5"
Diam. of Boiler - 60"
Number of Tubes - 278
Length of Tubes - 9'-10"
Diam. of Tubes - 2"
Note - Rotary is equipped with Westinghouse 9½" Air Pump and Pyle-National Electric Headlight.
Grate Area - 26 sq.ft.

DITCHERS Nº D-101, D-102

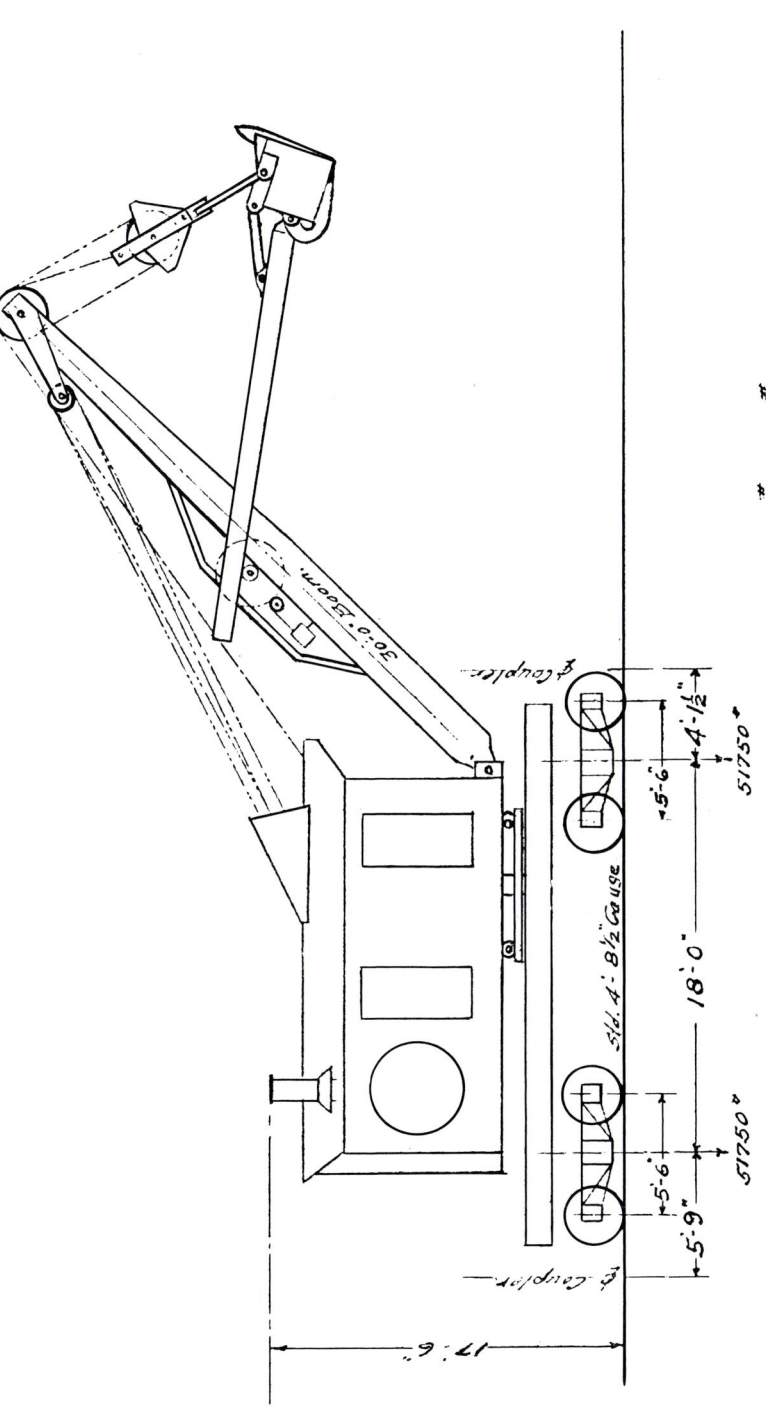

A.R.R.-BUCYRUS DITCHER #D-101, D-102
"SPECIFICATIONS"

Coal Capacity   - 1 Ton.
Water Capacity   - 500 Gallons.
Center to Center Trucks - 19'-0"
Trucks   - Arch Bar-Center to Center Bearings 6'-4"
Axles   - 5"x 9" Journals.
Wheels   - Eight 33" dia.
Couplers   - "Gould" Top Lift - Stub.
Draft Gear   - None.
Brakes   - Westinghouse.
Boiler   - 40" x 9'-7" Locomotive Type. Working Pressure.
No. of Tubes   - 93
Length   - approx 5'-0"
Dia.   "   - 2"
Ditcher Equipped with Pyle National Electric Headlight & 9½"x4½"x10"
Westinghouse Air Pump.

Bucyrus Ditcher #1 Self-Propelling
New Equipment
Built by   - The Bucyrus Co.
Placed in Service   - Anchorage 1920
Estimated Life   - 25 Years.
ENGINES-
   Main - 8"x 8"
   Boom - 6"x 6"
   Swing - 6"x 6"
Total Weight   - 103500# Approximate.
Dipper   - 1¼ Cu.Yds.
Spread of Jack Arms - 6'-6"
Maximum Height   - 29'-0"
   "   Width   - 11'-3"
Train Length   - 27'-10½"

Locomotives built before 1945 but placed in service in 1947. *The Alaska Railroad*

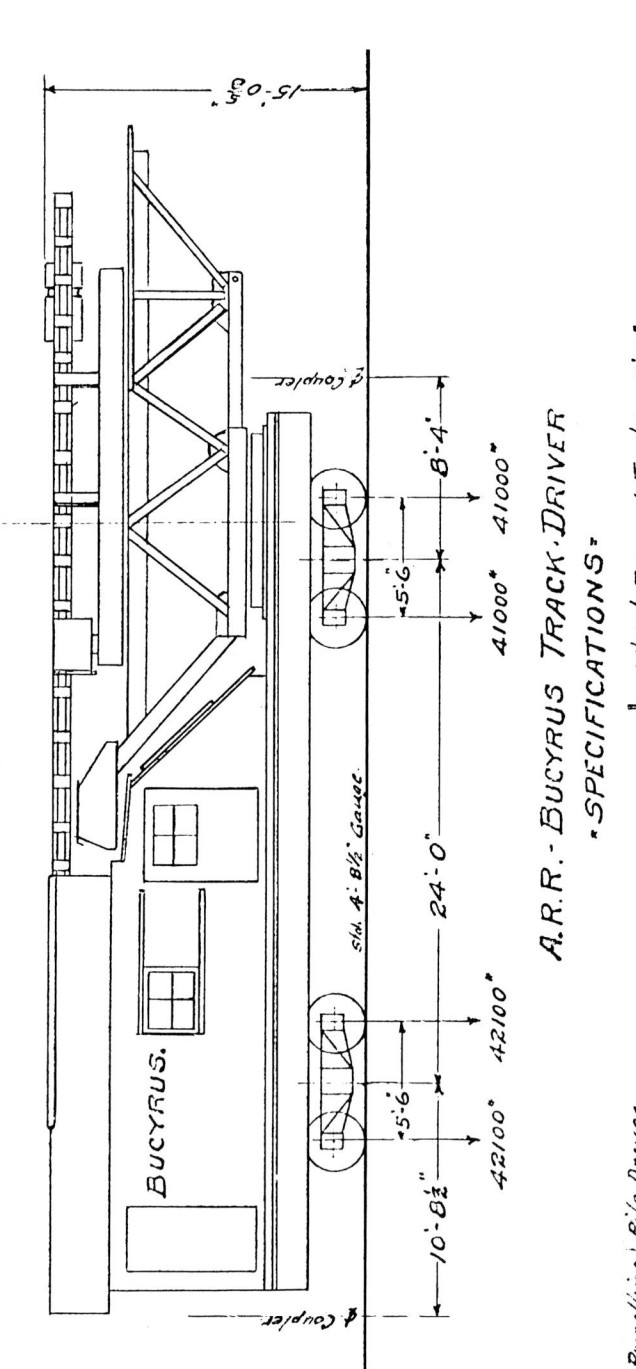

Nº 310 to Nº 320

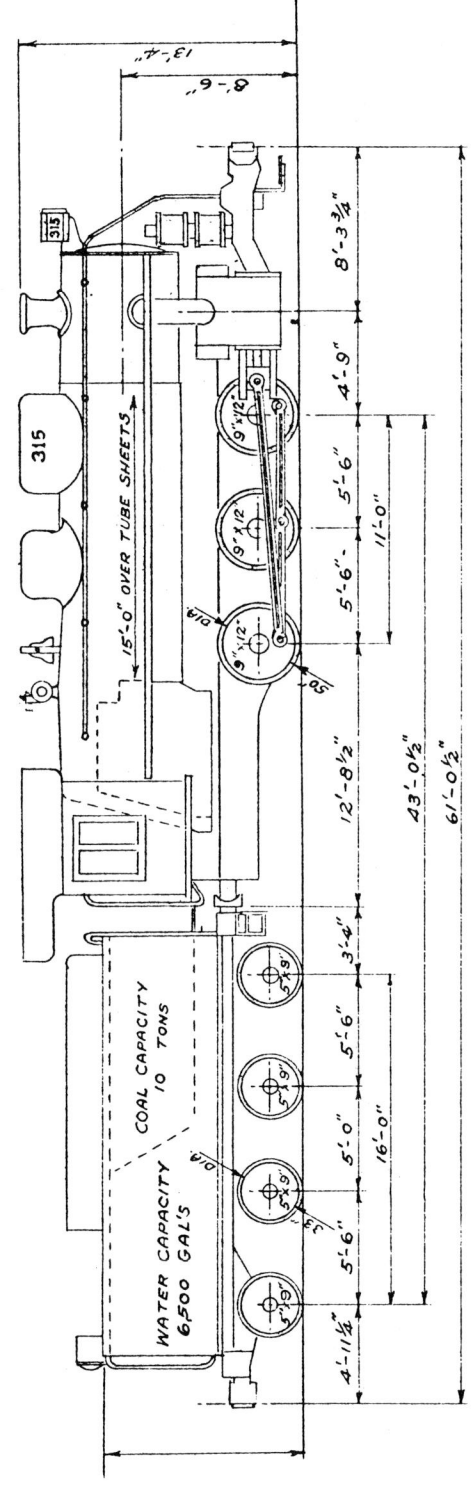

BUILT BY LIMA LOCO. WORKS	1943 & 1944
PURCH. FROM U.S. ARMY -- SURPLUS PROP.	
PLACED IN SERVICE	1947
TYPE:	0-6-0
WEIGHT ON DRIVERS W.O.	157,300 LBS.
WEIGHT OF TENDER LOADED	108,560 LBS.
TOTAL WT. ENGINE & TENDER LOADED	265,860 LBS.
CYLINDERS	21" x 28"
DIA. OF DRIVERS	50"
DRIVING WHEEL BASE	11'-0"
TRACTIVE POWER	40000
FACTOR OF ADHESION	

STEAM PRESSURE	190 LBS.
BOILER DIAMETER	67"
FIREBOX LENGTH	72 1/8"
FIREBOX WIDTH	66 1/4"
TUBES & FLUES	291 - (2" x 15'-0")
HEATING SURFACE	
TUBES & FLUES	2273 SQ. FT.
FIREBOX	122 SQ. FT.
ARCH TUBES	13 SQ. FT.
TOTAL	2408 SQ. FT.
GRATE AREA	33.1 SQ. FT.

TENDER TYPE 2-(4-WHEEL TRUCKS)
FUEL: Nº 310 TO 311   Nº 315 TO 320 COAL
       Nº 312 TO 314   OIL
TENDER COAL CAPACITY   10 TONS
TENDER OIL CAPACITY   Nº 312,313,314 1800 G.
TENDER WATER CAPACITY   6,000 GAL
                      Nº 317 & Nº 319
TENDER COAL CAPACITY   12 TONS
TENDER WATER CAPACITY   8000 GALS.

AKEY 4-47

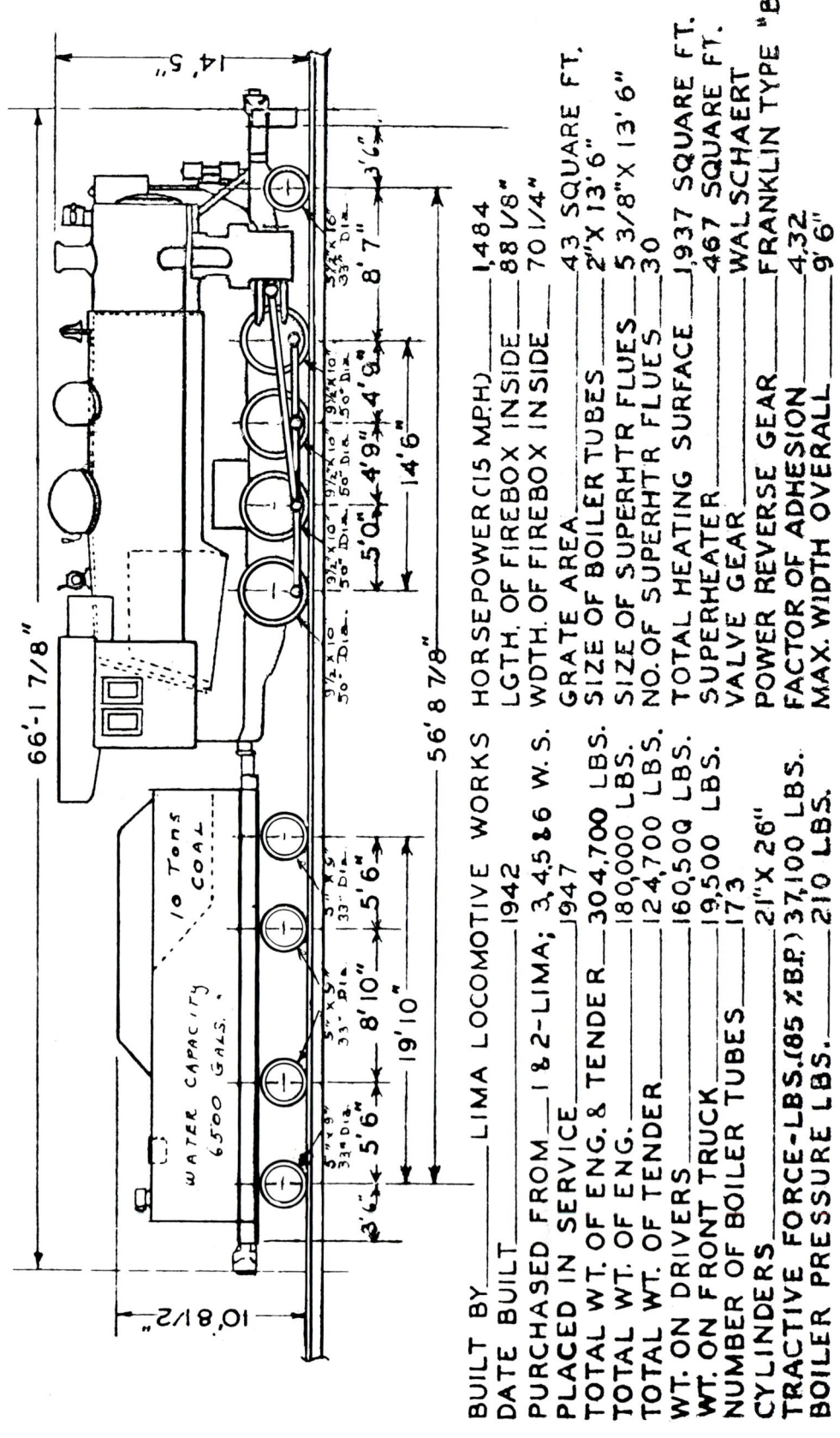

400 CLASS CONSOLIDATION TYPE

BUILT BY	LIMA LOCOMOTIVE WORKS
DATE BUILT	1942
PURCHASED FROM	1 & 2–LIMA; 3,4,5 & 6 W.S.
PLACED IN SERVICE	1947
TOTAL WT. OF ENG. & TENDER	304,700 LBS.
TOTAL WT. OF ENG.	180,000 LBS.
TOTAL WT. OF TENDER	124,700 LBS.
WT. ON DRIVERS	160,500 LBS.
WT. ON FRONT TRUCK	19,500 LBS.
NUMBER OF BOILER TUBES	173
CYLINDERS	21"X 26"
TRACTIVE FORCE–LBS.(85 % B.P.)	37,100 LBS.
BOILER PRESSURE LBS.	210 LBS.
HORSEPOWER (15 MPH)	1,484
LGTH. OF FIREBOX INSIDE	88 1/8"
WDTH. OF FIREBOX INSIDE	70 1/4"
GRATE AREA	43 SQUARE FT.
SIZE OF BOILER TUBES	2"X 13'6"
SIZE OF SUPERHTR FLUES	5 3/8"X 13'6"
NO. OF SUPERHTR FLUES	30
TOTAL HEATING SURFACE	1,937 SQUARE FT.
SUPERHEATER	467 SQUARE FT.
VALVE GEAR	WALSCHAERT
POWER REVERSE GEAR	FRANKLIN TYPE "B"
FACTOR OF ADHESION	4.32
MAX. WIDTH OVERALL	9'6"
SUPERHEATER	ELESCO TYPE "A"
AIR PUMP	ONE 8 1/2" WESTINGHOUSE #150-D
STOKER	NONE
LOW WATER ALARM	NONE
BRICK ARCH	AMERICAN SECURITY

ENG 403 – OIL–1800 GALS.

NOS 1100 TO 1107

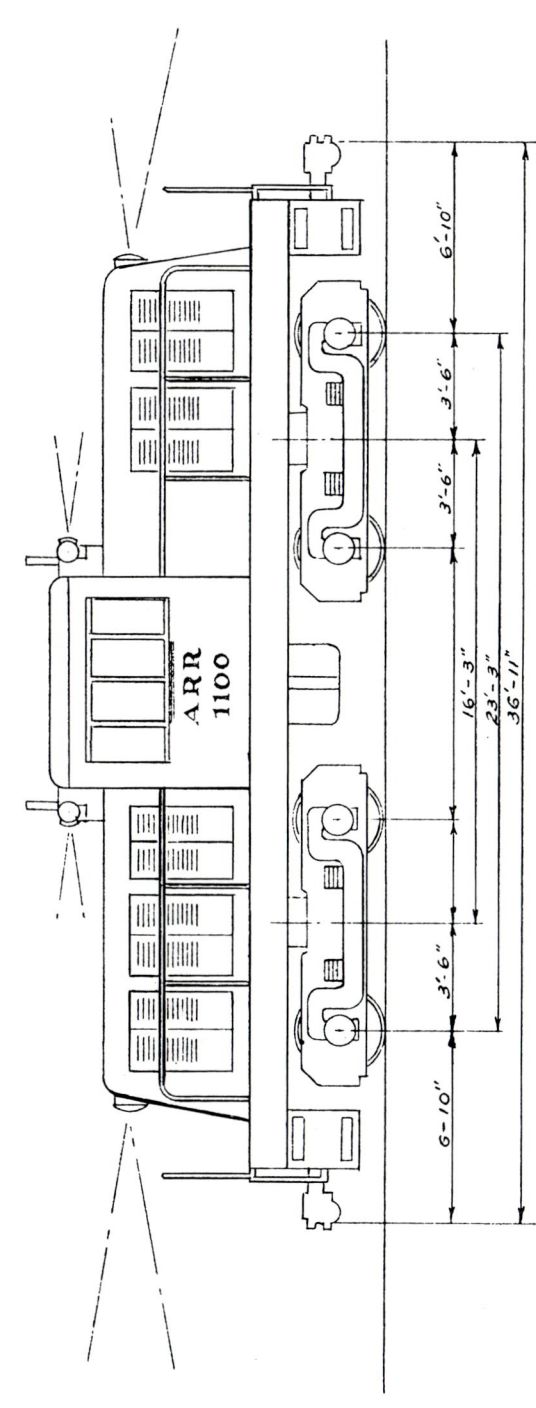

BUILT BY R.K. PORTER CO. DEC. 1942
TYPE: PORTER CUMMINS DIESEL
(2) 4-WHEEL SWIVEL TRUCKS
PURCHASED FROM SURPLUS PROP. U.S. ARMY
PLACED IN SERVICE   FEB. 1947
WEIGHT   130,000 LBS.
400 H.P.
2 HIGH SPEED GENERATORS
4 LOW SPEED MOTORS
TRACTIVE FORCE AT 30% ADHESION   39,000 LBS.
TRACTIVE FORCE CONTINOUS RATING
                                 5,600 LBS. AT 10 M.P.H.

WHEEL BASE - TRUCKS   7'-0"
TOTAL WHEEL BASE   23'-3"
LENGTH OVER BUMPERS   34'-0"
TRAIN LENGTH   36'-11"
HEIGHT   12'-0"
WIDTH   9'-6"

AKEY 4-47

LOCOMOTIVE CRANE L.C.-55

BUILT BY	INDUSTRIAL BROWN HOIST
DATE BUILT	1920
REBUILT BY	ALASKA R.R.-1964
PURCHASED FROM	INDUSTRIAL BROWN HOIST
PLACED IN SERVICE	1920
WHEELS	33"
JOURNALS	6½"X12"
WT. IN WORKING ORDER	205,780 LBS.
AIRBRAKES	"P" 12X12
AIR COMPRESSOR	GARDNER-DENVER ADK-1002
COUPLERS	"SIMPLEX" TOP LIFT
BATTERIES	32 VOLTS
ENGINE	CATERPILLAR
MODEL	D-333A
CYLINDERS	6

SUPPLIES:
FUEL 6.5 GALS.
MAX. OVERALL DIMENSIONS:
HEIGHT 16'-8"
WIDTH 10'-0"
TRAIN LENGTH 26'-10"
TAIL SWING 13'-4"
CAPACITY: 100 TONS - 17'-0" RADIUS - W/ JACK BEAMS
45 TONS - 25'-0" RADIUS - W/ JACK BEAMS
22 TONS - 16'-0" RADIUS - W/O JACK BEAMS
12 TONS - 24'-0" RADIUS - W/O JACK BEAMS

NOTE: CONVERTED TO DIESEL POWER - DEC. '64
BUCKEYE TRUCKS APPLIED - DEC. '64

War, and an Era's End

The Whittier cutoff was Ohlson's greatest, and his final, triumph. Opened in 1943, the cutoff met the ocean at the new port of Whittier on Passage Canal, an arm of Prince William Sound. Then it ran west 14.2 miles across the narrow neck of the Kenai Peninsula to Portage at the head of Turnagain Arm. It was shorter by fifty-two miles than the line from Seward. Twice it tunnelled beneath the mountain spines. In 1944, by Ohlson's estimate, the cutoff allowed his railroad to carry "approximately 75 percent more freight traffic with existing equipment than would have been possible through the Seward Gateway."[1]

Ohlson long dreamed of the cutoff, but his vision became substance only because the nation's defense planners put a premium on Alaska in the last months before World War II. The army's enthusiasm swept aside the strident opposition from Seward, where town leaders correctly gauged Ohlson's eagerness to abandon the Seward-Portage line when the Whittier connection was finished. The military's blessing also blunted opposition to the $5,300,000 appropriation. Ohlson's triumph turned to disappointment when the Whittier line opened but the Seward-Portage route was not closed. Ickes ordered Ohlson to keep the Seward line in operation.

Long before Ohlson's day, railroaders pondered the rugged barrier between Turnagain Arm and Passage Canal. John E. Ballaine considered it but rejected building his Alaska Central there because of high construction costs and the unpredictability of Portage Glacier. The great ice mass could expand, form a natural dam, and drown the low valley between a shoulder of the Chugach Mountains on the west and a range of the Kenai Mountains on the east. The Alaska Railroad Commission (the one appointed by President Taft) dismissed the narrow portage in a sentence. The geography of the place was a closed book to its members, and they had no time to investigate it during their rapid tour of the territory.

The Alaskan Engineering Commission scrutinized the route despite its unannounced preference for the Seward-Fairbanks line. From June to September 1914, a seven-man topographical party carefully mapped the craggy country from Passage Canal to Turnagain Arm. The party noted Passage Canal's drenching rains but saw no obstacles to port, townsite, and terminal developments. Portage Glacier, the team reported, had receded and was no longer an obstacle to construction. A track through Kenai Peninsula's neck was possible if the railroad bored beneath the mountains 13,005 feet through the eastern mass, 4,960 feet through the western. The A. E. C.'s preliminary survey was so well executed that the line, completed twenty years later, covered almost exactly the same ground.

The A. E. C. merely surveyed the cutoff. Noel Smith argued that eventually the line should be built. As early as 1925, when The Alaska Railroad suffered under congressional threats of abandonment, Smith recommended constructing the Passage Canal line. Open the route to the bay, he suggested, then wait "several years"[2] to learn whether economic growth would justify maintenance charges on the line to Seward. The tone of Smith's recommendation suggested that, in his opinion, no development would materialize to keep the Seward-Portage route open. The next year Smith ordered a fresh survey of Kenai Peninsula's spiny neck. The second survey suggested lowering costs by eliminating the shorter, western tunnel in favor of looping the right-of-way around the mountain's toe, just a few feet above the margin of Portage Lake. In March 1928 two of Smith's assistants flew over the proposed route, making new visual observations and taking photographs. Two months later the general manager depreciated the Seward-Portage line and edged toward suggesting that it be closed. "We have avoided as much as possible any permanent construction because of the uncertainty of the continuance of this part of the railroad to Seward,"[3] he wrote to the secretary of the interior. By then it was spring, and Smith's days in the office of general manager were almost done. He dropped the project.

Shortly after he arrived in Alaska, Ohlson scotched all talk of building through from Passage Canal and abandoning Seward. "I do not think we are going to spend any time or money on studying the advisability of the Portage Bay [Passage Canal] line," he told his policy committee in October 1928. "The Seward gateway has come to remain. While we could shorten the line somewhat, Seward is on the map, and we would have difficulty getting away from it."[4] The difficulties of getting away from Seward seemed less severe after several years of clearing snow, mud, and rocks from the tracks just to keep Seward in touch with the rest of the railbelt. A decade after Ohlson declared that the cutoff would never be built, the general manager was planning intensive studies of the route from Passage Canal. He dispatched the railroad's geologist with a team of surveyors and a weather observer to the rugged portage site. By September 1939, he knew enough of their findings to announce a $4 million budget request for constructing the cutoff.

Anchorage, as well as Seward, would have been devastated had Ohlson realized his most cherished hopes for the new route. The tough Swede wanted to relocate the railroad's headquarters, shops, and commissary from Anchorage to the Passage Canal site. The proposal was rational railroading — it would have ended the "deadhead" haul of the line's own freight from the port to Anchorage — but it was political dynamite. Granting his railroader's rationality, the general manager had broached an impractical idea. If the storm against the cutoff raised by Seward's 949 souls is any gauge, the opposition from Anchorage would have been cyclonic. Besides, the tiny Passage Canal townsite, mountain-ringed, overcast, windswept, chilly, and rainy, bore no climatic comparison with Anchorage's high plateau. Ohlson awakened not even the faintest interest within the Interior Department.

The new line itself was another matter. With the department's tentative approval, Ohlson worked out a two-part rationale for the cutoff, touting the advantages of the portage route while baring the defects of the line from Seward. He argued that the project's estimated cost of $5,203,268 was a trifle compared with the potential benefits to Alaska. Shortening the line by fifty-two miles would move passenger trains into Fairbanks twenty-two hours ahead of the existing schedule. Shippers and consumers would enjoy lower freight rates, from a 30.11 percent reduction for Anchorage to a drop of 6.54 percent at McKinley Park and Healy. (Because of distribution point rates, the percentage at Nenana, Fairbanks, and river stations, though they were more distant, would be slightly higher — 7.36.) The new route was geologically and climatically feasible. Safe tunnels could be bored through the mountains, and all the glaciers in the area were receding. During fiscal year 1940, the rainfall approached deluge proportions — 199.37 inches — and snow fell six months of the year to a total of 192.10 inches. But Ohlson saw no obstacle to train or port operations. The weather observer stationed at Passage Canal, confirming previous reports, found the arm free of ice.

In Ohlson's view, the engineering comparisons between the existing Seward route and the projected Passage Canal line were all in the latter's favor. Trains from Seward struggled over two summits 700 and 1,063 feet above sea level. Total rise and fall was 2,880 feet. From Passage Canal, the rise and fall was only 221 feet, and no steep summits had to be surmounted. Concerning maximum grades, the overwhelming advantage lay with the portage route, .6 percent northbound and .45 percent southbound versus 2.2 percent both ways from Seward. Trains from Seward ground their wheel flanges against 6,004 degrees of curvature, with a maximum 16-degree curve in the tortuous Loop district. From

Passage Canal the total curvature was a mere 248 degrees and the sharpest curve, 6 degrees. The line with its tunnels of 13,075 feet (65 feet longer than the A. E. C.'s survey) and 4,960 feet could be completed within eighteen months. Military interest in Alaska gave Ohlson a valuable argument: the winding single track from Seward was vulnerable to sabotage and air strikes, while the Passage Canal line was relatively safe.

Ohlson's estimates of the savings offered by the new route were partisan but except in one instance appeared sound. The general manager's assurance that reduced rail rates from Passage Canal would destroy highway and water competition forever was bravado, not analysis. Granted that lower rail rates might have recaptured part of his $160,000 projection, Ohlson's experience with rate cutting against trucks and boats should have stilled his hopes of ending competitive forays. His other estimates were more solid. He would realize an estimated annual $247,400 saving on maintenance and operation after closing the Seward line. Anticipated freight savings to government agencies, including the new army post and air base at Anchorage and the new air base at Fairbanks, were $259,217 per year. The salvage value of materials and equipment on the Seward line, less the cost of recovery, was $319,450. The savings as Ohlson outlined them never were realized because the Seward route remained open and freight revenues through Whittier soared far beyond his peacetime projections. In 1945 he reported "that the Army, by the end of this year, will have saved in transportation charges the entire construction cost of the Whittier cut-off."[5]

Unjustified, excessive costs formed the gravamen of Ohlson's charge against the Seward line. Line stoppages took their toll of tracks, still vulnerable after almost twenty years' improvement. The Kenai Peninsula's heavy rains induced huge slides of mud and gravel during the autumn of 1938, closing the line for a total of six and one-half days on two occasions. Still more rebuilding would help, but it could not banish the Kenai's freakish weather, the real cause of the staggering costs. The estimated charge for replacing wobbly trestles with permanent structures from Seward to Portage was $929,000 in 1940. In 1944, because of inflation and skimpy maintenance during the interim, Ohlson revised his rehabilitation and maintenance estimates to $2,612,839, spread over four working seasons. In the same year, he estimated that bringing the Seward-Portage roadbed up to the standard of the rest of his line would reduce maintenance charges from $275,500 to $208,865.

What would be gained from the heavy construction expenses and the modest maintenance savings? Almost nothing, for in sad truth the Kenai Peninsula area tributary to Seward generated little traffic for the railroad. Nor was there any economic activity in the Kenai's heartland beyond a little mining, a little tourism, a little hunting and fishing. By 1940 a graveled highway ran parallel to the railroad from Seward northward to Moose Pass (mile 29), then jogged westward and north once more to the mining communities of Sunrise and Hope. What freight business there was between Seward and Moose Pass moved by truck. The highway could be linked to the railroad at Portage at an estimated cost of $500,000, or it could cross on Turnagain Arm over fills and a bridge from Sunrise to Bird for an estimated $1 million. Then Seward would not be denied its outlet to the north.

Ohlson answered the anguished wails from Seward by claiming that the move to Passage Canal would involve only about 400 railroad employees and their families. A few business men also would migrate to the new port. The balance of Seward's 941 residents would be unaffected. (Through error or perversity, Ohlson always deducted eight people from Seward's 1939 census figure.) The remaining population included about 100 children at the Jesse Lee Home. Ohlson maintained that nobody lived between Moose Pass and Portage. The census enumerator of 1939 did find 339 people in the Seward census district outside of the towns, as well as 84 residents of Moose Pass. Although the region was a bit more populous than Ohlson claimed, it was not teeming by any stretch of the imagination. At its most calamitous, closing the Seward line would have affected no more than one thousand people.

Seward's spokesmen took cold comfort in Ohlson's calculations of the effect of the cutoff on their town. Anxiety was endemic in Seward from 1939 through and after World War II, especially about the impact of closing the line on property values and town revenues. Much bitterness was generated, partly because the town and the general manager had carried on a running fight through the years. A squabble over Ohlson's refusal to build coal bunkers, an arsonist's attack on cars of imported ties, Seward's 1937 attempt to tax the tonnage moving over the railroad's dock, and Ohlson's persistent refusal to improve the dock all were grist for the mills of controversy.

The steamship companies' December 1931 cancellation of through rate shipments to Woodrow station, seven miles from Seward, seriously ruffled the relationships between railroad and town. Seward merchants customarily shipped bulky, lightweight goods to Woodrow then trucked them back, because the through rate and trucking charges were less than the local steamer rates to Seward. The steamship companies were understandably unenthusiastic about the arrangement. Ohlson was able to delay the steamer lines until after the furor over his own "Howell committee" rate increases quieted, but he could not prevent them from withdrawing their concurrence to the Woodrow rates. Although the railroad earned some revenue from the haul to Woodrow, the tonnage was so slight — 91.248 tons from December 1930 through November 1931 — that the extra loading and switching cancelled the income. The Seward Chamber of Commerce preferred to believe in Ohlson's surrendering substantial railroad revenues and assisting the steamer lines with their rate squeeze at Seward. The issue did not die, but rankled all through the 1930s.

Don Carlos Brownell, Seward's obstreperous mayor, heightened the conflict over Passage Canal. During his 1938 visit to Alaska, Secretary Ickes remembered the officious Brownell as the "busy mayor who wanted us to look at every building in his little town."[6] In 1939 Brownell sent Ohlson a preemptory letter demanding full information on the new route "at once."[7] Ohlson maintained his reputation for giving short shrift to any Alaskan who tried to tell him what to do. Refusing to answer Brownell, he wrote to the Seward city council: "In view of the various statements made by the signer of your letter, one Don Carlos Brownell, . . . in which he remarks that Alaska did not need The Alaska Railroad when it was built and does not need it now, I do not think that you are very much concerned over what happens to The Alaska Railroad, as you always will have your highway which your champion so loudly acclaims."[8] Brownell's personal attacks on Ohlson and his rambling, inaccurate statements about the railroad discredited Seward's cause.

Even the most rational arguments in favor of the Seward line helped little, for Ohlson had the better of it when it came to cost comparisons. In a broadside against the new route delivered from the House floor, Delegate Dimond insisted that the Seward line could be rehabilitated and protected from sabotage for a modest $1,500,000. Larger locomotives could overcome the steep grades in the Kenai Mountains. The Ohlson estimates of costs and savings were "romance," he snorted. As for the promised rate reductions, he declared on another occasion, "I simply do not believe a word of it."[9] The new line would cost double or more Ohlson's estimates, he asserted. Dimond attacked with vigor, but only Ohlson had precise estimates backed by a railroader's expertise.

Passage Canal's detractors impeached the proposed line on other grounds. The canal's weather was bad, they said, but Ohlson had figures showing the climate to be bearable, if sometimes unpleasantly damp and cool. The railroad was built to develop Alaska and not to show a profit, they insisted, but the lack of development along the Kenai Peninsula trackage mocked their words. It was true, as Seward's spokesmen stressed, that The Alaska Railroad suffered from slides, washouts, and glaciering on other sections besides the Seward-Portage route. They failed to mention that the general thrust of the line along Turnagain Arm and northward to Fairbanks could not be abandoned. The line from Seward could be. Anyway, the freaks of weather and geology were less severe along the other 404 miles than they were on the first 66.

Ohlson confounded his critics by ignoring them. With the army on his side during the uneasy days of the "phony war," he really needed no other allies. By 1940 the army had scrapped its modest plans for a limited defense of coastal Alaska in the Anchorage and Seward areas. Because the Aleutians pointed like a scimitar toward Japan, Alaska's strategic value rose with the escalating bellicosity in Japanese-American relations. The military usefulness of the windswept, fogbound Aleutians turned out to be largely theoretical, but their limitations were not then well known. Besides, Alaska was close to Siberia. The wisdom of having military forces near the enigmatic Soviet Union seemed incontestable no matter how the European-Asian wartime alliances finally sorted themselves out.

Alaska's enhanced military importance entailed a large role for army aircraft in protecting the navy. Air bases at Fairbanks (begun in 1939) and at Anchorage (begun in 1940) depended upon The Alaska Railroad to carry construction equipment, material, men, and supplies. The army's first shipments almost overwhelmed the Seward dock. The Seward-Portage line could carry the railroad's peacetime freight, but it was obviously incapable of handling much military traffic without a major reconstruction. In 1940 the War Department independently investigated the railroad's southern trackage to determine whether to rebuild the Seward route, to establish a port at Anchorage, or to build a line from Passage Canal. The surveying engineers opted for the Passage Canal line because it was safer from air attacks than the Seward route, and because Passage Canal was free of ice during winter when the Anchorage harbor filled with floating ice pans.

Ohlson urged the army to submit an estimate for the new line in its budget. Defense was an idea whose time had come, and a project treated cooly in Congress when proposed by Ohlson would receive a fair hearing if advanced by the army. "Oh, the crimes that are committed in the name of defense,"[10] cried Jed Johnson of the House Appropriations Committee when he discovered what had been done. Pressure from the War Department saw the measure through despite objections. In April 1941 President Roosevelt signed the appropriations bill authorizing the new route. In June the Corps of Engineers signed a contract with the West Construction Company of Boston. The work began in the autumn. "Holing through" ceremonies in November 1942 symbolized Ohlson's victory. The savor was so sweet for the aging general manager that he wished once more to retire, but he was persuaded to stay on through the war. Tracklaying by railroad and army crews continued into 1943. On June 1 the first of the daily-except-Sunday, passenger-and-freight trains rolled through the tunnels to Passage Canal.

Ohlson had his cutoff, but that was only half his battle. Shifting civilian cargoes to Whittier (the name of a nearby glacier, following Ohlson's suggestion, was applied to the new port) and closing the Seward line remained. The general manager lost his fight. The little town at the head of Resurrection Bay stayed defiantly on the map, because removing it was politically unwise. Politics aside, creating the facilities at Whittier to close down Seward was not an urgent wartime measure.

Politically speaking, opening Whittier was one thing, creating a commercial port there was quite another. The furor surrounding the Passage Canal project, and Seward's future, boded ill for wartime domestic harmony. The administration wished to ruffle no more congressional feathers. As Ohlson bombarded the Division of Territories and Island Possessions with his plans for the new townsite, the costs of the project mounted appallingly. The site of Whittier had to be cleared of boulders and alder bushes, and a complete utilities system had to be installed under the supervision of a well-salaried city manager. Then houses had to be built of materials critically scarce during wartime. The labor shortage compounded the problem. In October 1942 the army's Alaska Engineer Office decided that the Whittier townsite could not be built "without interfering with work of a military necessity."[11] By April 1943 Ohlson had surrendered all hope of transferring commercial freight to Whittier during the war.

The determined Swede by no means had abandoned his goal, and he continued planning for a postwar shift of his railroad's terminal from Seward to Whittier. "I think there is more than meets the eye in the most recent correspondence from the Colonel on the subject of through rates via the Whittier terminus,"[12] wrote a subordinate in the division of territories to its head, Benjamin W. Thoron. On Thoron's advice, Ickes took a firm stand with Ohlson. The Kenai would develop, the Secretary of the Interior told the general manager in January 1944, and the railroad was its only connection with the interior of Alaska. Congress would decide whether to abandon the Seward-Portage line. In the meantime, Ohlson should prepare estimates for bringing the line up to the standard of the rest of the railroad. Two months later Ickes issued a statement confirming Seward's permanence.

Ohlson was by then at his most crotchety and was more unwilling than ever to accept dictation about railroad operations. Too loyal and too wise to challenge his superior directly, he continued chipping away at departmental policy. Delay was one of his tactics. Not until June 1944 did the Division of Territories and Island Possessions have a full narrative estimate of rehabilitation costs on the Seward-Portage line. Then it came interspersed with Ohlson's familiar arguments against the Kenai Peninsula route. Second, the general manager exploited a tendency within the division to think of a highway linking Seward with Anchorage as a reasonable substitute for the railroad. Finally, he narrowly construed Ickes' demand that the Seward line remain open. Beginning in December 1944, Ohlson and Alaska Steam laid plans to move tourists through the Whittier gateway as part of an overall effort to reduce tourist travel time. While he did not arrange an "immediate"[13] transfer of commercial freight, he did insist that a once-weekly local service down the Kenai would fulfill Ickes' pledge to retain the port of Seward.

Ohlson, to his credit, was vigorously forthright in response to queries from the Interior Department. If he failed to press for the shift to Whittier, he wrote, "I would consider myself subject to a charge of malfeasance of [sic] office." Only if Ickes gave "positive instructions that all commercial traffic must be handled through the port of Seward until the highway construction is completed"[14] would Ohlson delay the transfer to Whittier beyond the earliest possible date. On September 12, 1945 — scarcely a month after the Japanese surrender — the army announced its intention to withdraw from Whittier within thirty days. The port facilities would then, under a 1943 agreement, be deeded from the War Department to Interior. Six days later Ohlson formally recommended shipping all through freight via Whittier as soon as adequate dock forces could be assembled.

The Division of Territories continued to take a dim view of the general manager's ambitions. If previous commitments were not enough, evidence indicated that Alaska Steam intended to raise its rates, canceling any reduction in rail charges from the new port. The division's acting director recommended against the change. On October 2, 1945, Ohlson lost his battle against the Seward line. A preemptory telegram from Interior told him not to route commercial freight through Whittier. The port at the head of Passage Canal was to serve only the army, not Alaska's postwar civilian population.

It was a bitter pill for the seventy-five-year-old general manager, but only one of many. Long before war's end, Ohlson's organization and his railroad were in shambles and moving from crisis to crisis. A coal famine in the coal-rich railbelt was the first, ironic crisis of the defense effort. It established a pattern increasingly familiar during the war years: the army's presence created a critical situation, the army helped to overcome it, and by its assistance, the army increased the railroad's dependence upon the military. The Army's heavy coal demands at Elmendorf Field near Anchorage, soon to be joined by Fort Richardson, forced the railroad to reopen its Eska mine during the autumn of 1940. Fortunately, Ohlson had revived the Geological and Mining Department back in June 1939 expressly to survey the Passage Canal route and to ready the Eska mine for full emergency production. He closed the mine again after two and one-half months of operation. Even with the backlog from Eska, the privately owned Evan Jones mine at nearby Jonesville could not meet the demands from all of its customers. The cantankerous general manager grumbled about Evan Jones' inefficient management, inadequate development, and underfinancing, but he reopened the Eska mine in 1941 and kept it open.

Ohlson's actions were not enough. As early as November 1941, the Anchorage city council complained of coal shortages. The council blamed federal agencies for preempting coal supplies and creating a fuel famine in town. The army, too, fretted about the quantity and quality of the coal it received while smarting under Evan Jones' reluctance to comply with federal laws regulating government contracts. The general manager encouraged new coal mines and miners' renewed interest in old ones. He openly subsidized one new lignite producer, a reputable gold miner, with an especially low freight charge. When the well-established Healy River Coal Corporation complained of his preferential treatment, Ohlson refused to rescind the special rate. "This rate was quoted in order to. . .get much needed coal into the Anchorage area," he replied, "and you should know that the Healy River Coal Corporation was quoted a very low transportation rate. . .during the early days in order [to] assist in the development of your mine."[15]

Expanded production could not match the army's demand, and it began importing coal — 18,000 tons during the first half of 1942. Importing continued despite soaring local production. In fiscal year 1940, the railroad hauled 113,980 tons of Alaska coal. The tonnage jumped to 173,067 in fiscal year 1943. In fiscal year 1944, Alaska coal movements again increased sharply, to a record 255,989 tons. During fiscal year 1945, haulage slumped slightly — to 225,887 tons — and the railroad carried no imported coal.

The coal importations embarrassed Ohlson. When he strove for increases in domestic production, however, he worsened the already serious shortage of competent miners. With military and civilian needs requiring more than the railbelt's output, the railroad had to rely on the dwindling force at Eska to supply most of its coal. Ohlson poured money into new buildings, for improved mining as well as for increased employee comfort, but the draft and soaring wartime wages elsewhere scattered the Eska crews. Despite intensive country-wide recruiting, the railroad had to accept as many as fifty soldiers a day to keep its mine in full production. Every major railbelt mine suffered a similar fate, and the army, eager for coal development, supplied soldier-miners to them all. By fiscal year 1944, 68 percent of Eska's miners were soldiers. They mined coal at Eska until April 1945.

Keeping the railroad operating was even more demanding than keeping boilers full of coal. The army's enormous shipments set new traffic records each year from 1940 through 1944, but they brought Ohlson little joy. The old man watched helplessly while the railroad he had reconstructed with paternal care fell to pieces under the pounding wheels of the long military freights. The tonnages told the story. From 157,904 tons in fiscal year 1939, the last nondefense year, successive yearly hauls were: 1940, 194,467 tons; 1941, 361,295 tons; 1942, 419,867 tons; and 1943, 461,484 tons. In fiscal year 1944, freight traffic set a record — 627,847 tons — dropping off to 549,248 during fiscal year 1945. Even with the decline, The Alaska Railroad carried almost three and one-half times as much freight at war's end than it had during 1939. In 1944 the traffic density reached 252,800, modest compared to peacetime densities on "stateside" short lines, but a record for The Alaska Railroad.

Ohlson could not hire a force large enough to move mountains of freight, keep rolling stock in repair, and maintain roadbed and bridges. Ties rotted, rails developed battered ends, and trestles sagged. In October 1942 the general manager complained that "it has been impossible to perform any ballast work or even patch ballast work for the past two years and the road bed is getting worse instead of improving."[16] Two months later the Alaska Defense Command began supplying men to the railroad's mechanical and section forces. The soldiers could not carry the load. From the Pearl Harbor attack to the end of February 1943, Ohlson lost some 600 employees, mostly to higher paying jobs. Another 100 men were drafted. It was devastating to a railroad with an average monthly employment of 687 in 1939. Obviously, the army's piecemeal help and frantic recruiting by several federal agencies were insufficient. To save the railroad, the Alaska Defense Command appealed for a railway operating battalion to plug the manpower drain.

The 714th Transportation Corps Railway Operating Battalion arrived on April 3, 1943, with a complement of 25 officers and 1,090 enlisted men. The War Department reluctantly kept the battalion on duty in the Far North until May 1, 1945, while gradually reducing its strength. On that date, stepped-up civilian recruiting by the War Manpower Commission allowed the War Department to reassign all but 100 workers. In August the last of the battalion left the railroad. During its stay, the 714th eased, but did not cure, the railroad's labor shortage. The battalion lacked car repairmen, machinists, boilermakers, and blacksmiths. Though the railroad's wages spiralled upward, they remained behind the highest pay for comparable jobs in the territory. Scarce housing in Anchorage discouraged family men. Federal labor recruiters were inclined to sign up anyone who seemed sentient and willing to go to Alaska. The situation improved only a little after the War Manpower Commission took charge in January 1945. By springtime the Anchorage jail overflowed with drunks and vagrants sent to work on the railroad. Angry protests from harassed officials in Anchorage brought some change for the better. Ohlson knew what the Anchorage officials were going through. During the last year of the war, he retained but two-thirds of the 1,800 employees sent to work on the railroad.

The general manager did what he could, and even hired six women section laborers at Cantwell (mile 319.5) during 1945. But his best was not good enough. The average civilian force of 1944 — 916 — compared favorably with 1939's average 687. But the labor supply had lost the elasticity enabling Ohlson to expand his forces during the critically important construction and maintenance months. In 1939 he hired an average 1,235 employees from May through September. During the same period of 1944, he could gather an average of only 958. Consequently, the deteriorating roadbed and bridges sent more and more trains bouncing off the tracks. Major derailments were three or fewer until fiscal year 1944, when six occurred. In August 1944 (fiscal year 1945) part of a wooden bridge collapsed beneath a work train, dropping the locomotive tender and a flatcar into Honolulu Creek at mile 288. A December derailment occurred near Nenana, when the rails spread apart underneath a passenger train, overturning two coaches and injuring thirty-eight passengers. The most embarrassing accident occurred on August 4, 1945, when a passenger engine pulling a party of congressmen left the rails near Seward. Dozens of minor derailments happened each year. Ohlson simply did not have the labor, materials, or equipment to keep his railroad in acceptable condition.

The army helped the railroad in other ways: by guarding the right-of-way, by longshoring its own freight while paying full government rates for many items, by transferring (for free) the river steamer *Barry K* and loaning two barges during fiscal year 1944, and by transferring (for payment) supplies, equipment, and buildings at Whittier after war's end. Ohlson gratefully acknowledged the army's free services. He could be grateful, too, for the army's reluctance to run his railroad. Just after Pearl Harbor, the War Department demanded — and got — authority to operate the railroad through orders to its general manager in the event of a local emergency. The Alaska Defense Command never invoked its authority. When confronted with the railroad's imminent physical collapse, army officers in Alaska worked to secure a railway operating battalion, shying away from complete responsibility for Ohlson's line.

Ohlson reciprocated, mostly by offering free or reduced rates on military shipments. Freight for bridge guards was carried free. In 1939 Ohlson reduced the railroad's proportion of the through rate 20 percent to Fairbanks and 25 percent to Anchorage on shipments of construction material and petroleum products from Seattle. In July 1943 he cut the carload rates on War Department shipments 12½ percent below the regular tariff. During the same month, the railroad began picking up the tab for the 714th Railway Operating Battalion, reimbursing the army for payroll and subsistence costs, plus 10 percent. During the war the railroad turned the McKinley Park Hotel over to the army to use as a recreational camp and ran weekly special trains to the park during most of 1943, 1944, and 1945. Ohlson allowed low furlough fares of 1¼ cents per mile (*versus* the regular 6 cents) to military passengers on leave who were traveling at their own expense. Neither his concessions nor rising costs dammed the river of black ink flowing over the railroad's books. In fiscal year 1944, the surplus topped $5 million, incredible income by prewar standards.

Profits pleased the general manager not at all. For one thing, they would have to be plowed back into rebuilding his crumbling line at war's end. For another, they were one more gauge of his dependance on the military. That dependance was bearable so long as Simon Bolivar Buckner, Jr. headed the Alaska Defense Command. Silver-haired General Buckner, tough and opportunistic, ran his command with verve and a flair for slicing through red tape. He and Ohlson understood each other. Buckner left Alaska in June 1944. Ohlson did not like his successor. In March 1945 the general manager disgustedly recounted a meeting at the home of a prominent Anchorage resident, where the new military commander had freely criticized Ickes and another Interior Department executive. Soured relations at the top emphasized the continual bickering at lower levels. Railroad employees accused soldiers of pilfering, while admitting that soldiers were not the only petty thieves. The army's refusal to cooperate in investigations of theft was more irksome. Quarrels between military men and civilians working side by side were commonplace.

Major equipment purchases somewhat eased Ohlson's wartime burdens. When the great Kennecott copper mine closed and the Copper River & Northwestern was abandoned in 1938, The Alaska Railroad purchased much of its rolling stock at bargain prices. In September 1942 the Alaska Yukon Navigation Company liquidated, selling its river equipment to the railroad. The ancient steamer *Yukon* and three barges were the only serviceable remains of the A. Y. N.'s once-mighty fleet. After studies of ventilation problems in the longest (eastern) tunnel of the Whittier cutoff, the railroad secured its first two diesel locomotives for use on Whittier runs. The locomotives arrived June 9, 1944 and were placed in service a week later. Late in 1945 Ohlson negotiated for five war surplus diesel-electric locomotives returning from overseas. During the war the railroad bought engines, equipment, and rolling stock. Occasional items were new, but most ranged in quality from usable to decrepit.

The war years witnessed a flurry of construction on Ohlson's line, almost all of it done by or for the army. A new dock at Seward, reconstruction of the Anchorage ocean dock, a branch line to Ladd Field at Fairbanks, and a bypass around the wobbly trestles in the Loop district were among the major projects. In September 1942 the railroad completed a new passenger station and general office building in the Ship Creek flat just north of downtown Anchorage. The gray reinforced concrete structure replaced both the old station and the frame office building in the yards — a sagging, drafty relic of construction days.

For all its activity, Ohlson's railroad was far removed from war action. It played no direct role in the bitter Aleutian campaign against the Japanese invaders of Attu and Kiska. Yet, railroad employees bore the blackouts, the censored mail, and the travel restrictions that were a civilian's lot in an overseas theater. Through the war years they formed the human component of the rail lifeline to central Alaska's military bases. The wisdom of the extensive military buildup in the territory could be questioned, but once the bases were built, they had to be supplied. The Alaska Railroad carried military freight from 1939 to after the end of the war, the year around, to the major military installations in mainland Alaska. Of course it could not reach all the scattered outposts, but it did connect with the river boats at Nenana and with airplanes at Anchorage and Fairbanks.

No other land route matched the railroad's record. The celebrated Alaska Highway, pioneered through in October 1942, was chiefly important as a supplier to military projects, including the airfields used by pilots ferrying aircraft to the Soviet Union. Military activities in northwestern Canada also received shipments via the highway. It carried at the most 350,000 tons during the peak year of 1943, well below the railroad's record 461,383 in 1944. The highway handled considerably less in other years. The rugged trucks, strung out along the 1,428-mile lane through the wilderness, never moved much through freight to Alaska. Most of what they hauled was unloaded at construction sites along the way. The Richardson Highway from Valdez to Fairbanks bore a significant tonnage — about 26,000 tons a year — only during the open seasons of 1942 and 1943. It was not militarily important after the 714th arrived to bolster the railroad's forces.

By the end of 1945, the seventy-five-year-old Ohlson was as exhausted as his railroad. He had resigned in the summer of 1943, but his resignation was merely a formality. He preferred to withdraw his retirement deductions rather than come under the provisions of the railroad's retirement act; thus, he had to leave government service before completing a full fifteen years. But the old man enjoyed the rumor and speculation surrounding his resignation too much not to exploit it. Before he left on a long vacation, he dangled the general managership before Cunningham and other railroaders in Alaska. Then he returned to his job with the understanding that he would serve through the end of the war.

Ohlson's last years on duty were an unhappy time of declining mutual respect between the railroad and other federal agencies in Alaska, of diminishing service to civilian customers, and of deteriorating labor relations. In October 1945 the embittered Ohlson forgot himself during a labor meeting and rushed across the room to shove and choke a representative of the train dispatchers. Sad as such incidents were, his finale was a time of hope. Even before war's end he was planning the physical reconstruction of his road. But that was for the future. On the first day of 1946 a new general manager officially took charge of The Alaska Railroad. Otto F. Ohlson, whose home for seventeen years lay above the sixtieth parallel, retired to Virginia.

Notes

Chapter 1

1. Falcon Joslin, "Possibilities of the Tanana," *Alaska-Yukon Magazine* 4 (1907): 292.

Chapter 2

1. *Congressional Record,* 65th Cong., 3d sess., 1919, 57, pt. 5: 4365.
2. U. S., Congress, House, Committee on the Territories, *Hearings on H. R. 5694,* 67th Cong., 1st sess., 1921, p. 329.
3. Quoted in Franklin Ward Burch, "Alaska's Railroad Frontier: Railroads and Federal Development Policy, 1898-1915" (Ph.D. diss., Catholic University of America, 1965), p. 195.
4. Most of Ballaine's voluminous testimony on Alaska affairs is a gross distortion, but the Perkins story seems credible. With the Alaska Central in receivership, Ballaine stood to lose all of his stock holdings. He was already feuding bitterly with the line's new management. To prevent the Alaska Central's collapse and to wrest control from the new management, he would have had to act swiftly, enlisting large capital. He would naturally appeal to Perkins. Ballaine made several more or less detailed accounts of the Perkins visit and conversations at different times. All of his recollections substantially agree. Perkins did visit Alaska with an entourage in the summer of 1909. According to John A. Garraty, Perkins' biographer, his visit involved a proposed Morgan copper and coal venture. The trip need not have been confined to that purpose. Garraty does not discuss Perkins' role in the Alaska Syndicate, nor does he mention the Guggenheim connection with the Morgan bank. See *Right-Hand Man: The Life of George W. Perkins* (New York: Harper & Brothers, 1960), pp. 227, 374. Quotations are from Ballaine's *Strangling of the Alaska Railroad* (Seattle, 1923), p. 9.
5. Taft is quoted in Martin L. Fausold, *Gifford Pinchot: Bull Moose Progressive* (Syracuse, N.Y.: Syracuse University Press, 1961), p. 30.
6. U.S., *Statutes at Large,* 1912, 37:512.

Chapter 3

1. U.S., Congress, House, Committee on the Territories, *Railway Routes in Alaska: Message from the President of the United States Transmitting Report of Alaska Railroad Commission,* 62d Cong., 3d sess., Doc. no. 1346, 1913, p. 116.
2. Ibid., p. 11.
3. *Congressional Record,* 63d Cong., 2d sess., 1913, 51, pt. 1:76.
4. 3 Mar. 1913, p. 1.
5. Brooks, Piper, and Dickeson are quoted in Burch, "Alaska's Railroad Frontier," on pp. 334, 335, and 328-29 respectively.
6. Quoted in Ernest Gruening, *The State of Alaska,* rev. ed. (New York: Random House, 1968), p. 187.
7. *Congressional Record,* 63d Cong., 2d sess., 1914, 51, pt. 2:1646.
8. *Fairbanks Daily News-Miner,* 12 Mar. 1914, p. 1.

9. U.S., *Statutes at Large,* 1914, 38:305; Gruening, *State of Alaska,* p. 187.
10. U.S., Department of the Interior, Alaskan Engineering Commission, *Reports of the Alaskan Engineering Commission for the period from March 12, 1914, to December 31, 1915* (64th Cong., 1st sess., H. Doc. 610, pt. 2, 1916), p. 63.
11. Ibid., p. 84.
12. Strong to D. K. Butler, 17 Feb. 1915, Papers of the Governors of Alaska, Federal Archives and Records Center, Seattle.
13. U.S., Department of the Interior, Alaskan Engineering Commission, *Annual Report of the Chairman to the Secretary of the Interior, from February 1 to December 31, 1915* (64th Cong., 1st sess., H. Doc. 610, pt. 2, 1916), p. 181.
14. Cotton to Lane, 24 June 1915, Record Group 126, National Archives.
15. 2 Dec. 1913, Governors' Papers, Federal Archives and Records Center, Seattle.

Chapter 4

1. *Alaska Railroad Record,* 27 Feb. 1917, 1:121.
2. Mears to Edes, 29 Apr. 1915, Headquarters Files, Alaska Railroad Archives.
3. Edes to R. J. Weir, 13 Apr. 1916, Record Group 126, National Archives.
4. Edes to E. C. Bradley, 13 Aug. 1918, ibid.
5. Mears to Edes, 21 April 1916, ibid.
6. Mears to Edes, 20 Mar. 1916, Headquarters Files, Alaska Railroad Archives.
7. Cotton, "Report to the Secretary of the Interior on the Alaska Railway," 1 Oct. 1916, Record Group 126, National Archives.
8. Edes to Mears, 11 Apr. 1917, Headquarters Files, Alaska Railroad Archives.
9. Edes to Mears, 10 Mar. 1916. ibid.
10. Riggs to Edes, 9 Dec. 1916, ibid.

Chapter 5

1. Edes to E. C. Bradley, 13 Aug. 1918, Record Group 126, National Archives; and "A. E. C. Report, 1920," app. A, p. 2.
2. Mears to Albert B. Fall, 7 Oct. 1921, Governors' Papers, Federal Archives and Records Center, Seattle.
3. Transcription, "Remarks made by Mrs. Lena Morrow Lewis, at Labor Hall, Anchorage, Alaska, May 1 (Labor Day) 1917," and meeting notes, n.d., Headquarters Files, Alaska Railroad Archives.
4. Edes to the Secretary of the Interior, 24 May 1917, and to H. A. Meyer, 23 June 1917, Record Group 126, National Archives.
5. Riggs to Edes, 14 July 1917, ibid.
6. Riggs to Edes, 14 July 1917; and to Meyer, 15 July 1917, ibid.
7. John H. Robinson to Andrew Christensen, 31 Jan. 1918, Headquarters Files, Alaska Railroad Archives.
8. Browne to Edes, 3 Aug. 1918, ibid.
9. Mears to Fall, 30 Sept. 1922, Governors' Papers, Federal Archives and Records Center, Seattle.
10. Gerig to Mears, 20 Dec. 1922, ibid.
11. U.S., Congress, House, Committee on the Territories, *Relief of Special Disbursing Agents of the Alaskan Engineering Commission: Hearings on H. R. 226,* 68th Cong., 1st sess., 1924, pp. 51-52, 54.
12. Mears to B. H. Barndollar, 12 Nov. 1921, Headquarters Files, Alaska Railroad Archives.
13. "A. E. C. Report, 1919," statement "Miscellaneous Traffic Statistics, Northern and Southern Divisions."
14. U.S., Congress, House, Subcommittee of Committee on Appropriations, *Hearing on Interior Department Appropriation Bill, 1924,* 67th Cong., 4th sess., 1922, pp. 794-95.

Chapter 6

1. Mears to Lane, 2 June 1915, Headquarters Files, Alaska Railroad Archives.
2. For the regulations and other forms see *A.E.C. Report, 1915,* pp. 208-10.
3. Christensen to Clay Tallman, 21 July and 9 Dec. 1915, Headquarters Files, Alaska Railroad Archives.
4. J. Horace McFarland, "City Planning—Minus," typescript, ibid.
5. Resolution of the Chamber of Commerce, Anchorage, 20 Aug. 1915; and Edes to Lane, 30 Aug. 1915, ibid.
6. Christensen to Tallman, 31 Aug. 1915, ibid.

7. Christensen to William A. Munly, 4 Jan. 1917, attachment no. 1, ibid.
8. Ibid., attachment no. 5, ibid.
9. Christensen to Edes, 2 Dec. 1916, ibid.
10. Christensen to Mears, 6 Dec. 1916, enclosing petition to H. E. Brenneman, U.S. Marshal, Valdez, n.d.; and to Edes, 20 Jan. 1917, ibid.
11. U.S., *Statutes at Large,* 1905, 33:61; Territory of Alaska, *Session Laws, Resolutions, and Memorials,* 1915, pp. 110-14.
12. Watts to Christensen, 16 Aug. 1916, Headquarters Files, Alaska Railroad Archives.
13. Strong to Edes, 11 Oct. 1916, ibid.
14. Edes to Christensen, 29 Dec. 1916, ibid.
15. Christensen to Edes and Mears, 6 Jan. 1917; and Edes to Christensen, 23 Jan. 1917, ibid.
16. Christensen to Edes, 5 Jan. 1916, ibid.
17. Watts to Christensen, 29 Oct. 1917, ibid.
18. Christensen to Tallman, 10 Dec. 1915, ibid.
19. Burton H. Barndollar to Mears, 29 Oct. 1920; and transcript of Barndollar's remarks, ibid.
20. *Fairbanks Daily News-Miner,* 7 Aug. 1916, p. 4.
21. Ibid., 24 Aug. 1916, p. 3; and 25 Aug. 1916, p. 1
22. Ibid., 26 Aug. 1916.

Chapter 7

1. Warren to Mears, 25 Sept. 1919, Headquarters Files, Alaska Railroad Archives.
2. Mears to R. V. [sic] Alexander, 22 Nov. 1919, ibid.
3. Warren to Mears, 29 Dec. 1919; and Mears to C. E. Dole, 21 Oct. 1919, ibid.
4. Mears to John H. Bunch, 10 Nov. 1922, ibid.
5. "Official Report of the Alaska Territorial Shipping Board," 18 June 1920, p. 16.
6. Mears to Rustgard, 14 Oct. 1922, Headquarters Files, Alaska Railroad Archives.
7. Quoted in Alaska Steamship Company, *Statement Concerning the Through Rates and Divisions with the Government Railroad in Alaska* (Seattle, 1923), p. 22.

Chapter 8

1. Wickersham to Daniel A. Sutherland, 21 June 1920, Sutherland Papers, University of Alaska Archives.
2. Quoted in *Alaska Daily Empire,* n.d., copy, Headquarters Files, Alaska Railroad Archives.
3. Lane to President Wilson, 9 Mar. 1918, Record Group 126, National Archives.
4. Ballaine to Lane, 21 May 1917, ibid.
5. *Congressional Record,* 65th Cong., 3d sess., 1919, 57, pt. 5:4365.
6. Quotations from Mears to John W. Hallowell, 14 Nov. 1919, Headquarters Files, Alaska Railroad Archives.
7. Anderson, "Railroad Engineering Under Sub-Arctic Conditions," copied 1964, p. 5.
8. Charles L. Mason to Judge Finney, 3 Mar. 1919, Headquarters Files, Alaska Railroad Archives.
9. Edes memorandum, 27 Jan. 1919, ibid.
10. Edes memorandum, 15 May 1919, ibid.
11. J. M. Aldrich to H. M. Gillman, 2 Oct. 1922, Record Group 126, National Archives.
12. Cotton, "Report to the Secretary of the Interior on the Alaska Railway," 1 Oct. 1916, Headquarters Files, Alaska Railroad Archives.
13. Mears to C. E. Dole, 23 Sept. 1915, ibid.
14. Quotations from *Congressional Record,* 65th Cong., 3d sess., 1919, 57, pt. 5:4363, 4366.
15. "United States *v.* Howard P. Curtis, Commissioner's Court, Nena [sic] precinct, fourth division, Territory of Alaska," transcript, 17 June 1918, p. 42.
16. Edes to Riggs, 1 Aug. 1918, Headquarters Files, Alaska Railroad Archives.
17. John W. Hallowell to Mears, 6 Dec. 1919, Record Group 126, National Archives.
18. Lane to Pollok, 17 July 1918 ; and Anne Wintermute Lane and Louise Herrick Wall, eds., *The Letters of Franklin K. Lane* (Boston: Houghton Mifflin Co., 1922), pp. 290-91.
19. Ibid.
20. Ballaine to Lane, 21 May 1917, and to the President, 7 Mar. 1918, Record Group 126, National Archives; and *Strangling of the Alaska Railroad* (Seattle, 1923), p. 44.
21. *Congressional Record,* 65th Cong., 3d sess., 1919, 57, pt. 5:4365.
22. Lane, "Memorandum on the Alaskan Railroad," Record Group 126, National Archives.

23. Ibid.

24. Preston to Mears, 27 Oct. 1921, Headquarters Files, Alaska Railroad Archives.

25. Rate committee, Anchorage Chamber of Commerce to Gerig, Browne, and Barndollar, 25 Nov. 1921, ibid.

26. Wickersham to Lane, 8 Jan. 1919, Record Group 126, National Archives.

27. Lane, "Memorandum on the Alaskan Railroad," ibid.

28. Ibid; and Edes memorandum, 15 May 1919, Headquarters Files, Alaska Railroad Archives.

29. Mears to Sherman Rogers, 21 Nov. 1922, Headquarters Files, Alaska Railroad Archives.

30. *Congressional Record,* 66th Cong., 3d sess., 1921, 60, pt. 1:1010.

31. H. A. Meyer to James A. Wilkinson, 14 July 1917, Record Group 126, National Archives.

Chapter 9

1. Board of Road Commissioners for Alaska, "Report Upon the Construction and Maintenance of Military and Post Roads, Bridges, and Trails, Alaska," excerpt, U.S., Army, Chief of Engineers, *Annual Report for the Fiscal Year Ending June 30, 1923* (Washington: Government Printing Office, 1923), pt. 1:2101.

2. U.S., Congress, House, Subcommittee of Committee on Appropriations, *Hearings on Sundry Civil Appropriation Bill for 1919,* 65th Cong., 2d sess., 1918, 1:1162.

3. Bone to Work, 8 Dec. 1923, Governors' Papers, Federal Archives and Records Center, Seattle.

4. Gotwals, transcript of speech to Anchorage Chamber of Commerce, 14 Aug. 1923, Headquarters Files, Alaska Railroad Archives.

5. *Alaska Weekly,* 26 Oct. 1923.

6. Landis to J. H. Hughes, 4 Feb. 1924; and 9 May 1924; Headquarters Files, Alaska Railroad Archives.

7. Committee on Policy of The Alaska Railroad, minutes, 30 Nov. 1923, Governors' Papers, Federal Archives and Records Center, Seattle.

8. Noel W. Smith to Scott C. Bone, 23 Sept. 1924, ibid.

9. Cunningham to Landis, 14 Jan. 1924, Headquarters Files, Alaska Railroad Archives.

10. F. H. Chapin to Landis, 5 Jan. 1924, ibid.

11. Work to Bone, 1 Nov. 1923, Governors' Papers, Federal Archives and Records Center, Seattle.

12. Bone to Work, 13 Mar. 1924, ibid.

13. Work to Barndollar, 1 July 1924; and Barndollar to Bone, 4 July 1924, ibid.

14. Smith to Work, Nov. 1924, an early draft of the "preliminary report," 1 Nov. 1924, Headquarters Files, Alaska Railroad Archives.

15. *Seattle Post-Intelligencer,* 9 Sept. 1924.

Chapter 10

1. Smith to Work, 1 Nov. 1924, Headquarters Files, Alaska Railroad Archives.

2. Smith to Thompson, 25 Sept. 1925, ibid.

3. Work to Smith, 7 Oct. 1924; 9 Sept. 1925; and 12 Oct. 1925, ibid.

4. Smith to Transportation Committee, Chamber of Commerce, in *Anchorage Daily Times,* 12 Nov. 1924.

5. *Seattle Post-Intelligencer,* 7 Oct. 1924; and 8 Oct. 1924.

6. Ibid., 31 Aug. 1925.

7. Ibid., 17 Oct. 1925, 18 Nov. 1925; and Work to Smith, 12 Oct. 1925, Headquarters Files, Alaska Railroad Archives.

8. Smith, General Circular no. 25, 18 June 1925, Headquarters Files, Alaska Railroad Archives.

9. Smith to Work, 30 Apr. 1926, ibid.

10. Transcript of conference, 2 Sept. 1927, Record Group 126, National Archives.

11. Ibid.

12. Smith to Work, 16 Sept. 1927, Headquarters Files, Alaska Railroad Archives.

13. Mears to Gerig, 9 Jan. 1921, ibid.

14. Ummel to H. M. Gillman, Jr., 15 May 1926, ibid.

15. Ummel to Smith, 9 Sept. 1926, ibid.

Chapter 11

1. *Seattle Times,* 14 Jan. 1936.

2. Ohlson to E. J. Duggan, 31 Oct. 1935, Headquarters Files, Alaska Railroad Archives.
3. Snell to Ickes, 16 June 1933, Record Group 126, National Archives.
4. Smith to Work, 21 Sept. 1928, Headquarters Files, Alaska Railroad Archives.
5. Ohlson to Wilbur, 16 May 1930, ibid.
6. *Congressional Record,* 70th Cong., 1st sess., 1928, 69, pt. 3:2675.
7. Ibid., 71st Cong., 2d sess., 1930, 72, pt. 11:11502, 12165. Deficits from fiscal year 1928 through 1930 were: $799,095.86 on revenues of $1,338,854.86; $916,599.21 on revenues of $1,449,823.95; and $1,213,155.78 on revenues of $1,186,551.41, Department of the Interior, "Circular of Information Regarding The Alaska Railroad," 1 Feb. 1940, p. 15, Headquarters Files, Alaska Railroad Archives.
8. U. S., Congress, Senate, Special Select Committee, *Report on the Investigation of the Alaska Railroad,* 71st Cong., 3d sess., 5 Jan. 1930 [sic 1931], pp. 8, 10.
9. Wilbur to Howell, 3 Jan. 1931, Record Group 126, National Archives.
10. Wickersham to Sutherland, 20 Nov. 1930, Sutherland Papers, University of Alaska Archives.
11. The Alaska Railroad, "Annual Report, 1932," report of the general manager, p. 8.
12. Chamber of Commerce of Seward, Alaska, resolution, 8 Oct. 1929, copy Headquarters Files, Alaska Railroad Archives.
13. *Seward Daily Gateway,* 23 Sept. 1931, p. 4.
14. U. S., Congress, House, Subcommittee of Committee on Appropriations, *Hearings on Interior Department Appropriation Bill for 1933,* 72nd Cong., 1st sess., 1932, p. 1008.

Chapter 12

1. R. J. McKenna to Ohlson, 23 Mar. 1932, Headquarters Files, Alaska Railroad Archives.
2. Ohlson to H. H. Edgerton, 14 July 1939, ibid.
3. U. S., Department of the Interior, "Report of the Committee Appointed by the Secretary of the Interior to Review the Rates and Policies of The Alaska Railroad" [the Thoron report] (Washington, 1947), p. 190.
4. Ohlson to Wilbur, 31 Mar. 1932, Headquarters Files, Alaska Railroad Archives.
5. Thoron report, p. 62.
6. Ohlson to Wilbur, n. 4.
7. Ohlson to Philip Clough Nelson, 19 May 1932, Headquarters Files, Alaska Railroad Archives.
8. Interview with John E. Clark, Fairbanks, 30 May 1968.
9. James D. Cunningham to E. K. Burlew, 25 Jan. 1934, Record Group 126, National Archives.
10. Ibid.
11. Ohlson to Wilbur, 28 Oct. 1932, ibid.
12. Jack Warren to Ickes, 5 Oct. 1933, ibid.
13. *Fairbanks Daily News-Miner,* 26 Oct. 1940, p. 8.
14. Ohlson to Nelson, n. 7.
15. H. H. Porter to Ohlson, 4 June 1934; and Ohlson to Porter, 5 June 1934, Headquarters Files, Alaska Railroad Archives.
16. Ohlson to Ickes, 14 July 1933, Transportation Files, ibid.
17. Ohlson to Carl Lomen, 28 Apr. 1931, Headquarters Files, ibid.
18. Ohlson to C. I. Fitzgerald, 26 Nov. 1937, ibid.

Chapter 13

1. T. B. Wilson to Ohlson, 15 May 1934, Headquarters Files, Alaska Railroad Archives.
2. Ohlson to Ickes, 6 July 1934, ibid.
3. Ickes to Ohlson, ibid.
4. Ohlson to Anchorage Chamber of Commerce, 2 Nov. 1936, ibid.
5. Ohlson to Ernest Gruening, 31 Dec. 1936, ibid.
6. *Seward Gateway,* 11 Feb. 1937, p. 2; and C. C. Garland to Ickes, 3 Mar. 1937, Headquarters Files, Alaska Railroad Archives.
7. Ohlson to L. W. Baker, 24 Sept. 1938; and to J. D. Nelson, ibid.
8. *Fairbanks Daily News-Miner,* 23 Dec. 1936.
9. Mrs. J. S. Johnson to Ohlson, 8 Aug. 1935, Headquarters Files, Alaska Railroad Archives.
10. Thoron report, p. 39.
11. Ickes, *The Secret Diary of Harold L. Ickes: The Inside Struggle 1936-1939* (New York: Simon and Schuster, 1954), 2:446.
12. Ohlson to H. Jean White, 28 Oct. 1936, Headquarters Files, Alaska Railroad Archives.

13. Ohlson to Ruth Hampton, 7 May 1942; and 10 July 1942, ibid.
14. Ohlson to Burlew, 25 Apr. 1935, ibid.
15. Ohlson to Gruening, 25 Sept. 1938; and to the Secretary, 10 May 1939, ibid.
16. Ohlson to Wilbur, 24 Dec. 1931, ibid.
17. Harry B. Mitchell to Robert Ramspeck, 25 June 1935, ibid.
18. Ohlson to Ickes, 7 Mar. 1935, ibid.
19. Quoted in Dimond to Ickes, 3 Jan. 1934, Dimond Papers, University of Alaska Archives.
20. Ibid.
21. McCarl to Ickes, 13 July 1934, ibid.
22. Ohlson to Gruening, 6 May 1936, Headquarters Files, Alaska Railroad Archives.
23. Ohlson to S. E. Lancaster, 22 Jan. 1930, ibid.
24. Ohlson to Gruening, 21 Dec. 1934, ibid; and Thoron report, p. 114.

Chapter 14

1. The Alaska Railroad, "Annual Report, 1944," p. 13.
2. Smith to the Secretary of the Interior, 25 Sept. 1925, Record Group 126, National Archives.
3. Smith to Work, 10 May 1928, ibid.
4. "Minutes of Meeting—Committee on Policy," 15 Oct. 1928, Headquarters Files, Alaska Railroad Archives.
5. Ohlson to Jack B. Fahy, 23 July 1945, ibid.
6. Ickes, *Diary*, 2:441.
7. Brownell to Ohlson, 20 Dec. 1939, Headquarters Files, Alaska Railroad Archives.
8. Ohlson to City Council, Seward, 26 Dec. 1939, ibid.
9. *Congressional Record*, 77th Cong., 1st sess., 1941, 87, pt. 3:2470. Dimond to Gruening, 9 Aug. 1940, Dimond Papers, University of Alaska Archives.
10. U. S., Congress, House, Subcommittee of the Committee on Appropriations, *Interior Department Appropriation Bill for 1942*, 77th Cong., 1st sess., 1941, pt. 1:947.
11. D. O. Givens to Earl D. McGinty, 12 Oct. 1942, Headquarters Files, Alaska Railroad Archives.
12. John G. Evans to Thoron, Record Group 126, National Archives.
13. Ohlson to Hampton, 17 June 1944, Headquarters Files, Alaska Railroad Archives.
14. Ohlson to Fahy, n. 5; and to Mr. Arnold, 20 Sept. 1945, ibid.
15. Ohlson to A. E. Lathrop, 20 Feb. 1942, ibid.
16. Ohlson to Guy J. Swope, 9 Oct. 1942, Annual Report Files, ibid.

Bibliographical Essay

Introduction

The exigency of publication forced me to excise the extensive documentation and most of the material on economic development contained in the original manuscript. Those who wish to review the documentation and the original version of this study may consult the carbon copy typescript at the Library of North Texas State University.

My view of Alaska's resources is basically that one or two abundant natural resources have, since the purchase from Russia, given rise to the myth of the Alaskan treasure house. Furs, fisheries, gold, timber, and oil, each in its turn, have spurred the romance of an abundant last frontier. The traditionalist interpretation of Alaska's history holds that there is no myth—widespread resource development would have been greater were it not for the policies of the federal government, the large economic interests in Alaska, or both. The revisionist argument, to which I subscribe, is that the federal government's aid to Alaska has been, at least in some specific instances, more than enough to increase the material prosperity of the Great Land. Therefore, the reasons for the failure of Alaska's agriculture, coal, and other resources to develop significant markets must lie partly in the paucity, poor quality, or inaccessibility of the resources themselves.

Anyone wishing other published expositions of my view should read the following articles: "The Alaskan Engineering Commission and a New Agricultural Frontier," *Agricultural History* 42 (1968):339-50; "Alaska's Past, Alaska's Future: The Uses of Historical Interpretation," *Alaska Review* 4 (1970):1-11; and "Alaska Steaks for California Tables," *The Alaska Journal* 5 (1975):205-10. I hope that other articles exploring the relationships between The Alaska Railroad and resource development will follow.

Archival Sources

The Alaska Railroad's own archives are an indispensable source for any historical study of the railroad or of the development of central Alaska. The Headquarters Files have survived fires, deliberate removals, and cleanup campaigns to form the nucleus of a remarkably candid and complete record of the railroad. The following files also were important and are listed in the approximate order of their usefulness: Headquarters Case, Headquarters Transfer, Transportation, Real Estate and Contract, Barndollar, and Publicity. The Annual Report Files contain not only the annual reports and their appendices, they also include letters and memoranda relating to subjects contained in the annual reports. The annual reports are the source for the operating statistics used in the text. When I studied them, most of the Archives were located in the basement of the passenger station at Anchorage. The bulk of them have since been removed to the Federal Archives and Records Center, Seattle.

At the National Archives, Record Group 126, the Records of the Office of Territories, comprises the major collection of files consulted for my study and virtually the only ones pertaining to this book. Within the group, portions of the 9-1 files relating to Alaska and all of the 18 files, the Central Classified Files Relating to The Alaska Railroad, were consulted. The National Archives railroad material is partly mirror image of the railroad's Headquarters Files of correspondence with the Interior Department. Both, however, contain many important letters and memoranda not shared with the other.

The third major archival source is the Papers of the Governors of Alaska at the Federal Archives and Records Center, Seattle. At the University of Alaska Archives I obtained useful information from the papers of Frederick Mears, Anthony J. Dimond, and Dan Sutherland. The collections of John E. Ballaine and Charles R. Garfield at the Archives Division, as well as the Seattle Chamber of Commerce scrapbooks and other materials in the Northwest Collection, Suzzallo Library, University of Washington, also were useful.

Government Documents

So many government documents were used in this study that listing them with even the briefest evaluation would consume several pages. Interested readers should consult the notes to this volume, the notes to the carbon copy cited in the introduction, and a splendid dissertation indispensable to a full understanding of pre-1915 Alaska rail issues: Franklin Ward Burch, "Alaska's Railroad Frontier: Railroads and Federal Development Policy, 1898-1915" (Catholic University of America, 1965).

Background (Chapters 1-3)

Survey histories of Alaska abound, although almost all of them were written before the newer revisionist monographs and articles began to appear. They are traditionalist in interpretation and are organized around political issues and chronologies. Two of the best are Jeannette Paddock Nichols, *Alaska: A History of Its Administration, Exploitation, and Industrial Development During Its First Half Century Under the Rule of the United States* (1924; reprint ed., New York: Russell & Russell, 1963), and Ernest Gruening, *The State of Alaska*, rev. ed. (New York: Random House, 1968).

The gold rushes were the pivot for much of Alaska's twentieth-century history. Pierre Berton, *The Klondike Fever: The Life and Death of the Last Great Gold Rush* (New York: Alfred A. Knopf, 1958), is a masterful evocation of the Klondike rush. Briefer on the Klondike, but more comprehensive, is David B. Wharton, *The Alaska Gold Rush* (Bloomington: Indiana

University Press, 1972). The best comprehensive study is also the most recent: William R. Hunt, *North of 53°: The Wild Days of the Alaska-Yukon Mining Frontier, 1870-1914* (New York: Macmillan Publishing Co., Inc., 1974). Cautious, sensible stampeders are the subject of Carl L. Lokke, *Klondike Saga: The Chronicle of a Minnesota Gold Mining Company* (Minneapolis: University of Minnesota Press, 1965). An outstanding inclusive study of Alaska's history, geography, and climate contains important gold rush observations: Alfred Hulse Brooks, *Blazing Alaska's Trails,* ed. Burton L. Fryxell (Caldwell, Idaho: University of Alaska and Arctic Institute of North America, 1953).

The best summary of pre-Alaska Railroad rail developments in Alaska is Burch, "Alaska's Railroad Frontier," fully cited in "Government Documents" above. The Copper River & Northwestern is treated in the context of Alaska Syndicate investments in Robert Alden Stearns, "The Morgan-Guggenheim Syndicate and the Development of Alaska, 1906-1915" (Ph.D. diss., University of California, Santa Barbara, 1967), and with special emphasis in Lone E. Janson, *The Copper Spike* (Anchorage: Alaska Northwest Publishing Company, 1975). The Alaska Central-Alaska Northern history is stridently related in two pamphlets by John E. Ballaine, *Alaska Central-Alaska Northern Railway* (Seattle, 1911); and *Strangling of the Alaska Railroad* (Seattle, 1923). For the Tanana Valley line see Duane Koenig, "Ghost Railway in Alaska: The Story of the Tanana Valley Railroad," *Pacific Northwest Quarterly* 45 (1954): 8-12.

Four standard works on the Ballinger-Pinchot controversy are Alpheus T. Mason, *Bureaucracy Convicts Itself: The Ballinger-Pinchot Controversy of 1910* (New York: Viking Press, 1941); M. Nelson McGeary, *Gifford Pinchot: Forester-Politician* (Princeton: Princeton University Press, 1960); Samuel P. Hays, *Conservation and the Gospel of Efficiency: The Progressive Conservation Movement, 1890-1920* (Cambridge: Harvard University Press, 1959) and James Penick, Jr., *Progressive Politics and Conservation: The Ballinger-Pinchot Affair* (Chicago: University of Chicago Press, 1968). Hays and Penick are especially good on the ideas of the conservation movement. For an Alaska emphasis see Nichols, *Alaska*; and Herman Slotnick, "The Ballinger-Pinchot Affair in Alaska," *Journal of the West* 10 (1971): 337-47.

The Alaskan Engineering Commission (Chapters 4-7)

Most nongovernment studies of the A. E. C. also deal with The Alaska Railroad; however, several of them deserve special emphasis here. Indispensable for its photographs of all phases of the railroad is Bernadine LeMay Prince, *The Alaska Railroad in Pictures, 1914-1964,* 2 vols. (Anchorage: Ken Wray, 1964). The A. E. C.'s organizational structure is carefully reviewed in Joshua Berhardt, *The Alaskan Engineering Commission: Its History, Activities and Organization,* Institute for Government Research, Monographs of the United States Government no. 4 (New York: D. Appleton and Company, 1922). Nellie Neal Lawing, *Alaska Nellie* (Seattle: Chieftain Press, 1940) touched on the railroad's procedures. Two unpublished M.A. theses, Miriam Myrtle Reinhart, "Secretary Franklin Knight Lane and the Alaska Railroad Problem" (University of Washington, 1926) and Benjamin B. Christopher, "The Alaska Railroad, 1915-1951," (Duke University, 1951) are useful.

The A. E. C.'s townsite work is mentioned in Merle Colby, *A Guide to Alaska, Last American Frontier,* Federal Writers' Project, American Guide Series (New York: The Macmillan Company, 1939). A history of Anchorage in the booster tradition, and distorting the relationship between railroad and town, is Evangeline Atwood, *Anchorage: All-America City* (Portland, Ore.: Binfords & Mort, 1957). Good on Anchorage and its area from prehistoric times to the present is Morgan Sherwood, ed., *The Cook Inlet Collection: Two Hundred Years of Selected Alaskan History* (Anchorage: Alaska Northwest Publishing Company, 1974).

Maritime matters involving Alaska need much more judicious treatment than they have yet received. Most shipping studies, such as Giles T. Brown's finely crafted *Ships That Sail No More: Maritime Transportation from San Diego to Puget Sound, 1910-1940* (Lexington: University of Kentucky Press, 1966), exclude Alaska, although Brown recounts the formation of the Pacific Steamship Company. A curious and idiosyncratic, but valuable study is Gordon Newell, ed., *The H. W. McCurdy Marine History of the Pacific Northwest* (Seattle: Superior Publishing Company, 1966). A candid pamphlet from an often-censured source is Alaska Steamship Company, *Statement Concerning the Through Rates and Divisions with the Government Railroad in Alaska* (Seattle, 1923). Stearns, "The Morgan-Guggenheim Syndicate" includes important material on "Alaska Steam."

John E. Ballaine was the A. E. C.'s most rabid critic. See his *Strangling of the Alaska Railroad.* James Wickersham ran a close second. For biographical information on Wickersham see Hunt, *North of 53°;* Wickersham's *Old Yukon: Tales-Trails-and Trials* (Washington: Washington Law Book Co., 1938); Gruening, *State of Alaska;* and Nichols, *Alaska.* Lane's attitudes and concerns are expressed in Anne Wintermute Lane and Louise Herrick Wall, eds., *The Letters of Franklin K. Lane* (Boston: Houghton Mifflin Co., 1922); and Bill G. Reid, "Franklin K. Lane's Idea for Veteran's Colonization, 1918-1921," *Pacific Historical Review* 33 (1964): 447-61.

For Yukon River steamboating see Lois Delano Kitchener, *Flag Over the North* (Seattle: Superior Publishing Company, 1954); and William R. Siddall, "The Yukon Waterway in the Development of Interior Alaska," *Pacific Historical Review* 28 (1959): 361-76.

The Alaska-Pacific Northwest portions of President Harding's trip are recounted in many places, including the *New York Times,* 10-28 July 1923; Herbert Hoover, *The Memoirs of Herbert Hoover: The Cabinet and the Presidency, 1920-1933* (New York: The Macmillan Company, 1952); Robert K. Murray, *The Harding Era: Warren G. Harding and His Administration* (Minneapolis: University of Minnesota Press, 1969); and Francis Russell, *The Shadow of Blooming Grove: Warren G. Harding in His Times* (New York: McGraw-Hill Book Company, 1968).

The Alaska Railroad (Chapters 8-14)

The pictorial history by Prince continues as an invaluable source. Edwin M. Fitch, *The Alaska Railroad* (New York: Frederick A. Praeger, Publishers, 1967) is standard for the post-1945 period, but also makes useful observations on earlier times, especially the Ohlson era.

The hero of the dash to Nome is sanctified in Elizabeth M. Ricker, *Seppala: Alaskan Dog Driver* (Boston: Little, Brown and Company, 1930).

Some ideas and attitudes of the men who helped to shape the destiny of The Alaska Railroad may be gleaned from Noel W. Smith, "Our Alaska Railroad," *Scientific American* 134 (1926): 151-53; Thomas R. Bullard, "From Businessman to Congressman: The Careers of Martin B. Madden" (Ph.D. diss., University of Illinois at Chicago Circle, 1973); Howard H. Quint and Robert H. Ferrell, eds., *The Talkative President: The Off-the-Record Press Conferences of Calvin Coolidge* (Amherst: University of Massachusetts Press, 1964); Ray Lyman Wilbur, *The Memoirs of Ray Lyman Wilbur, 1875-1949*, ed. Edgar Eugene Robinson and Paul Carroll Edwards (Stanford: Stanford University Press, 1960); and Harold L. Ickes, *The Secret Diary of Harold L. Ickes: The Inside Struggle 1936-1939* (New York: Simon and Schuster, 1954). Ernest Gruening's perspective on the Ohlson years is in his *Many Battles: The Autobiography of Ernest Gruening* (New York: Liveright, 1973).

The Seattle-Alaska aspects of the maritime strike are mentioned in Brown, *Ships That Sail No More* and Newell, *McCurdy Marine History*.

Brian Garfield, *The Thousand-Mile War: World War II In Alaska and the Aleutians* (Garden City, N.Y.: Doubleday & Company, Inc., 1969) treats some aspects of the defense effort in the Far North. Even though they are government publications, and in a category usually excluded from this essay, some volumes of *The United States Army in World War II* published by the U. S. Department of the Army, Office of the Chief of Military History, deserve special mention. They are: Stetson Conn, Rose C. Engelman, and Byron Fairchild, *Guarding the United States and Its Outposts* (1964); Karl C. Dod, *The Corps of Engineers: The War Against Japan* (1966); Joseph Bykofsky and Harold Larson, *The Transportation Corps: Operations Overseas* (1957); and Stanley W. Dziuban, *Military Relations Between the United States and Canada: 1939-1945* (1959).

Index

Advisory Council (Anchorage), 108
Alaska Advisory Committee (later Alaska Interdepartmental Committee), 156
air travel to Alaska, 1, 215-16
Alaska Agricultural College and School of Mines, 202, 203, 231
Alaska Central Railway; see Alaska Northern Railroad
Alaska Defense Command, 259-60
Alaska Labor Union, 44, 76
Alaska Highway, 1, 261
Alaska homestead and railroad act of 1898, 4
Alaska Loyal League, 76
Alaska Northern Railroad, 6-8
  condition of, when purchased by government, 30
  coal discoveries of survey teams of, 14
  government purchase of, 7, 17, 28, 30
  survey of, by A.E.C., 27-29
Alaska Pacific Railroad, 1
Alaska Railroad Act, 26-27
Alaska Railroad Commission, 23-24
Alaska Railroad Employees' Protective Association, 149, 213
Alaska Railroad Record, 76, 81
Alaska Railroad, The
  Alaska Defense Command and, 259-61
  comptroller general and, 173, 174-75, 236
  cost of, through 1923, 142
  deficit, reduction of, 180
  equipment of, 38, 87, 237, 260-61
  free freight of, 87
  free passes, abolition of by attorney general, 173
  name of, 83
  passenger traffic of, 86-87, 208
  revenues of, 1925-28, 180; 1932, 208; 1934-39, 238
  schedules of, 1924-28, 180
  tonnage of, 86-87, 161, 259
  through service established, 79
Alaska Railroad Townsite Regulations, 102
Alaska Road Commission
  consolidation of, with A.E.C., 85-6, 156, 159
  Chatanika branch of A.R.R., closing of, and, 197
  maintenance of roads and, 207, 210
  tolls for trucks and, 211
  transfer to Interior Department of, 210
Alaska Steamship Company, 5, 123
  A.E.C. and, 208
  Alaska Syndicate, ownership of company, 15, 123
  joint rates/through rates of 1923 and, 126, 128
  sailings in 1919 of, 123
  loading and handling, criticism of by A.R.R., 230-31
  maritime strikes against, 227-32
  Ohlson and, during strikes, 229-30
  tonnage carried by, 123
  requirements of tonnage to A.E.C., 125
  rate reductions to A.E.C. and, 126, 172
  weight/measurement system and, 127-28
Alaska Syndicate, 5, 14-17
Alaska, University of; see Alaska Agricultural College and School of Mines
Alaska Yukon Navigation Company (previously American Yukon Navigation Company), 260-61
Alaskan Engineering Commission, 27-28, 37
Alaska Steam and, 124, 126, 130
commissaries of, 45, 148-49
Congressional appropriations and, 45-46
construction and, 39-41, 45
construction camps, conditions in, 45
cost of railroad and, 142
criticism of A.E.C., 135-50
divisions of, 37-38, 80-81
expansion of, 42, 46-48, 81, 102-04, 106-09, 111
  accounting department, 47
  general storekeeper, 47
  health and sanitation, 46, 48, 103
  Land and Industrial, 81, 102
  law enforcement, 104, 106
  lighting systems, 103
  schools, 106-07
  telephone and telegraph, 42, 103
  water system, 103
housing of, 45
labor and, 42, 148
medical care of, 45
merger with Alaska Road Commission, 85-86, 156, 159
mining and, 143
Portage Bay route study, 27, 253
purchasing office of, 38
rates of, 42, 144-46
relations with other government departments, 86
relations with steamship companies, 124
riverboats of, 179, 237
Alice, riverboat, 179, 237
American Bridge Company, 79, 82
American Yukon Navigation

Company (subsequently Alaska Yukon Navigation Company), 83, 84
Anchorage
  city dock of, 47, 171
  complaints about commissary, 149
  early history and geography of, 101-03
  gambling and, 104-05
  government town, as, 103
  incorporation of, 103, 109-10
  General Land Office survey, 102
  port of, 170-72
  prostitution and bootlegging in, 104-05
  schools of, 106-08
  school board investigation in, 147
  telephones in, 103
  utilities in, 103
  townsite office in, 103, 108-09
Anchorage Chamber of Commerce, 108, 146, 158
Anchorage Daily Times, 213
Anderson, Anton, 8, 40, 137
Arctic, steamship, 229

Bain, H. Foster, 84
Ballaine, John E.
  Alaska Central/Alaska Northern and, 6
  Alaskan Engineering Commission, criticism of, 135, 136, 137
  Alaska Syndicate and, 15, 16
  cost estimates of, 136
  damage suit against A.E.C. and, 40
  development of Alaska, ideas for, 143
  Portage Bay and, 6-7
  route selection of, 6-7
  Strangling of the Alaska Railroad and, 136
  weight/measurement system and, 136
Ballinger-Pinchot controversy, 16-17, 28
Bangor & Aroostook Railroad, 232
Barndollar, Burton H., 162, 201
Barry K, riverboat, 260
Berger, Heinie, 212-13, 214
Board of Road Commissioners; see Alaska Road Commission
Boxer, motorship, 229, 234
Bone, Scott C., Governor, 158, 162
Brandeis, Louis, 17
Bridges, Harry, 228
Brill car, 174-75, 180, 208
Brooklyn Daily Eagle tour party, 158
Brooks, Alfred H.
  Alaska Advisory Committee

and, 156
Alaska Railroad Commission and, 23
development board, opinion of, 155
evaluation of Alaskan coal beds of, 14
Klondike gold rush calculations of, 3
Browne, Frederick D.
  Fairbanks fuel famine and, 79
  influenza in Northern district and, 77-78
  investigations of, 140-41
  labor policies of, 77, 141
  line construction and, 137, 141
  Nenana townsite and, 81
  reorganization, 1919, and, 80
Brownell, Don Carlos, 256
Buckner, Simon Bolivar, Jr., 260
Bunch, John H., 173
Bunnell, Charles, 202

Carmack, George, 2
Christensen, Andrew, 103-05, 141
  school director, Anchorage, 105, 107
  townsite auction, Anchorage, and, 102
  townsite auction, Nenana, and, 110
Clark, John E., 210
Coal
  Alaska Central survey discoveries of, 14
  Coal land laws, 16-17
  Lane, Franklin K. and, 25
  locations of mines, 14, 23
  Navy and, 14
  Roosevelt, Theodore, and, 7-8, 14
  World War II and, 258-59
commissary, 148-49
Committee on Policy of The Alaska Railroad, 159, 162, 196
Competition
  airplanes and, 215-16
  passengers and, 208
  responses to, by Alaska Railroad, 208, 209-10
  river boats and, 214-15
  shipping, ocean-borne freight and, 212-14
  support of truckers by Alaskans and, 209
  tolls on highways and, 210-11
  trucks and, 207-11
complaints, 231
Comptroller General, 212, 236. See also McCarl, John.
Congress, United States, 45-46
construction, 38-39, 157
  appropriations and, 143
  cost of, 142, 143
  completion of, 39, 78, 79, 83
  Edes' comments on, 142

Panama equipment and, 38
priorities of, 38
Coolidge, Calvin, 170
Copper River & Northwestern Railroad, 5
  Alaska Railroad Commission and, 23-24
  Alaska Syndicate and, 5, 6
  construction of, 5-6
  equipment purchased by Alaska Railroad, 260
  maintenance of, 5, 6
  rates of, 6, 24
  route of, 5
Cotton, Joseph, 30, 139
Cox, Leonard M., 23
Crook, steamship, 38, 124-25
Cunningham claims, 16-17
Cunningham, J. T., 176-77
  Alaska Steam and, 230
  Anchorage port closure, estimates of cost of, 171-72
  attempted dismissal of, by Landis, 162
  Berger, Heinie and, 213
  competition and, 209
  1934 maritime strike and, 228
  1936 maritime strike and, 228
  Northern Division tour of, 81
  snowslide, 1921, role in, 78-79
Curry, 175, 181
Curry, Charles F., Congressman, 85, 147

Davis, riverboat, 84, 179
Dawson, 3, 4
Delaney, J. J., 139
development of Alaska, 25
  Alaska railroad act and, 30
  Alaskan Engineering Commission and, 28
  gold rushes, roles in, 2, 3
  Lane, Franklin K., and, 25, 141-42, 155
  withdrawal of coal land, effect on, 14
Dickeson, Oliver L., 26
Dimond, Anthony, 234-36, 256
Discoverer, motor vessel, 212
Dole, C. E., 172, 178
Duluth, South Shore & Atlantic Railroad, 232

Edes, William C., 27, 37
  Alaska Northern and, 40
  Congressional appropriations, 1917, and, 46
  labor, 1916, and, 43-44, 75
  political appointments of, 146-47
  resignation of, 80, 138
Eklutna River power project, 175, 200
Elliott Highway, 198
Elliott, Malcom, Major, 197
Elmendorf Field, 258
Eska, 258-59
Evan Jones mine, 258

Fairbanks, 8, 13
Fairbanks Daily News-Miner, 25, 110, 169
Fairbanks Exploration Company, 180, 197-200
Fall, Albert B., 83, 85
Ferrill, Fred C., 81
Fort Richardson, 258
Free, Arthur M., Congressman, 173-74

General W. C. Gorgas, steamship, 209
Gerig, William, 80, 84, 144
Girdwood, 111
gold rushes, 3, 4
Good, James W., Congressman, 85
Gotwals, John C., 156-58, 162
Great War; see World War I
Gruening, Ernest, 232

Haines, 2
Hampton, Ruth, 232
Harding, Warren G., 85, 86
Healy River Coal Corporation, 258
Heney, Michael, 4
"home rule" bill, 1912, 17-18
Hoover, Herbert, 85, 201
hospital, Anchorage, 45, 237
Howell Committee, 198
  Anchorage Light & Power Company and, 200-01
  coal, evaluation of, 200
  failure of recommended rate increases by, 202
  Hoover administration and, 201
  members of, 198-99
  recommendations of, 199, 201
Howell, Robert B., 198-99, 200

Ickes, Harold L., 196, 253, 256-57
  Alaska Steam and, 208
  highway tolls and, 211
  labor legislation and, 236
  opinion of Alaskans of, 232
  Ohlson and, 227, 229
  visit of, to Alaska, 256
Industrial Workers of the World, 43-44, 76-77
Influenza, 1920, 77-78
Ingersoll, Colin M., 23

Jacobs, riverboat, 84, 237
Jarvis, David H., 15
Jones, Wesley M., Senator, 158
Joslin, Falcon, 8

Kendrick, John B., Senator, 199
Klondike, 2

labor
  Alaska Labor Union and, 44
  A.E.C. philosophy of, 42
  disputes with Smith over wage increases, 176
  Economy Act and, 236
  eight-hour law and, 43, 44, 45
  Fairbanks district strike and, 76-77
  forty-hour week and, 235-36
  general strike, 1916, and, 42-43
  leave and retirement benefits of, 235-36
  1934 maritime strike, 227-28
  1936 maritime strike, 228
  1920 wage and operating agreement and, 176
  Ohlson and, 227-28
  Smith, gains made during tenure for, 177
  "Sunday court," 44
  wages and, 42-43
Ladd Field, 238
Lake Francis, motor vessel, 214
Landis, Lee H., 159-60
  accounting, procedure changes of, 160
  economy drive of, 160-61
  personnel policy of, 161-62
  resignation of, 162-63
  tourism and, 160
Lane, Franklin K., 28, 144
  hopes for Alaska of, 141-42
  development and, 25, 155
  interview with John Ballaine of, 136
  opinion of commissioners of, 141
  rate-making power of, 144-45
Lathrop, Austin E., 148
Lestor, Charles, 76, 77
Lewis, Lena Morrow, 76
Lomen, Ralph, 215
Lost Slough, 137

McCarl, John R., 174-75, 236
McManamy, Frank, 199
Madden, Martin B., Congressman, 139, 148
maintenance, 156, 157, 237-38, 255
maritime strikes, 227-28
Matanuska
  coal beds of, 14, 110
  government colonization project in Valley, 231
Mayo mines, 84
Mears, Frederick, 27, 28, 139, 148
  Anchorage and, 101-03, 147
  eight-hour law and, 43, 44, 45
  gentleman's agreement and, 84
  reorganization and, 80-81
  relieved of duty, 84-85
  "Sunday court" and, 44
  steamship transportation, comment on, 125
Merrillat, Charles F., 14
Metzdorf, Dewey W., 178
"Midnight Sun," launch, 81
Modjeski & Angier, 82
Mondell, Frank, Congressman, 14
Moore, John J. C., 177
Moose, 111

Morrow, Jay J., 23
Nenana, riverboat, 237
Nenana, 110-11
Nenana River, 137
"New Golden Belt Line Tour," 158
Nordale, Arnold, 141
"North Nenana Limited," 79
"North Pacific Study," 128
North Star, motorship, 227, 229, 230, 234
Northern Commercial Company, 83, 179
  boats of, on river, 179, 215
  Chatanika branch of Alaska Railroad and, 198
  contract with Alaska Railroad and, 203, 215
  Northern Navigation Company of, 83

Ohlson, Otto F., 155, 195
  airplane travel and, 215, 229-231
  Chatanika branch closing and, 196, 197, 198
  coal and, 258-59
  commissary and, 234
  competition and, 207-08, 210-11, 212-14, 216
  economy drive of, 196, 202-03, 233
  fiscal responsibility of, 196
  General Accounting Office, ruling of, and, 212
  labor and, 233-37, 259-60
  labor legislation and, 234-37
    forty-hour week and, 235-36
    retirement and leave benefits and, 234-35
    wages and, 233
  maintenance of railroad and, 203, 237-38, 259-61
  1934 maritime strike and, 227-28
  1936 maritime strike and, 203, 228
  Platinum mine and, 195
  political appointees and, 233
  Portage Bay and, 254
    economic advantages of, 254-55
    maintenance of, 255
  Seward, charges against of, 255, 258
  railroad schedule, changes of, 208
  rates and, 201-03, 208-09
  retirement of, 261
  riverboat replacement of, 237
"Omineca," riverboat, 39

Pacific Steamship Company, 123, 230
Panama Railroad, 87
Parks, George A., Governor, 177, 197
Passage Canal; see Portage Bay
Payne, John Barton, 81, 156
Peters Creek, 42

277

Pinchot, Gifford, 16, 17
Platinum, 195
policy committee; see Committee on Policy of The Alaska Railroad
Pollok, Allan, 141
Portage Bay; see also Whittier
  Alaska Northern Railroad and, 6-7
  Army investigation of, 257
  Corps of Engineers and, 257
  geography of, 253-54
  Smith, Noel W. and, 253-54
  strategic value of, 256-57
  weather and disadvantages of, 254, 256
Post Office Department, 86, 229
Preston, George, 146
Price, Thomas C., 148
rates, 144-46, 232
  Anchorage port closure and, 172
  Army, free shipments for, 260
  free passes and, 173
  Howell Committee recommendations and, 201-02
  increases of, 202
  local rates of railroad, criticism of, 143-44
  passenger, 208
  reductions of, 203, 231-32
  special tariffs, 209
  steamship lines and, 127-28
  weight/measurement, 126-28
  Western Classification, 128, 145
  World War II and, 260

Richardson Highway, 210, 261
Richardson Highway Transportation Company, 208, 210
Richardson, Wilds P., 135-36
Riggs, Thomas, 27, 80
  condition of Tanana Valley Railroad, comments on, 47
  I.W.W. strike and, 76-77
  irregularities in accounts of, 140
  Nenana, comments on founding of, 110
River Boat Service, 237
  boats of, see under individual names
  established, 83
  "gentleman's agreement" and, 84
  Howell Committee rates and, 201-02
  Northern Commercial Company and, 179
  Smith, Noel W., and, 178-79
  tonnage of, 84, 179
  traffic of, 86, 179
Roosevelt, Franklin D., 227, 257
Roosevelt, Theodore, 7-8, 14
Rustgard, John, 129-30

St. Michael, 3, 83
schools, Anchorage, 106-07, 108, 109

Seattle Chamber of Commerce, 38, 159
Seward, 2, 25-26
  Alaska Northern, as base for, 6, 7
  construction base at, for A.E.C., 37
  dock fire at, 40
  general headquarters moved from, 48
  maintenance along line from, 254
  Ohlson and, 255
  reaction to Portage Bay cutoff of, 254, 255
  subdivision lots sold by A.E.C. in, 111, 204
Seward Chamber of Commerce, 204
Seward Daily Gateway, 204, 229
Ship Creek, 6, 28-29, 111
Smith, Noel W., 169, 170
  Anchorage city dock and, 171
  analysis of railroad of, 174
  Army withdrawal and, 175
  capital expenditures of, 174
  development policies and, 169
  diptheria epidemic, 1925, and, 175
  economy drive of, 169
  Eklutna River power project and, 175
  labor relations of, 170, 175-76
  maintenance of railroad and, 174, 179-80
  Portage Bay and, 172
  port at Anchorage and, 170-72
  purchasing department, Seattle, disputes with, 177-78
  relationship with Hubert Work, 170
  River Boat Service and, 178-79
  steamship rate negotiations and, 172
  wildlife refuge and, 175
Snell, Harold L., 196
Special Select Committee on Investigation of The Alaska Railroad; see Howell Committee
Steese, James G., 155-56
  Alaska Road Commission and, 156
  Chairman of Alaskan Engineering Commission, 84-85, 156
  maintenance and, 156-57, 159
  "New Golden Belt Line Tour" and, 158-59
  River Boat Service and, 158
  squatters and, 159
  uniforms for railroad employees and, 158
Strangling of the Alaska Railroad, 136
Strong, J. F. A., 29, 107
Sutherland, Dan, 175

Taft, William Howard, 16, 17, 25
Talkeetna, 111, 143
Tallman, Clay, 102
Tanana Valley Railroad
  construction and equipment of, 8, 9, 79-80
  earnings of, 8
  purchase of, by A.E.C., 8, 47
  rates of, 8
Tacoma, 227-28
Tacoma Chamber of Commerce, 229
Taylor, Edward, Congressman, 204
Thompson, W. F., 169
Thoron, Benjamin W., 257
Thoron report, 232
Townsite regulations; see Alaska Railroad Townsite Regulations
Thomas, John, Senator, 199
Troy, John W., 229, 233
trucks, 207
  competition of, 207-08
  hazards to, 209-10
  route of, 207
  tolls and, 210-12
"tunnel boats," 39
Turnagain Arm, 39-40
Turnagain District, 39

Ummel, Jacob, 178, 229

Valdez, 2, 207
Van Gundy, E., 162
Valdez & Yukon Railroad, 1

Warren, H. P., 125
Wasilla, 111
Watts, J. G., 104
  assessments and, 108-09
  public schools, Anchorage, and, 107
Western Classification; see rates
Wheeler, Burton K., Senator, 172-73
White Pass & Yukon Railway
  American Yukon Navigation Company, 83. See also Alaska Yukon Navigation Company
  construction of, 4
  meaning of, for Alaska, 4
  river boat service of, 83, 84
  tonnage of, 4, 5
  U.S. government tax on, 4
Whittier, 2, 253, 257
Wickersham, James
  Alaska Road Commission and, 135-36
  author of Alaskana, 135
  criticism of A.E.C. and, 138
  Howell Committee, influence on election of, 202
  judge of Third Judicial District, 135
  railroad bills and, 25, 30
  Riggs, Thomas, and, 135

Wilbur, Ray Lyman, 196, 201, 232
Wilson, Woodrow, 26
  announcement of "western" route, 27, 29
  government control of railroads and, 25
  purchase of Alaska Northern railroad and, 30
Work, Hubert, 84, 159, 162
  Committee on Policy of The Alaska Railroad and, 159, 162
  "Friday letters," to, 170
  Landis, Lee H., opinion of, 162
  Smith, Noel, appointment of, 162-63, 170
World War I, 75-76
World War II
  Alaska Railroad and, 257-61
  coal shortage during, 258-59

Yukon River, 2, 4, 83-84, 179, 237

Railroad in the Clouds *was printed on a 70 pound Mead offset enamel paper by Pruett Press/O'Hara Corporation of Boulder, Colorado. The type was set in Souvenir Light by B. Vader Phototypesetting, Inc., of Fort Collins, Colorado. The smyth sewn case binding was furnished by Roswell Bookbinding of Phoenix, Arizona. The original watercolor was created by Howard Fogg, the dust jacket design by Jim Kifer. The book's interior was designed by Dianne Kedro.*

```
TF25                                    180421
.A4
.W54     Wilson
         Railroad in the clouds
```

Randall Library – UNCW
TF25.A4 W54   NXWW
Wilson / Railroad in the clouds : the Alaska Railr

3049002378643